Experience
Rating
in Unemployment
Insurance

JOSEPH M. BECKER, S.J.

Experience Rating in Unemployment Insurance:
An Experiment in Competitive Socialism

THE JOHNS HOPKINS UNIVERSITY PRESS
BALTIMORE AND LONDON

Manufactured in the United States of America

The Johns Hopkins University Press, Baltimore, Maryland 21218
The Johns Hopkins University Press Ltd., London

Library of Congress Catalog Card Number 72-4026
ISBN 0-8018-1429-4

Library of Congress Cataloging in Publication data will be found on the last printed page of this book.

Contents

Tables

Table   Page

Appendix A

Table   Page

General Tables

CHARTS

Preface

In turning to the field of social security, a quarter of a century ago, I was attracted by the opportunity this field provides to study the interaction between individual and social responsibility. The way a society combines these two in its institutions goes far to determine the character of its economy. Within the social security system, my attention was early caught by a device used in unemployment insurance that was unique to the United States and that epitomized the choice between individual and social responsibility. This device was experience rating and it was extremely controversial.

Over the years I often considered attempting an evaluation of experience rating, but was deterred partly by the difficulty of the task and partly by the degree of emotion surrounding the issue. This issue divides the friends of unemployment insurance among themselves, and civil wars tend to be the bitterest. Finally, realizing that the years were passing and that I would have to make the attempt soon or never, I embarked on the study of which the present book is the result.

The book will be of interest primarily to those who are acquainted with the social security system, especially unemployment insurance. Among these are specialists in government (state and federal) and in labor and management circles. Tax specialists also may find some interest in this intensive investigation of a particular tax. In the academic world, writers of textbooks and teachers of courses in labor economics and in social welfare will find here the information needed to correct numerous misunderstandings that occur in earlier treatments of the subject.

For him who must read as he runs, the first and last chapters have been written so as to convey the gist of the study. The reader of these two chapters will understand the questions that had to be asked and at least the essentials of the answers that have been given.

I wish to express my appreciation to The Ford Foundation and to the Earhart Foundation for their financial assistance in carrying through this study. Neither foundation is in any way responsible for the views expressed herein.

I am deeply indebted to the many state unemployment insurance agencies and to the many firms whose cooperation provided the "stuff" of the study; I wish I could acknowledge my indebtedness to each by name. The assistance of the Massachusetts Division of Employment Security was especially valuable. The Division supplied the materials for an entire chapter (Chapter 7) and was helpful in many other ways.

The entire project owes much, also, to a team of ten consultants—in government, industry, and academia—who read the manuscript in its various versions and provided valuable insights and corrections. Michael Santoliquido and Lucy Santoro provided analytical and clerical assistance of the highest quality. The Jesuit Center for Social Studies provided indispensable facilities for the work.

Jesuit Center for Social Studies
Georgetown University
February 2, 1972

Experience
Rating
in Unemployment
Insurance

Issue of Experience Rating

Nature of Experience Rating

In the United States the major public program in aid of the unemployed is unemployment insurance,[1] which pays several billions of dollars annually in unemployment benefits. These benefits are financed almost entirely by a federal-state payroll tax levied on employers. The federal government levies the tax in the first instance, but any state may—and all states do—levy a similar tax by which its employers may offset the federal tax. Furthermore, a state may tax a given firm at a rate lower than the federal rate and the firm may still claim the full offset if the basis for the lower rate is the firm's favorable experience with unemployment.[2]

Unemployment insurance has the essential characteristics of group insurance, of which it is a form. The "insurance company" is the state, and the insured are the employees, who have the right to draw benefits. The employer in effect purchases the insurance by paying his tax to the state. In group insurance it is common practice to require a firm to pay a lower or higher insurance premium (tax) as its employees represent a greater or lesser risk to the insurance fund. The practice of varying the tax rate in some relation to the experience of the individual firm is called "experience rating."

The alternative to experience rating is the uniform tax, under which every firm pays the same tax rate regardless of the degree of risk it represents to the fund. The choice between a uniform tax and an experience-rated tax is a basic decision in constructing a system of unemployment insurance. Of all the countries that have made this decision, only the United States has chosen experience rating. The choice was made only after bitter controversy and it continues to be the object of intense criticism. Has the choice been a wise one? Or, assuming a decision to make use of experience rating to some degree, have we chosen the right degree? These are the questions on which the present study attempts to

---

1. Its official title is "unemployment compensation," a term that reflects an early controversy, described elsewhere in the chapter, between "reserves" and "insurance." The neutral term "compensation" was applicable to both systems.
2. For a fuller explanation of this offset and its relation to experience rating, see Appendix B.

1

throw some light by assembling the available evidence for the chief advantages and disadvantages alleged to accompany experience rating.

Significance of Experience Rating

Experience rating is part of, and draws some of its importance from, the larger and deeper conflict between the "individualistic" and the "socialistic" approaches to the solution of the problems of our society. Although both these terms are vague and tend to have pejorative connotations, they are still the most convenient terms available. Other terms are less objectionable only to the extent that they are even less clear. By each of these terms is meant here not a concrete social structure but merely a characteristic approach—a general tendency to solve problems by reliance on individual responsibility or on social responsibility. In relation to the choice between experience rating and a uniform tax, the alternatives take the form of a requirement that each firm meet its own costs or a requirement that employers share each other's burdens.

Although all societies make simultaneous use of both approaches, they tend to exhibit a preference for one or the other. This preference, exercised repeatedly in area after area of a society's life, imparts a clearly distinguishable character, a recognizable national life style. The relationship of experience rating to this deeper issue may explain why the experience-rating controversy carries such a high emotional voltage. Despite the absence of hard evidence for most of the alleged effects of experience rating, positions have been held with great tenacity. As Edwin Witte remarked a decade after the main battle had been concluded: "Differences of opinion among the champions of the institution are so extreme as to disrupt lifelong friendships" [1, p.21]. According to former Secretary of Labor Willard Wirtz, experience rating was a line dividing the two major interest groups in our society. "I would like to make clear first, complete recognition of the fact that experience rating has become a kind of symbol in this area whether you are for it or against it, and very largely the line divides labor and management. I have gone into it fairly deeply, to the point I would like to divorce myself entirely from the symbolism of it" [2, p. 349]. The opposing camps may see experience rating as one battle in a continuing war. In this explanation a large part of the experience rating issue, as with many other social issues, lies beneath the surface.

The choice between the more individualistic, competitive approach and the more socialistic one had to be made repeatedly in the series of decisions which brought unemployment insurance into existence in the United States. We first had to decide whether to have compulsory unemployment insurance at all. Such a program represents a socialistic intervention in the individualistic market. We made the socialistic choice in 1935. Next we had to decide whether to locate financial responsibility in the national government or to require each state to be responsible for its own program. We made the more individualistic choice of separate state programs. We had also to decide on the kind of tax to be levied in support of the program. The more general the tax, the more socialistic are its effects. For the most part, we have chosen the most narrowly focused of all possible taxes, a payroll tax payable only by employers subject to the law.[3] Next we had to decide whether to tax each employer at a uniform rate or to vary the rate with individual employer experience. Generally, we have made the more individualistic choice of experience rating.

The final decision, which is continually being remade, is on the degree of experience rating. By the degree of experience rating is meant the closeness of the relationship between an employer's experience with unemployment and his tax rate. The original Wisconsin program was 100 percent experience-rated, whereas in the state of Washington, before 1970, the degree of experience rating approached zero. In between there are many actual, and an indefinite number of possible, gradations. In general, as illustrated in Chapter 5, the states have stopped far short of complete experience rating. In all state programs there is a substantial amount of sharing of the burden of unemployment benefit costs.[4] In what might be termed characteristic American fashion, after grafting some individualistic branches onto the socialistic vine of unemployment insurance, we proceeded to graft some socialistic twigs onto the branches.

This location of the issue of experience rating within the larger context of the individualistic-socialistic tension is not meant to imply that concrete decisions affecting the program are usually made in these formal terms. Legislators, labor leaders, and employers do not typically favor or oppose experience rating because they deem it "individualistic" or "socialistic." They are more likely to make their decisions because they see it in terms of concrete advantages or disadvantages as it affects themselves or their constituents. Nevertheless, it remains true that in making such decisions they are as a matter of fact favoring a more individualistic or a more socialistic approach and are thus modifying, however imperceptibly, the "mix" in our society. Moreover, in all probability they (and the author and reader?) are temperamentally inclined to favor one approach over the other, and this basic inclination affects the way they weigh and interpret evidence. In some situations, where the evidence is partial or is qualitative rather than quantitative, this basic inclination may be decisive. As John Henry Newman remarked, "In any enquiry about things in the concrete, men differ from each other, not so much in the soundness of their reasoning as in the principles which govern its exercise." And these first principles are "hidden for the very reason they are so sovereign and engrossing. They have sunk into you,

3. No state has ever used general revenues. (The District of Columbia did so briefly at the very beginning of the program and the federal government does so, of course, for the coverage of government employees.) As of 1970, only three states (Alabama, Alaska, New Jersey), with 5.2 percent of the total covered employment, also levied a small tax on employees.
4. The very act of setting a maximum tax rate, for example, assumes that some high-cost firms will be partly subsidized by other firms.

they spread through you; you do not so much appeal to them as act upon them" [3].

Need for Study

The decisions that have been made regarding the unemployment insurance tax are not irrevocable. The social debate has remained very much alive, and serious proposals are made from time to time to further modify or to eliminate experience rating. One of the earliest of such attempts was the "McCormack amendment" of 1939, which would have granted each state the freedom[5] to vary its employer taxes on any basis it chose (rather than solely on the basis of individual experience) but would have simultaneously imposed federal benefit standards. A similar proposal was contained in H.R. 8282, the 1965 bill of the Johnson administration. Had H.R. 8282 become law, the retention or elimination of experience rating would have become a burning political issue in most states.

Even more numerous have been proposals to change the *degree* of experience rating in existing laws. Some of the proposals seek to lessen the degree, some to increase it. One of the more dramatic examples of the latter was the prolonged impasse in the state of Washington, where all substantive unemployment insurance legislation was blocked for more than a decade (1959-69) because management wanted a system with more experience rating, while labor preferred to sacrifice needed benefit improvements rather than accept a greater degree of experience rating. (In 1970 a compromise was effected whereby benefits were considerably liberalized and the degree of experience rating somewhat increased.)

If, as was suggested above, judgments on experience rating are greatly affected by one's predisposition to favor the individualistic or socialistic approach, may not a study like this one, which is a search for "evidence," be largely a useless performance? If the greater part of the experience-rating issue lies beneath the surface, as with an iceberg, can it be reached by the light of "evidence?" Further study of experience rating, in itself, may have little influence on decisions.

Two considerations weigh against this pessimistic conclusion. All economies are mixed in the sense that they use both the individualistic and the socialistic technique, depending on which seems better to suit a given situation. Decisions have to be made, therefore, which depend mainly on the concrete details of the particular situation. Hence, additional light thrown on the concrete situation may influence the final decision—to abolish or keep experience rating, and if it is kept to increase or decrease its degree.

---

5. As explained in Appendix B, the only legal alternative to charging all firms 2.7 percent has been to use some form of experience rating.

Further, although the greater part of an iceberg is below the surface, not all of it is. At least a part is within the reach of the sun's rays. While former Secretary of Labor Wirtz recognized that experience rating was a symbol, he also recognized the desirability, as he put it, of divorcing himself from the symbolism so as to be able to analyze the merits and demerits of experience rating itself. In short, because decisions on experience rating are not foreordained by political predispositions, there would seem to be room for a study such as this, which attempts to shed additional light on the actual effects of experience rating.

Origins of Experience Rating

To see the issue of experience rating in perspective, as well as to observe how the issue has changed over time, it will be helpful to review the origins of experience rating in this country. The review may be the briefer because a number of recent full histories are available. The writings of Edwin Witte [1], [4] and Arthur Altmeyer [5] provide the accounts of eye-witnesses, as does also a brief article written in 1967 by Paul Raushenbush [6]. Daniel Nelson's history of the origins of unemployment insurance [7], told mainly from the viewpoint of the struggle over experience rating, is a very useful account that describes fully the roles played by all the major participants, such as John B. Andrews and his American Association of Labor Legislation. Roy Lubove's book [8] has a chapter on unemployment insurance that situates the issue of experience rating in the deeper tension between voluntarism and compulsory social insurance.

Among the earlier writings on experience rating, the debate between Feldman-Smith [9] on the one side and Lester-Kidd [10] on the other, is very informative. Also, a series of articles by Harry Malisoff [11] describes in considerable detail the establishment of the original state unemployment insurance programs.[6] But if one could read only two authors, the choice would surely be Raushenbush [15], [16], [17] and Rubinow [18], [19], [20]. These two authors are the most reliable guides to the real issues in the early debate over experience rating.

Outside the United States, experience rating has very little history. The German and Austrian experiments mentioned in Chapter 3 ended almost as soon as they began. The British experiment lasted longer but encountered the insuperable difficulty of prolonged serious depression. Moreover, in all three of them, the government and the employee also contributed to the fund, so that the role of experience rating was limited to the part represented by the employer tax. Finally, the rating was done, not on the basis of individual employer experience,

---

6. The best of the textbooks are easily those by Eveline M. Burns [12 and 13] and that of Haber and Murray [14].

but on the basis of "industry" experience.[7] It is safe to say that neither British nor European experience has any significant light to shed on the current debate in this country.

For our purpose, the history of the debates over experience rating may be reviewed most conveniently under four headings: The Wisconsin approach, the alternatives to the Wisconsin approach, the compromise between these two approaches effected in the Social Security Act, and the continuing debate.

The Wisconsin Approach

An early obstacle to any system of unemployment benefits was a prevalent assumption that unemployment was attributable to some defect in the individual. This obstacle became less formidable as recognition grew that the problem of unemployment was mainly a problem of the institutions of an industrial society. Beveridge contributed notably to this recognition by his early book, whose title accurately expresses its theme, *Unemployment, A Problem of Industry* [21].

The old obstacle thereupon assumed a new form. Management argued that if unemployment was indeed a problem of industry, then it should be left to industry. Certainly, it should not be turned over to government, for that would be to foster (dread word) socialism. Supporting this position was a contemporary development in the United States, the growth of Scientific Management. During the first two decades of the twentieth century, there were heady expectations of what modern management could accomplish through the "rationalization" of industry. The New Emphasis movement among leading employers, especially in New England, had the élan of a crusade (see Chapter 10).

Like a good Judo practitioner, John R. Commons of Wisconsin took advantage of this trend in management[8] and made the strength of his opponents work for him. Was unemployment a problem to be solved not by government but by industry? Very well, let industry face up to its responsibility: let it transform at least part of the social cost of unemployment, borne largely by the unfortunate individuals who became unemployed, into a regular cost of doing business. Commons's explicit proposal was contained in the Huber Bill, introduced in the Wisconsin legislature in 1921. This bill broke with tradition in assessing the cost

7. Both Raushenbush [6] and Rubinow [20, p. 84] were perceptive enough to see early that it was much more difficult to rate industries than to rate individual firms, but it was Raushenbush who was the main force opposing all proposals to substitute industry-rating for the rating of individual firms. He was arguing this point with John B. Andrews as early as 1930, in connection with the latter's "American Plan."

8. It was a trend congenial to Commons's own inclinations. Commons was above all the "reasonable" man [22, pp. 29, 30]. Commons contributed significantly to the Americanization of the labor problem in the sense that he helped formulate an intermediate ground of worker interest which rejected equally the atomized individualism of classical economics and the class struggle of the socialists [23].

of the proposed unemployment benefits entirely on the employer.[9] The fund accumulated from employer contributions would be pooled (available to all eligible claimants), but each employer's contribution rate would vary in some proportion to his own experience with unemployment. Thus, this first Wisconsin bill had the essential financing features that today characterize practically all existing state unemployment insurance laws: a pooled fund financed by an experience-rated employer tax.

Helped by the heavy unemployment of the period, the Huber Bill came close to passing one house in 1921. It was reintroduced with various modifications session after session in the Wisconsin legislature, but never again came as close to passage. Opposition to any form of unemployment benefits increased rather than diminished. In the meantime, as John R. Commons grew older and became immersed in other problems, leadership in the campaign for unemployment insurance was taken over by his students, especially Paul A. Raushenbush and Harold Groves. In 1930 Philip F. LaFollette, son of the famous senator, called in Groves and Raushenbush, along with Elizabeth Brandeis, told them that he planned to run for the Wisconsin governorship, and asked them to prepare an unemployment insurance bill which he could advocate.

Since the main obstacle to a compulsory program of unemployment benefits was still the stigma of a "socialistic dole," Harold Groves conceived the idea of pushing the logic of the original Commons approach one step further—to individual employer reserves. Each firm would be required to accumulate a reserve proportioned to the number of its employees, and this reserve would be usable only by that firm's employees, whose benefits would terminate when the reserve was exhausted. This would be merely to require all firms to do what some of the more progressive firms were already doing.[10] Such a plan was, Raushenbush wrote to John B. Andrews in 1931, "conceptually consonant with American individualism, modified by social responsibility." Groves and Raushenbush drafted a bill to achieve this objective, and Groves, who was an assemblyman, introduced it in the Wisconsin legislature in 1931.

The Groves bill became a major issue in the state, and the campaign for it was intense and long. The supporting arguments used—essentially the same as those used for the Huber Bill—are faithfully reflected in the statement of public policy which prefaced the law as finally enacted and which is shown in Appendix D.[11] The primary reason for having an unemployment benefit program is to aid the unemployed, on whom "the burden of irregular employment now falls directly

9. The first unemployment insurance bill in the United States, introduced in Massachusetts in 1916, was largely a copy of the 1911 English law and provided for contributions from the employer, from the employee, and from the government.

10. For some examples of such firms, see [7, Chapter 3].

11. It was written by Paul Raushenbush, who later also wrote the statement of public policy for the model draft bill which was distributed by the Committee on Economic Security and was adopted by many states.

and with crushing force." Two reasons are then given for financing such a program by means of individual employer reserves: to make the (partial) support of unemployed workers a regular cost of doing business and to give employers an additional incentive to prevent unemployment. The order in which the first and third reasons are given bears out the 1933 statement of Paul Raushenbush: "So the main emphasis of the Wisconsin law was placed on compensation as a right for those unemployed through no fault of their own, and supplementary emphasis was laid on the maximum possible inducement to regularization of employment" [15, p. 111].

A twelve-page pamphlet arranged in question-and-answer style, prepared principally by Raushenbush and used extensively during the 1931 campaign for the Groves bill, spells out in more detail the reasons supporting the bill's enactment. Of the thirty questions and answers given in the pamphlet, the first five establish the unemployed worker's need for help. The next three enforce this conclusion by indicating the inadequacies of the existing public provision of aid.

The next three answers establish industry's responsibility to meet this need for help. The point is first made that many firms had been able to continue the payment of dividends during the decline of 1929-30 because they had accumulated reserves for that purpose; the conclusion is then drawn that firms should accumulate reserves in order to continue the payment of at least partial wages to employees whom they had to lay off. The next four answers (12-15) justify the enactment of a law to compel employers to accumulate such reserves. It is not until the sixteenth question that the prevention of unemployment is even mentioned, and then it is immediately connected with the more fundamental obligation of business to bear (a part of) the cost of even unavoidable unemployment, because it is a "real cost of doing business" (Question 17).

It is necessary thus to stress the philosophy underlying the Wisconsin law in order to restore balance to what has become a distorted historical picture. The small size of the benefits provided in the Wisconsin bill and the emphasis accorded the stabilization effect during the campaign for the bill, did not reflect a wrong view of unemployment insurance objectives, but were dictated by political necessity: these were needed to persuade the Wisconsin legislature to step out in front of all the other states. Surmounting apparently impossible obstacles, the campaign succeeded, and the Groves bill was enacted into law in January 1932, to become the first compulsory unemployment compensation law in the United States.[12]

Other Approaches

Since the Wisconsin position was toward one end of the individualistic-socialistic spectrum, there was room for an indefinite number of degrees of

---

12. The collection of taxes was postponed until business conditions should have improved. Further, the entire law was to remain inactive if a specified number of firms

disagreement and for alternative proposals. At the far left of the spectrum, for example, there was the Lundeen bill, introduced into Congress in 1934, which would have paid unemployment benefits to all unemployed persons over the age of eighteen years for as long as they were out of work, and would have paid a weekly benefit at least equal to the full prevailing local rate of wages. Originally introduced by the Communists, the Lundeen bill attracted vigorous support from many other groups, especially the social workers. It helped to break down resistance to the idea of unemployment benefits and had the effect of making other approaches look more reasonable and acceptable.

The chief alternative to the Wisconsin approach, however, was more moderate and originated in Ohio. It was developed in the influential *Report of the Ohio Commission on Unemployment Insurance.* Authored mainly by I. M. Rubinow, this 1932 document rejected the Wisconsin law primarily on the ground that the benefits it provided were uncertain and inadequate. According to the report, the benefits were uncertain because unemployed workers could draw only against their own employer's reserve, which might become exhausted; and they were inadequate in both amount and duration primarily because revenue was obtained from only the employer. To provide adequate benefits it was necessary, according to the report, to obtain a contribution at least from the employee and preferably also one from the government. The report proposed a plan that would pay higher benefits for a longer time than the Wisconsin plan, would be financed by taxes on both employer and employee, and would pool contributions in a common fund available for all eligible claimants. Partly in deference to the popularity of the Wisconsin approach and partly because Rubinow saw some genuine merit in the idea [19, p. 455], the Ohio plan envisioned some possible future provision for experience rating.

Despite the advantage of coming after Wisconsin had established a precedent, the Ohio bill based on this report failed of enactment. Other bills in other state legislatures also failed of enactment in 1932 and 1933—a reminder of the political stringency under which the original Wisconsin campaign had to operate. However, the Ohio plan attracted an influential following and provided the chief alternative to the Wisconsin approach during the debate that filled the period between the enactment of the Wisconsin law in January of 1932 and the enactment of the Social Security Act in August 1935.

Limitations of the Early Debate

In retrospect it is possible to see that during the debate some of the relevant issues were exaggerated or misunderstood or overlooked. The argument that experience rating might prevent unemployment was overstressed by the Wis-

---

established voluntary plans paying benefits equal to those provided by the law. That condition was accepted at the last minute as the necessary price of enactment. The first law did not come easily.

consin school. Although other arguments for experience rating were developed, especially its effect on the allocation of resources (see Chapter 3), in the dust raised by the prevention controversy they tended to be obscured. Likewise, the Wisconsin school tended to overstress the virtues of individual employer reserves, failing to recognize adequately that the essential values of experience rating could be obtained even with a pooled fund. Both the prevention argument and the argument for individual employer reserves were probably a necessary tactic in 1931, but they were defended so strongly during the succeeding period that the dividing line between tactic and principle was obscured.[13]

The opponents of the Wisconsin school also gave an excessive amount of attention to the issue of unemployment prevention. Partly, this was a natural response to the Wisconsin stress. Partly, it was an inevitable reaction in the context of the great depression, when individual efforts to prevent unemployment were obviously so futile. But partly also, it may have been a debating tactic. Disliking experience rating for other reasons, the opponents chose to attack it on this vulnerable ground, even when the issue of prevention was irrelevant to their argument.

For example, the key Wisconsin agrument, that experience rating would affect the allocation of resources, was most frequently met by the rebuttal that it was "unfair" to give a lower tax rate to a bank than to a construction firm. Why unfair? Because neither firm was "responsible" for its respective unemployment record. In what sense were they not responsible? Because the difference in unemployment experience stemmed from the very nature of the economic activity in which the firm was engaged and was therefore beyond the firm's control. But, since the employer's ability to control unemployment is irrelevant to the allocation argument, such a response had to be either a misunderstanding of the argument, or an avoidance of the argument, or a denial of the argument's fundamental assumption, namely, that our society has chosen the free market as its major mechanism for the allocation of resources (see Chapter 3). In most cases, the main reason for the response was probably not the third one.

The Wisconsin-Ohio debate is sometimes described as "individual reserves versus insurance" and this is a correct designation. Another description, "prevention versus adequacy," is less accurate but has a foundation in the historical context in which it was used. But the commonest description, "prevention versus insurance" [8], easily leads to misunderstanding: it seems to convey the impression that "prevention" and "insurance" are contraries; whereas in principle neither term excludes the other.

None of these formulations should be understood, as they often seem to be, as synonymous with "experience rating versus a uniform tax." In other words, much of the original Wisconsin-Ohio debate has little relevance for the precise

13. For example [24, p. 8]. In any case, the deepening depression was changing the balance of political forces, and the use of such arguments as a tactic may not have been as justifiable in 1935 as it had been in 1931.

issue of experience rating versus a uniform tax, which is the only issue under consideration in the present study. It is necessary to make this point, because there has been a marked tendency to carry forward the terms of the early debate into the current period, even when they are no longer relevant.

During the period of debate preceding the passage of the Social Security Act, a major issue was whether to have a single national program of unemployment benefits or to have separate state programs. At that time experience rating was linked politically with the federal-state issue, and attitudes toward experience rating were affected by the other contemporary conflict.[14] Although these two issues were often intermingled in the debate, there is no relation in principle between the two. In principle, both a federal system and a state system could use either a uniform tax or an experience-rated tax.

The early debates were often incomplete. Thus the Social Security Board could write in an official document prepared in 1939 and distributed to the states in 1940: "Implicit in the interpretation of section 1602 (a) (1) of the Internal Revenue Code is the principle that any experience rating plan must be designed to accomplish, through differentiation of rates as between employers, *one or both of the only known objectives of experience rating*, namely the promotion of stability of employment, and/or a fair allocation of the cost of unemployment compensation" [25, p. 1] (emphasis supplied). In the discussions of that period, other possible effects of experience rating were often ignored.[15]

The Social Security Act

The debate came to a temporary halt with the passage of the Social Security Act, which in effect required every state to enact an unemployment insurance law, but permitted each state wide latitude in its choice of a financing system. For the most part, the states preferred a combination of the Wisconsin and Ohio approaches, favoring pooled funds supported by an employer tax, experience-rated.

As of 1937, when all the states had enacted unemployment insurance laws, forty-four of them had elected to establish pooled funds, while only seven had established a form of individual employer reserves.[16] Of these latter, four (Indiana, Kentucky, Oregon, South Dakota) had established "partially pooled" funds, in which one-sixth of the fund was pooled and five-sixths was kept in individual reserves. These partial pools may properly be considered the beginnings of the "common account" discussed later (Chapter 2). Wisconsin joined this group in early 1937 by amending its law to provide for a "balancing account," from

14. Both sides held the conviction, probably correct at that time, that a single national program would have a uniform tax. Currently, however, the political relation between the two issues is much more ambiguous.

15. In a 1941 talk, however, Raushenbush lists four objectives of experience rating [26].

16. The seven were: Indiana, Kentucky, Nebraska, Oregon, South Dakota, Vermont, and Wisconsin [27, p. 399]. North Carolina joined this group in 1939.

which benefits could be paid to the employees of any employer whose account was exhausted.[17]

As of the end of 1937, forty-four state laws taxed only the employer, while seven levied a tax also on the employee.[18] This avoidance of employee taxes stemmed not only from the Wisconsin influence but also from the opposition of organized labor.

In 1937 forty states (thirty-three of them with pooled funds) provided for some form of experience rating, while eleven states did not.[19] About three-fourths of the states with experience rating had chosen the reserve-ratio system, which most closely reflects the total experience of the individual employer. These early elections of experience rating probably represented a choice in principle. The states had not yet been faced by the situation, which became common later, of funds growing beyond the size the states desired, with no device available for reducing the inflow except experience rating.

Debate Continued

After the passage of the Social Security Act, the debate over experience rating moved into the separate states, which had various options open to them. In 1940 the states embarked on an extensive discussion of experience rating under the auspices of the Interstate Conference of Employment Security Agencies (ICESA), which appointed a committee of five[20] to make a thorough study of the subject and report at the 1940 annual meeting.

This ICESA discussion took place in the context of a contemporary problem that greatly influenced the form of the debate. The unemployment insurance funds had grown at an unanticipated rapid pace; many voices were raised to say that the reserves were becoming excessive. To the extent that the problem was real, it was obviously open to two solutions—improve benefits or decrease taxes. In the dozen states which had a uniform tax of 2.7 percent, demands were made to introduce experience rating in order to achieve a lower average tax. But even in states which had experience rating, there was pressure to reach the goal of tax reduction by a more direct route.

In 1939 John McCormack of Massachusetts proposed to amend the Social Security Act to permit a state to reduce the 2.7 percent unemployment insur-

17. Actually, Wisconsin had the beginnings of such a Common Account as early as 1935, when the unused reserves of firms that went out of business were used—by administrative decision—to pay benefits to the employees of an employer whose reserve was exhausted. By good fortune, Wisconsin never had to deny benefits to a claimant because his employer's account was exhausted.

18. The seven were: Alabama, California, Kentucky, Louisiana, Massachusetts, New Jersey, Rhode Island. Several states which had enacted an employee tax earlier had repealed the provision by this time [11, pp. 412-13].

19. The eleven states without experience rating were: Georgia, Hawaii, Maine, Maryland, Massachusetts, Mississippi, New York, North Carolina, Pennsylvania, Rhode Island, and Virginia. Nine of these had a provision in the law to study experience rating.

20. The members of the committee were: Clemens J. France, chairman (Rhode Island), William R. Curtis (North Carolina), T. Morris Dunne (Oregon), Paul A. Raushenbush (Wisconsin), Paul L. Stanchfield (Michigan).

ance tax by means other than experience rating. This demand was made although tax rate variations were already in actual operation in four states in 1940
and would begin in fourteen additional states during 1941 and in twenty-one
more states during 1942. Thus the McCormack amendment, as it came to be
known, represented an unwillingness even to wait for the tax reductions that
experience rating would certainly bring. The McCormack amendment was clear
evidence that reduction in the size of the state average tax was not simply the
result of experience rating. Although historically experience rating has been the
only available method of reducing the average tax, in the absence of experience
rating there would have been a demand for some other method.[21]

Insofar as "excessive" reserves really existed, the problem was obviously open
to the alternative solution of improving the meager benefits then provided by
most of the state programs. At the urging of Arthur Altmeyer, the McCormack
amendment was modified to include federal standards governing the levels of
benefits and reserves, and in this form it was passed by the House [5, p. 104].
Vigorously opposed by a number of state administrators, it was rejected by the
Senate in June 1939. Thus, experience rating remained the only available
method of reducing income. Because the alternative to reducing taxes, by any
method, was to liberalize benefits, the ensuing 1940 debate tended to take the
form of "experience rating versus benefit adequacy." Although this formulation
may have had substantial validity in the historical context of 1940,[22] it seems to
have had less validity thereafter (see Chapter 9). But chiefly this formulation
must be watched lest it lead to the false assumption that in the absence of
experience rating the average state tax would have remained at the standard rate
of 2.7 percent, with the resulting funds available for benefit liberalization.

Labor joined the 1939–40 debate with vigor. A long article in the *American
Federationist* [28] provided what still represents the most thorough presentation of labor's case against experience rating. All relevant issues were discussed,
including the charge that experience rating causes employers to protest claims
unnecessarily. (By this time, the states were paying benefits and issues relating to
administration were coming to the fore.) Labor presented its views also at the
1940 ICESA meeting. Robert Watt, speaking for the American Federation of
Labor, described experience rating as "this utterly stupid and destructive form
of sabotage of unemployment insurance" [29, p. 74], while Joseph Kovner of
the Congress of Industrial Organizations agreed that "merit rating threatens the
entire system of unemployment compensation" [29, p. 72].[23]

21. See, for example, the developments in the nonexperience-rated Railroad Unemployment Insurance program, as described in Appendix E.
22. Developments in Puerto Rico in 1970 were a replay of the 1940 situation on the
mainland (see below).
23. Thirty years later, another article in the *American Federationist* showed that labor
was still strongly opposed to experience rating: "Any objective view of the system reveals
that, on balance, experience rating in the unemployment system has proved ineffective as an
employment stabilizer, created needless and bitter conflict between workers, management
and employment security personnel, and deprived the system of needed income by permit-

The ICESA Committee on Experience Rating produced three extensive reports, which were discussed at the 1940 annual meeting. The *Unanimous Report* [31] presented the positions on which all members of the committee could agree. It is significant that this report began by (1) strongly recommending substantial benefit liberalization and (2) warning against a too-easy conclusion that reserves were excessive for even current benefit provisions. Although the members of the committee disagreed among themselves on the issue of experience rating, they were unanimous in these two recommendations. The committee thus made it clear that the issues of benefit liberalization and adequate reserves were separable in principle from the issue of experience rating.[24]

It was only after thus clearing the ground of possible misunderstandings that the *Unanimous Report* proceeded to discuss the possible effects, desirable and undesirable, of experience rating. Paul Raushenbush, who drafted this report, found himself in the same ambiguous position he had occupied during the debate preceding the Social Security Act—in the middle, waging a fight on two fronts. He was defending the socialistic position that more adequate benefits were needed and that this should be the first charge on "excessive" reserves, at the same time that he was defending the individualistic proposals for state freedom from federal standards and for an experience-rated employer tax. The *Unanimous Report* also warned the states that if they adopted experience rating they might have to raise the maximum tax for some employers to the extent they lowered the tax for others.

The *Majority Report* [33] was signed by Curtis, France, and Stanchfield. Two of these men were from states (Rhode Island and Michigan) which had been experiencing a benefit-cost rate of over 2 percent and were concerned about their competitive position with respect to states with lower cost rates. The *Majority Report* argued that experience rating should be allowed only if accompanied by federal benefit standards and that there should be some sharing of unemployment insurance tax funds nationally. The greater part of the argument was directed to establishing that unemployment was generally beyond the control of the individual employer.[25] The conclusion was then drawn that firms with low benefit-cost rates should not be "rewarded" with low tax rates nor should firms with high benefit-cost rates be "punished" with high tax rates. In answer

---

ting the application of grossly inadequate tax rates to a constantly dwindling tax base" [30, p. 17].

24. A recognition of the distinction in principle between these issues is contained in the statement of Joseph Kovner of the CIO, made to the ICESA Committee on Experience Rating: "Perhaps our objections to employer experience rating would not be so serious, as a matter of principle, if it were not for the fact that all of these schemes, with perhaps some exceptions, tend to prejudice the amount of funds available for the payment of benefits" [32, p. 2].

25. This emphasis on what is essentially the stabilization effect of experience rating has continued on down through much of the literature dealing with experience rating (see Chapter 10).

to the objection that a firm should meet its own costs, even those which flow from the nature of its operations and are beyond its control (the allocation effect of experience rating), the report argued:

> The majority members of the Committee are of the opinion that experience rating cannot be justified by the argument that it equitably allocates the social cost of compensated unemployment. In the first place, it cannot be demonstrated that the payroll tax becomes a part of the price of finished goods and services. In the second place, even if the payroll tax could be shifted forward, it is not certain that such shifting would be desirable. In the third place, the majority members feel that there is a basic inconsistency between providing an incentive to stabilize and allocating social costs. An experience rating scheme must do one or the other; it cannot do both. [33, p. 50]

These reasons are discussed in Chapter 3.

The *Minority Report* [34] developed the arguments in favor of experience rating. Reflecting the then current situation, it also devoted much space to the discussion of the related but distinct issue of federal-state relations. It also urged the wisdom of postponing judgment on experience rating until there had been a chance to test it in operation. This report was signed by Raushenbush (its author) and Dunne.

The three reports were the main item of business at the 1940 ICESA meeting. Although no formal action was taken on the reports by the Conference, the discussion at the meeting and the subsequent actions of the states clearly indicated support for the Raushenbush-Dunne position rather than for the France-Curtis-Stanchfield position. (It is not clear, however, how much of this support stemmed from the experience-rating issue and how much from anti-federal sentiment.)

It occasionally happens that scientists come upon some unchanged tribe in a remote part of the world which provides them with the opportunity to study mankind in its early stages of development. In somewhat the same way, Puerto Rico provides an opportunity to see how the issue of the average state tax was intertwined with experience rating in the early years of the program. Puerto Rico still (1971) does not have experience rating. Puerto Rican employers, led by the larger manufacturing firms, have begun a campaign to introduce experience rating. The setting is an almost perfect replay of the 1939-40 episode described above. As the Puerto Rican reserve fund keeps growing, a choice becomes possible between limiting the inflow through lower taxes or increasing the outflow through more liberal benefits. In this situation employers are proposing the inauguration of experience rating and supporting their proposal with two arguments: experience rating will stabilize employment for workers and will lower taxes for employers [35].

In this situation it is easy to understand how anyone opposed to experience rating would direct his attack to these two arguments. Yet in doing so he would be missing the genuine issues involved in experience rating and would be charging windmills. Although stabilization is a genuine effect of experience rating, it is one of the lesser effects. The level of the average state tax is, as was just explained, not an issue in principle at all. Puerto Rico could adopt experience rating and still raise exactly the same sum of money as it would raise with a uniform tax. But because of the historical accident that experience rating is the only method available to vary the tax, and because employers will certainly attempt to lower the level of the average tax simultaneously with the introduction of experience rating, the two issues are actually, for the time being at least, closely intertwined. These were the terms on which the early battles were fought, a historical fact that unfortunately still colors much of the literature dealing with the issue of experience rating, although except in Puerto Rico it is a situation which has long since lost its meaning.

After more and more states had chosen experience rating (forty by 1940, all by 1947), its discussion mainly took the form of criticism of the existing situation, with periodic federal proposals to modify it. Arthur Altmeyer, the chairman of the Social Security Board, changed from a supporter to a severe critic of experience rating [5, pp. 179,n., 258]. The most recent proposal to modify the system, made in 1965 by the Johnson administration in the form of H.R. 8282, was essentially similar to the McCormack amendment of 1939.[26]

Structure of Experience Rating

Principles

Experience rating was defined as a technique for varying the unemployment insurance tax in *some* relation to the taxpayer's experience with the contingency insured against. There are, therefore, degrees of experience rating which depend on the structure of the actual tax system.

The degree of experience rating in a given tax system is determined primarily by three factors: (1) the definition of experience; (2) the measurement of experience; and (3) the translation of this experience into a tax rate. Decisions on each of these depend partly on administrative convenience and cost, and partly on the relative weights to be assigned the various objectives of experience rating. A given procedure may favor the attainment of one objective at the cost of impeding the attainment of another. There is nothing paradoxical in this; it is the usual limitation attaching to the use of a single instrument to attain multiple objectives.[27]

26. The part of H.R. 8282 dealing with experience rating aroused so much opposition that it was omitted from the 1969 version (H.R. 12625) lest its inclusion endanger the rest of the bill.
27. The objectives of experience rating are identical with its possible effects, insofar as these are intended. The main possible effects are listed later in the chapter.

Definition of experience. The *Unanimous Report* of the 1940 ICESA Committee on Experience Rating listed seven possible ways of defining an employer's "experience" with unemployment [31, p. 34]:

1. Variation in the number of persons on the payroll
2. Variation in the number of man-hours of employment
3. Variation in payroll
4. Total number of separations
5. Compensable separations
6. Benefit wages
7. Benefit payments

The last three in the list express experience in terms of benefits, or benefit derivatives, charged against employers.[28] As may be seen from Table A-1, nearly all the states have chosen one of these three as the index of experience.[29] Most states (42) have chosen benefit payments, which was the index recommended by both the Federal Bureau of Employment Security and the Interstate Conference of Employment Security Agencies.

The choice of benefits as the index of employer experience implies the adoption of a point of view that has significance for nearly every other decision to be made in the construction of an experience-rating system. The employer is viewed as assuming some liability for the payment of the taxes needed to support the benefits provided by the state law under the conditions prescribed in the law. This liability is incurred by the very act of paying wages to a covered worker.

Currently, as may be seen from Table A-1, only one state uses the system of compensable separations and only five states use the system of benefit wages.[30] The chief limitation on these two systems is that they do not measure the duration of benefits; one week of benefits has the same significance for an employer's experience as twenty or thirty weeks. Nine states have chosen the benefit-ratio plan and thirty-two the reserve-ratio plan. Both reflect the duration of benefits but the reserve-ratio plan measures much more fully the entire period of an employer's experience in the program.

In the reserve-ratio system, the reserve credited to the individual firm is not, of course, "owned" by that firm, but is merely a bookkeeping device.[31] The

28. "Compensable" separations are merely separations that result in the payment of benefits. "Benefit wages" are merely the wages of beneficiaries. For a fuller description, see Appendix B.

29. Only Alaska, Utah, and Washington currently (1970) use a different index of experience. Alaska and Utah use the payroll variation system entirely; Washington uses it partially. For a description of this system, see Appendix B.

30. This system was promoted in the early days of the program by Frank Cliffe, then of the General Electric Company, to simplify administration at a time when the states had a minimum of administrative expertise. He himself considered the system to be inferior to the reserve-ratio system.

31. However, the condition of the firm's reserve is an economic asset or liability, usually transferrable with the business, that is part of the net worth of the firm.

state's fund is completely pooled and is available for the payment of benefits to any eligible claimant, no matter what the condition of any individual firm's "reserve." Apart from this important difference, the reserve-ratio system embodies the basic concept of the original Wisconsin employer-reserve system. A firm is conceived to have the obligation of accumulating a reserve for the payment of unemployment benefits much as it accumulates reserves for other business costs. Because the reserve-ratio system is the main focus of this study, as explained below, the remaining discussion of structure will apply principally to that system. However, most of what is said will apply also to the other methods that use benefits as an index of experience.

Measurement of experience. The choice of benefits as a measure of an employer's experience with unemployment requires that decisions be made regarding the charging of benefits against the appropriate employers. The chief decisions are two: (1) What benefits are to be charged? (2) Against which employer are they to be charged?

A completely experience-rated system would, of course, charge every benefit to the account of some individual employer. "Anything less represents a departure from the experience-rating principle itself" [36, p. 53]. But no system is completely experience-rated, and all state laws provide for the noncharging of some benefits. For example, some states do not charge the employer's account for dependents' benefits, or for benefits paid to an employee who quit the employer. Also, as explained in Chapter 2, some states, in effect, "uncharge" benefits previously charged by writing off part of the negative balances of deficit firms.

The reasons for the charging or noncharging of benefits are much the same as for having or not having experience rating at all. At the point where the advantages of experience rating are considered to be outweighed by offsetting disadvantages, the charging of benefits will be curtailed and thus the degree of experience rating in the system limited. The states have made, and unmade, judgments regarding the noncharging of benefits in a wide variety of situations, and the pattern of noncharging will probably never become stable. The significance of noncharging is discussed more fully in Chapter 2 and its extent is indicated in Chapter 5.

After deciding what benefits are to be charged, the state must decide against what employers to charge them. This decision presents a problem only in the case of those claimants who have more than one employer in their base period.[32] From scattered sample studies, it would seem that on the average about one-fourth of all claimants have multiple employers in the base period. Are all the base-period employers to be held equally liable for the benefits paid to their

32. This is the period, usually a year, during which the claimant worked in covered employment and established his right to draw benefits from the fund.

common employee, or is one employer to be held more liable or liable earlier than another?[33] The states have given various answers to this question. Currently (1970) of the forty-eight states which charge benefits or benefit derivatives, ten charge only one employer (the most recent or the principal employer) while the other thirty-eight states charge all the employers in the base period—either in inverse chronological order (twelve states) or in proportion to the wages earned with each employer (twenty-six states). The most popular method, the allocation of charges among all base-period employers, was recommended by the ICESA Experience Rating Committee and has an easily understood rationale.[34] As Taulman Miller explains:

> It is a basic element of American unemployment compensation theory and practice that benefits are based on wages earned. It then follows that liability for benefits should be inherent in the payment of wages, and benefits should be charged against all employers from whom wages have been earned during a stipulated base period. This line of reasoning means that when an employer hires workers and pays them wages he accepts a contingent liability for benefit charges in the event of the future unemployment of anyone of those wage earners. This is a perfectly logical view, and, to those who accept it, benefit charges on account of voluntary quits and misconduct discharges do not seem unreasonable or inequitable. [36, p. 58]

This method of charging is indeed "perfectly logical" from the viewpoint of attaining the allocation objective; but if a state preferred to emphasize the objective of employment stabilization, it would probably choose to charge the most recent employer.

With respect to the allocative effect of experience rating, the precise method of charging multiple employers is probably of only minor importance. The problem is limited, first of all, to the minority (one-quarter) of claims that involve multiple employers in the base period. Among even this restricted group of claims, it is likely that most charging methods produce substantially the same effect. An early study made by the Bureau of Employment Security of the different effects produced by various charging methods reached the conclusion that over 85 percent of the firms in the sample would have been assigned identical tax rates under most of the charging methods [36, p. 61]. The method of charging may, however, have more significance for the effects of experience rating on administration and employment stabilization.

Tax as function of experience. The final step is the conversion of an employer's "experience" into a tax rate. This step involves three choices: the range

33. For detailed discussions of this problem, see [37, pp. 16–28] and [36, pp. 53–63, 90–94].

34. It was also recommended, even earlier, by the Social Security Board: "The basis for experience rating should be an assumption of employer liability by reason of the payment of the wages on which benefit rights are based" [37, p. 20].

between the minimum and the maximum tax rate, the number of intermediate tax rates between the minimum and the maximum, and the span of reserve ratios assigned to a given tax rate. The longer the range, the more numerous the intermediate tax intervals, and the narrower the spans of reserve ratios—the more sensitively will the tax structure reflect differences in individual employer experience. The shorter the range, the fewer the intermediate tax rates, and the wider the spans of reserve ratios—the less will the tax structure be characterized by experience rating.

Three major economic considerations explain the universal policy of limiting the maximum tax rate. First, unlimited liability for unemployment costs might act as a deterrent to hiring and thus hamper the achievement of full employment. Second, the very high tax rates which would be imposed on some firms under a rule of unlimited liability could push them below the level of minimal profitability.[35] Third, one purpose of an insurance pool is to provide security at a lower cost than if each employer had to accumulate adequate reserves of his own. Insurance accomplishes this purpose by a sharing of the risk: each employer accepts a small certain loss in exchange for a large uncertain loss. Although it is reasonable to proportion the tax to the risk involved, the measurement of this risk is fraught with uncertainty.[36] The past experience of an individual firm, especially of a small firm, provides only a rough approximation of the risk which that firm represents. This uncertainty should be carried by the fund, not by the individual firm. A limitation placed on the maximum tax achieves this goal.

The above economic reasons for limiting the range between the minimum and the maximum tax rates are logical and probably exert an important influence on actual decisions. But there are also an indefinite number of possible political factors that may affect the outcome, and in many situations the political consideration may be dominant. For example, the maximum tax may remain well below what economic logic would recommend merely because the chairman, or a couple of key members, of the legislative committee responsible for unemployment insurance come from a district with a high-cost industry. Although it is difficult to generalize about the operation of politics in unemployment insurance, the possible importance of this protean factor must always be kept in view.

The choice of a minimum tax above zero is dictated primarily by the consideration that this is a *social* insurance program and therefore some sharing of burdens is to be expected. On the assumption that a given tax increment is less burdensome at the lowest end of the range than at any point above, the lowest-cost firms might reasonably be required to bear part of the burden of the

---

35. Against these first two reasons it can be argued that in a perfect market and over the long run the workers not hired by the less efficient firms would be hired by the more efficient firms. But markets are not usually perfect, and short-run effects can be important.

36. As explained in Chapter 3, it is necessary to distinguish between *insuring* against uncertain losses and *subsidizing* certain losses.

higher-cost firms. Although the assumption is of dubious validity, it is used when politically convenient.

Legislative Profile

No two states are identical in their experience-rating provisions. Moreover, these provisions are very complex and subject to frequent change. Hence, to provide a history of all the changes that have taken place in experience-rating provisions in the life of the program would be a major research project in itself. But it is possible to obtain a hill-top view of the major features of the landscape today, as well as to record a few of the more significant changes in experience rating that have taken place in the past.

Choice of experience rating. A fairly clear picture is available of the stages by which the various states have selected an experience-rating system. The situation as it stood in 1937 was given earlier in the chapter. Table A–1 shows developments from 1938 through 1969. Changes were frequent in the first few years, primarily because the initial decisions had been made hurriedly, under pressure, with a minimum of information. By 1941, however, a more stable pattern had emerged. Thirty-eight states had opted for an experience-rated tax system while thirteen had chosen a uniform tax system. The notable increase in 1945 and 1948 in the number of states with experience rating reflected the pressure of bulging reserves accumulated during the war and the availability of experience rating as the only practical mechanism for lowering the average tax rate below 2.7 percent. It also reflected a growing employer interest in the administration of unemployment insurance and its connection with experience rating. In July 1948 Mississippi became the last state to adopt experience rating. After 1941, by which time a stable pattern had been established, only one state (Alaska in 1955) dropped experience rating from its law. Alaska restored experience rating in 1960.

Ten other states suspended the operation of experience rating for one or more years because of the weakness of their funds. As Table A–2 shows, Rhode Island and Washington accounted for most of the suspensions, but even New York was forced to suspend on two occasions. The largest number of states to suspend in any one year was six, in 1963. Altogether, experience rating was suspended for forty-nine state-years.

Type of system. A number of states which had chosen the reserve-ratio system in the rush of the early years shifted later to other systems, so that by 1941 the reserve-ratio system was the choice of only twenty-three states. Thereafter, its popularity revived, until by 1954 it had attained its original total of thirty-two states.

It remained at this level throughout the rest of the period. As of 1970, these thirty-two states included two-thirds of all covered employment. After 1941 only two states abandoned the reserve-ratio system—Pennsylvania in 1960 (partially) and Oregon in 1964.

In 1948 five states adopted the new payroll-decline system. These had been the final holdouts, and when they did adopt experience rating, it was in a form least open to its alleged undesirable effects.[37] Rhode Island in 1960, Mississippi in 1969, and Washington in 1970 changed under pressure to a more sensitive system of experience rating, so that by 1970 only Alaska and Utah retained a pure payroll-variation plan. Utah, while retaining the payroll-variation system, had adjusted it several times so as to cause seasonal employers to bear a larger part of their benefit costs. This was done each time by increasing the weight given to *quarterly* payroll variations.

In 1958 Kentucky became the last state to abandon all features of the original employer-reserve system and become completely pooled. The other individual-reserve states adopted the completely pooled reserve system as follows: Oregon in 1939; Indiana, Vermont, and Wisconsin in 1945; Nebraska and South Dakota in 1948; North Carolina in 1953.

Tax rates. The single most important determinant of the degree of experience rating in a given law is the range between the minimum and maximum tax rates. In a completely experience-rated system, the minimum would be zero and there would either be no maximum or else the payment of benefits would be discontinued under specified circumstances. The extent to which the actual tax rates in a given law approach this norm is one measure of the degree of experience rating in that law. Table A-12 shows, for years in which the *Comparison* [39] was published, the maximum possible tax rate in each state.[38] The table shows that initially about half the states heeded the recommendation of the *Unanimous Report* of ICESA that there should be some tax rates above 2.7 to compensate for the reduced tax rates below 2.7. During the war years, when reserves accumulated and pressures for tax reduction built up, the states responded by lowering the maximum tax rate, even for those firms which were not paying their way. As of 1951, only eight states had a maximum tax rate above 2.7 percent.

A subsequent weakening of reserves, a development of actuarial expertise (Chapter 2), the growing complaints of stable employers about the burden laid on them of subsidizing other employers, and the widening gap between taxable wages and the wages on which benefits were based, led gradually to the adoption

37. In introducing the payroll decline system in early 1943, the Bureau of Employment Security explained to the states that in this system, "the interests of the worker and employer are not placed in direct opposition, as is the case when every benefit payment made to a claimant affects adversely an employer's record" [38, p. 6].

38. If a state has more than one schedule of tax rates, this table shows the highest rate in the least favorable schedule. It does not necessarily follow that this was the rate effective in the indicated year. It merely indicates what the rate could have been if conditions required it.

of higher maximum tax rates. As of 1969, thirty-nine states had a maximum tax rate above 2.7 and nine of these had a rate of 4.5 or higher.[39] Only twelve states retained the original maximum of 2.7 percent.[40]

The minimum tax rate is one of the more revealing features of a state law.[41] A state which has a minimum tax rate of zero has clearly adopted experience rating in principle, because it has moved as far as it is possible to go in this direction toward complete experience rating. A minimum tax rate above zero has the same significance for employers whose benefit-cost rate is consistently below the minimum tax rate that the maximum tax rate has for employers whose cost rate is consistently above the maximum tax rate: It offers them little or no incentive to do any of the things (desirable or undesirable) that experience rating is said to encourage.[42] As Table A-13 shows, the number of states with a zero rate was ten in 1938, had dwindled to four by 1941, but had increased again to fifteen by 1960. The economic and political reasons for the increase after 1941 have not been ascertained. The explanation probably lies in a decreasing unemployment problem, or an increasing esteem for experience rating, or a combination of the two. As of 1969, ten of the fifteen states with a zero minimum also had a maximum tax rate of 4 percent or more.[43] These states seem to have applied experience rating to a greater degree than the average state.[44]

As may be seen from Table 4-7, even in prosperous 1967 only 2.6 percent of taxable payrolls had been assigned a zero tax rate. Although this percentage may have been higher in 1968 and 1969 (at the time of writing these data were not available) the increase was probably not great. It seems safe to say that unemployment insurance in the United States has made little use of the zero tax rate. However, a quarter of all taxable payrolls were taxed at a rate of 0.5 or less.

As to the number of intermediate rates between the minimum and maximum, the historical trend has been to increase their number and thus to increase the

39. The nine were: Delaware, Florida, Georgia, Idaho, Michigan, Minnesota, North Carolina, Ohio, and Texas.

40. The twelve were: Connecticut, District of Columbia, Kansas, Louisiana, Mississippi, Nebraska, Oklahoma, Oregon, Utah, Virginia, Washington, and Wyoming. Puerto Rico had a uniform tax rate of 2.7 percent.

41. The term "minimum" may have several meanings. It may mean the lowest possible rate that is provided by any of the various schedules that go into effect as the fund rises or falls; or it may mean the lowest rate available in a given schedule. Or it may mean the lowest rate actually assigned in a given year. Finally, in states which have a subsidiary tax (defined later), it is necessary to distinguish the minimum which does and the minimum which does not include the subsidiary tax. In this discussion, "minimum" is used in the sense given first above unless otherwise specified.

42. From the viewpoint of experience rating, one of the results of having a Common Account with a subsidiary tax is the increased freedom to adopt a minimum tax rate of zero in the experience-rated part of the tax structure (see Chapter 2).

43. The ten states were: Florida, Iowa, Kentucky, Michigan, Missouri, New York, Ohio, Pennsylvania, South Dakota, Wisconsin.

44. The qualification "seem" is required because some of these states (Michigan, New York, Ohio, Pennsylvania, and Wisconsin) also make some use of a flat subsidiary tax.

degree of experience rating in the system. However, the states differ widely in this respect (see, for example, Table 4-6).

The degree of experience rating[45] is affected also by the size of the taxable wage base in relation to total wages, but the situation here is too complicated to permit of more than a few generalizations. It is helpful to think of all firms as belonging to one of four types (A, B, C, or D) as shown in the diagram:

	High-wage	Low-wage
High-cost	A	B
Low-cost	C	D

If the wage base used for taxes remains unchanged, while the wages used for calculating benefits are increasing (a common situation historically), and if everything else, including the maximum tax, remains unchanged, the degree of experience rating in the system will probably decrease. If the taxable wage base is increased, while everything else remains unchanged, high-wage firms (A and C) will be affected more than others; but whether this will increase or decrease the degree of experience rating in the total system will depend on a great variety of factors. It may happen, for example, that the increase in the degree of experience rating among firms of type A is offset by a decrease in the degree of experience rating among firms of type C. Many other combinations of results are possible, and there will usually be differences between short-run and long-run results. Thus, while an increase in the maximum tax will always increase the degree of experience rating in the system—a result that may or may not be desirable—an increase in the taxable wage base may increase, decrease, or maintain the existing degree of experience rating, depending on a great variety of factors.[46]

Other developments. In 1954 the federal government covered its employees under the state unemployment insurance system; some local and state governments have done likewise. The federal government also covers ex-servicemen under the state unemployment insurance systems. Governments are not taxed like other employers, but are required to finance only such benefits as are paid under these special programs. Such an arrangement is, of course, 100 percent experience-rated. Substantially the same financial arrangement was made available as an option to nonprofit institutions when they were covered by the passage of H.R. 14705 in 1970. This same bill provided for extended benefits to be paid during recessions and to be financed by a joint federal-state contribu-

45. It will be recalled that by "degree of experience rating" is meant the closeness of the relationship between the benefit-cost rates of individual employers and their respective tax rates.

46. The issue of the size of the taxable wage base was discussed at many places in the 1965 hearings on H.R. 8282; see, for example [2, p. 863, pp. 1235-36]. A fuller treatment of the issue may be found in [40].

tion. Some of the states have arranged to raise their part of the joint contribution by a flat tax, some by an experience-rated tax. As of March 1972, the latter group comprised twenty-eight states with 52 percent of the covered workforce.

Summary. Currently (1971), all states have pooled funds; all but three (Alabama, Alaska, and New Jersey) tax only the employer;[47] and all jurisdictions but Puerto Rico have some form of experience rating. Thus both Wisconsin and Ohio (Raushenbush and Rubinow) have made their contribution to the final structure of the unemployment insurance system.

Since 1935 there have been many legislative changes, some of them increasing, some of them lessening the degree of experience rating in the total system. On the whole, the degree of experience rating probably increased—as more states adopted an experience-rating system of some kind; as more states shifted to the reserve-ratio type of system; as the range between minimum and maximum tax rates grew; and as the number of intermediate rates grew. The main offsets to these developments have been the growth in some states of noncharged benefits and of ineffectively charged benefits.

Study of Experience Rating

Claims and Counterclaims

The social debate that has swirled around experience rating since its inception has generated a series of claims and counterclaims about its desirable and undesirable effects. The six principal effects are listed below and provide the natural structure of the study. They are listed here in an order that permits the showing of three important subgroups.

Effects of experience rating on:

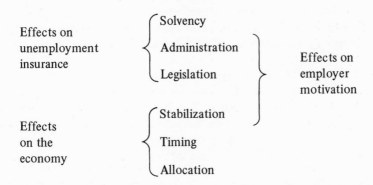

---

47. Alabama taxes the employee only when the state fund drops below a predesignated level. In early 1970 the governor of Alaska asked the legislature to eliminate the employee

One group comprises the effects of experience rating on the unemployment insurance program itself, while another group comprises the effects on the economy. The third group comprises the effects which are mediated by conscious employer activity and can occur only to the extent that experience rating motivates employers to do or refrain from doing something. The other effects, on the contrary, may occur even if employers are unaware of experience rating.

The order in which the effects are treated in the book requires only a brief explanation. Although the effect on solvency is the least important of the six, it is treated first because it offers a convenient opportunity to present background material helpful to an understanding of the other effects. The remaining effects are treated in the order of their current importance,[48] starting with the effect on the allocation of costs and resources.

The first, basic, and inevitable effect of experience rating is to integrate the cost of unemployment benefits into the system of prices through which the market mechanism allocates resources—that is, to make unemployment benefits a regular cost of doing business. The other effects are derivatives of this one and can occur only to the extent that the allocative effect occurs (or is believed to occur). Nevertheless, this is a distinct effect that must be appraised in its own right. Because of its central importance, and also because it is often misunderstood, a full chapter (Chapter 3) is devoted to developing its rationale. Two additional chapters (4 and 5) present the basic data—on benefit-cost rates and tax rates—involved in the discussion of the allocation effect of experience rating.

The effects of experience rating on the unemployment insurance program itself have always been part of the debate, but over time their relative importance has grown. This has been especially true of the effect of experience rating on employer participation in the administrative process. Both friend and foe of experience rating now lay great stress on this effect. Three chapters (6, 7, and 8) are required for a full discussion of the effect on administration.

Another aspect of experience rating involving employer motivation is its impact on employer participation in the legislative process. Although this effect is obviously very important, it is also, unfortunately, very difficult to appraise. As so often happens, the more crucial an issue the less amenable it is to exact measurement and demonstration. What light that can be shed on this issue is provided by Chapter 9.

A third alleged effect of experience rating involving employer motivation is the incentive it provides to stabilize employment. The stabilization issue has lost some of the importance accorded it in the early stages of the debate over experience rating, but it remains a significant issue. It is examined in Chapter 10.

Another way in which experience rating may stabilize employment—besides changing the allocation of resources and influencing an employer's production

---

tax on the ground that the fund did not need it. It would seem, therefore, that in these two states the employee tax is a matter not of principle but only of financial expediency.

48. In the early discussions of experience rating, which make up the larger part of the extant literature, the effect on stabilization was accorded the greatest attention.

and personnel policies—is to counteract the swings in general economic activity called the business cycle. Although to the student of fiscal policy this effect of experience rating on the timing of the tax tends to become the whole issue involved in experience rating, to the legislators who make the decisions, and to the specialists who advise the legislators, this has never been a crucial issue in the debate over experience rating, and hence is treated last.

With respect to each of these six effects, the study attempts to answer two questions: (1) What is the extent of the effect? (2) Is the effect desirable? In combination, these two supply the answer to the central question: Is experience rating desirable?

The scope of the study does not extend, therefore, to the general problem of financing unemployment insurance, nor even to the entire problem of experience rating.[49] Its single objective is to assemble the available evidence for the principal claims and counterclaims that have emerged from the social debate over the desirability of experience rating.

In its early stages, the debate over experience rating was intertwined with three other major issues—individual employer reserves, independent state systems, and sole reliance on the employer tax. None of these was ever a part of the experience-rating issue in principle, and currently none is a live political issue. Hence this study accepts the system as it now stands[50]—with pooled reserves, separate state laws, and almost sole reliance on an employer payroll tax—and merely asks how the tax burden in such a system should be distributed.

The Principle of Limits

Where possible, the study examines a representative sample. But frequently a representative sample—of states, periods, industries, experience-rating systems—was not possible, either because the data were not available on a uniform basis or because the available data were too vast to be handled with limited clerical assistance. In such cases, recourse was had to that useful research tool—the limiting case.

As Aristotle has observed, the nature of anything may be observed most clearly in its most developed specimen. Since the focus of this study is on the effects of experience rating, it would seem to follow that the study can reach significant conclusions by concentrating on those situations where experience rating is most developed and its effects most pronounced. Here, if anywhere, the effects should be most visible. This approach explains, for example, the concentration of the study on the reserve-ratio system of experience rating, which, as explained above, is the most likely to produce all the effects, good and bad,

49. It does not, for example, discuss the technical problems involved in the construction of an experience-rating system, nor analyze the differences between the various systems, nor provide a complete history of experience rating developments in the United States.

50. If the nature of unemployment insurance itself should be changed along the lines once outlined by Eveline Burns [41, pp. 11, 15] so as to emphasize its "social" element more and its "insurance" element less, experience rating would lose much of its logic.

alleged to follow upon experience rating.[51] It also explains the emphasis of the study on the experience of the most active firms.

The use of the limiting case leads to such conclusions as "Effect X was at least this great" or "Effect Y was no greater than this." Such conclusions, while far from exact, are nonetheless useful. Many of our social decisions must be made with no more light than that provided by such generalized guide-lines.

Probably the simplest and most satisfactory way of conceiving the focus of this study is to assume the position of the state legislator who must decide whether to increase or decrease the degree of experience rating in his state's law, or even to eliminate experience rating entirely in favor of a uniform tax,[52] and who would like to know what are the present effects of experience rating in his own state. What help would he—or, more likely, his technical adviser—find in this study?

He would be instructed in what to look for in his own state, and he would find some guidance in how to look for it. Also, he would learn to what extent evidence for a given claim or criticism is lacking and could weight such a claim or criticism accordingly. But principally he would learn what the evidence is for the effects of experience rating "at the limit," that is, in situations where these effects are likely to be most pronounced.

If he concludes that the net effect of experience rating is good in such situations, he is likely to conclude that the net effect in his own state is also probably good and therefore that the degree of experience rating in the state law should be retained or even increased. If, on the other hand, he concludes that the net effect of experience rating is undesirable in those situations where its effects are clearest, he may decide that the probabilities warrant a lessening of the degree of experience rating in his own state.

Many other considerations, of course, including those of a purely political nature, must be weighed before our legislator can make an intelligent judgment on a concrete proposal; but the evidence provided by this study will properly be part of the factors entering into this decision. The goal of this study is a modest one—not to supply the definitive answer to the question, "Is experience rating desirable?" but to narrow somewhat the limits within which intelligent men of good will may agree the answer lies.

51. This system has also considerable representative value, inasmuch as it is the current (1970) choice of thirty-two states embracing about two-thirds of all covered workers.
52. As would have been permitted by H.R. 8282, the 1965 proposal of the Johnson administration.

Solvency of the Fund

The main concern of this chapter is with the effect of experience rating on solvency. Does experience rating, as claimed, provide an automatic mechanism to assure solvency? Or does experience rating, as charged, tend by its nature to reduce the fund and threaten solvency?

An unemployment insurance fund is solvent when it is adequate to pay the benefits specified in the state law. Although the definition of "adequate" has always been disputed, and although any definition must vary as between states because of state differences in industrial composition and in benefit provisions, there is general agreement that at least those funds are insolvent which borrow in order to meet their obligations.[1] By this minimal norm of solvency, three states have encountered insolvency in the history of the program. Alaska, Michigan, and Pennsylvania borrowed from the federal "Reed Fund" during the course of the 1958-59 recession. Three additional states (Delaware, Oregon, and West Virginia) had so depleted their reserves at this time as to become eligible for federal loans if they had chosen to apply. The three borrowing states eventually repaid their loans, Michigan without ever actually using any of the borrowed funds. Any effect that experience rating may have had on actual insolvency has therefore been confined within relatively narrow limits, even on the unlikely assumption that the financial difficulties of these states were traceable primarily to experience rating. Indeed, the chief conclusion of the chapter is that *in principle* experience rating has no effect on solvency.

Before developing this main theme further, it may be useful to comment briefly on the reverse relationship—the effect of solvency on experience rating. Experience rating has its widest scope when the fund is most clearly solvent and its smallest scope when the fund is threatened. At the limit, experience rating is usually suspended completely.

In the history of the program, experience rating has been suspended for forty-nine state-years and repealed for five state-years (Table A-2) because sol-

---

1. The agreement, though general, is not universal. There have always been a few voices raised in praise of planned deficit financing. In 1942 Ewan Clague, then head of the Bureau of Employment Security, directed the attention of all state administrators to the possibility of deficit financing [42, p. 3]. Some use of deficit financing was recommended by Eveline Burns in 1945 [41, p. 5] and by the Senate Advisory Council on Social Security in 1949 [42, p. V-7].

vency was endangered. It should be noted that if the increased taxes resulting from the suspension of experience rating are credited to employer accounts during this period, they will eventually result in greater rate reductions for some employers when variable rating is resumed. In the strictest sense, experience rating is completely suspended only in those instances when the contributions do not operate to reduce future tax rates for individual firms. This would be the case, for example, in states that do not have a reserve-ratio type of formula, or in states which have some form of the Common Account described later.

Nature of the Issue

The attainment of solvency is obviously the first and fundamental objective of any unemployment insurance financial structure. Whether the tax system be uniform or experience-rated, the same fundamental steps must be taken to assure solvency: First, future economic developments must be anticipated and translated into unemployment rates. The amount of compensable unemployment is by all odds the chief factor determining the cost of the system, outweighing all other factors combined [43, p. 12]. Next, unemployment rates must be translated into benefit-cost rates in the light of current and anticipated benefit provisions.[2] Finally, these benefit-cost rates must be expressed as the average tax rate needed over a period of time.

In the early years of unemployment insurance the historical principle of "replenishment" was used rather than the actuarial principle of "expectation." Later, actuarial studies of expected costs became more common. In 1947, after the confusion of the reconversion period had subsided, the Bureau of Employment Security established a Financial Studies Branch to work with the states on the problem of solvency. At about the same time, the Interstate Conference of Employment Security Agencies appointed a committee on long-run financing. In 1950–51 this committee, under the chairmanship of Paul A. Raushenbush, completed a voluminous report of 220 pages which comprised the best thinking on the subject up to that date.

At about this time, also, the states began to make long-range financial studies of their respective programs. Based on the pioneering monograph of W. S. Woytinsky [44] and usually carried out with the assistance of Michael Wermel of the Bureau of Employment Security, such studies were completed and published by practically all states during the period 1951–53. These studies, which the states have enlarged and updated from time to time, are dramatic evidence of how far the actuarial science of unemployment insurance has come since the early 1930's, when the Metropolitan Life Insurance Company was "proving"

---

2. The estimated annual average cost rate is the product of two ratios:

$$\frac{\text{average weekly benefit amount}}{\text{average weekly taxable wage}} \times \frac{\text{average compensable unemployment}}{\text{average covered employment}}$$

that unemployment was not insurable, and when the actuarial societies were in agreement that no unemployment insurance plan could meet "standards of actuarial soundness" [20, p. 74]. In more recent years, Harry Malisoff has updated the discussion on the insurability of unemployment [45] and has further developed the technique of cost estimation in unemployment insurance [46]. However, the techniques involved are complex, and in 1970 it could still be said that the most frequent weakness in the capabilities of the states was in the realm of cost estimating.

Although these studies of solvency open a fascinating field, the temptation to explore the subject must be resisted, since it has only tangential significance for the issue of experience rating. In principle, experience rating as such has no necessary relationship to solvency. An experience-rated tax and a uniform tax are alike in this, that either can produce whatever income is required for solvency. For a quarter of a century all states have been alike in being experience-rated, but they have differed greatly in their financial history and record of solvency. Solvency and experience rating are essentially distinct issues: where the one looks only to the size of the total tax, the other looks only to its distribution among taxpayers.

Alaska provides an interesting example of this difference between the two issues. At the beginning of the year 1960, Alaska taxed all its employers at a uniform rate of 2.9 percent. In the course of the year, the state amended its law to provide for experience rating and a variable tax. But the new experience-rated system was actuarially designed to produce an *average* state tax of 2.9 percent. Thus the previous uniform tax and the new experience-rated tax produced the same amount of income and had the same implications for solvency. The only difference made by the change from a uniform to an experience-rated tax was in the *distribution* of a given total tax burden.

Instrument of Tax Reduction

Although distinct in principle, the issues of experience rating and solvency have been linked historically in two ways. The first relation is rooted in the twin facts that experience rating has been the only instrument available for reducing taxes below the "standard" rate of 2.7 percent (Appendix B) and that practically every threat to solvency has been preceded by a history of tax reduction. When the war ended in 1945 the states found themselves with high reserves which continued to grow after the reconversion period. In this situation, when pressures for lower taxes became insistent, although most states managed their financial affairs responsibly, some followed the easy path of satisfying all sides by raising benefits and lowering taxes simultaneously.[3] This was the easier to do

3. As early as 1936, W. R. Williamson, who was later the chief actuary of the Social Security Board, expressed his apprehension of just such a legislative pattern: "Whether they

because of the relatively undeveloped state of unemployment insurance actuarial science at the time.

Some states reduced the requirements for given rates, or added lower minimum rates, or eliminated rates above 2.7 percent, or added new schedules of lower rates applicable when fund balances reached specified levels. As reserves were drawn down and automatic mechanisms were about to go into operation to raise taxes, some legislatures took direct action to prevent these safeguards from performing their function. For example, Pennsylvania acted thus in 1956, Oregon in 1958, and Delaware and Maryland in 1959.

As Table 2-1 shows, of the six states eligible for federal loans in 1958, all had maintained an average tax rate lower than their average benefit-cost rate during the preceding decade, and five of them had reduced their average tax rate significantly below the "standard" rate of 2.7 percent. Five of these states could have avoided the worst of their financial troubles by an increase of their average tax rates during the decade of less than 1 percent (Delaware, by an increase of only 0.3 percent). Clearly, this financial crisis was due not so much to overwhelming benefit costs as to a record of unwise tax reductions.

Table 2-1. Average Benefit-Cost Rates[a] and Tax Rates,[a]
Six States, 1949-58

State	Average annual benefit-cost rate 1949-58	Average annual tax rate 1949-58
United States	1.6	1.3
Alaska	3.6	2.5
Oregon	2.2	1.5
Pennsylvania	2.1	1.4
Michigan	2.1	1.6
West Virginia	1.9	1.1
Delaware	0.9	0.6

Source: Staff paper prepared for the Federal Advisory Council, October 27, 1959 (mimeo.), p. 2.

[a]Benefits and taxes as percents of taxable wages.

Since experience rating has been the only mechanism available for reducing taxes below the standard 2.7 percent, whatever reductions have occurred and whatever effects these reductions have had on solvency are attributable in a sense to experience rating. But this is a relationship, not of principle, but only of historical accident. In the absence of experience rating, some other method would undoubtedly have been devised to enable states with excessive reserves to

[administrators of unemployment insurance] can resist the temptation to reduce the rates of contribution at the very time when their continuance is relatively easy [in prosperous years] may determine the solvency of the plan" [47, pp. 37-38].

lower their average tax rates below the standard 2.7 percent. The incident of the 1939 McCormack amendment narrated earlier (p. 12) and the history of Railroad Unemployment Insurance (see Appendix E) underline the truth of this crucial proposition.

The original choice of 2.7 percent had been made in the dim, early light of the meager statistics on unemployment available at that time,[4] and the significance of this "standard" diminished rapidly in the growing light of experience. Instead of the modest benefits of the original laws costing 2.7 percent of total wages, the liberalized benefits provided by the frequently amended state laws proved to cost only about 1 percent (Table A-3). It may assuredly be argued that many states should have provided more liberal benefits; but these were, as a matter of fact, the levels of benefits the states chose to establish, and they adjusted their tax levels to fit these benefit levels.

Adjustments were made as the reserves of some states ballooned to clearly excessive size. At the end of 1950 the average state reserve was sufficient to pay benefits (at the average 1946-50 benefit-cost rate) for 5.7 years, even if no further taxes were levied and no interest were received on existing reserves [48, p. 7]. For Iowa this figure was 23.6 years. In 1953 this figure was twenty-five years for Colorado and twenty-seven years for Texas. As Horwitz had warned in 1938 [49], and as the McCormack amendment had demonstrated in 1939, the states needed, and were certain to secure, some method of varying their tax rates. States that lowered taxes under experience rating irresponsibly or ignorantly presumably would have followed the same general course under the other alternative of a tax uniform for all employers in a given state at a given time but variable over time.

A discussion of experience rating that proceeds by comparing the total taxes collected under experience rating with what would have been collected under the "standard" 2.7 percent rate is dealing with a largely fictitious issue. This is a mathematical exercise leading to no significant conclusion. Yet it is a frequent exercise. Service companies regularly make this comparison by way of demonstrating to a client how much they have "saved" the firm in taxes. The federal Bureau of Employment Security and some of the states have frequently published tables showing the difference between what would have been produced by an average tax of 2.7 percent and the amount actually produced "under experience rating." The implication seems to be that this is the amount "lost" to the system by experience rating. The comparison between the two amounts is some-

---

4. As participants in the decisionmaking process recall the original line of reasoning, it began with the judgment that a 3 percent tax (on total payrolls) was about the maximum industry could stand in that depressed period. Of this, about 10 percent (0.3 percent of payrolls) would be needed for administrative expenses, leaving 2.7 percent for the payment of benefits. Uncertain as to what level of benefits this amount of money would support, the government actuaries recommended a very conservative approach.

times made even in academic writings, as when Teple and Nowacek use the difference between the two amounts as the measure of "the extent and importance of the system" [50, p. 377]—meaning by "the system," experience rating.

Labor regularly makes the explicit charge that experience rating has resulted in inadequate financing and, as a consequence, in inadequate benefits. The possible effect of experience rating on benefit adequacy is indeed a genuine issue; however it is the issue not precisely of solvency, but of legislation, and is more appropriately discussed in Chapter 9. Here it suffices to repeat that a simple comparison between the "standard" 2.7 percent and the actual average tax rate sheds little light on any genuine issue, including the issue of benefit adequacy, because the comparison rests on the invalid assumption that the 2.7 rate is "standard" in some normative sense and that this standard would have been maintained in the absence of experience rating.

Uncharged Benefits

Although in principle experience rating does not differ from a uniform tax in its effect on solvency, may there not be some characteristics of experience rating which endanger solvency in practice? The qualified affirmative which must be given to this question constitutes the second, and more significant, historical relationship between experience rating and solvency.

By definition, experience rating relates taxes to individual employer experience, and nearly all states measure "experience" in terms of benefits charged to employer accounts. It follows that if some benefits are paid that are not effectively charged to some employer's account, an imbalance will tend to develop between the fund's inflow and outflow. Uncharged benefits open a gap in the foundations of experience rating and imperil the principle that the degree of experience rating on the benefit side and on the tax side must balance. Benefits that are not charged to any employer's account should be balanced by income that is not credited to any employer's account. To the extent that the system includes some benefit costs which are outside the experience rating mechanism, it must also include some income which is outside the experience-rating mechanism.[5]

The principle is simple, there are many ways of applying it, and most states have applied it successfully. Nevertheless, there is always the danger that the principle will be overlooked, and this constitutes a potential threat to solvency not similarly present in a uniform tax system. The danger is the greater as the psychology of experience rating leads the taxpayer to think in terms only of costs for which he individually is "responsible" and to resist the payment of taxes that do not meet this norm. The danger is further aggravated to the extent

5. The Bureau of Employment Security voiced this warning as early as 1944 [51, p. 22].

that "responsibility" is defined in the narrow sense of ability to control unemployment.

All states pay some benefits which are not effectively charged to an employer's account.[6] Data on the extent of these uncharged benefits are presented in Chapter 5; here it suffices to describe the two kinds of such benefits. It should be noted that uncharged benefits have significance for all the alleged effects of experience rating. They are described here rather than elsewhere merely because solvency is the first effect to be discussed.

Noncharged Benefits

The first species of uncharged benefits is generally termed "noncharged benefits" and consists of those benefits that have never been charged to any employer's account.[7] Noncharged benefits take a variety of forms.

For example, charges may be omitted if benefits are paid in error and not recovered; or if an earlier determination granting benefits is reversed; or if benefits are paid to an individual taking approved training; or if the separating employer has employed the claimant for only a very brief period. As of 1970, six of the eleven states with dependents' allowances did not charge such benefits to individual employer accounts; such noncharges are second in size only to those connected with disqualifications.

The extended benefits provided by the employment security amendments of 1970 are 50 percent state financed. As of March 1972, twenty-eight states had arranged to charge these extended benefits to the accounts of individual firms and thus make them a part of the state's regular experience rating system. The remaining twenty-four states[8] had arranged to noncharge these benefits.

By far the most important noncharges in both size and significance are those connected with disqualifications, and these have been growing. In 1945 only four states had provisions for the noncharging of benefits connected with disqualifications;[9] in 1970 thirty-six states had such provisions.[10]

---

6. Except in one state (Wisconsin) for a part of one year (1936) there have always been legal provisions for the payment of such benefits.

7. The writing off of negative balances (see below) is the equivalent of noncharging. It is a kind of delayed noncharging.

8.

Arkansas	Maine	Oregon
California	Massachusetts	Pennsylvania
Connecticut	Michigan	Rhode Island
District of Columbia	Minnesota	South Carolina
Hawaii	Mississippi	South Dakota
Idaho	Nevada	West Virginia
Illinois	New Mexico	Wisconsin
Kansas	North Carolina	Wyoming

These twenty-four states include about 48.3 percent of all covered employment.

9. Maine, Minnesota, New Hampshire, West Virginia.

10. Only twelve states charged all benefits connected with disqualifications: Colorado, District of Columbia, Illinois, Iowa, Louisiana, Maryland, Michigan, New Jersey, New York, North Dakota, Virginia, Wisconsin.

Noncharged benefits may be connected with disqualifications in two ways. In the usual situation, the claimant is disqualified for a number of weeks in connection with his separation from employer X, serves out the disqualification period, and then draws benefits which though based (wholly or partially) on wages earned with employer X are not charged against the account of employer X. In the other situation, the claimant is not disqualified at all, yet his benefits are noncharged. For example, under some state laws an employee may quit his job "for good cause" and be immediately eligible for noncharged benefits. This situation is usually described as noncharging in "potentially" disqualifying circumstances.

Noncharged benefits would seem to be in conflict with the provision that no reduced rate is to be granted an employer except on the basis of his experience with unemployment (see Appendix B). In *Unemployment Compensation Program Letter No. 78*, dated December 29, 1944, the Bureau of Employment Security informed the states that the Social Security Board had interpreted this provision to require, not that *all* benefits be charged, but only "that those which are charged assure a reasonable measure of the experience of employers with respect to unemployment risk." This administrative decision, which has never been challenged, in effect loosened the federal standard regulating experience rating and allowed the states additional freedom to decide what degree of experience rating they would have.

All noncharged benefits, but especially those related to potential disqualifications, represent a clear and explicit decision to limit the operation of experience rating. The commonest rationale offered for the limitation is linked with the stabilization issue: The employer should not be charged for unemployment for which he was not "responsible"—that is, which he could not prevent. But, in reality, the main reason back of most noncharging provisions is their link with the legislation issue: If the employer is not charged, he will not be so insistent that the law contain strict disqualification provisions.[11] Labor therefore tends to favor noncharging. In earlier years most employers also generally welcomed an extension of noncharging. Then the more sophisticated among them began to preach to their fellows that any tax saving was, and had to be, illusory, since all benefits paid—whether charged or noncharged—had to be replaced by tax income. Hence, where noncharging has been curtailed or eliminated, it has usually been with the active support, or even on the initiative, of employers. The em-

---

11. In a legislative manual prepared for the use of the states, the Bureau of Employment Security reminded the states that noncharging is an alternative to severe disqualifications: "Since omission of charges for benefits in such circumstances [quit for good personal cause] has been found consistent with the provisions of section 1602 (a) (1) and (3) of the Federal Unemployment Tax Act, such restrictive disqualification provisions are not necessary to prevent the charging of benefits when charging benefits to a specific employer does not appear reasonable under the theory of employer responsibility for an individual's unemployment" [52, p. C-60]. Probably the earliest recognition of this possible use of noncharging appears in a 1936 article by Elizabeth Brandeis [53, p. 60].

ployer service companies, on the other hand, favor the broader extension of noncharging provisions, which increase their opportunity to "save" a client some taxes.

Ineffectively Charged Benefits

The other species of uncharged benefits consists of those which are charged against an employer whose reserve is exhausted and who is already paying the maximum tax.[12] The charging of such benefits is ineffective in the sense that it neither draws on past accumulated taxes (reserves) nor triggers additional current taxes. It merely results in the accumulation of a "negative reserve" on the part of the firm charged. Hence, like noncharged benefits, ineffectively charged benefits pose a threat to solvency not adequately met by the experience-rating mechanism.

The charging of such benefits may be temporarily or permanently ineffective. If the charges always remain against the account of firm X, they may be only temporarily ineffective. Although they are ineffective as of a given time, they may become effective later. Firm X may eventually pay off its total debt to the fund. Or firm X may eventually be absorbed by a firm with a positive reserve that will more than offset X's negative balance.[13]

But many states have the practice of writing off ("forgiving") negative reserves, and then the charged benefits represented by these negative reserves are permanently ineffective. The practice of writing off negative reserves is identical in its effect with the practice of noncharging benefits. Where noncharging neutralizes current benefits, the writing off of negative reserves neutralizes past benefits. Both practices prevent the experience-rating mechanism from triggering the tax flow required to offset the payment of benefits.

The chief reason usually given for writing off negative reserves is to safeguard those effects of experience rating which depend on employer motivation.[14] If an employer sees no hope of ever getting out of debt to the fund and thus achieving a lower tax rate, he will have none of the incentives that experience rating is supposed to provide. But if his debt is systematically cut back to a specified size (expressed as a percentage of his taxable payroll) his hope of someday attaining a lower tax rate may be kept alive. Thus the decision to write off negative reserves represents a choice between effects of experience rating: a diminished

12. Also, benefits charged against firms that are no longer in the state. Construction companies frequently move into a state only for the duration of a job. By the time their laid-off employees are filing for benefits the company has left the state. (To counter this situation, Michigan has enacted a special maximum tax payable by such companies.)

13. Neither contingency is very likely, but they do occur. See, for example, the experience of Company E shown in Chart II, Chapter 11. Although at one time in the period shown this company had a negative balance, it eventually repaid its debt.

14. Often, some political trade-off is involved. For example, to get high-cost employers to agree to an increase in the maximum tax, they may be offered a write-off of accumulated negative balances.

effect on the allocation of costs is accepted in order to maintain presumed desirable effects on administration, legislation, and stabilization.[15]

Wisconsin was the first state to adopt this technique. By a 1937 amendment to its law, it provided that negative balances would be written off annually down to 4 percent (later changed to 10 percent) of the negative employer's taxable payroll. Some other states adopted similar provisions later. Although no complete listing of states with such provisions is available, the following are examples of states which, as of 1970, wrote back negative balances to the indicated percentages.[16] The lower the percent, the greater, of course, is the write-off. A few states have adopted such provisions and later rescinded them, as they

Pennsylvania	0%	Rhode Island	4.2%
New York	2%	Ohio	5%
Massachusetts	3%	Wisconsin	10%

changed their evaluation of the relative importance of the different effects of experience rating. Also, although Michigan and California normally accumulate negative balances indefinitely, on occasion each has proclaimed a year of jubilee and written off all negative balances to give employers a fresh start. Michigan did so in 1957 (in exchange for employer agreement to a 50 percent increase in the maximum tax rate), and California did so in 1966.

Ineffectively charged benefits result primarily from a too-low maximum tax rate. In general, the states have been slow to adopt the recommendations of the Bureau of Employment Security and the Interstate Conference of Employment Security Agencies that experience rating be made to work in both directions—not only lowering taxes for some employers, but raising taxes for others. Although the original 2.7 percent "standard" rate was chosen during a period of deep depression and was based on a minimum of statistical information, it tended to become the top state rate. Once established it acquired a kind of sanctified stability which enabled it to persist for many years in some states. Still, by 1970, all but eleven states had broken out of the mold and had established a maximum tax rate above the original 2.7 percent.

If total wages were taxed, the extent of ineffectively charged benefits would be a function simply of the maximum tax rate. But ever since 1939 the taxable wage base has been less than total wages and hence has been a separate, independent factor making for a possible increase in the amount of ineffective benefit charges. The average benefit amount tends to grow in some proportion to total wages, while tax rates are applied only to taxable wages. A difference in the

15. But in a situation such as described in the preceding footnote, even the allocative effect of experience rating may be increased—because of the increase in the maximum tax, not otherwise attainable.

16. Among the states which do *not* write off negative balances but accumulate them indefinitely are the following: Arkansas, California, Indiana, Kentucky, Michigan, New Jersey, North Dakota, South Carolina.

movements of the two bases tends to produce a discrepancy between outflow and inflow and to affect the size of reserves.[17]

Ineffectively charged benefits combine with noncharged benefits to make up that proportion of total benefits which represent pooled or shared costs. Part of the taxes paid by positive-balance employers go to finance these pooled costs, and recognition is growing that this part should not be credited to individual reserve accounts.[18] On their face, the employer reserve accounts represent taxes paid into the fund and not used.[19] To the extent that they have in fact been used to pay pooled benefit costs they should not be credited to individual employer accounts. When they are so credited they create fictitious ("paper") reserves which in the aggregate exceed the balance of the fund. But the sum of the parts cannot really be greater than the whole!

In Pennsylvania, for example, the whole fund disappeared under an avalanche of deficit accounts at the same time that employers generally had vast paper reserves to their credit. In 1959 Pennsylvania employers had $700 million to their credit, while there were actually only $100 million in the fund. Thus each dollar credited to individual accounts was worth only about 15 cents.[20] Many other states had a similar experience, though not to the same extent. For example: In 1958, in Indiana, the sum of employers' positive experience accounts was approximately $26 million greater than the actual trust fund balance [54, p. 46]. In 1963, in Tennessee, the sum of employer credits was approximately $165 million, while the balance in the fund was only about $65 million, so that one dollar of employer credit was worth about 39 cents [55, p. 30].

The Common Account

In a reserve-ratio system, there are various ways of providing income to match noncharged and ineffectively charged benefits, but the most direct and accurate way is to set up a separate account to which all such benefits are charged and to which a corresponding proportion of total income is credited.[21] Since this in-

17. As of January 1970, almost half of total wages covered by unemployment insurance were outside the taxable wage base. More than half the states (twenty-nine) still retained the taxable wage base of $3,000 set by the federal government in 1939; of the twenty-two states which had raised the base, only five had acted before 1960. However, in 1970 Congress enacted H.R. 14705, which raised the taxable wage base to $4,200, effective January 1, 1972.

18. An excellent discussion of this and of related propositions is contained in five "Technical Papers," Series R #24, prepared by the Research and Statistics division of the California Department of Employment over the period 1961-70.

19. Reserves credited to the accounts of firms are not in any sense "owned" by the firms to which they are credited, but are merely an accounting device used to determine tax rates.

20. The growth in this disproportion was gradual and could have been prevented. In 1954 a dollar credited to an employer's reserve was worth 81 cents; in 1956, 56 cents; in 1959, 15 cents; and in March 1961 it was worth nothing—the fund was bankrupt.

21. For a discussion of this device see Michigan [55, p. 19] and New York [57, pp. 40-41] (see also [58, p. 48]).

come is not credited to individual employer accounts, it avoids the accumulation of fictitious employer reserves and the consequent premature triggering of lower tax rates.

The device goes by a variety of names in the states which use it (see below). It is called here the Common Account to indicate its function of registering those benefit costs and taxes which have been made—by state law—a common obligation of all covered employers. The Common Account is not a separate fund; it is only a bookkeeping device designed to make clear what is happening to the fund and to trigger the tax flow needed to replenish the fund for benefits not automatically financed through the experience-rated provisions of the tax schedule.

The Common Account is debited with noncharged benefits, ineffectively charged benefits,[22] and other minor charges. The income credited to the Common Account arises from a number of sources: interest earned by the fund, positive reserves remaining in closed accounts, and various other small sources such as penalties and repayments.[23] If these "regular" sources prove inadequate to balance the charges made against the Common Account, an additional levy is made upon employers.[24] In most states, the levy takes the form of a subsidiary tax which is added to current tax rates, but in Rhode Island it takes the form of a transfer of employer reserves to the Common Account.[25] This is equivalent to a levy on past taxes (a kind of "un-crediting" of tax payments previously credited) and of course affects only firms with positive reserves. From the viewpoint of experience rating, the method of adding a special tax has two advantages over the method of transferring reserves: (1) It makes the extent of subsidy more measurable and hence more visible. (2) Because it imposes the additional levy on all employers, including those with negative balances, it lessens the extent of the subsidy.

The prototype of the Common Account is perhaps the "partial pool" established by states which originally adopted the individual employer reserve system (see Chapter 1). The pooled part of the total fund was available for the payment of benefits to claimants whose firm's account was exhausted. Unlike the Common Account, however, the partial pool was not a mere bookkeeping device. It

22. The states with Common Accounts vary in their definition of ineffectively charged benefits. Some states (for example, California and Michigan) charge to the Common Account all negative balances, while other states (for example, New York, Ohio, and Wisconsin) charge only that part of the negative balances that have been written off ("forgiven").

23. In Massachusetts the Common Account is also automatically credited with any firm's reserve which is in excess of 13 percent of taxable payrolls. Such a provision represents a very explicit move away from experience rating.

24. A simpler, but less flexible, procedure is followed by West Virginia, which allocates the first 0.7 percent of each employer's tax to the general account and not to his individual reserve account. This unvarying tax is levied automatically, rather than in proportion to varying needs.

25. In Wisconsin a firm with a positive balance has the option to pay an additional tax or to have a portion of its reserves transferred. New York made some use of the transfer method during the period 1958–63; Massachusetts used the transfer method exclusively until 1970, when it changed to the method of an additional tax.

was a separate fund in the sense that these unchargeable benefits could continue to be paid only as long as there was a positive balance in the pooled fund.

The development of the partial pool into the Common Account may be illustrated in the case of Wisconsin. Starting with no provision for pooling in its 1932 law, by 1935, when it began to pay benefits, Wisconsin provided for a small pool made up of reserves left in closed accounts. This sufficed to save the state from ever having to deny a benefit because an employer's reserve was exhausted.

In 1937 the resources of this pool were enlarged by an amendment to the law allocating interest earned by the fund to a "balancing account."[26] In 1939 the state recognized that interest earnings might not always be sufficient, and the law was again amended to require that when the balancing account dropped below a specified figure ($500,000), an additional tax was to be levied on all employers and the proceeds credited to the pool. Before this provision was ever applied, it was changed by a 1941 amendment: When the balancing account dropped below $2,000,000, *reserves* were to be *transferred* from the accounts of employers to the balancing account. In 1945 Wisconsin changed to a completely pooled fund,[27] but retained the device of the balancing account, whose critical level was raised to $10,000,000 by a 1957 amendment.

In 1963–64 the balancing account dropped below $10,000,000, and the state for the first time had to call on employers for additional funds. The transfer of reserves was announced in early 1964, but led to such an outcry that the very first act of the 1965 legislature was to suspend the transfer until a different provision could be devised. Later in the year the law was amended to provide that positive employers could choose between having their reserves transferred or paying an equivalent additional tax, but negative employers would have to pay the additional tax. The safety level of the balancing account was raised several times, until eventually it was tied automatically to changes in total (not taxable) covered wages. As of 1970, the critical level of the balancing account was 0.4 percent of total covered wages.

Wisconsin seems to have been the only one of the original individual reserve states to retain the device of the separate account when changing from individual reserves to a pooled system. Some states, however, which always had completely pooled funds, later adopted the device of the separate account within the pooled fund. As of 1970, the following states were known to have adopted the Common Account under the indicated titles and on the indicated dates:

26. This change was initiated by the employer members of the Wisconsin Advisory Council.

27. The fund requirements for individual reserves were very high: five times the largest amount of benefits paid in the most recent three-year period. It was expected that very high benefits would be paid during the reconversion period. Hence a very large reserve would have to be accumulated after the reconversion period, and experience rating would practically disappear for some years. The requirements for the pooled type of fund were much easier to meet.

Wisconsin	Balancing Account (1937; 1945)
New York	General Account (1951)
Massachusetts	Solvency Account (1951)
Michigan	Solvency Account (1954)
Rhode Island	Solvency Account (1958)
California	Balancing Account (1961)
Ohio	Mutualized Account (1963)

Although the device of the Common Account is available only to reserve-ratio states, some benefit-ratio states have the equivalent in their use of an "adjustment factor" to raise experience-rated taxes sufficiently and automatically to cover pooled costs. As of 1970, four states—Florida (1957), Pennsylvania (1960), Mississippi (1964), Wyoming (1964)—made use of such a device. Allowing for procedural differences, the adjustment factor operates essentially as follows: The noncharged and ineffectively charged benefits paid during the preceding fiscal period are expressed as a percentage of the taxable wages of that same period, and this percentage is added uniformly to all employer tax rates. Thus if the total of noncharged and ineffectively charged benefits is 0.5 percent of taxable wages, the tax rates of all employers are increased by 0.5 percent. The adjustment factor is essentially similar to the Common Account in that it divides the tax system into separate, distinguishable parts, of which one is experience-rated while the other is not.

The Common Account and the adjustment factor are not the only methods of providing income to cover pooled benefit costs. For example, the interest earnings of the fund fulfill this function in the states (nearly all of them) which do not credit this interest to the individual employer accounts. Or, again, the regular tax schedules may be geared to produce individual employer reserves with sufficient "excess" to cover whatever pooled costs occur. For example, a minimum tax may be imposed on all employers no matter how good their individual experience may be. Or, even if the minimum tax is allowed to drop to zero, the reserve requirements at all tax levels may be sufficiently "excessive" to provide the subsidy needed for the negative accounts. So long as the state average tax rate equals the state average benefit-cost rate, it is certain that the pooled costs are being financed in some fashion. What the device of the Common Account does is to provide a specific, automatic, and somewhat more accurate method of performing this task. As California observed:

> The balancing tax has introduced a highly illuminating concept. If pursued, it can achieve an elegantly straightforward fulfillment of the objective of actuarial balance. The balancing tax was introduced into the statute with the view, obviously, of achieving an offset to the so-called "socialized" cost. ... If it were adequate for that purpose, then the remainder of the financing would consist of nothing more or less than each employer meeting his own charged benefits, up to the fixed maximum tax rate, with

some mechanism for smoothing contribution changes over a period of time. [58, p. 48]

The Common Account has significance not only for the issue of solvency, but for the issue of experience rating itself. Seen from the viewpoint of experience rating, the device of the Common Account has several advantages. (1) It helps to maintain the normal structure of tax differentials among employers. An employer whose regular rate is 1 percent may have to pay a total rate of 2 percent during the period that the subsidiary tax (credited to the Common Account) is 1 percent; but, if that happens, then the employer whose regular rate is 2.7 percent will pay 3.7 percent for that same period. For the negative-account employer, it is as though the maximum tax rate were raised. (2) The Common Account facilitates the use of a zero minimum tax. Since the only function of a minimum tax above zero is to finance pooled costs, the need for such a tax is obviously lessened by the operation of a Common Account. This is a consideration of some importance to experience rating because a minimum tax rate above zero may offer no more incentive to some low-cost employers (those whose benefit-cost rate is significantly below the minimum tax) than does the maximum tax rate to some high-cost employers. (3) The Common Account increases the visibility of pooled costs and provides a useful measure of the degree of experience rating in the system (see, for example, Table 5-1). However, to some proponents of experience rating, these advantages are outweighed by the danger that the Common Account may encourage a habit of thinking that will eventually undermine the principle of experience rating itself.

Allocation of Costs I: *Claims and Counterclaims*

PART I: THE CLAIMED EFFECT

Nature of the Claim

The most basic advantage claimed for experience rating is that it accords with our society's choice of the free market as the major mechanism for the allocation of resources.

The case for this claim may be set out in the form of a loose sorites: (1) As its main mechanism for the allocation of resources our society has chosen the free market. (2) The market works the more efficiently as market prices more accurately reflect the full costs of production. (3) The costs of production are reflected in market prices, the more fully as the unemployment tax is the more completely experience-rated. (4) Thus experience rating accords with society's choice of the market as the main mechanism for the allocation of resources.

The final step in the argument produces a fifth and crucial proposition: (5) Since experience rating thus accords with society's fundamental economic choice, it occupies a position of presumptive favor. Although the presumption is rebuttable by specific evidence, in the absence of such evidence the allocation effect of experience rating enjoys the benefit of the doubt. To put this proposition in a slightly different form: When specific evidence of undesirability is not obtainable (the usual case), the desirability of the allocative effect of experience rating is assailable only by denying the first proposition of the sorites, which is almost universally accepted.[1]

Despite its central importance, the allocative effect of experience rating has received less explicit attention than almost any other effect.[2] A discussion that starts with the allocative effect tends to veer off almost immediately in the

1. In his 1970 presidential address to the American Economic Association, Wassily Leontief was stating the common view of economists when he said: "Our free enterprise system has rightly been compared to a gigantic computing machine capable of solving its own problems automatically" [59, p. 6].
2. For example, one long and otherwise balanced article on experience rating dispatches this effect in two short paragraphs [50, p. 379], and still another relegates it to a footnote [41, p. 13, n. 41].

direction of other related effects, especially the "stabilization" effect, with which it is frequently confused. As a result, the discussion reaches no conclusion on this precise issue—the effect of experience rating on the allocation of costs and hence of resources. As a way of keeping this precise issue in focus, it is helpful to assume at this point that there are no other effects of experience rating. Suppose that experience rating has no effects whatsoever on administration, legislation, stabilization, timing, or solvency. There would still be this question to answer: What is the impact of experience rating on the allocation of resources, and is the impact desirable? Other effects of experience rating, if they occur, may offset or support this effect. But the effect of experience rating on the allocation of costs and therefore of resources is distinct and separate from all other effects and is therefore to be evaluated in its own right.

Definitional Clarifications

At the outset it may be advisable to guard against certain common misunderstandings of the nature of this claim. This claim for experience rating does not rest on a value judgment—that the market is actually the best allocator—but merely on the historical fact that (wisely or not) our society has chosen the market as the main mechanism for the allocation of resources. In what is one of the better analyses of experience rating, Taulman Miller properly relates the allocation effect to "desirable social policy"; but he then reduces that policy to "fairness" and dismisses the whole issue by saying: "Discussions of fairness or equity become deeply involved with subjective value judgments, and the temptation to drop the matter of experience rating and equitable cost allocation at this point is strong" [36, pp. 24-25]. Although the value judgments which support a society's institutions are subjective, the actual choice of one institution over another is an objective historical fact. Thus, it is not "a subjective value judgment" but an objective fact that our society has chosen the market as its main mechanism for the allocation of resources.

This claim does not undertake to establish that the effect of experience rating on the allocation of resources is significant; still less does it undertake to predict what the effect will be in any given set of circumstances. The strategic importance of the claim lies elsewhere, namely in the proposition that experience rating enjoys a preferred position as the result of our prior, basic preference for the market.

Neither does this claim rest on the assumption that the free market is our only mechanism for the allocation of resources. The claim recognizes that every modern economic society is "mixed"—in the sense that it makes use both of controls and of the free market—and that the degree to which we rely on the market varies from situation to situation. In time of war or under the threat of runaway inflation, we allow the market much less freedom than we do during more normal times. Even in more normal times we allow the market much less freedom in the allocation of resources to some industries—to the liquor and tobacco industries, for example—than to other industries. Moreover, during the last fifty years we have set up many permanent social structures whose net effect has been to limit the free operation of the market. The enactment of a compulsory unemployment compensation program itself is one in a long list of such actions. However, each such action had to overcome, usually with great difficulty, the favorable presumption that the market enjoyed. Presently, it remains true that the dominant style of American economic life as compared, say, to the dominant style of Russian economic life is its reliance on the free market as the major mechanism for the allocation of its resources.

The history of the 1971 price controls established by the Nixon administration illustrates both the presumptive favor enjoyed by the market and the possibility of overturning the presumption. The whole inclination of the Nixon administration and of the country generally was to avoid controls. When they were finally embraced it was with great reluctance and on a temporary basis. Even then, organized labor declared it would not cooperate if government insisted on exercising final control over the decisions of the tripartite policy committees. The institutional values illustrated here are typically American. Intervention in the market will be accepted, but it must be justified each time in each specific situation. The presumption is in favor of the market.

The claim obviously rests on an assumption of employer responsibility for unemployment, but the meaning of "responsibility" must be carefully defined. The responsibility that is relevant hery is not limited to the employer's ability or inability to control unemployment. This point must be made emphatically, because failure to recognize it has been the source of frequent confusion in discussions of the allocative effect of experience rating.[3]

A helpful illustration is at hand in the history of workmen's compensation. In Europe, the development of this program proceeded by three stages: (1) It was recognized that the employer's responsibility extended to injured workmen in cases where it was the employer's fault and (a later development) that the burden of proof was on the employer to establish that the accident had occurred without any negligence on his (the employer's) part. (2) Accidents that happen through no one's fault, but are the expected consequences of certain industrial processes, are also the employer's responsibility. This became known as the "trade risk" and became accepted as a regular cost of doing business, just as the repair of inanimate machinery was accepted as a regular cost of doing business. (3) Finally, the employer was held responsible for compensating all injuries, even those caused by some negligence on the part of the employee.

The "responsibility" relevant to the allocative effect of experience rating includes responsibility for the "trade risk." It may even include responsiblity for unemployment traceable to some employee action. Suppose, for example, that a state law provides benefits without disqualification to a claimant who quit his

---

3. For a recent example, see [14, p. 368].

job for a compelling personal reason, or it provides benefits after a temporary disqualification to a claimant who was discharged for cause; then if an employer chooses to do business in that state, he may be considered to have assumed responsibility for this business cost, much as he does for costs occasioned by other state laws governing minimum wages, maximum hours, safety devices, and so forth.

Finally, this claim (for the desirability of the allocative effect of experience rating) need not rest on any particular theory of the shifting and incidence of taxation.[4] Recognizing that the final incidence of the unemployment insurance tax depends on many variable factors and usually cannot be known except by an exhaustive study of each particular situation, this claim does not undertake to predict what that final incidence will be. On the contrary, it belongs to the essence of the claim to accept whatever effect is finally produced by the operations of the market. This faith in the market is disprovable; but the proof offered must suffice to establish (1) what the final incidence of the tax is and (2) that this incidence is undesirable.

These two steps cannot be established in general but only in particular cases, and even then only with considerable difficulty; for the shifting and incidence of taxes is a field of utmost complexity. In 1933 that keen and balanced analyst, Isaac Rubinow, wrote: "No definite answer to the problem of the incidence of the cost of social insurance is acceptable to all theorists, though it has been discussed in Europe for several decades" [18, p. 86]. And he added, three years later: "The pragmatic student is forced to the conclusion that [tax] shiftings probably take place in all possible directions" [20, p. 78]. The operative word is "pragmatic"; Rubinow was not an economic theorist, but he was a good judge of when a theory had sufficient support to be a political force.

Two decades later, Eveline Burns reviewed the debate on incidence and reached much the same cautious conclusion [13, pp. 161–62]. Although Richard Lester argues plausibly that the employer generally can shift little of the tax [63, pp. pp. 65–67], a recent study by John A. Brittain [64] concludes that payroll taxes are borne ultimately by labor. And so the debate continues. The early warning of Carl Shoup, a specialist in the field of payroll-tax incidence, "that the complexity of the economic effects of taxation is commonly underestimated" seems still relevant.[5]

Prices and Social Costs

In the performance of its function as the chief allocator of resources, the market operates the more efficiently as prices reflect costs more accurately. In this context, "prices" are understood in the most general sense, so as to include

4. For typical examples of such an erroneous assumption, see [60, p. 222], [61, p. 723], [62, p. 349].

5. [65, p. 59; see also his strong statement on p. 51.] And see his more recent work, [66, passim].

not only the prices paid by the consumer for the final product but also the prices paid to the factors of production in the form of wages and profits. (This obvious point is mentioned only because it is so frequently overlooked in the literature dealing with the allocation effect of experience rating.) Only to the extent that prices mirror actual costs can the transactions of the market achieve an allocation of resources that accords with the actual values held by the buyers and sellers in the market. Therefore, to the extent that the maintenance of unemployed workers is a cost of production, it should be reflected in the prices associated with the productive activities that gave rise to the unemployment.

It may easily happen that a large part of the cost of unemployment is hidden and not adequately reflected in the prices through which the market operates. [6] Except to the extent that wage scales are adjusted to reflect the risk of unemployment—and all studies show that such adjustments, even when they occur, are uncertain and partial—the support of the unemployed worker is a "social" cost borne largely by the discarded worker, with some assistance from the community in the form of welfare. In the absence of unemployment benefits, the cost of unemployment resembles such other social costs of production as the expense of purifying—or enduring—industrially polluted water and air.[7] A system of unemployment benefits financed by a payroll tax operates to transform a social cost into a business cost, changing a part of the hidden cost of unemployment into a more visible and measurable magnitude capable of being related more directly to market prices.

The decision to inaugurate a compulsory system of unemployment benefits represents an intervention in the workings of the free market based on a judgment that the market is producing undesirable results. But the choice of an experience-rated payroll tax over alternative sources of funds represents a particular kind of intervention, the kind which is characteristic of the Antitrust Division of the Department of Justice. The object of such intervention in the market is to improve the market, that is, to improve the efficiency of the price system through which the market works. Such intervention is in accord with the principle that prices should accurately reflect the cost of production in order for purchases to direct productive resources and capacities into uses consistent with the preferences of purchasers.

Presumptive Favor

An example at this point may serve to sharpen the issue under discussion here. Suppose that firms in the construction industry in Massachusetts were to

6. The discussion here is limited obviously to the money cost of unemployment. Although other costs of unemployment, including psychological and political costs, may be even more significant, they are not relevant here.

7. For some typical discussions of "social costs" see [67, Part II, Ch. 9], [68, pp. 377–78], [69, pp. 70–74]. The last named source is a general discussion of the effect of unemployment compensation taxes on the allocation of resources. See also Richard Musgrave's conclusion that "... it may well be desirable (on grounds of efficient allocation)

be assessed the full cost of the unemployment benefits drawn by their employees. During the decade 1957-67, the annual cost for the industry averaged 6.2 percent of taxable wages and was much higher, of course, for some construction firms. In all probability a continuing cost of this size would have some significant market effects, even though they might not be exactly measurable.

Wages in the construction industry might be lower than they otherwise would be, and this effect might lead, in turn, to a smaller or less skilled labor force. Profits might be lower, with the possible consequence that investment in this industry might be less. Bids submitted for construction projects might be higher and, as a result, fewer projects might be started. Purchasers of buildings might have to allocate more of their total funds to this purpose and hence have less to spend on other commodities and services. Many other combinations of results are possible, including such a successful shifting of the tax to other industries that the construction industry itself would remain unaffected and unchanged.

This claim (for the desirability of the allocative effect of experience rating) does not rest on the ability to prove what results would actually follow from the application of (any given degree of) experience rating to the construction industry. Rather, the claim rests on the general proposition that the market is to be considered the best allocator of resources, short of positive evidence to the contrary, and that the market works most efficiently when prices most accurately reflect costs. Hence, any line of action that makes for more accurate pricing enjoys a position of presumptive favor; whereas any other line of action must bear the burden of proof and produce positive evidence that a less accurate pricing system will produce a better allocation of resources. Of course, when such positive evidence to the contrary is available, as it sometimes is, the presumption falls.

Thus, the nature of this claim is derivative. What validity it possesses derives from a prior, more fundamental choice of society. The claim merely unfolds the implications of that basic choice of the market as the principal mechanism for the allocation of resources. To the extent that one accepts this choice, one is inclined to approve the allocative effect of experience rating, except where positive evidence is available that the net effect of experience rating on the allocation of resources in a particular situation is undesirable.[8]

The importance of this position of presumptive favor can hardly be overrated. As noted above, it is extremely difficult, usually impossible, to trace the effects of a small economic quantity like the unemployment insurance tax and to establish what the final incidence is. Given this difficulty of producing proof—

---

to have them [particular industries] bear the cost of seasonal unemployment and of certain types of structural unemployment" [70, p. 37].

8. Although it should be obvious, it may be necessary to point out at this point that approval of the allocative effect of experience rating does not necessarily imply approval of experience rating in general. There may be other, and undesirable, effects of experience rating that outweigh the allocative effect.

for or against the allocative effects of experience rating—the position of presumptive favor will often be decisive.

History of the Claim

A review of the history of this claim will serve to set it in perspective and thus guard against the tendency, so marked in the literature of experience rating, to slight the discussion of the central issue involved here. Such a review will also help dispel the notion that this issue is of recent origin. The impression is sometimes conveyed that the allocation effect was a later discovery, or even invention, by the advocates of experience rating, to take the place of the stabilization issue after that issue had lost its popularity.[9] But in fact, this issue has been prominent since the earliest discussions of unemployment insurance.

Foreign Experience

The first compulsory unemployment insurance law was established by Britain in 1911. Initially the contribution rate was uniform for all firms, but, as Beveridge approvingly notes, "provision was made for keeping the accounts so as to show how each industry was paying in and drawing out; after seven years there was to be a valuation of the fund and it was contemplated that there should then, in the light of experience, be a revision and differentiation of contributions by trades" [21, p. 269]. Twenty years after unemployment insurance had been established, Beveridge reviewed the British experience and made a number of recommendations, among them the following: "Measures of some kind must be taken to make trades which have excessive unemployment, as a result not of war dislocation but of their own methods, set their house in order and pay till they do so for their own reserves of labour" [71, p. 47]. Here, clearly distinguished, are the two issues so frequently confused: "set their house in order" (stabilization) and "pay for their own reserves of labour" (accurate costing). Shortly before, in 1929, Pigou also had expressed some concern over the implications of the British unemployment insurance system for the allocation of resources: "The risks of unemployment being much more serious in highly fluctuating industries, such as engineering and shipbuilding, than in comparatively stable industries, such as railway service, a general flat-rate scheme will favour industries of the former class and will tend to push an unduly large number of persons into them" [72, p. 369].

The Austrian unemployment insurance system of 1920 included a form of experience rating, under which contributions varied by industry. A schedule was established consisting of three classes of industries classified according to their unemployment risk: the high-risk class, composed mainly of the building industry and the hotel and restaurant industries; the average-risk class; and the low-

9. For example, [62, p. 349], [7, p. 221]. However, a marked shift of emphasis did occur.

risk class, which included such groups as banks and insurance companies [73, p. 28]. The system was abandoned because the basic assumptions underlying the schedules proved unsound[10] and also because the workers' organizations were opposed to it. The scheme had been adopted primarily not so much to promote stabilization as to achieve a more equitable distribution of costs; but labor considered these differentiated contributions divisive and a threat to industrial solidarity.

American Academicians

In the United States the voice of Justice Louis D. Brandeis was one of the earliest and clearest in asserting the responsibility of employers toward the unemployed:[11]

> For every employee who is steady in his work there shall be steady work. The right to regularity in employment is co-equal with the right to regularity in the payment of rent and the payment of interest on bonds, in the delivery to customers of the high quality of product contracted for. No business is successfully conducted which does not perform fully the obligations incident to each of these rights. Each of these obligations is equally a fixed charge. No dividends should be paid unless each of these fixed charges has been met. The reserve to insure regularity of employment is as imperative as the reserve for depreciation, and it is equally a part of the fixed charges to make the annual contribution to that reserve. No business is socially solvent which cannot do so. [74, p. 1]

In the last sentence Brandeis states succinctly—and strongly—the goal of transforming the social cost of unemployment into a business cost. He would seem to accept even the possibility of a firm being forced to close because it was unable to carry this cost.

The Wisconsin school, although generally associated only with the issue of stabilization, was always very insistent also on the issue of the allocation of resources. According to the late Harold Groves, John R. Commons would start a lecture on social costs by holding up a chair and announcing: "There is blood in this chair." He meant that among the costs of producing the chair were the costs borne by the injured, the retired, and the unemployed workers. Commons would then go on to argue that the prices governing the chair's production should reflect this "blood" cost.

Writing during the period of debate preceding the passage of the Social Security Act, Harold Groves and Elizabeth Brandeis[12] consistently stressed the need to transform the social cost of unemployment into a business cost. For example,

10. Principally the assumption that nearly all firms in a given industry would have a generally similar experience with unemployment. (See footnote 15 below.)

11. Although the quotation speaks only of "regularity of employment," in the rest of the article Brandeis makes clear that the "reserve" mentioned was to supply (some) wage income when regular work was not available.

12. Daughter of Justice Louis D. Brandeis and wife of Paul A. Raushenbush.

in 1934 they wrote: "The plant with widely fluctuating employment repeatedly dumps some or all of its workers upon the community. Unless these workers can be utilized at such times in other concerns, they must be supported by somebody. Correct cost accounting requires that this should be done by the concern for which they are in effect a labor reserve. Otherwise, such a concern is not paying the full cost of its production" [75, p. 40].

Paul A. Raushenbush, a key figure in the experience rating controversy and probably the most influential propagator of the system, has always given great emphasis to the effect of experience rating on the allocation of resources. Because of his central position in the history of experience rating, it may be appropriate to present several examples of his position. In 1933 he wrote: "Just as employers are now required by law to pay workmen's compensation for accidents, so they should in future pay limited unemployment compensation to laid-off workers. Both accidents and unemployment are *industrial* hazards and genuine production costs to be prevented where possible but compensated where unavoidable. The time must come when those business units which fail to meet the true social costs of their irregular operation will no longer be considered either socially or financially solvent" [16, p. 72]. In this statement he combines Beveridge and Brandeis. Like Beveridge, he succinctly distinguishes the alternatives ("costs to be prevented where possible but compensated where unavoidable") and like Brandeis, he pushes the employer's obligation to the limit ("will no longer be considered either socially or financially solvent").

In a 1933 address to the International Association of Government Labor Officials,[13] after describing the characteristic features of the Wisconsin program, with its extreme form of experience rating, Raushenbush said: "There are two main reasons for those features. The first I might mention is that there ought to be a proper allocation of cost. Good social cost accounting ought to be used" [15, p. 114]. It was only after developing this reason at some length that Raushenbush came to the second reason, the "regularization of employment." There was an interesting interchange at the 1940 ICESA convention between Milton Loysen, then director of the New York unemployment insurance agency, and Paul Raushenbush. Loysen wanted to know if experience rating would still be desirable if it had no "incentive effect" (on employment stabilization) but only had the effect of "an equitable distribution of cost among industries." Raushenbush replied emphatically the experience rating would "still be worthwhile economically" [29, pp. 94, 95].

---

13. This address still reads very well. It is marked by a sense of balance and realism that recommends it even today, after thirty-five years of actual experience with unemployment benefits. It somehow manages to avoid all the exaggerations it could have fallen into so easily at that early date. Of the employment stabilization objective, for example, Raushenbush claimed no more than: "It is an emphasis upon more regular employment by the individual employer who has some control over that problem—how much we do not know, but he has some, certainly, and probably more than he has yet used" [15, p. 115].

This same emphasis is to be found in a letter written as early as 1938 to George Bigge, a member of the Social Security Board.

> So far as the substance of your remarks is concerned, my most important criticism is that you make a fragmentary or incomplete (and therefore incorrect) assumption as to the purpose of merit rating or experience rating.
> You apparently assume that the *sole* purpose of experience rating is to encourage employers to provide more regular employment. (I hasten to say that you have lots of company in making this limited assumption, including many members of the Board's staff.) . . . In my judgment, the basic assumption or major premise is incorrect—and confused and uncertain thinking about concrete experience rating proposals is the natural result.
> As we see it, experience rating has 2 *objectives*:—(a) to charge every employer with the costs of his own unemployment (i.e. benefits paid, based on employment by him); and (b) to encourage steadier employment [76, p. 1].

The complaint that Raushenbush voices of the Board and its staff in those early years could be repeated of many writers on experience rating during the thirty succeeding years.

It was not a complaint that could be voiced, however, of all the Board's staff (see below, p. 56) nor of Isaac Rubinow, the chief opponent of the Wisconsin school. On this issue Rubinow shows his usual balance. He could see some value in experience rating in terms of its market effect. He recognized that rate variation reflects "the normal desire or effort to achieve some sort of fair proportion between the degree of hazard and the rate of contribution upon industry as the hazard-carrying factor" [20, p. 79]. He indicated that he shared this desire when he wrote: "The essential justice of the claim for some rate differentiation need not be denied" [20, p. 83].

In his classic work, *The Quest for Security* (1934), Rubinow lists a set of unemployment benefit standards which he says he shares with Paul H. Douglas, another leading opponent of the Wisconsin school, and which include provision for some form of experience rating: "Though fully recognizing all the technical difficulties of adjusting the contribution to the degree of unemployment hazard in each industry or branch of industry, I recognize both the moral and practical value of such adjustment and I believe, therefore, that in the administration of the act provisions should be included to make such adjustment possible after necessary statistical data have been obtained" [19, p. 455].

Although granting "the essential justice of the claim for some rate differentiation," Rubinow felt that "the whole question in American discussion has been given consideration entirely out of line with its intrinsic importance" [20, p. 83]. In support of this judgment, Rubinow ventured the estimate: "If reliable statistics of distribution of all industries according to cost of unemployment insurance were obtainable, it would probably be found that some ten percent or twenty percent would be between the legal minimum and maximum limits and the rest either below the minimum or over the maximum. What is the scientific or social value of such a limited degree of rate adjustment" [20, p. 83]? As the data of Chapter 4 show, the spread of rates has been rather different from that anticipated by Rubinow.[14]

Another early and influential figure in the debate over unemployment benefits was William M. Leiserson, who in 1913 anticipated by two decades Raushenbush's statement of the objectives of experience rating: "Here is the problem for the social engineer—to make employment constant, and, where constant work is impossible, to place the burden of unemployment on the industry where it belongs" [77, p. 112]. Later (1933) Leiserson said even more strongly: "If industry can't support such people [the unemployed], then those industries ought to be chucked into the Atlantic ocean" [7, p. 184]. In the first quotation he clearly distinguishes between the stabilization and the allocation effects, and in the second quotation he pushes the allocation effect to its extreme limits.

Management and Labor

The early (1940) ICESA Committee on Experience Rating (see Chapter 1) received conflicting statements on the objectives of unemployment compensation from representatives of two leading employer associations. The representative of the National Association of Manufacturers expressed the narrow view of unemployment compensation that was frequent in those early days: "The position of our association has been . . . [that] . . . the underlying principle of this legislation is the prevention of unemployment, not the compensation of it" [32, p. 25]. The representative of the United States Chamber of Commerce expressed a more balanced view, making compensation the "basic purpose" of the system and recognizing the social-cost argument as the "underlying principle" of the tax structure. "The basic purpose of unemployment compensation legislation is to provide a system of temporary benefit payments to employees who have lost their jobs through no fault of their own. . . . The underlying principle is that the costs of such benefits are a proper charge upon production and distribution" [32, p. 15].

Among management spokesmen on the issue of experience rating, one of the best known was Emerson Schmidt, for many years director of the economic research department of the Chamber of Commerce of the United States of America. Writing in 1945 and listing the reasons for supporting experience rating, Schmidt gave first place to the effect of experience rating on the alloca-

14. However, in this connection it should be noted: (1) Much of the discussion outside of Wisconsin was in terms of rate differentiation by industry, not by individual firm. (2) Rubinow had in view the half-dozen pooled-fund plans that had been enacted by 1936, including the Ohio plan in which the minimum was 1 percent and the maximum tax was 3.5 percent of payroll.

tion of resources: "(1) The risk of unemployment varies widely among different industrial classifications and among employers within a specific classification; therefore in a free-consumer-choice society the cost and price structure of each such classification . . . should be made to reflect this variation" [78, p. 242].

Labor spokesmen, although generally opposed to experience rating in unemployment insurance, have often espoused the social-cost argument on which experience rating rests. In 1919, according to Daniel Nelson, some American labor unions "found a parallel between their ideas and the work of the British Building Trades Parliament, which was engaged in a nationwide bargaining campaign to win recognition of unemployment benefits as a direct cost of production" [79, p. 83]. Charles M. Hay, spokesman for railway labor in the 1938 hearing on unemployment insurance, argued: "We contend that if the railroads must operate seasonally, if they must from time to time hire temporary or irregular workers, they must accept a social responsibility to provide unemployment benefits. . . . Railroads have tools and machinery which they use only seasonally. They have not yet had the temerity to ask the community to store them at community expense when not in use by the railroads. They willingly care for their idle machinery. They should be willing to take the same care of their idle men" [80, p. 257]. Since the railroad industry does not have a common pocketbook, this argument would logically extend to the individual companies in the industry.

The early AFL was, of course, strongly market-oriented, even to the point of opposing, until 1932, any form of governmental unemployment insurance program. The CIO, although more socially inclined than the AFL, could on occasion appeal to the market and to the social-cost argument. For example, in 1955, when the United Auto Workers (CIO) was attempting to negotiate the first plan of Supplemental Unemployment Benefits (SUB), its spokesman argued:

> One effect of wage guarantees is to minimize social losses flowing from irresponsible management action with respect to technological change. The guarantee transfers to the books of the employer part of the cost of his actions that are now borne as social costs. To the extent that the costs as well as the gains resulting from managerial decisions are more adequately reflected on the employer's books, there is greater likelihood that those decisions will be sound from the over-all economic standpoint as well as from the narrow and selfish standpoint of the individual corporation. [81, p. 5]

Labor has generally adopted the position that all employers must meet minimum standards of employee remuneration, even though this may impose a relatively greater burden on some employers than on others. One might therefore expect labor to hold each employer responsible for paying whatever insurance premium is required to provide a stipulated amount of protection against unemployment. That labor generally has not adopted this position is probably due not so much to rejection of the market effect of experience rating as to labor's apprehension that experience rating has other—undesirable—effects. Quite possibly, if there were no effect of experience rating other than its impact on the allocation of resources, American Labor would favor experience rating, or at least not oppose it. The same may probably be said of most academicians who oppose experience rating. One must speak here only in terms of probabilities because, as mentioned before, the typical discussion of experience rating does not stay with this precise issue long enough to reach a clear conclusion.

Government

The federal Bureau of Unemployment Compensation quite early (1938) distinguished between the allocation and stabilization issues and gave primacy to the former. In a research memorandum which was written to provide guidance for the states and which is still one of the best pieces written on experience rating, the Bureau explained seven principles that should govern any experience rating system. The first principle listed was: "1. The system should be based on the most accurate measurement of the individual employer's experience with unemployment among his workers, rather than on any measurement of individual merit. Not only is merit not susceptible to accurate measurement but since so many external factors affecting stability of employment may far outweigh the individual employer's efforts, a system based primarily on 'merit' would also be unattainable" [37, p. 1]. The Bureau explained to the states that "the *chief* effect of experience rating is to assess a larger share of the social cost of unemployment against the unstable industries" [37, p. 5, emphasis supplied], and logically observed: " 'Experience rating' then seems to be a more descriptive name for the matter in hand than 'merit rating' " [37, p. 4]. Here, early in 1938 was a clear, semiofficial statement of the basic nature of experience rating that both Wisconsin and Ohio (Raushenbush and Rubinow) would have accepted.[15]

Anticipating this federal document, some of the earliest state unemployment insurance laws described the underlying "public policy" in terms of the allocation of social costs. For example, the original (1935) California law stated: "The benefit to all persons resulting from public and private enterprise is realized in the final consumption of the goods and services. It is contrary to public policy to permit the supply of consumption goods and services at prices which do not

15. This early document also made the following realistic observation on the proposal, common at that time, to use industry classification for rating purposes:

> It is an unwarranted assumption that employers producing the same type of product or offering the same type of service are subjected to similar unemployment risks. For example, the shoe manufacturer who makes work shoes has a much easier task of regularization than one who manufactures a line of shoes in which the vicissitudes of style tend to prevent regularization. Hence, any broad grouping fails to produce a norm against which individual employers can fairly be rated. On the other hand, if industry classifications with a State are drawn so fine as to limit each category to a group of employers engaged in the same type of business and confronted with similar market conditions, the result would be so close to no classification at all that in effect almost every employer would be treated separately. [37, pp. 3–4]

provide against that harm to the population consequent upon periods of unemployment of those who contribute to the production and distribution of such goods and services" [81, Art. 1, Sec. 1]. The first unemployment benefit program in the United States was, of course, that of Wisconsin in 1932. For this reason, as well as because Wisconsin has played a unique role in the development of experience rating, its "Public Policy Declaration" has special significance. This earliest Wisconsin law did include unemployment prevention among its objectives—but in a subordinate position to the objectives of protecting the wage earner and properly allocating the social cost of unemployment (see Appendix D).

Summary

Edwin E. Witte was responsible for the form and content of the Social Security Act as much as any one person could be. Often called the "father of social security," he continued to participate in the development of the social security programs after their enactment. Writing in 1940 and reviewing the development of unemployment insurance up to that point, Witte included a discussion of experience rating. It is significant, coming from him, that he began by relating experience rating to the fundamentals of the American economy. His statement may serve as a summary of all the preceding:

> This brings me to the final major issue in unemployment compensation today—experience rating. No other question is more of a headache to the administrators or has provoked more controversy among the theorists.
>
> There are good theoretical arguments on both sides of this question. To me the weight of the theoretical arguments seems to be in favor of experience rating. I hold this view not so much because I believe that experience rating will operate to reduce unemployment, but because I believe that the adjustment of contribution rates to the varying risks of unemployment of different industries and establishments is in accord with prevailing American concepts. In all other "insurances" in this country, rates are adjusted to the risk. Our private economy is grounded upon the concept that each industry should stand on its own feet. Honest cost accounting requires that all costs be ascertained and properly allocated to the commodities produced or services rendered. An industry which operates intermittently occasions great costs to its employees and to society through its methods of operation. Whether it can or cannot operate more regularly, the unemployment which arises by reason of its intermittent or irregular operation is a cost which should be charged to the establishment producing the goods or services and which gets the profits of the enterprise. Every reason that can be advanced for contributions from employers only—and in all but six states [three, in 1970] all contributions come from the employers—logically leads to variable contribution rates, rates adjusted to risk and costs. In a socialistic economy it might be proper to have all industry collectively bear the costs of unemployment; in a private economy, where the profits go to particular entrepreneurs, all costs of production should be borne by the particular establishments, and these should

include the unemployment compensation costs, as well as all other costs.
[83, pp. 274-75].

For our purpose, all the quoted statements regarding the effect of experience rating on the allocation of costs and thus on the allocation of resources may be summarized in four propositions: (1) This effect is distinct from other effects (especially stabilization), and the question of the desirability of experience rating would have to be answered in terms of this effect even if there were no other effects. (2) This is the primary effect of experience rating. (3) This effect is not a recent discovery, but has always occupied a prominent place in the discussion of the principles governing unemployment benefits. (4) Because it accords with our society's fundamental economic choice—the choice of the market as the chief mechanism for the allocation of resources—this effect enjoys a preferred position in the sense that it is to be presumed desirable unless there is positive proof of the opposite.

PART II: THE COUNTERCLAIMS

The claim that experience rating has a desirable effect on the allocation of costs and resources is challenged on both general and particular grounds, and it will be convenient to consider the challenges in that order.

General Counterclaims

Although the general challenges are the more significant, since they relate to fundamentals, they are also less clear. In the entire literature dealing with experience rating, it is difficult to find an explicit, developed critique of the allocation claim. There are many general statements that it is "unfair" to give a "bonus" (a low tax rate) to a firm that is by nature stable and to impose a "penalty" (a high tax rate) on a firm that is by nature unstable.[16] But the underlying reasoning is not developed. As a result of this lack of developed discussion of the allocation effect, it is difficult to know to what extent this claim is rejected. It may be that very few critics of experience rating reject this claim exactly as it was presented in the preceding section. *If the allocation effect were the only effect*, opponents of experience rating might be largely confined to firms with above-average costs.[17]

16. For example: "It hardly seems fair that these employers—the least able to pay—who have poor experience ratings, largely as a result of the economic nature of their business, should be punished" [2, p. 1482, statement of J. Bill Becker, president of the Arkansas State AFL-CIO].

17. Although obvious, it is worth pointing out that at any given time, firms accounting for one-half of all taxed payrolls stand to gain, while firms accounting for the other half stand to lose, by a change from experience rating to a uniform tax, or from a uniform tax to experience rating. As used here, "firm" is to be understood as including all the factors of production—owners, managers, workers.

Logically, the first general counterclaim should be directed against the first proposition in the sorites on which the claim is based. According to the proposition, our society has chosen the market as its main mechanism for the allocation of resources. While this proposition cannot be denied, it needs to be qualified. Our society has shown a growing willingness to have its government modify the action of the market. Increased governmental intervention in the market has been one of the outstanding features of our history during the past fifty years.

Given this long-run willingness of our society to *increase* the degree of governmental intervention, it would seem that the presumption in favor of the market has been weakened. To modify the market is no longer to attack a sacrosanct, untouchable institution; it is merely to take another step on a road along which we have already traveled far. Although each act of intervention still needs to be justified by specific evidence, the weight of evidence required is becoming less. To use a distinction of the ethicians: It is not necessary to follow the course that enjoys the greater probability; one is free to choose any course that has some solid probability. Since the area is growing within which one may find a solidly probable reason for intervening in the market, the presumption favoring the market is weakening.

This qualifying counterclaim has obvious validity. Nevertheless, it leaves the original claim essentially whole. The presumption still favors the market, and each act of intervention must be supported by specific evidence of its greater desirability. And this kind of evidence still remains difficult, usually very difficult, to establish.

Sometimes an objection directed against the allocation effect of experience rating is based on a particular conception of the nature of insurance. Typical of many similar statements is the following: "In some respects merit rating conflicts with the fundamental objectives of insurance. By apportioning the cost of unemployment compensation among employers according to the amount of their unemployment, merit rating restricts the spreading of the risk and thus runs counter to the basic purpose of insurance" [84, p. 61].[18] The question of what premium to charge the employer who purchases the insurance requires a distinction between two kinds of pooling—insurance and subsidy. In insurance pooling it is known in advance that there will be some redistribution of the pooled resources—some of the insured will draw out of the pool much more than they put in—but it is not known what the pattern of redistribution will be and no particular pattern is intended. Insurance is rooted in risk, and risk by definition implies uncertainty. There can be insurance only where there is uncertainty.

In subsidy pooling, a pattern of redistribution is foreseen and intended. It may be known, for example, that the risk of unemployment is much greater for

18. The statement that experience rating "restricts the spreading of the risk" must be interpreted carefully. According to Rubinow, insurance is "soundest and most economical when it covers the widest spread of people subject to the risk" [85, p. 13]. This is a much more accurate statement than the statement, so often encountered, that insurance pools good and bad risks.

most firms in the construction industry than for most firms in the banking industry. If all firms are nevertheless charged the same premium, there will be a foreseen and intended redistribution of funds in favor of high-cost firms, for example in the construction industry, at the expense of low-cost firms, for example in the banking industry. In relation to the allocation of resources, the result of such pooling is not, strictly speaking, insurance but subsidy. Both kinds of pooling and redistribution may occur in the same system, as they do in the unemployment insurance system, but they represent different objectives and are to be evaluated by different norms. If the subsidy is intended as an economic aid to high-cost firms, its discussion belongs to this chapter, which deals with the allocation of resources. In this case, the desirability of the subsidy must be proved against the presumption enjoyed by the market. If the subsidy is intended for other reasons (for example, to lessen the opposition of high-cost firms to a liberalization of benefits), its discussion belongs to other chapters (for example, to Chapter 9, which deals with legislation).

There was a time when the original Wisconsin–Ohio debate was carried on in terms of "reserves" versus "insurance," by which was meant individual employer reserves versus pooled reserves. But this particular controversy, which turned on the *degree of protection to be provided for the employee*, has been a dead issue for thirty years. All programs now have pooled reserves, all of which are available to all eligible claimants, and the only issue is whether to finance the pool by means of a uniform tax or by means of a tax that varies with the individual employer's experience. The latter method is clearly compatible with insurance, for most insurance premiums vary in proportion to the risk insured against.[19]

Sometimes the objection is raised that the claim for the allocation effect of experience rating is inconsistent with the claim for the stabilization effect [32, p. 11],[14, p. 343]. According to this objection, the allocation effect assumes that the employer will shift the tax to the consumer, while the stabilization effect assumes that, unable to shift the tax, the employer will be under pressure to escape the tax by avoiding unemployment. Hence "there is a basic inconsistency between providing an incentive to stabilize and allocating social costs. An experience rating scheme must do one or the other; it cannot do both" [33, p. 50]. This objection is so groundless that one wonders how it could have been repeated so often in the literature.[20]

In the first place, the claim for the allocation effect does not depend on any particular theory of tax shifting. The claim doess *not* rest on an assumption that the cost is passed on to the consumer of the final product or service. That may occur, but alternatively the cost may be absorbed by one or all of the suppliers

19. In discussing this issue, Edwin Witte said: "Viewing unemployment compensation as basically an insurance institution, I believe that experience rating is necessary to equitably distribute compensation costs" [83, p. 284].

20. It probably stems from an original, and correct, observation by Paul Douglas [86, p. 147] which seems to have been picked up and misapplied by a succession of writers.

(labor, management, investors) of the product or service. As explained earlier, this claim accepts, without specifying, whatever final result the market produces. Second, there is no inconsistency in assigning both objectives to experience rating, either as alternatives or as partially realizable simultaneously. Faced with a cost, an employer will try to eliminate it and/or shift it. What experience rating does is face him with the cost. What he does with the cost is usually unascertainable. The correct relationship between the two effects has been stated clearly by Beveridge, Brandeis, Raushenbush, Leiserson, and others (see above). In Leiserson's words: "Here is the problem for the social engineer—to make employment constant, and, where constant work is impossible, to place the burden of unemployment on the industry where it belongs" [77, p. 112].

Particular Counterclaims

In addition to general criticisms, there are some that are directed at more specific aspects of the allocation effect of experience rating. Three in particular are worth noting: that the allocative effect of experience rating is too small, is inaccurate, and imposes too great a burden on some firms.

Effect Too Small

It is sometimes asserted that the differences in employer costs attributable to experience rating are too small to have any significant effect on the allocation of costs and, hence, of resources.

The statement may be understood in two senses, one more fundamental than the other, but both of them important. The statement may mean that the various economic activities do not differ significantly among themselves with respect to experience with unemployment; as a result, the differences in benefit-cost rates between individual firms are too small or too irregular to justify differentiated taxes. This is the most fundamental possible objection to the claim under discussion in this chapter; for the claim is based on exactly the opposite premise, that cost differences *are* significantly large and regular. To resolve this issue, information on cost rates is needed. While such information is not readily available, enough such data are assembled and analyzed in Chapter 4 to support a reasonable judgment on the validity of this criticism.

More often the objection seems to refer to tax rates. No matter how large the differences in benefit-cost rates might be, if the differences are not as a matter of fact reflected in tax rates[21] the actual effect of experience rating on the individual firms may be, as the objection states, "too small." The norm of smallness is, of course, relative. A tax difference that may be too small to determine the location of a new firm may be large enough to limit the expansion of a seasonal

21. To the extent that differences in tax rates are smaller than differences in cost rates, the charge is directed against a lack of experience rating rather than against experience rating as such.

firm or hasten the demise of a declining firm.[22] The charge that the tax differential of experience rating is "too small" may be inconsistent with one or other of the five charges listed later, all of which state that experience rating imposes "too great" a burden on some firms. In any case, an evaluation of these charges must begin with an examination of the actual differences in tax rates as between firms. Data on tax rates are fairly abundant and are examined in Chapter 4.

Inaccurate Cost Allocation

It is sometimes charged that experience rating fails to establish an accurate relationship between an employer's unemployment experience and the tax he pays, and hence fails to achieve the more accurate price pattern which is its aim. Ewan Clague lists a number of such inaccuracies and concludes: ". . . the average employer's tax rate in unemployment compensation is now largely the result of fortuitous factors which affect his business in ways which he can neither understand nor overcome" [87, p. 63]. The key word is "largely," for the issue is one of degree. Since experience rating inevitably achieves a closer correspondence between full costs and market prices than does a uniform tax, this criticism must mean: Is the increase in accuracy worth the bother of establishing the system of experience rating? An evaluation of this criticism depends on cost/tax ratios, and considerable data on such ratios are provided in Chapter 5.

This objection, it should be noted, is directed not against experience rating as such, but against the absence of experience rating in the existing tax system. The remedy for this defect is simply more experience rating. Sometimes this objection takes the form of charging the existing tax system with inconsistency or irrationality in not carrying the principle of experience rating to its logical extreme. But normally any social technique—like the progressive income tax, or the division of governmental powers, or experience rating—has disadvantages as well as advantages, and the normal procedure is to use the technique only up to the point where its advantages begin to be outweighed by its disadvantages.

The data analyzed in Chapter 5 assume that the benefits which determine the numerator of the cost/tax ratio have been accurately charged to the proper firm. But often, the criticism continues, this is not the case. Some benefits are not charged against any firm, while others are charged inaccurately, that is, are charged against firms not responsible for the unemployment. The extent of noncharging is examined in Chapter 5, while the various meanings of employer "responsibility" were described above (p. 46) and the rationale underlying the charging of multiple employers in the base period was explained earlier (p. 19).

Voluntary contributions. A recent treatise on experience rating repeats early charges that the allowance of voluntary contributions constitutes an internal

---

22. It may also be large enough to have some of the other effects claimed for experience rating (on administration, legislation, stabilization), but these effects are matters for other chapters.The present chapter is concerned only with the allocation of resources and the economic health of the firms directly affected by such allocation.

contradiction in experience rating: "The most important conceptual departure from experience rating . . . is the admissibility of voluntary contributions. Voluntary contributions, in effect, remove the sanction of law from the theoretical foundations of experience rating" [55, p. 29]. This charge seems to stem from a conception of experience rating as reflecting only the firm's ability to control unemployment—the stabilization issue. Whether or not the charge applies to the stabilization effect, it does not apply to the allocation effect. In a reserve-ratio tax system[23] voluntary contributions normally affect only the timing of a firm's contributions, not the eventual amount. For all firms other than those at the maximum tax rate (and those at a minimum rate that is greater than zero) the "natural tax rate" tends to cause taxes to at least equal the benefits charged to any given firm (see Appendix B). To grant a firm some flexibility in the arrangement of its cash flow accords with the conception of the unemployment insurance tax as a cost of doing business.

Effect Too Hard on Some Firms

A series of objections states that experience rating is "too hard" on certain classes of firms: small firms, new firms, manufacturing firms, declining firms, seasonal firms. These objections include, as usual, two propositions: that experience rating has the alleged effect and that the effect is undesirable [29, p. 84].

Small firms. To the extent that the federal and state governments wish to protect small firms in their competition with larger firms, this objection enjoys a position of presumptive favor. If experience rating works to the disadvantage of the small firm, the effect may be presumed to be undesirable unless there is positive evidence to the contrary. This objection takes three forms: (1) Under experience rating the small employer bears a disproportionate part of the tax burden; i.e., his cost/tax ratio is lower. (2) Whether that is true or not, small firms tend to pay higher tax rates than do large firms. (3) Under experience rating the tax rates of small firms tend to fluctuate widely from year to year. These charges are evaluated in the light of available data in Chapters 4 and 5.

New firms. Haber and Murray voice a common charge that "new employers bear a disproportionate share of the cost of unemployment insurance under experience rating" [14, p. 343]. New firms must accumulate experience during one to three years, depending on the state law, before they are "rated," that is, are eligible for an experience-rated tax. During this period they pay the standard tax (usually 2.7 percent), which may be higher or lower than the tax paid by their established competitors.[24] Hence during this period new firms may be

23. All but one of the twenty-five states permitting voluntary contributions are reserve-ratio states. The exception (Minnesota) uses the benefit-ratio system.

24. The 1970 unemployment insurance amendments (H.R. 14705) provided that under specified conditions any state that wished could allow new firms to enter the program with an initial tax rate of 1 percent.

disadvantaged or advantaged with respect to the older firms, depending largely on whether they are in a low-cost or high-cost industry. This charge, also, is to be evaluated in the light of the data provided in Chapters 4 and 5.

Durable-goods manufacturing. It is said that firms in this industry tend to pay a higher-than-average tax. This effect of experience rating is said to be undesirable for two reasons: "[these firms] are the cornerstone of the business and employment structure and are unstable for reasons beyond their control" [55, p. 25].[25] As to the first reason, considerable evidence would be required to establish that firms which are the cornerstone of the economy and which can afford to pay higher-than-average wages cannot pay their way with respect to the relatively minor cost of unemployment taxes. As to the second reason: Although ability to control unemployment is relevant to the stabilization effect of experience rating, it is not relevant to the allocation effect.

Declining firms. It is charged that experience rating imposes too heavy a burden on the firm that experiences a prolonged decline in the demand for its product. Such a firm must pay an unusually high tax when its ability to pay is unusually impaired. A burden that a healthy man will carry easily is onerous for an ailing man.

Although the general good is not always served by prolonging the existence of a dying firm, the inevitability of termination is usually not clear; moreover, in our society there is a general reluctance to add the straw that may break the camel's back. Perhaps, as a typical compromise, existing unemployment insurance laws have set a maximum tax that may be higher than desirable for some firms, though it is lower than desirable for most high-cost firms. The concrete circumstances of time and place are decisive. Each state must decide according to the circumstances of its own economy how it wishes to tax firms with secularly declining payrolls.

Seasonal firms. The operations of firms strongly marked by seasonality pose problems that relate to all the effects of experience rating examined in this study. Here we are concerned with only the market or allocation effect.

The charge that experience rating imposes "too great" a burden on seasonal firms rests on the argument that seasonal industries cannot afford to pay their way in the unemployment insurance system and that curtailed seasonal industries mean a curtailed total amount of available employment. This is the argument, for example, of Joe Davis, president of the Washington State AFL–CIO, a long-time and effective opponent of experience rating. Employment in the state of Washington is characterized by more than average seasonality, and the Wash-

25. In this 1964 treatise, the author was quoting approvingly a 1940 report of the ICESA [33, pp. 41–42].

ington unemployment insurance law imposes a lesser penalty on seasonal operations than does any other state.[26] Mr. Davis argues that it is better to provide part-year work than none and fears that a high unemployment insurance tax would prevent Washington's many seasonal firms (for example, logging, fishing, canning) from providing as much employment as they now do.

Each state will decide for itself in the light of its own total situation whether and to what extent it wishes other industries to subsidize the more seasonal industries. That is, it will decide to what extent it wishes to intervene in the market and change the allocation of resources that the market working in terms of full costs might have produced. Chapter 5 provides some data on the extent of existing subsidies. The point of the present chapter has been that in each case the desirability of intervening in the market must be established.

---

26. Washington measures a firm's experience with unemployment by annual payroll declines. A seasonal firm that has as large a payroll this year as last year may qualify for the lowest tax rate, even though it may have laid off all its employees each year. Many seasonal firms do, as a matter of fact, qualify for the lowest tax rates.

Allocation of
Costs II:
Cost Rates and
Tax Rates

Introduction

The preceding chapter developed the claims and counterclaims that have been made respecting the effect of experience rating on the allocation of costs and, hence, of resources. Chapters 4 and 5 present data useful for the evaluation of these claims and counterclaims. The data pertain to benefit-cost rates (benefit payments as a percent of taxable payrolls), tax rates (taxes as a percent of taxable payrolls) and their relationships. The data are organized around two topics, the potential and the actual extent of experience rating: How much experience rating could there be and how much experience rating is there? This kind of information is pertinent, obviously, not only to the allocation effect but to all the other effects of experience rating. It helps to establish the limits within which any of the alleged effects of experience rating could possibly occur. But chiefly these data pertain to the allocation effect.

Another way of viewing the organization of the data in these two chapters is to see them as seeking answers to three more specific questions. First, how large and how regular have been the differences in benefit-cost rates among firms? Enough to establish the possibility of meaningful differences in tax rates? Second, how large have been the differences in the actual tax rates? Enough to have economic significance? Third, what has been the relationship between the two rates—how accurately or inaccurately, and for what kind of firms, have tax rates reflected cost rates? Answers to these questions are a necessary, though not a sufficient condition for determining the answer to the ultimate question whether to maintain or increase or decrease the existing degree of experience rating and thus to retain or change the existing allocation of costs.

The original decisions on experience rating had to be made with a minimum of information on the patterns of unemployment and hence with a minimum basis for estimating what the allocation ot costs would be as among individual firms under various systems of experience rating. Now, thirty-five years later, there is a great accumulation of such data. Indeed, the accumulation is so great that only a large task force could hope to codify it and analyze it comprehensively. What this chapter does is select from this mountain of data portions which have particular significance for the alleged effects of experience rating, especially the effect on the allocation of costs and resources.

The data are subject to limitations, several of which are general in nature and are properly mentioned at the outset. First, although the data are sometimes fairly representative in the sense that they reflect a large proportion of total experience under the program, more often they are "limiting" rather than representative. That is, they suffice only to establish the upper and lower limits within which the answers probably lie. This qualification stems partly from the unavailability of some data, especially benefit-cost data, and partly from limited research resources, which enforced a selective approach.

Second, the available data are not in ideal form. The ideal data would be the cost rates and tax rates of individual firms for the whole period during which each firm was in the program. Such data are desirable because only the individual firm has a pocketbook and pays taxes. Many tables do show the distribution of fir. is or their payrolls according to the experience of the individual firm, and a few other tables show at least whether the individual firms have a positive or negative balance (are or are not paying their way). But these data are usually limited to a single year and do not permit us to follow the experience of the individual firm from one period to the next. Hence, while they furnish information on the size of the differences between firms at a point of time, they do not reveal how regular (predictable) such differences may be. To secure some light on the regularity or stability of the differences between firms, it is usually necessary to make use of proxy data, chiefly averages by industry or by size of firm. These averages may be used only as approximations to the experience of the individual firms included in the classification; for within each industry or size group there are firms whose individual experience differs greatly from the average of the classification. This limitation affects especially the cost-tax comparisons of Chapter 5.

Third, although data that cover a period shorter than total experience are necessarily ambiguous, especially when used for the construction of cost/tax ratios, frequently data are available only for such shorter periods. Moreover, because of limited research resources, the use of available data covering longer periods had to be restricted to the larger industrial groups. Thus, data for eleven-year averages had to be limited mostly to major industrial divisions. When data were presented in greater detail, they generally had to be limited to experience covering fewer years for fewer states.

The tables presented in Chapters 4 and 5 and in Appendix A proceed from the more general to the more detailed experience (a gain), but at the same time they go from longer to shorter periods of experience (a loss). They are utilized to the fullest advantage when used to supplement each other. What the longer periods of experience lack in detail is partly supplied by the tables reflecting shorter experience, and what the more detailed tables lack in duration is partly supplied by the tables reflecting less detail. In combination, the tables throw considerable light on past experience. One who assimilates the history contained in these tables, while he will still lack much pertinent information, will be in a very much better position to estimate the limits within which the answers probably lie.

Finally, a word of warning is necessary regarding interstate comparisons. A wide variety of factors go to explain the differences between states. These factors include legal provisions, industrial patterns, and administrative procedures. If the reader wishes to venture on interstate comparisons beyond those made in the text, he may do so safely only on the basis of an intimate knowledge of all these factors in each of the states compared.

Benefit-Cost Rates

If the investigator of experience rating could have only one piece of information, he would probably choose information about the benefit-cost rates of individual firms, for such rates are the building blocks of an experience-rated system. Knowledge about benefit-cost rates (often termed simply "cost rates") is essential to an intelligent decision whether to have an experience-rated system at all and, if so, what degree of experience rating to have.

There are two situations in which an experience-rated insurance program would make little sense: if the cost rates of all firms were the same or if the rates varied in completely random fashion. If all firms had the same cost rate, experience rating would produce exactly the same result as a uniform tax, and there would be no reason to assume the greater administrative cost of experience rating. If cost rates varied in completely random fashion, there would be no basis for differentiating between one firm and another in terms of the degree of risk represented by each firm. Again, a uniform tax rate would be the more reasonable choice. The closer that actual experience approaches either of these extremes (cost rates differing very little or almost randomly) the weaker is the case for experience rating in an insurance program.

The situation which most favors the choice of an experience-rated system is one in which the cost rates of firms differ significantly and regularly. In order to adjust the premium to the risk, which is the essence of experience rating, the insurer must be able to calculate the risk; and to do that he must be able to find significant and regular differences in experience. The larger and the more regular the differences, the more reason there is to regard the unemployment insurance tax as one of the normal costs of doing business and to integrate the tax with the market. The first task, therefore, is to see how large and how regular, or how small and irregular, are the differences in benefit-cost rates between different economic activities. Although the examination of such data is a somewhat tedious task, it is indispensable for an evaluation of this first and most fundamental effect of experience rating. Indeed, the reader would be well advised to steep himself in the details of the data provided here and in Appendix A to a much greater extent than limitations of space permit us to do in this chapter.

As was observed in Chapter 1, the principle of experience rating found its first application in the decision to establish separate state programs and to hold each state financially responsible for its own benefit costs. Table A-3 shows average benefit costs by state for almost three decades. The length of the period allows chance fluctuations to be offset and thus permits fundamental economic differences to become visible. The (arithmetical) average cost rate for the United States was 1 percent of (total) wages; the median rate was about the same. Since wages do not include fringe benefits, the cost of unemployment benefits as a percentage of total labor costs is even smaller than these ratios indicate [63, pp. 58, 59]. As a percentage of total production costs the ratios would, of course, be smaller still. The costs are much smaller than one would have expected who had read only the early debates over the burden that would be imposed by unemployment benefits. Except for Alaska, whose proportion of the nation's covered employment is miniscule and whose economy is exceptional in many ways, no state had an average cost rate as high as 2 percent of total wages.

Although no state had a high rate as compared with earlier expectations, some states had much higher rates than others. The upper third of the states had an average cost rate about twice that of the lower third of the distribution. The most costly state (Rhode Island) had a cost rate four times that of the least costly states (Virginia and Texas).

To the extent that interstate cost differences are traceable to differences in benefit provisions, rather than to differences in the states' economies, the issue raised belongs in the chapter on legislation rather than here. However, it is almost certain that the differences chiefly reflect basic economic characteristics. There is general agreement among actuarial experts that the level of unemployment is by far the major factor in determining benefit costs. Michael T. Wermel, who more than any other individual was involved in the actuarial studies made by the various states, illustrated this proposition on one occasion as follows:

> About two years ago, I was asked the question: "What would be the difference in cost among the various states in the Nation if all of them had exactly the same benefit formula?" For comparative purposes I took a formula containing the proposed Federal standards which at that time provided, among other things, for a $30 maximum weekly benefit amount, dependents' allowances, and twenty-six weeks' uniform duration. I computed the cost on the basis of such a formula for every State in the Union for that year and I found that the range between the highest cost State and the lowest cost State remained very wide. Whereas under the existing State laws the range for that year—that was '49—was from something like 0.4 percent to 6.2 percent, under this uniform formula the range would have been from 0.7 percent to 8.0 percent, so that costs in the highest cost State would still be more than eleven times higher than in the lowest. This suggests very strongly that the basic cost determinant is really the rate of compensable unemployment [43, p. 12].

There is some support for this position in Table A-3, which shows the rank of states according to cost rates and their unemployment rate. Although the periods of the two series are not identical, and although the latter series is influenced by differences in the procedures used by the states in counting claims, especially partial claims, there is, nevertheless, a rough correspondence in the ranking of the states by the two series of data. The third of the states with the highest cost rates had an average unemployment ranking of twelve, while the third of the states with the lowest cost rates had an average unemployment ranking of forty-one.

Two conclusions suggest themselves from this general view of interstate differences during most of the life of the program. First, the cost differences are primarily the result of fundamental economic differences and have the characteristics of other business costs of regularity and predictability. Second, the cost rates of even the more costly states are not so high as to constitute a major burden.[1]

Industry Groups

State averages conceal more than they reveal of industrial differences. Much greater differences in cost rates appear when such rates are calculated for industrial divisions within a state, as is done in Table A-5.[2] The eleven states in the table include about 45 percent of all covered employment and exemplify states of varying size, cost rate, geographical location, and type of experience-rating system. There is, therefore, considerable representative value attaching to the experience of these states. The eleven-year period, 1957-67, is long enough to allow fundamental economic differences to show through and includes two recessions and an extended period of prosperity. It is immediately evident that the average cost rates for the first three industrial divisions in the table are appreciably higher, while the last four industrial divisions are appreciably lower, than the state average for all industries. Manufacturing, the largest single division, is usually closest to the state average. In every state, the division of finance-insurance-real estate usually has the lowest cost rate.

If more states were added to Table A-5, would the general results be the same? It is highly probable that they would. Table A-6 shows the experience of five additional states during 1961 (a depression year) and 1967 (a prosperous year). The general pattern is clearly the same—the averages of these two years generally approximate the eleven-year averages of Table A-5. The inclusion of four states (Maine, Massachusetts, Pennsylvania, and Utah) in both tables per-

1. It would be difficult to prove that the high-cost states are incapable of carrying the cost. Of the states that had a benefit cost of 1.3 or more, only one (North Dakota) had a per capita income in 1968 below the national average [88, p. 188].

2. Benefit-cost rates for different industries within a given state are comparable because they are based on taxable not total wages. Taxable wages are the same for every firm in the state. Hence if the cost rate of firm A is 1 percent and the cost rate of firm B is 2 percent, it is correct to conclude that firm B represents twice as great a risk to the fund and would need to pay a tax rate (also based on taxable wages) twice that of firm A in order for each to pay its way in the system. The ratios of practically all the tables used in Chapters 4 and 5 are based on taxable wages.

mits the reader to make a rough comparison between the impressions conveyed by the two tables. Construction and mining have costs much above average, manufacturing is at about average, while the remaining divisions are significantly below average. The lowest cost experience is again in the division of finance-insurance-real estate. There is evidently a high degree of predictable regularity in the differences between industries.

The list below, compiled from Table A-5 and from the 1961 data in Table A-6, shows the difference between the industry with the highest cost rate and the cost rate of finance-insurance-real estate, which is generally the lowest. Most of these differences are clearly large enough to be significant items of cost in most situations.

State and years 1957-67	High	Low[3]	Difference
California	7.1 (agriculture)	1.2	5.9
Maine	5.4 (mining)	0.5	4.9
Massachusetts	6.2 (construction)	0.8	5.4
New York	5.7 (construction)	0.9	4.8
Ohio	5.6 (agriculture)	0.6	5.0
Oregon	3.2 (construction)	0.6	2.6
Pennsylvania	6.7 (mining)	0.8	5.9
Utah	2.8 (construction)	0.5	2.3
Virginia	1.8 (agriculture)	0.2	1.6
Washington	8.6 (agriculture)	1.2	7.4
1961			
Alaska	4.8 (construction)	1.0	3.8
Michigan	8.9 (construction)	0.5	8.4
Minnesota	8.9 (mining)	0.5	8.4
Mississippi	5.2 (construction)	0.5	4.7
Wisconsin	9.2 (mining)	0.3	8.9

Although more revealing than statewide averages, these industrywide averages still conceal many significant and persistent differences. Table A-7, for example, shows cost rates for industries at the two-digit level. Partly because cost data at this level are not generally available, and partly because the statistical task of constructing eleven-year averages at this level of differentiation becomes burdensome, the table is limited to three states. Its scope is widened somewhat by Table A-8, much as Table A-5 was widened by Table A-6.

3. Rates shown are for finance-insurance-real estate, the division for which the rate is usually the lowest.

Manufacturing, which appeared "average" before is now seen to encompass a range of economic activities with widely differing cost rates. The six-state listing below, which draws on Table A-7 and the 1961 data of Table A-8, shows some of the high and low rates for manufacturing industries. Apparel and textiles, along with leather and lumber, are consistently among the highest, while chemicals and printing along with instruments and ordnance, are consistently among the lowest.

Manufacturing

State and years 1957–67	High-cost	Low-cost	Maximum difference
New York	7.2 (apparel)	1.2 (tobacco)	5.9
	5.4 (textiles)	1.3 (chemicals)	
	5.0 (leather)	1.3 (ordnance)	
Ohio	3.1 (primary metals)	0.6 (printing)	2.5
	2.8 (textiles)	0.9 (chemicals)	
	2.5 (furniture)	1.0 (ordnance)	
Pennsylvania	4.9 (tobacco)	0.9 (printing)	4.0
	3.9 (textiles)	1.3 (instruments)	
	3.6 (apparel)	1.4 (chemicals)	
1961			
California	8.3 (lumber)	0.5 (ordnance)	7.8
	6.4 (apparel)	1.5 (printing)	
	5.8 (food)	1.8 (chemicals)	
Massachusetts	8.0 (apparel)	1.5 (printing)	6.5
	6.0 (leather)	1.7 (chemicals)	
	4.9 (textiles)	1.7 (paper)	
Minnesota	6.7 (lumber)	0.6 (paper)	6.1
	5.1 (transportation equipment)	0.7 (instruments)	
	5.0 (apparel)	1.1 (printing)	

Construction also is seen to encompass industry groups with very different cost rates. In New York, for example, where the special trade contractors have a cost rate of 4.7, the general contractors have a cost rate of 8.9 percent. Within the transportation-communication-utilities division, the range of cost rates is from 0.5 to 2.2, while in the service division it is from 1.0 to 3.1. Likewise, the cost rate of the real estate group is almost twice that of the average for its industrial division. The range of rates in Ohio and Pennsylvania are essentially similar to those in New York for the same industrial groups.

As would be expected, the maximum differences between rates increase as the comparison is made between smaller, more homogeneous industry groups. Thus where the maximum difference between industry *divisions* in New York was 4.8 (Table A-5), at the two-digit level (Table A-7) it was 8.4 (the average for general contracting was 8.9 and for utilities was 0.5). It is interesting to note the differences in cost rates for the successive steps in the industrial process relating to the same product. For example, in New York the manufacturers of transportation equipment had a cost rate of 3.0 while those who sold the finished product and those who repaired it had cost rates of only 1.3 and 1.4. Likewise, the manufacture of apparel showed a cost rate of 7.1, while the retailing of apparel had a cost rate of only 2.2. A uniform tax rate would prevent these differences from being reflected in prices.

It is worth noting, in Tables A-6 and A-8, that the differences in cost rates between the various economic activities persist through periods of both high and low unemployment. The absolute differences diminish in good times, but the same industries remain in the high and in the low categories.

Average cost rates at even the two-digit level conceal many significant differences. This is illustrated in Table A-9 which shows cost rates at the three-digit level in three states (California, Massachusetts, and New York) in one year (1967), for a selection of industries for which data were available and in which the differences were particularly marked. Within the group of special trade contractors, for example, plumbing and electrical work are seen to have much lower cost rates than painting and plastering. Within the food group, firms that do canning and preserving have very much higher cost rates than does the average food processor.

In the apparel group, hats and fur goods are marked by more than double the average cost rate for the group. In women's and misses' outerwear—where style changes are important—the cost rates are much higher than in either women's and children's undergarments or men's and boys' furnishings. The different kinds of transportation equipment have significantly different cost rates—and so forth. In all probability, these examples, taken from three states for one year, are roughly indicative of what would be found if similar three-digit data were available for all states for all years.

Three New York tables show, not the averages for industry groups, but the actual distribution of individual firms and payrolls. These are the kind of data one would like to have for every state for every year. Table 4-1 provides an overall view of the distribution of cost rates, while Tables 4-2 and 4-3 provide information on possible industrial explanations of the distribution. The distinction in these latter tables between positive-balance and negative-balance firms introduces a helpful duration element that partially compensates for the restriction of the data to a single year; the condition of the reserves of most of these firms reflects the experience of past years.

As Table 4-1 shows, firms and payrolls were scattered all along this range of cost rates, but the great majority had cost rates of less than 1 percent. Indeed, 71.5 percent of the firms in this prosperous year of 1967 had cost rates of less than 0.5 percent. This is the typical picture of a successful insurance program, with most of the insured drawing very little from the common fund in any one year.[4]

Table 4-1. NEW YORK: Percent Distribution of Firms and Taxable Payrolls, 1967, by Benefit-Cost Rate[a]

Benefit cost rates	Firms	Taxable payrolls
Totals	100.0	100.0
0.0 percent and under 0.5 percent[b]	71.5	46.0
0.5 percent and under 1.0 percent[b]	4.1	18.4
1.0 percent and under 1.5 percent[b]	3.0	8.6
1.5 percent and under 2.0 percent[b]	2.2	5.1
2.0 percent and under 4.0 percent	5.9	11.8
4.0 percent and under 6.0 percent	3.2	3.5
6.0 percent and under 8.0 percent	2.1	2.0
8.0 percent and under 10.0 percent	1.5	1.3
10.0 percent and under 12.0 percent	1.1	0.9
12.0 percent and under 14.0 percent	0.9	0.6
14.0 percent and under 16.0 percent	0.7	0.4
16.0 percent and under 18.0 percent	0.6	0.4
18.0 percent and under 20.0 percent	0.5	0.2
20.0 percent or more	2.8	0.8

Source: Calculated from Unemployment Insurance Tax Rates, 1968, Division of Employment, Department of Labor, New York State (Albany, January 1969), Tables 17 and 18, and data provided by New York Division of Employment.

[a] Benefit charges as percent of taxable payrolls.

[b] Distributions of small percentages of negative-balance firms and their benefit cost rates included herein have been estimated.

The distribution of cost rates in Table 4-1 is a picture of what, in general, the distribution of tax rates might look like if the New York system were completely experience-rated. Some firms might be paying tax rates twenty times greater than those of other firms. On the other hand, if the system used a uniform tax, all firms would be paying about 1.8 percent, the average cost rate of the state that year. Thus the potential significance of experience rating in this one state for this one year was the difference perfect experience rating would make between a tax rate of 1.8 percent and some rate lower or higher. For the 71.5 percent of all firms (with 46 percent of the payrolls) which had cost rates under 0.5 percent, perfect experience rating would result in their paying a tax

4. By contrast with the experience of the average firm, in the apparel industry in 1967 only 18 percent of the firms had cost rates below 0.5 percent (not shown in the table).

rate averaging about 1.3 percent (1.8-0.5) of payrolls less than they would have paid under a uniform tax. A part of the political appeal of experience rating probably derives from this large constituency of potentially advantaged firms.

Tables 4-2 and 4-3 show the distribution of firms and payrolls by industry. In the generally high-cost construction industry, there were two clearly differentiated groups—58.4 percent of the firms which had built up reserves and the 41.6 percent whose reserve accounts showed a negative balance. The positive-balance firms experienced a range of cost rates that ran from over 4 percent to less than 2 percent.[5] The negative-balance firms also included a few firms with cost rates (for that one year) of under 2 percent but their range of costs extended upward to over 20 percent. At the other end of the cost spectrum, in the low-cost industry of finance-insurance-real estate, over 80 percent of all firms had cost rates under 0.5 percent and only 1 percent of all firms had cost rates as high as 20 percent (not shown in table). Nonetheless, there are some firms scattered at various cost rates all along the range.

Additional data, pertaining to particular states in particular years, might be cited from some of the state actuarial studies conducted in the 1950's[6] These additional data all confirm the conclusion that the various economic activities are marked by predictable differences in average cost rates and that, as the economic activity is defined more precisely, the range of differences increases while maintaining most of its predictability.

The sparseness of cost data may be supplemented by the use of tax data "at the limit." That is, firms paying the maximum tax may be viewed as having a cost rate at least that high, and probably higher, while firms paying a minimum tax above zero may be viewed as having a cost rate at least that low, and probably lower. Tables A-15, 16, 17 and 4-6 and 4-7 may all be used in this manner. Individual states are likely to have, or can easily compile, much additional data on tax rates, even if their information on cost rates is limited.

Size Groups

The only information on benefit costs by size of firm were provided by New York, which regularly publishes such data, and by Massachusetts, which made a special compilation for the purposes of this study. As may be seen in Tables 4-4 and 4-5, the average cost rate of the smallest firms tends to be much higher than the average cost rate of the largest firms. Thus in both Massachusetts and New York the smallest firms had a cost rate of 2.5, while the largest firms had a cost rate of only 0.5. More significant, perhaps, is the tendency of small firms to cluster at either end of the cost spectrum. Their costs tend to be either much above or much below the average cost. This is only to be expected: because they

5. Despite their belonging to a generally high-cost industry, over half (52.5 percent) of all construction firms had a cost rate in 1966 of less than 2 percent (not shown in table).
6. Among many others, see the study by Massachusetts in 1950 [89], by Indiana in 1956 [90], and by Kansas in 1961 [36].

Table 4–2. NEW YORK: Distributions of Positive- and Negative-Balance Firms by Industry, by Cost Rate,[a] Year Ending December 31, 1966

Industry division or group	Number of firms — All firms (Number)	All firms (Percent of all firms)	Positive-balance firms (Percent of all firms)	Negative-balance firms (Percent of all firms)	Positive-balance firms: Total-all cost rates	Under 2%	2% and under 4%	4% and over	Negative-balance firms: Total-all cost rates	Under 2%	2% and under 6%	6% and under 10%	10% and under 20%	20% and over
Totals–all industries	363,263	100.0	85.1	14.9	100.0	91.3	5.3	3.4	100.0	8.4	28.0	20.7	24.1	18.8
Contract construction	28,234	100.0	58.4	41.6	100.0	85.7	8.4	5.9	100.0	6.1	26.7	22.0	25.8	19.4
Manufacturing	40,063	100.0	70.9	29.1	100.0	85.1	10.9	4.0	100.0	5.7	34.3	21.4	23.4	15.2
Durable goods	11,736	100.0	85.7	14.3	100.0	88.6	8.0	3.4	100.0	12.2	43.0	20.4	14.6	9.8
Nondurable goods	28,327	100.0	64.8	35.2	100.0	83.2	12.4	4.4	100.0	4.6	32.9	21.4	25.0	16.1
Apparel	10,811	100.0	42.2	57.8	100.0	74.4	20.1	5.5	100.0	3.2	28.6	21.7	28.1	18.4
Men's and boys' suits and coats	339	100.0	54.0	46.0	100.0	77.6	14.8	7.6	100.0	2.6	32.7	26.2	29.5	9.0
Women's and misses' outerwear	4,191	100.0	40.6	59.4	100.0	70.4	23.4	6.2	100.0	2.9	31.0	23.8	27.3	15.0
Women's and children's undergarments	659	100.0	60.8	39.2	100.0	76.8	19.5	3.7	100.0	4.7	50.8	23.9	15.2	5.4
Hats, caps, millinery	524	100.0	13.7	86.3	100.0	73.6	18.1	8.3	100.0	1.5	15.7	15.9	33.5	33.4
Fur goods	1,187	100.0	25.2	74.8	100.0	82.6	13.7	3.7	100.0	2.1	16.9	18.5	35.0	27.5
Transportation, communication and utilities	11,365	100.0	86.1	13.9	100.0	89.8	6.8	3.4	100.0	12.1	30.4	19.4	20.9	17.2
Wholesale and retail trade	128,321	100.0	88.5	11.5	100.0	90.5	5.6	3.9	100.0	11.2	27.1	20.3	22.3	19.1
Finance, insurance, and real estate	39,140	100.0	94.1	5.9	100.0	94.1	3.2	2.7	100.0	10.8	24.4	18.9	24.1	21.8
Services and miscellaneous industries	112,991	100.0	89.7	10.3	100.0	93.8	3.6	2.6	100.0	8.7	24.0	19.7	25.8	21.8

[a]Cost rate = benefit payments as percent of taxable payroll.

Source: *Unemployment Insurance Tax Rates, 1967*, New York State Department of Labor, Division of Employment, Research and Statistics Office (Albany, 1968)

Table 4-3. NEW YORK: Distributions of Taxable Payrolls[a] of Positive- and Negative-Balance Firms by Industry, by Cost Rate,[b] Year Ending December 31, 1966

Industry division or group	Taxable payrolls[a] in 000's				Percent distributions by cost rate									
	All firms		Positive-balance firms	Negative-balance firms	Taxable payrolls of positive-balance firms				Taxable payrolls of negative-balance firms					
	Amount	Percent of all firms	Percent of all firms' taxable payrolls	Percent of all firms' taxable payrolls	Total—all cost rates	Under 2%	2% and under 4%	4% and over	Total—all cost rates	Under 2%	2% and under 6%	6% and under 10%	10% and under 20%	20% and over
Totals—all industries	$16,497,955	100.0	86.2	13.8	100.0	89.9	8.1	2.0	100.0	6.0	45.9	23.5	19.0	5.6
Contract construction	1,042,087	100.0	41.5	58.5	100.0	76.0	18.1	5.9	100.0	2.2	41.2	30.4	21.9	4.3
Manufacturing	6,317,690	100.0	84.5	15.5	100.0	88.8	9.4	1.8	100.0	5.2	47.7	20.9	19.2	7.0
Durable goods	3,021,455	100.0	94.9	5.1	100.0	90.3	9.1	0.6	100.0	8.4	71.2	13.0	6.5	0.9
Nondurable goods	3,296,235	100.0	75.0	25.0	100.0	87.1	9.8	3.1	100.0	4.6	43.2	22.5	21.6	8.1
Apparel	904,717	100.0	47.3	52.7	100.0	71.6	24.7	3.7	100.0	3.6	37.4	23.6	25.0	10.4
Men's and boys' suits and coats	91,595	100.0	66.7	33.3	100.0	87.4	11.7	0.9	100.0	1.0	46.4	21.9	28.8	1.9
Women's and misses' outerwear	385,844	100.0	38.3	61.7	100.0	65.2	29.7	5.1	100.0	3.2	33.7	25.5	26.1	11.5
Women's and children's undergarments	76,567	100.0	65.1	34.9	100.0	67.4	28.0	4.6	100.0	12.5	59.7	18.8	7.9	1.1
Hats, caps, millinery	29,907	100.0	12.4	87.6	100.0	63.8	26.0	10.2	100.0	1.1	15.8	18.6	37.3	27.2
Fur goods	31,756	100.0	18.2	81.8	100.0	65.8	30.5	3.7	100.0	1.8	27.2	24.6	35.5	10.9
Transportation, communication and utilities	1,500,229	100.0	92.2	7.8	100.0	95.5	3.9	0.6	100.0	28.1	54.2	8.9	6.8	2.0
Wholesale and retail trade	3,722,799	100.0	93.2	6.8	100.0	89.8	7.9	2.3	100.0	8.3	48.5	23.4	14.5	5.3
Finance, insurance and real estate	1,537,292	100.0	97.3	2.7	100.0	95.5	3.4	1.1	100.0	7.5	39.5	30.2	18.5	4.3
Services and miscellaneous industries	2,351,331	100.0	88.5	11.5	100.0	88.3	9.6	2.1	100.0	5.6	45.3	22.6	21.0	5.5

Source: *Unemployment Insurance Tax Rates, 1967*, New York State Department of Labor, Division of Employment, Research and Statistics Office (Albany, 1968).

[a] Taxable payrolls for year ending September 30, 1966.
[b] Cost rate = benefit payments as percent of taxable payroll.

have few employees, they may go along for years without a compensable separation and hence without any benefit charges. But if even one employee is separated and draws benefits, the result may be a precipitate rise in the employer's cost rate.

As the Massachusetts data (Table 4-4 and Table A-11) show, among the firms with a positive balance, the smaller firms have lower cost rates than large firms, but among the negative-balance firms, the smaller firms have the higher cost rates. Although these latter are a relatively small part of the total, their rates are so high that they dominate the average for their group. For example, 82.8 percent of the smallest firms had an average cost rate of only 0.2, the lowest of all the groups; but the remaining 17.2 percent had such a high rate (14.2) that the average for the entire size group was 2.5, the highest of all the groups.

The New York data (Table 4-5) illustrate the wide variation of experience within each size group. Some very low-cost and some very high-cost firms appear in every size group. These data also confirm the characteristic tendency of small firms to cluster at either end of the cost spectrum. Thus the great majority (87.4 percent) of the smallest firms had positive balances, and nearly all (95.6 percent) of these had cost rates under 2 percent. Only a small minority (12.6 percent) had negative balances, but over half of these had cost rates above 10 percent.

Thus, to the question: "Do smaller firms tend to have higher cost rates?" the answer must be twofold. No; the great majority of them have lower than average cost rates. But yes; a small minority has such high rates that the average for the group exceeds the average for all groups.

Although both the Massachusetts and the New York tables show only one year's experience, the separation of positive and negative firms introduces the factor of reserves and hence an element of duration. The pattern revealed here probably has a significant degree of stability. This inference is confirmed by Table A-10 which shows the experience of New York firms over six years. In each year, the smallest firms had a higher average cost rate than did the largest firms.

This review of cost data by size of firm suggests two general conclusions. First, classification by size of firm is not so important as classification by industry. The differences in cost associated with size, while significant, are not so large as the differences associated with industry. Second, the largest firms tend to have the lowest cost rates and thus to represent the least risk to the fund. The smallest firms, which tend to cluster at the extreme ends of the cost spectrum, as a class tend to have higher than average cost rates. For this reason they would represent a greater risk to the fund were it not for the fact that, although numerous, they account for only a small part of taxable payrolls. For example, in Massachusetts, which has coverage of one or more, the smallest firms were 52.5 percent of all firms but accounted for only 4.0 percent of taxable payrolls and 7.8 percent of all benefits (Table 4-4 and Table 5-7).

Table 4-4. MASSACHUSETTS: Average Benefit-Cost Rates,[a] Year Ending September 30, 1967, by Size of Taxable Payroll, All Rated Employers, Positive Accounts, and Negative Accounts

	All rated employers					Positive-balance accounts					Negative-balance accounts				
		Firms		Taxable payrolls			Firms		Taxable payrolls			Firms		Taxable payrolls	
Size of taxable payroll	Average cost rate	Number	Per cent of total	Amount (in 000's)	Per cent of total	Average cost rate	Number	Per cent of total	Amount (in 000's)	Per cent of total	Average cost rate	Number	Per cent of total	Amount (in 000's)	Per cent of total
All size groups	1.3	103,404	100.0	$5,659,309	100.0	0.6	86,919	100.0	$5,036,046	100.0	6.6	16,485	100.0	$623,263	100.0
Less than $10,000	2.5	54,296	52.5	228,323	4.0	0.2	44,933	51.7	192,096	3.8	14.2	9,363	56.8	36,227	5.8
10,000- 24,999	1.6	23,551	22.8	372,416	6.6	0.4	20,163	23.2	319,028	6.3	8.4	3,388	20.5	53,388	8.6
25,000- 49,999	1.6	11,407	11.0	400,365	7.1	0.5	9,803	11.3	344,155	6.8	7.6	1,604	9.7	56,210	9.0
50,000- 99,999	1.6	6,658	6.4	464,606	8.2	0.6	5,696	6.6	397,001	7.9	7.0	962	5.8	67,605	10.9
100,000- 249,999	1.6	4,523	4.4	693,318	12.3	0.6	3,787	4.4	577,930	11.5	6.2	736	4.5	115,388	18.5
250,000- 499,999	1.6	1,531	1.5	525,638	9.3	0.7	1,276	1.5	439,515	8.7	6.1	255	1.6	86,123	13.8
500,000- 999,999	1.3	805	0.8	555,281	9.8	0.6	689	0.8	475,302	9.5	4.9	116	0.7	79,979	12.8
1,000,000- 2,499,999	1.2	410	0.4	617,767	10.9	0.7	362	0.4	551,096	11.0	5.3	48	0.3	66,671	10.7
2,500,000- 4,999,999	0.8	126	0.1	431,831	7.6	0.6	118	0.1	407,759	8.1	3.9	8	0.1	24,072	3.9
5,000,000- 9,999,999	0.9	58	0.1	386,010	6.8	0.7	54	*	359,055	7.1	3.0	4	*	26,955	4.3
10,000,000-24,999,999	0.8	29	*	434,281	7.7	0.6	28	*	423,635	8.4	3.0	1	*	10,646	1.7
25,000,000-and over	0.5	10	*	549,474	9.7	0.6	10	*	549,474	10.9	—	0	0.0	0	0.0

Sources: Tabulations furnished by the Massachusetts Division of Employment Security (Boston 1969).

*Less than 0.05 percent.

[a]Cost rate = benefit charges as percent of taxable payrolls. (During the year ending September 30, 1967, 18 percent of all benefits paid were noncharged.)

Table 4–5. NEW YORK: Distributions of Positive- and Negative-Balance Firms by Size-of-Taxable-Payroll Group,[a] by Cost Rate,[b] Year Ending December 31, 1966

| | All firms | | | Positive-balance firms | Negative-balance firms | Percent distributions by cost rate | | | | | | | | | |
| | | | | | | Positive-balance firms | | | | Negative-balance firms | | | | | |
Size of taxable payroll	Number; or amount in 000's	Average cost rate	Percent in size group	Percent in size group	Percent in size group	Total—all cost rates	Under 2%	2% and under 4%	4% and over	Total—all cost rates	Under 2%	2% and under 6%	6% and under 10%	10% and under 20%	20% and over
Total—all size groups	363,263	1.8	100.0	85.1	14.9	100.0	91.3	5.3	3.4	100.0	8.4	28.0	20.7	24.1	18.8
Under $10,000	203,723	2.5	100.0	87.4	12.6	100.0	95.6	1.8	2.6	100.0	10.7	15.0	15.8	27.1	31.4
10,000– 24,999	78,573	2.1	100.0	84.4	15.6	100.0	87.3	7.4	5.3	100.0	7.3	33.5	26.4	23.7	9.1
25,000– 49,999	37,690	2.2	100.0	83.0	17.0	100.0	83.2	12.2	4.6	100.0	6.5	42.8	24.2	20.0	6.5
50,000– 99,999	21,796	2.7	100.0	78.2	21.8	100.0	82.4	14.4	3.2	100.0	5.1	43.3	24.5	19.5	7.6
100,000– 249,999	13,878	2.8	100.0	74.5	25.5	100.0	83.6	14.3	2.1	100.0	4.6	46.0	23.7	19.9	5.8
250,000– 499,999	4,178	2.3	100.0	79.1	20.9	100.0	87.6	11.3	1.1	100.0	4.1	49.3	25.2	18.4	3.0
500,000– 999,999	1,865	1.7	100.0	84.5	15.5	100.0	91.3	7.3	1.4	100.0	4.5	57.5	20.0	15.2	2.8
1,000,000– 2,499,999	995	1.5	100.0	87.9	12.1	100.0	91.2	7.9	0.9	100.0	5.0	50.0	30.0	13.3	1.7
2,500,000– 4,999,999	323	1.2	100.0	90.7	9.3	100.0	95.2	4.1	0.7	100.0	0	53.4	30.0	16.6	0
5,000,000– 9,999,999	123	1.1	100.0	94.3	5.7	100.0	94.8	3.4	1.8	100.0	0	57.2	14.3	28.5	0
10,000,000–24,999,999	88	0.8	100.0	96.6	3.4	100.0	95.3	3.5	1.2	100.0	33.3	66.7	0	0	0
25,000,000 and over	31	0.5	100.0	100.0	0	100.0	96.8	3.2	0						

Source: *Unemployment Insurance Tax Rates, 1967*, New York State Department of Labor, Division of Employment, Research and Statistics Office (Albany, April 1968).

[a] Taxable payrolls for year ending September 30, 1966.
[b] Cost rate = benefit payments as percent of taxable payroll.

The Lesson of Cost Rates

The principal conclusion to be drawn from this historical pattern of cost rates is that they provide support for treating the cost of unemployment benefits as a regular cost of doing business. Like other business costs, the costs of unemployment benefits vary significantly and regularly with the type of economic activity with which they are associated. One can predict with a high degree of probability, for example, that in state after state, and year after year, the firms in the construction industry will draw much more out of the fund per covered worker than will the firms in the industry of finance-insurance-real estate. That within construction, the special trades group will draw out less than will other groups. That within the special trades, electrical work and plumbing will be much less costly than painting and plastering. One can predict that the service industries will be relatively more costly than finance-insurance-real estate, but less costly than manufacturing. One can predict that within manufacturing, heavy durables, like steel and autos, and seasonal activities, like canning and apparel, will draw out more per covered worker than printing or chemicals or instruments. One can safely predict that within apparel manufacturing, men's suits and women's undergarments will be less costly than hats or fur goods or women's outerwear.

It should be recalled that these data are averages for groups of firms and are only proxies for the more desirable data, namely, those that show the experience of individual firms. Within each industry the individual firms are distributed widely around the industry averages (Table 4-2) and thus within each industry there will be firms that are paying their way and firms that are not paying their way. Since industries are not taxed, but only individual firms, of what use are industry averages? Only this, that they provide some basis for judging the distribution of cost rates for individual firms.

The differences among the industry averages clearly are rooted in the natures of the respective economic activities. These regular differences persist over time and hold for firms at the two-digit and three-digit levels. It seems logical, therefore, to assume that similar differences exist to a significant extent at the level of the individual firm. To what extent? If eleven-year average cost rates could be obtained for individual firms, would the differences between firms be as large and as predictable as they are in the eleven-year averages for industry groups? The range of differences for individual firms would certainly be greater (see, for example, Tables 4-1 and 4-2). The degree of stability (predictability) of the differences would certainly be less, but would probably remain high.[7] Most firms, in most years, could predict with considerable probability, and within a narrow range, what their next year's cost rate would be.

7. The degree of predictability would be greater for the larger firms, which comprise the bulk of the program, than for the smaller firms, which, though numerous, account for only a minor fraction of total payrolls (as exemplified in Table 4-4).

To summarize: It is likely that the anticipations of individual firms with regard to their cost rates show great differences and that these anticipations are generally fulfilled. The existence of such significant and stable cost differences supports a tentative conclusion that experience rating unless it is objectionable for other reasons, is the appropriate arrangement for an economy in which the market is the principal instrument for the allocation of resources. On the other hand, since the individual firm cannot be certain that those anticipations will be fulfilled in its own case—for the competitive market poses an inescapable, constantly present risk—the use of the *insurance* technique is indicated. A combination of considerable risk with considerable predictability provides the typical situation suitable for an insurance program financed through differentiated premiums. Although no firm can ever know with complete certainty, most firms in most years can predict with considerable probability what their year's cost rate will be.

Tax Rates

Although cost rates determine the potential degree of experience rating, the actual degree is determined by tax rates. The employer's cost is not what his employees draw from the fund but what he pays into the fund.[8] To see how experience rating has actually been working, it is necessary to look at the behavior of tax rates.

All the effects which are attributed to experience rating are dependent upon the pattern of tax rates. The allocation of costs and resources will be that produced by the taxes which firms actually pay. Likewise, the motivation of employers to participate in legislation or administration or to stabilize employment is directly dependent on their tax rates. Finally, the effect of experience rating on the business cycle is entirely a matter of the timing of taxes. In a word, the limits within which the claims and charges about experience rating can possibly be true are set by the degree of experience rating in the system, and the degree of experience rating is determined by the pattern of tax rates.

The tax data have been arranged to answer two general questions. First, how large and how regular are the differentials in the tax rates actually levied on employers? The larger and the more regular the tax differentials, the more likely it is that experience rating has significant effects. Second, what kind of firms are paying the higher and the lower rates? This knowledge is needed for decisions to retain the existing distribution of the tax burden, or to increase the degree of experience rating and thus make more firms pay more of their own way, or to decrease the degree of experience rating and thus provide more firms with more of a subsidy.

8. However, in the reserve-ratio and benefit-ratio systems, for firms between the minimum and maximum tax rates, these two flows tend to an equilibrium position where they are approximately equal (see Appendix B).

Industry Groups

From Table A-5, which shows eleven-year averages for industry divisions, it is clear that the tax differentials are sufficiently regular to justify the conclusion that they stem from fundamental differences in the economic activities to which the tax rates apply. It would be safe to wager that the average tax in the construction industry will be higher than the average tax in the finance industry. Table A-6 serves as an extension of Table A-5. Although tax rates for single years are uncertain guides in themselves, they gain in significance when they are found to be generally similar to the eleven-year averages of the previous table. It is also significant that the interindustry differences persist whether the period be a time of recession or a prosperous year.

Industry averages conceal, of course, the differences in tax rates facing the actual taxpayers, which are not industries but individual firms. Table A-7 illustrates how the differences in rates grow larger as the industry classifications are narrowed. In Ohio, for example, where the greatest difference between industry divisions in Table A-5 is 1.8, in Table A-7 the difference between "Other General Contractors" and "Electric, Gas and Sanitary Services" is 2.7. The lessons of this table are extended to three additional states by Table A-8. Although the latter table supplies data for only two years, a general similarity in results to the eleven-year average supplies a reasonable basis for concluding that if similiar eleven-year averages were calculated for these states the results would be substantially the same. The greatest difference in tax rates shown in Table A-8 is that of Minnesota in 1967, where the group "Other General Contractors" was taxed at a rate of 4.0, while several manufacturing groups were taxed at a rate of only 0.7.

Table A-9 shows tax rates for industry groups at the three-digit level. Although for cost rates differences were noticeably greater at this level than at the two-digit level, the same was not equally true of tax rates. The reason, of course, is the limiting effect of the maximum tax, which prevents variations in cost rates from being fully reflected in the tax rates.

Tables A-15, 16, and 17 are the equivalent of dividing larger industry divisions into smaller units. They extend this process to its limit, the individual firm. They show the distribution of individual taxpayers *within* each major industry division. The tables reveal a significant range of rates within each industrial division, whether the division as a whole has a high or a low average rate. To take New York as an example: In the construction industry, although two-thirds of the firms are taxed at a rate of 3.0 percent or higher, 10.9 percent of them are at the minimum rate, with other firms at all the rates between. Contrariwise, in finance-insurance-real estate, although nearly half of the firms are at the minimum rate, 19.8 percent of them are taxed at a rate of 3.0 percent or higher, and again there is an even scattering of firms at all the intervening rates. The distribution of all industries combined conveys the impression of a fairly sensitive experience-rating system. Firms are fairly evenly distributed at all the tax rates between 0.9

and 2.9. However, there is a noticeable concentration of firms at the lowest and highest rates. More than a quarter (28.0 percent) were taxed at the minimum rate of 0.8, while more than a third (35.5 percent) were in the 3.0–3.3 rate interval. To achieve a greater degree of experience rating in the New York system, the minimum would have to be lowered and the maximum would have to be raised.

Oregon used experience rating to a lesser degree than did New York. As Table A-16 shows, Oregon had a higher minimum, a lower maximum, and fewer rate intervals. As a result, two-thirds of all employers were at either the maximum or the minimum rate. However, there is the same basic picture of significant variation within each industrial division. Massachusetts (Table A-17) resembles New York more closely than it does Oregon.

Although not reproduced here because of its large size, a table was constructed for Massachusetts showing the distribution of tax rates within *two-digit* industrial groups. Within each group, the same fundamental pattern was revealed: firms were distributed along the tax spectrum from the minimum to the maximum. The exact pattern differed, of course, for the various groups; but in every group, whether it had a high or a low average tax, there were some firms at every tax-rate interval. Firms at the three-digit level probably exhibit a similar spread of tax rates. It should be noted that, as a general principle, tax differences become the more potent as incentives for the individual firm as the industrial group to which the firm belongs is the more homogeneous.

Table 4-6 presents a different view of the spread of tax rates. For eleven states and two years, the distribution of tax rates is shown according as firms were paying the minimum, the maximum, or were in between these two extremes. Obviously, experience rating can operate to produce differentiated tax rates only over the interval determined by the floor of the minimum rate and the ceiling of the maximum rate. Thus the greater the proportion falling between the minimum and the maximum, the greater, other things being equal, is the degree of experience rating. In the majority of cases over half of the firms were paying a tax between the minimum and maximum rates. In 1967 only two states (Illinois and Virginia) taxed less than half their firms at rates between the minimum and maximum, and in both cases the reason was a heavy concentration of firms at the minimum rate. Ohio in 1967 taxed over three-quarters of the firms and over 90 percent of the payrolls at rates between the minimum and maximum.[9] Bunching at the maximum rate always indicates a lack of experience rating; but bunching at the minimum must be interpreted in the light of the level at which the minimum has been set. A bunching of firms at a minimum of zero may indicate a high degree of experience rating, while a bunching at a relatively high minimum, such as that of California or of Pennsylvania, indicates a lack of experience rating.

9. Table 4-6 also shows the range between the minimum and maximum rates in these states. The narrowest ranges were in California (2.1) and Main (2.2), while the widest ranges were in Florida (4.5), Wisconsin (4.2), and Ohio (4.1).

Carefully studied, Table 4-6 will provide the reader with a reliable, if rough, "feel" for the degree of experience rating in the program in recent years. Experience rating resulted in about this much tax dispersion among the firms covered by the system. However, the table reveals nothing about the crucial distribution of rates between the minimum and maximum. For this, it needs to be studied in conjunction with Tables A-15, 16, and 17, and especially with Table 4-7.

Table 4-7 shows the complete distribution of tax rates for all firms in all states for 1967. It provides the best single view of how experience rating allocated the tax costs of unemployment benefits in the country in that prosperous year. The table conveys an overall impression of a tax system of considerable sensitivity. In most states, experience rating had produced a significant dispersion of tax rates. Although there is considerable concentration in two intervals (1.0-1.8 and 1.9-2.6), this is partly a statistical accident reflecting the width of these intervals. In actuality, employers were taxed at many different rates within these intervals—see, for example, New York and Massachusetts in Tables A-15, 16, and 17.

About 20 percent of all payrolls were taxed at or above the "standard" rate of 2.7, while about 25 percent were taxed at a rate of 0.5 or less. The difference in taxes paid by these two groups ranged between 2 and 3 percent of taxable wages. Since under a uniform tax the difference would be zero, experience rating changed the competitive position of these firms, on the average, by 2 or 3 percent of taxable wages. While the significance of a tax differential of this size varies from situation to situation—depending on such factors as the proportion that taxable wages are of total wages, the proportion that labor costs are of total costs, and the rate of profit—in no situation would such a differential be completely negligible. It belongs among the multitude of other small costs which the firm earnestly seeks to minimize, because together they constitute an appreciable part of its total costs and thus affect its success in the competitive struggle for resources.

The tax differentials are smaller among the remaining 55 percent of the firms which are in the central section of the distribution. Even for these firms, however, the range is between 0.5 and 2.7, and in most situations this is a significant difference. In large corporations, which have most of the payroll and workers, an increase in the tax rate of a fraction of 1 percent is likely to elicit an inquiry from the finance department directed to the personnel department or to the employee benefits department asking for an explanation. In some firms, the unemployment insurance tax may loom large in relation to profits, and a drop in the tax rate from 2 percent to 1 percent may mean a significant increase in profits.[10]

10. Six large manufacturing firms calculated, for the purpose of this study, the average ratio of their unemployment insurance taxes to their net profits during the decade 1960-70. The ratios ranged from 3 percent to 7 percent. A study of a food-service firm in Illinois, employing about 400 in 1963, found that in several years the unemployment insurance tax was larger than the firm's profits [91, p. 33]. The firm was still in operation in 1970.

Table 4-6. Percent Distribution of Rated Employers and Their Taxable Payrolls by Tax Rate,[a] 1962 and 1967, Selected States

	California		Florida		Illinois		Maine		Massachusetts	
	1962	1967	1962	1967	1962	1967	1962	1967	1962	1967
Number of rated employers	199,083	222,622	34,877	39,429	78,492	81,873	6,762	6,957	100,054	103,83
Percent distribution of employers by rate:										
At minimum	7.9	.7	34.8	43.7	27.0	50.4	16.1	31.0	22.2	19
At maximum	34.1	26.7	19.2	2.2	30.0	1.4	25.3	16.1	16.1	10
In between	58.0	72.6	46.0	54.1	43.0	48.3	58.6	52.9	61.7	70
Amount of taxable payroll of rated employers (in millions of dollars)[b]	12,198	15,247	2,288	3,239	7,582	9,410	490	593	4,227	5,44
Percent distribution of taxable payroll by rate:			INA				INA			
At minimum	1.1	0.1		24.3	5.1	40.8		29.1	7.3	5
At maximum	29.8	18.0		2.0	18.9	0.2		14.9	12.8	6
In between	69.2	81.8		73.7	76.0	59.0		56.0	79.9	88
Rates in effect:										
Minimum rate	2.2	1.6	1.1	0.0	0.1	0.1	1.4	0.5	1.1	0
Maximum rate	3.5	3.7	2.9	4.5	4.0	4.0	2.7	2.7	3.9	3
Steps in schedule	12	19	19	55	40	40	14	16	15	15

Sources: Statistical tables published by the employment security agencies of the respective states, supplemented by correspondence with them; also statistical tables published by, or obtained from, the Bureau of Employment Security, U.S. Department of Labor.

As may be seen in Table 4-7, the states differ considerably in the degree to which their programs are experience-rated. Michigan, Ohio, Illinois, Florida, and Minnesota make the fullest use of the higher rates, distributing payrolls among the higher tax rates without notable bunching. New York makes considerable use of tax rates above the standard 2.7, but allows the tax payments to bunch in the interval ending at 3.5. Alaska, North Dakota, Pennsylvania, and Vermont permit notable bunching in the interval 4.0-4.4. Most of the other states make less use of the higher rates. The states which permit the greatest bunching of taxes are in the northwest—Oregon, Utah, and Washington—where seasonal industries play a large role. Florida, Ohio, and Wisconsin, which make more than average use of the rates in the upper range also make more than average use of the rates in the lower range and hence cover the entire spectrum of rates.

Table 4-8 supplements Table 4-7. While lacking the depth of detail of that table, it supplies more temporal breadth. It shows the distribution of taxable wages by tax rates during the period 1959-67 for the program as a whole. In each of these years there was a significant range of tax rates from less than 1

Mississippi		New York		Ohio		Pennsylvania		Virginia		Wisconsin	
1962	1967	1962	1967	1962	1967	1962	1967	1962	1967	1962	1967
12,050	12,270	327,092	298,870	75,325	86,394	166,909	160,542	25,110	28,117	31,082	34,940
6.0	33.7	2.0	32.7	13.3	14.4	19.0	5.4	47.1	69.2	34.8	25.8
10.8	8.3	17.1	14.3	25.1	8.1	32.7	18.2	11.9	3.4	7.3	7.1
83.2	58.1	80.9	53.0	61.6	77.5	48.3	76.4	41.0	27.4	57.9	67.1
631	944	14,576	15,441	6,657	8,290	7,700	10,210	1,804	2,493	2,431	3,142
8.0	8.3	3.6	22.9	3.0	4.6	5.6	0.3	13.8	31.0	18.7	6.0
5.8	7.0	16.0	12.9	27.3	3.7	41.0	13.4	11.0	3.0	7.1	5.7
86.2	84.7	80.4	64.2	69.7	91.7	53.3	86.3	75.2	66.0	74.2	88.3
1.0	0.1	2.1	0.8	0.6	0.1	2.0	1.0	0.1	0.1	0.0	0.0
2.7	2.7	4.2	3.3	3.2	4.2	4.0	4.0	2.7	2.7	3.6	4.2
7	27	15	19	17	18	21	31	27	27	9	12

[a]Rates include supplementary taxes not credited to employer reserves, in states where such taxes are assessed.

[b]Taxable payroll figures are for the twelve-month periods ending at the computation dates for the 1962 and 1967 rates. Such computation dates vary by state and for the same state may differ as between the two years.

percent to 4 percent or more. On the average, the categories "below 1.0" and "above 2.7" combined, accounted for about 50 percent of the payrolls. As the average rate declined, the distribution shifted from the higher tax rates toward the lower. Even in 1967, however, 16.2 percent of payrolls were taxed above the "standard" rate. Contrariwise, even in 1963, following the 1961 recession, 19 percent of payrolls were taxed at less than 1 percent.
less than 1 percent.

Tables 4–7 and 4–8 are ideal insofar as they relate to individual firms, rather than to industry averages. They are seriously limited, however, insofar as they tell us nothing about the regularity with which firms remain in the same tax bracket. This table must be supplemented by the previous tables. In the light of the previous tables, it is reasonable to assume that this distribution of tax rates results primarily from differences in the nature of the economic activities involved and hence exhibits considerable stability.

One direct measure of the stability with which firms remain in high-cost or low-cost brackets is provided by Table 4–9, a special compilation provided by

Table 4-7. Percent Distribution of Taxable Wages of Active Accounts Eligible for Experience Rating by Tax Rate, Type of Experience-Rating Plan, and State, Rate Years Beginning in 1967

Percentage distribution by employer contribution rate

Type of plan and state[a]	Taxable wages amount (in 000's)	0.0	0.1	0.2	0.3	0.4–0.5	0.6–0.9	1.0–1.8	1.9–2.6	2.7	2.71–3.1	3.2–3.5	3.6–3.9	4.0–4.4	4.5 and
Total, 51 states	$144,265,674	2.6	6.9	3.7	5.5	6.6	14.8	23.9	16.1	3.7	6.9	3.3	3.5	2.1	.4
Reserve ratio plan															
Arizona[b]	1,014,414	3.1	2.9	0.5	4.1	5.6	16.9	27.3	15.0	4.2	9.5	4.4	5.0	1.2	0.3
Arkansas[b]	941,610				6.8	5.5	13.2	48.5	15.3	5.0	5.7				
California	15,246,979				33.7	12.9	17.2	15.6	7.1	0.7	4.9	9.0	21.0	8.0	
Colorado[b]	1,211,857	79.4				6.6		8.1	38.6	7.4	15.9				
District of Columbia[b]	818,447		53.2			15.0		18.4	2.6	13.9					
Georgia	2,775,501				8.7	13.3	20.8	48.0	6.7	10.8			[c]	0.2	
Hawaii	601,219						20.5	49.5	11.7	1.9	2.8				
Idaho	403,147						8.9	39.7	37.6		9.8			3.0	
Indiana[b]	3,932,143		10.2		6.3	11.2	20.7	37.5	3.9	5.5	[c]				
Iowa[b]	1,468,177	37.9	8.1	10.0	11.3	20.2	3.8	0.4	1.4	0.5	[c]				
Kansas[b]	1,092,335	2.8		1.5	1.7	11.6	27.9	38.3	4.3	1.8					
Kentucky[b]	1,492,084	29.3					30.9	11.8		11.9		8.0			
Louisiana[b]	1,821,921					29.1	21.2	12.4	2.4	20.0					
Maine[b]	593,445				42.4		23.8	26.7	5.6	21.6					
Massachusetts	5,449,307						9.3	35.4	22.4	14.9	22.9				
Michigan[b]	7,856,888	[c]	[c]	[c]		13.3	18.4	49.7	6.7	2.1	1.3		1.6	3.6	3.2
Missouri[b]	3,037,190	15.8	35.3		18.6		13.8	11.6		2.1			4.9		
Nebraska[b]	750,661		11.5	7.1	20.5	29.5		14.0	2.5	0.1					
Nevada	421,464						15.1	38.1	26.8	14.9					
New Hampshire	509,691			29.5		15.8	11.4	24.5	13.6		0.9	4.4			
New Jersey[b]	5,107,115						16.4	35.0	18.0	1.5	12.8		17.8		
New Mexico	438,184		26.3		12.8		25.7	20.1	4.2	1.5	9.5				
New York[b]	16,326,141						26.0	27.2	13.7	1.4	19.5	12.2			
North Carolina[b]	3,235,953				18.3	14.2	23.6	20.4	13.0	2.1	0.8	0.6	0.6	0.4	
North Dakota[b]	211,909							60.9	17.8	3.0	2.7	2.1	1.4	11.3	
Ohio[b]	8,299,925						31.0	27.2	7.8	6.2	5.1	1.0	1.4	2.0	
Rhode Island	789,264		4.6	1.5	3.5	12.0	31.0	50.2	25.0	3.3	10.1	1.0	5.3		0.8

Distribution of taxable payroll (dollars) and percent distribution by employer contribution rate, by State and type of experience-rating plan.

State	Taxable payroll	Percent distribution by contribution rate (read left to right)
South Carolina[b]	1,514,319	43.4 34.4 8.8 11.9 0.4 0.5 0.1 0.5
South Dakota[b]	217,576	53.0 20.5 16.2 2.3 0.8 0.8 7.1
Tennessee	2,514,475	12.8 24.5 44.7 9.7 4.0 2.9 1.8 0.6 2.3
West Virginia[b]	1,109,321	13.1 7.4 6.3 14.4 19.0 2.9 1.7 0.6 6.6
Wisconsin[b]	3,141,910	6.0 8.0 23.6 40.6 8.9 2.9 1.8 (c) 0.1
Benefit wage ratio plan		
Alabama	21,508,643	30.4 19.5 10.6 16.9 9.3 7.9 2.3 2.3 0.4 (c) (c) 0.1
Delaware	1,865,170	26.2 27.7 6.7 59.0 20.6 5.5 4.5 12.3 0.3 0.1
Illinois	499,716	40.8 22.7 11.8 6.9 8.6 7.1 2.7 1.8 0.8 0.2
Oklahoma	9,409,728	57.9 12.0 6.5 6.5 3.8 1.2 0.7 0.1 0.2 0.1
Texas	1,254,291	30.0 18.0 10.9 12.3 13.3 12.3 3.6 6.9 3.5 0.2
Virginia	5,986,905	31.0 4.7 19.7 22.5 12.4 5.0 1.9 3.0 3.0
	2,492,833	
Benefit ratio plan		
Florida	22,128,931	3.8 3.2 2.8 8.0 2.4 13.9 22.4 24.3[d] 19.5[d] 2.5 1.6 8.2 1.2
Maryland	3,239,460	24.3[d] 19.5[d] 15.5 9.7 10.7 10.1 5.5 1.5 0.1 0.4 0.2 0.3 2.0
Minnesota[b]	2,352,332	57.3 16.7 12.8 12.8 5.1 1.1 6.6 0.8 0.6 0.4 6.5
Mississippi	2,935,969	8.3 13.4 11.4 57.3 12.7 2.8 1.5 0.8 0.6 0.8
	943,762	21.2 20.2 13.9 4.5 7.0
Oregon	1,619,045	50.0 40.1 9.9
Pennsylvania[b]	10,594,281	31.4 37.1 2.1 5.8 4.3 2.8 16.5
Vermont	272,889	26.9 26.8 8.8 17.8 9.1 10.6
Wyoming[b]	171,193	28.8 42.8 10.2 2.4 2.9 12.9
Payroll variation plan		
Alaska	3,303,305	18.5 76.1 0.3 0.8 1.7 1.6 1.0
Utah	279,592	19.6 19.6 0.1 9.8 19.5 19.4 12.1
Washington	673,570	82.5 17.4 0.1
	2,350,143	99.6 0.4
Other plans		
Connecticut[e]	2,980,223	1.5 13.5 40.7 35.4 9.0
Montana[b,e]	2,646,267	10.9 43.1 37.8 8.3
	333,956	13.0 34.6 21.4 16.5 14.6

Source: Tabulation furnished by the Office of Actuarial and Research Service, Manpower Administration, U.S. Department of Labor.

[a] States classified by type of plan in effect at end of 1967.
[b] Includes effects of voluntary contributions made toward credit for 1967 rates and of subsidiary and additional taxes where applicable.
[c] Less than 0.05 percent.
[d] In Florida the 24.3 percent consist of 13.5 percent with a 0 rate and 10.8 percent with rates of 0.01–0.04 percent; the 19.5 percent consist of 9.9 percent with rates of 0.05–0.09 percent and 9.6 percent with a 0.10 percent rate.
[e] Connecticut has compensable separations formula; Montana, a combination of benefit contribution experience and payroll decline.

Table 4-8. Percent Distribution of Taxable Wages of Rated Accounts by Tax Rate, All States, for Years 1959-67

Year	Average tax rate	Percent distribution of taxable wages by tax rate													
		Total	0.0	0.1	0.2-0.5	0.6-0.9	1.0-1.8	1.9-2.6	2.7	2.71-3.1	3.2-3.5	3.6-3.9	4.0+	Below 1.0	Above 2.7
1959	1.71	100.0	2.6	2.9	14.5	14.4	30.6	16.0	11.1					34.4	7.9
1960	1.88	100.0	2.2	3.4	11.1	10.1	28.6	17.2	11.2	5.6	2.6	1.3	6.7	26.8	16.2
1961	2.06	100.0	1.5	2.8	9.5	10.6	26.7	17.4	9.7	6.8	5.2	2.2	7.8	24.4	22.0
1962	2.36	100.0	1.4	2.2	6.1	8.4	14.6	23.3	10.2	13.1	5.1	8.1	7.5	18.1	33.8
1963	2.31	100.0	1.2	2.3	5.8	9.7	19.8	18.4	7.6	10.5	8.8	6.0	9.9	19.0	35.2
1964	2.21	100.0	1.3	2.8	7.1	9.9	22.9	16.6	7.3	9.4	10.1	5.0	7.6	21.1	32.1
1965	2.11	100.0	1.1	3.2	8.9	11.7	21.5	20.8	7.1	7.3	7.0	5.5	5.9	24.9	25.7
1966	1.90	100.0	1.7	3.9	12.3	11.9	26.6	19.1	4.7	5.6	3.9	6.2	4.2	29.8	19.9
1967	1.61	100.0	2.6	6.9	15.8	14.8	23.9	16.1	3.7	6.9	3.3	3.5	2.5	40.1	16.2

Sources: 1959-61: *The Labor Market and Employment Security*, U.S. Department of Labor, Bureau of Employment Security; 1962-66: *Unemployment Insurance Review*, U.S. Department of Labor, Manpower Administration; 1967: data provided by U.S. Department of Labor, Manpower Administration, Office of Actuarial and Research Service.

Table 4–9. MASSACHUSETTS: Percent Distribution of Employers Who Had Been Subject to the Massachusetts Employment Security Law Continuously, 1960–68 (by Portion of 9-Year Period in Which Their Tax Rates Were above Average; at or below Average; at Maximum; at Minimum)

Period applicable	Total of col. (3) and col. (7)		Employers whose rates were above average		Employers whose rates were at maximum[a]		Employers whose rates were at or below average		Employers whose rates were at minimum[b]	
	Number	Percent of total employers	Number	Percent of total employers (67,986)	Number	Percent of total employers (67,986)	Number	Percent of total employers (67,986)	Number	Percent of total employers (67,986)
	(1)	(2)	(3)	(4)	(5)	(6)	(7)	(8)	(9)	(10)
Entire 9-year period	29,847	43.9	13,407	19.7	2,215	3.3	16,440	24.2	1,417	2.1
8 years only	10,009	14.7	3,894	5.7	1,362	2.0	6,115	9.0	1,631	2.4
7 years only	9,283	13.7	4,070	6.0	1,356	2.0	5,213	7.7	2,303	3.4
6 years only	9,403	13.8	4,392	6.5	1,475	2.2	5,011	7.4	2,834	4.2
5 years only	9,444	13.9	4,806	7.1	1,756	2.6	4,638	6.8	3,425	5.0
Total employers	67,986	100.0	30,569	45.0	8,164	12.0	37,417	55.0	11,610	17.1

Source: Tabulation furnished by the Massachusetts Division of Employment Security.

[a]Will also be included in col. (3).
[b]Will also be included in col. (7).

Massachusetts, which tracked individual firms through a nine-year period, 1960–68. The interpretation of this unusual table should consider that the points of reference used by the table—the average rate, the minimum rate, the maximum rate—probably result in an understatement of the degree of stability. A firm that moved back and forth across the average line from one year to the next, but by very small amounts, would show in the table as very unstable, whereas it was in fact quite stable. The same would be true of a firm that dropped very slightly below the maximum or rose very slightly above the minimum.

Almost half (43.9 percent) of the 67,986 firms had remained in the same general category during the entire nine-year period: 19.7 percent had remained above average, while 24.2 percent had remained below average. More than 85 percent had remained in the same general category for at least six of the nine years. Twelve percent had remained at the maximum most of the time and 3.3 percent had remained at the maximum for all nine years. The corresponding proportions which had remained at the minimum were 17.1 percent and 2.1 percent.

The general impression conveyed by the table is one of a significant degree of stability of experience—enough, for example, to incline a commercial insurance company to think in terms of differentiated premiums, rather than of a uniform premium.

Size Groups

A frequently expressed objection to experience rating is that it tends to burden the smallest firms with the highest tax rates. While data by size group is much less abundant than data by industry, the available information provides little support for this charge. Table 4–10 shows the national average tax rates by size group in five years for which such data were available. The first and clearest impression conveyed by the table is that differences in tax rates by size of firm are much less than differences by industry. The highest and the lowest tax rates differed by less than 0.4 percent. Also, the tax rates of the smallest firms differed from the tax rates of the largest firms by about only 0.2 percent. To the extent that these five years are typical, it must be concluded that size is not a major determinant of a firm's tax rate. The smallest firms tend to have a tax rate that is somewhat higher than the average but is not the highest among all groups. The very largest firms tend to have a tax rate that is below average but is not the lowest among all groups. The highest tax rates tend to occur in the middle-sized firms, those with payrolls between $100,000 and $500,000. The lowest tax rates tend to occur in the next-to-the-largest groups.

Table A–10 reflects the experience of only one state (New York) but covers a different period. Although the comparison cannot be exact because the size intervals differ, these New York data generally confirm the national experience. For example, the difference between the lowest rates and the highest rates, as

Table 4-10. National Average Tax Rates for Rated Employers
by Size Groups, Selected Years, 1957-67

Size of taxable payroll	Estimated average assigned employer tax rate (percent)				
	1957	1958	1959	1960	1967
All size groups	1.23	1.22	1.54	1.79	1.56
Less than $10,000	1.31	1.30	1.66	1.72	1.66
$10,000- 24,999	1.27	1.20	1.45	1.55	1.49
25,000- 49,999	1.24	1.18	1.44	1.59	1.48
50,000- 99,999	1.29	1.23	1.52	1.70	1.62
100,000- 249,999	1.35	1.30	1.60	1.82	1.74
250,000- 499,999	1.36	1.33	1.61	1.87	1.71
500,000- 999,999	1.32	1.30	1.58	1.86	1.64
1,000,000- 2,499,999	1.26	1.23	1.52	1.80	1.59
2,500,000- 4,999,999	1.17	1.13	1.46	1.74	1.46
5,000,000- 9,999,999	1.10	1.12	1.45	1.76	1.37
10,000,000-24,999,999	1.06	1.03	1.43	1.73	1.39
25,000,000 and over	1.09	1.24	1.67	2.10	1.46

Sources: 1957–"The Labor Market and Employment Security," November 1959; 1958, 1959, 1960–"The Labor Market and Employment Security," March 1962; 1967–Calculated from data received from U.S. Department of Labor, Manpower Administration, Office of Actuarial and Research Service.

also the difference between the rates of the largest and smallest firms, averaged less than 1 percent. Also, the tax rates of the smallest firms only slightly exceeded the average rate for all firms.

The experience of Massachusetts in 1967 (Table A-11) also resembles the national experience. The division of firms into positive-balance and negative-balance firms makes clear a fact which is generally true of small firms, namely, that they tend to have either the lowest or the highest tax rates. Among firms with positive balances, the smallest firms had the lowest tax rate (1.8), but among negative-balance firms, the smallest firms had the highest tax rate (3.4 percent). In this respect the tax rates of the small firms resemble their cost rates (Table 4-4 and 4-5).

The tendency for small firms to concentrate at either end of the tax-rate spectrum is brought out even more clearly in Table A-18, which shows for Ohio the distribution of tax rates *within* size groups. Where only 8.1 percent of all firms were at the maximum tax rate, among small firms this percentage was 10.0. The concentration at the lower end of the range is even more marked: where only 14.4 percent of all firms were at the minimum tax rate, among small firms this percentage was 20.9 percent. By contrast, the largest firms were under-represented at both the maximum and minimum tax rates. The tendency for small firms to cluster at the ends of the tax rate spectrum is understandable. With only a few employees, a firm is likely to go through a year with no layoffs; but even one layoff may represent a third of its total work force and have a serious effect on its tax rate.

Other scattered pieces of evidence support the conclusion that small firms do not usually have the highest tax rates. An analysis of tax rates in 1946 for thirty-two states showed employers with payrolls of $5,000 or less paying an average tax rate of 0.98 when the average tax rate for firms of all sizes was 1.03 percent [92, p. 15]. The 1951 New York Hughes Report presented 1949 data for ten states by size of firm [57, p. 45] and showed the small accounts as having the lower tax rates. A study of Indiana data for the period 1943-53 reached the conclusion: "The proposition that size, in itself, tends to produce a favorable experience rate is severely shaken by this new evidence" [90, p. 121]. This Indiana study took the interesting further step of distributing firms by tax rates within two-digit industries by size of payroll, thus lessening a possible correlation of industry with size of firm. The study concluded: "If the effect of industry is eliminated by considering separately firms within each 2-digit industry, the hypothesis of linear correlation significantly different from zero is rejected for practically all industries" [90, p. 128].

Although adequate data are not available to quantify the proposition, it is undoubtedly true that the tax rates of small firms tend to fluctuate more violently than those of large. Several ways of handling this problem are available. One technique, used by some states, is to limit the change in tax rates from one year to the next. Another technique is the current (1970) Illinois provision whereby the maximum tax rate for the small firm is limited. Illinois firms with a payroll under $20,000 may not be taxed above the standard rate of 2.7 percent. Still another possible technique is to group small employers and assign to all of them the average rate for the group. New York considered this step at one time [93, pp. 8, 9], but the proposal lacked support, even among the small firms themselves.

Conclusions

Although the size of a firm is not an important determinant of its tax rate, the nature of the activity performed by a firm evidently is. Different kinds of activities clearly tend to be associated with different tax rates. It is possible to predict with virtual certainty that the average tax rate of specific industries will be higher than that of other specified industries. This *regularity* of tax differentials as between industries lends some support to the claim that experience rating makes the costs of unemployment benefits a regular cost of doing business and thus integrates this cost with the free market.

Tax differentials may be regular without being significant. Their significance depends on their *size*. The largest differential is between the firms at the minimum rate and the firms at the maximum rate; for the firms in the middle distribution the differential (between them and firms on either side) is about half this large. Table 4-7 offers a convenient view of the degree of differentiation in a recent year.

It is evident that the tax differential produced by experience rating is not normally a major item of cost. It is also evident, on the other hand, that the tax is not a negligible cost item. Harold Keller, Commissioner of Commerce of New York State from 1947 to 1954, called unemployment insurance "the most costly tax paid by business to the State government" [94, p. 3]. It belongs to that multitude of small costs whose total a firm tries earnestly to control because in sum they affect the firm's position in competition with other firms in the industry and in competition with other industries for the consumer's dollar.

For example, I have encountered situations in which the financial officer of a company wanted to know the cost of a proposed action in terms of unemployment insurance taxes. It might be that there was thought of closing a plant or a store; or that a decision had to be made between working the entire labor force part-time or laying off some employees and working the rest full-time. In several contract negotiations that I happened to observe, the unemployment insurance unit was called upon to supply an estimate of the cost of agreeing to certain demands of the union with respect to pensions, holidays, pregnancy layoffs, or vacations. The unemployment insurance cost would always be just one of a number of costs, of course, and would rarely be the decisive cost; but it was one of the costs requiring calculation.

In 1960 a large national retail food company bought a small processing plant in Georgia. This plant had a large negative balance, and Georgia does not write off negative balances but accumulates them indefinitely. The negative balance of this small plant was so large that it raised the tax rate of the company's entire Georgia operation to the maximum. The company spent over $50,000 working off this negative balance, and because of this increased cost attributable to unemployment insurance taxes the cost-accounting department had to revise its estimate of the cost of canning pimentos and to raise its estimate of the price that would have to be charged for pimentos.

I have encountered situations in large corporations where the introduction of internal experience rating (see Chapter 12) was opposed by the accounting department on the score that unless the share of the unemployment insurance tax allocable to each unit was known in advance it would not be possible to set up the budget for each unit. While the objection has doubtful validity, it is another indication that the unemployment insurance cost has some economic significance.[11]

Again, where internal experience rating has been introduced, it has sometimes had its origin in the complaints of low-cost operating units that they were bearing the costs of other units in the company. On the contrary, internal

11. Service companies are often asked by their clients to estimate the firm's tax rate for the coming year because the firm wants to include the tax in its budget. Evidently, this cost is not negligible.

experience rating has sometimes been rejected because of a fear that some units would be burdened with an "unfair" cost. In either case, the differential unemployment insurance cost was perceived as a significant economic magnitude.

For two decades the federal government refused to cover its own employees under unemployment insurance; most state and local governments still do not cover their employees. The reluctance of governments to assume the burden of the unemployment insurance tax is a particularly eloquent testimony to its economic significance.

Many other indications of firms' awareness of this cost are noted in the chapters dealing with employer participation in administration (Chapters 6, 7, 8) and employer efforts at employment stabilization (Chapter 10) and in Appendix C, which describes employer attempts at tax avoidance. Perhaps the simplest way of summing up in general terms the market significance of the tax differentials produced by experience rating is to say that if private companies sold unemployment insurance policies, as the Metropolitan Life Insurance Company once proposed to do, they would certainly charge differentiated premiums. Also, a firm seeking to purchase such a policy would certainly concern itself with the premium charged and would choose among competing insurance companies partly on this basis.

Allocation of Costs III: *Cost/Tax Relationships*

Although benefit-cost rates and tax rates have meaning in themselves, they attain their fullest significance in their relation with each other. They then reflect the essential character of experience rating, which is to vary tax rates in some relation to benefit-cost rates. As noted previously, all effects of experience rating are possible only to the extent that experience rating exists, and experience rating exists to the extent that taxes mirror benefit costs. Information on the cost/tax relationship is therefore fundamental to any evaluation of the effects of experience rating.

Cost/Tax Ratios

For a given firm the cost/tax relationship is defined as the ratio of the benefits drawn by the employees of the firm to the taxes paid by the firm.

Information on cost/tax ratios is limited to those situations for which similar data are available on both cost rates and tax rates. Since fewer data are available on cost rates than on tax rates, the extent of information on cost/tax ratios is determined by the availability of cost-rate data. Cost/tax ratios are subject, of course, to all the limitations inherent in the cost and tax data on which such ratios are based. These limitations are noted at the beginning of Chapter 4, which also offers a warning regarding interstate comparisons of cost rates and tax rates. This warning applies equally—indeed, especially—to cost/tax ratios.

The ideal data would cover the entire period during which a firm was subject to the law and would show that firm's total contributions (taxes and interest earned on taxes) and the total benefits paid to that firm's employees. The actual data usually fall short of this ideal in a number of ways.

First, as noted previously, many of the data are in the form of averages for firms grouped by industry and size. These averages identify only the *group* which is subsidizing or is being subsidized, that is, which has an average cost/tax ratio much below or above unity. It must be borne in mind that within each group there are many firms whose individual ratios are very different from the group average. Within *every* group therefore there will be some firms that are subsidizing and some that are being subsidized. Hence the strictly correct statement is not that one industry is subsidizing another industry, but that low-cost firms (in all industries) are subsidizing high-cost firms (in all industries). The group averages have only the significance accorded them in the discussion of cost rates and summarized at the end of that discussion (see pp. 81-82).

Second, even the averages may not be entirely accurate. On the tax side, for example, the data may not include special taxes, such as those credited to a Common Account, and the data usually omit the interest earned by previously contributed employer taxes held in reserves. These limitations tend to overstate the cost/tax ratio. On the benefit side, the data sometimes show not all benefits paid but only benefits charged to employer's accounts. If substantial amounts of benefits are noncharged, as happens in some states, the cost/tax ratio tends to be understated. On both the tax and benefit sides, the period for which data are available is usually less than the total period.

To avoid getting lost in a multitude of tables, it may help the reader to recognize that all the tables are intended to provide answers to one or both of two questions: (1) How close to balancing are benefits and taxes? That is, what degree of experience rating is there? (2) To the extent that benefits and taxes do not balance, who is subsidizing whom?

To judge from Table A-5, which shows eleven-year averages by major industry divisions, the program worked to produce a predictable redistribution in favor of the first three industry divisions in the table at the expense of the last four. The cost/tax ratio of manufacturing usually came closest to unity. The lowest ratio was that of finance-insurance-real estate, while the highest was that of agriculture-forestry-fisheries. Of the subsidized industries, construction is the most important because of its substantial size. In Massachusetts and Utah, construction took out two dollars for every dollar it contributed. Only in Virginia was the average ratio of construction less than unity.[1]

Table A-6 extends these conclusions to five additional states. Although only two years are shown, the average of these two—one a recession year and the other a prosperous year—is generally close to the eleven-year average of Table A-5.[2] The industries with the high and the low ratios are generally the same as in the preceding table. Hence the relationships between industries reflected in Table A-6 may be accorded cautious credence.

Table A-7 illustrates the differences that appear among industries at the two-digit level, where the units of experience are more homogeneous. Some manufacturing activities characteristically have average cost/tax ratios that are two and three times as large as those of other activities. The apparel industry especially has a consistently high ratio; in New York it took out more than two dollars for each dollar it contributed to the fund. In the construction division,

1. During the period covered by the table, Virginia's population grew very rapidly, especially in the area contiguous to Washington, D.C., and construction consequently prospered. The milder climate of Virginia may also have been a contributing cause of this lower cost/tax ratio. Finally, it should be noted that the ratios of all industry divisions are lower in Virginia than in the other states.

2. However, the ambiguity of a cost/tax ratio for a single year is exemplified by the significant differences between these two years.

the average ratio of general contractors was much above the division's average, while the ratio of the special trade contractors was significantly below average. In the transportation-communication-utilities division, utilities had a much lower average ratio than transportation. The firms which sold apparel had a lower average than did the firms that made apparel. The firms which sold and serviced automobiles had a much lower average ratio than did the auto producers. Real estate is revealed as having a much higher cost/tax ratio, although still low, than the other economic activities with which it is classified. The ratios of services are shown to vary from the relatively high averages for hotels to the relatively low averages for medical services.

Table A-8 helps to extend the scope of the previous table to three additional states. The relationships between the industries are, in general, similar to those shown in Table A-7. One of the more extreme contrasts in experience is between banking and "other general contractors" in California and Minnesota. In California some medical and legal services may be paying some of the unemployment benefits of the motion picture industry.

Table A-9 extends the investigation a step further into the three-digit industries and illustrates how at each level of differentiation there are economic activities with substantially different cost/tax ratios. If these data are fairly representative, and scattered bits of similar data indicate that they are, the plumbing and electrical construction firms are more likely to be among the subsidizers, while painting and plastering firms are more likely to be among the subsidized. In apparel manufacturing, practically none of the groups is paying its way, but some have cost/tax ratios three and four times as high as those of other groups in the same industry. Table A-19 illustrates, for New York, how persistent, and hence predictable, such unbalanced ratios can be.

Tables A-10 and A-11 throw some light on the charge that under experience rating small firms bear a disproportionate share of the total burden. The New York data indicate that usually the smallest firms have the highest cost/tax ratios and the largest firms have the lowest ratios, with the usual "hump" manifest in the middle range. That is, as groups, the smallest firms are the subsidized and the largest firms are the chief subsidizers. The Massachusetts data cover only one year but tell the same general story.

The Massachusetts data (Table A-11) also reveal the marked differences that exist among firms within any size group and thus illustrate the ambiguity inherent in the use of group averages. For example, among the smallest firms, 44,933 had an average cost/tax ratio of only 14.8 in the same year that 9,363 of them had a ratio of 418.6. In each of the other size groups there are, likewise, firms with very high and very low cost/tax ratios. Thus in answer to the question, "Are small firms taken as a group subsidized or subsidizing?" one would have to say that they are both the leading subsidizers, with a cost/tax ratio of 14.8, and also the most subsidized, with a ratio of 418.6. Another way of answering the question is to observe the proportion of each size group which had a negative balance. By this norm one would judge that the smallest firms were the most likely to be negative and not paying their way (17.2 percent), while the largest firms were the least likely (0 percent).

This review of cost/tax ratios leads to four general conclusions: (1) There is a great deal of subsidy-type pooling in the program: Cost/tax ratios depart from unity by wide margins, even when averaged over a decade. (2) The degree of subsidy within classifications is greater than between classifications. While it is correct to say that as groups the finance industry subsidizes the construction industry and the largest firms subsidize the smallest, it is more meaningful to say that the low-cost firms in every industry and of every size subsidize the high-cost firms in all industries and of all sizes. (3) The size of a firm is less of a determinant of its cost/tax ratio than is the industry to which the firm belongs. (4) The stability of interindustry differences in cost/tax ratios, even at the three-digit level, supports an inference of some stability in the differences between individual firms. The reasoning used to support the inference is the same as that used in Chapter 4 (pp. 81–82).

Common Account

The question: "How much experience rating is there in the unemployment insurance system?" cannot be answered by any single statistic. Although in principle cost/tax ratios can supply an adequate answer, in practice the data on such ratios are incomplete and need to be supplemented by whatever additional information may be available. One such supplement is to be found in the operations of the Common Account, which was described in Chapter 2.

In those few states which use the device, the Common Account provides a fairly reliable measure of the degree to which the tax system is *not* experience-rated. The measure applies "at the limit": since all the operations of the Common Account are mutualized, *at least* this much of the system is not experience-rated. In practice, the measure supplied by the Common Account will usually be quite close to the actual measure.[3] It is probably the simplest and clearest of the available measures for gauging the degree of experience rating in a state's unemployment insurance tax system.

The operations of the Common Account may be used as such a measure on either the tax or the benefit side. Table 5-1 shows operations on the tax side for five states during various periods. Whatever income is credited to the Common Account is not credited to individual employer accounts and hence is outside the experience-rating system.[4] Table 5-1 shows the amounts credited to the Common Account as a proportion of the total fund income.

3. Probably the principal socialized element not reflected in the Common Account on the income side is any "excess" in the reserves required of firms in order to be eligible for reduced tax rates. It is very difficult, however, even to define such excess, let alone measure it.
    4. As will be recalled (Chapter 2), the two main sources of income credited to the Common Account are: (1) the interest earnings on the fund; (2) a subsidiary tax or a

Table 5–1. Credits to Common Account as Percent of Total Credits to Fund, for Years 1955–69, Selected States
(Amounts in 000's)

Year	California[a] Total credits to fund	California Credits to Common Account Amount	California Percent of total credits to fund	Michigan[b] Total credits to fund	Michigan Credits to Common Account Amount	Michigan Percent of total credits to fund	New York[c] Total credits to fund	New York Credits to Common Account Amount	New York Percent of total credits to fund	Ohio[b] Total credits to fund	Ohio Credits to Common Account Amount	Ohio Percent of total credits to fund	Wisconsin[a] Total credits to fund	Wisconsin Credits to Common Account Amount	Wisconsin Percent of total credits to fund
1955	$ 163,985	$ 19,060	11.6	$ 70,348	$ 8,653	12.3	$ 229,802	$ 34,754	15.1						
1956	183,152	25,075	13.7	69,703	8,231	11.8	235,004	35,129	14.9						
1957	186,404	32,127	17.2	105,601	20,230	19.2	277,338	108,846	39.2						
1958	168,938	27,171	16.1	124,295	35,415	28.5	286,855	68,395	23.8						
1959	257,081	23,241	9.0	125,395	27,810	22.2	283,424	99,905	35.2						
1960	309,584	42,731	13.8	156,897	28,693	18.3	345,542	92,579	26.8				$ 42,200	$ 6,500	15.4
1961	320,211	57,454	17.9	152,194	27,587	18.1	410,475	126,484	30.8				44,400	6,100	13.7
1962	473,923	93,984	19.8	160,637	26,969	16.8	506,686	206,059	40.7				43,000	5,900	13.7
1963	508,805	99,261	19.5	174,658	36,438	20.9	808,503	260,672	32.2				47,200	6,100	12.9
1964	525,618	105,286	20.0	202,682	49,009	24.2	468,348	136,870	29.2				48,900	6,500	13.3
1965	537,444	115,907	21.6	192,461	65,131	33.8	519,100	193,505	37.3	$210,713	$ 39,323	18.7	55,700	12,700	22.8
1966	572,240	200,266	35.0	194,383	60,868	31.3	483,111	174,770	36.2	192,105	42,254	22.0	60,900	11,700	19.2
1967	572,448	214,435	37.5	181,853	55,313	30.4	401,273	95,281	23.7	153,756	17,650	11.5	65,100	13,200	20.3
1968	607,446	233,991	38.5	150,167	29,720	19.8	419,245	110,555	26.4	107,414	2,215	2.1	59,900	18,100	30.2
1969	587,013	253,336	43.2	150,996	31,400	20.8	405,628	107,453	26.5	89,817	73	0.1	62,700	13,800	22.0
Totals	$5,974,292	$1,543,325	25.8	$2,212,270	$511,467	23.1	$6,080,334	$1,755,976	28.8	$753,805	$101,515	13.5	$530,000	$100,600	19.0

Sources: The data in this table were derived mainly from periodic and special reports issued by the employment security agencies of the respective states. In some cases where the data were not available in published form they were supplied by the agency as requested.

[a]Calendar year.

[b]Fiscal year ending June 30.

[c]1955–62: fiscal year ending June 30; 1963: 18-month period ending December 1963; 1964–69: calendar year. For the year 1956–57, the credits to the General Account included some $42 million transferred from accounts of employers who had discontinued operations.

By this measure, Ohio had a relatively high degree of experience rating during the short period covered by the Ohio data, especially since 1967. The very high degrees shown for 1968 and 1969 are to be explained partly by the Ohio policy of crediting interest earnings to individual employer accounts.[5] In Ohio there is no large automatic flow of interest earnings to the Common Account, such as there is in the other states of the table. Interest earnings tend to increase in periods of prosperity, as reserves grow. Wisconsin and Michigan have the next lowest proportions of nonexperience-rated income, while New York and California have significantly higher proportions. In California the proportion credited to the Common Account generally increased throughout the decade 1959–68. The Massachusetts average (not shown in the table)[6] was the highest. In Massachusetts, during the period 1952–69, 38 percent of total income was credited to the Common Account. (Thus only 62 percent was experience-rated.) In the five-year period 1965–69, the proportion credited to the Common Account increased each year until by 1969 more than half (52 percent) of total income was credited to the Common Account, while only 48 percent was experience-rated. In Ohio in that same year 99.9 percent of the income flow was experience-rated.

Nearly all the credits and debits to the Common Account are due ultimately to noncharged and ineffectively charged benefits. Likewise, the degree to which cost/tax ratios depart from unity is explained primarily by noncharged and ineffectively charged benefits. A review of experience under these two headings may help, therefore, toward a fuller understanding of Table 5-1,[7] as well as of the cost/tax ratios previously discussed.

Noncharged Benefits

Most noncharged benefits arise in connection with disqualifications. The other sources of noncharges (see Chapter 2), while numerous, are minor. In states with sizable amounts of noncharges, from 75 percent to 95 percent of all

---

diversion of reserves. It should also be recalled that the operations of the Common Account for any one year may be ambiguous and may need to be interpreted in relation to other years.

5. This provision was enacted in the period following World War II, partly and perhaps primarily as a way of lessening the rate of income flow to an over-large fund. The crediting of interest increased employers' balances, which in turn had the effect of lowering employers' tax rates.

6. Because Massachusetts operated its Common Account by a transference of reserves instead of by a supplementary tax, annual changes in the account do not have the same meaning as for the states in the table. The average over a period of years is comparable, however, to the averages of the other states. (In 1970 Massachusetts adopted a supplementary tax in place of its former policy of transferring reserves.)

7. For example, since Michigan and New York have practically no noncharged benefits (Table 5-2), the operations of the Common Account in these states reflect almost entirely the impact of ineffectively charged benefits. In California and Massachusetts, on the other hand, noncharged benefits are an important explanatory factor in the behavior of the Common Account.

noncharged benefits are paid in connection with situations that involve actual or potential disqualifications.[8] Since most of these disqualifications involve the quitting of a job, the issue of noncharging is principally, though not entirely, the issue of how to charge the benefits paid to claimants who have quit a job. The principal alternatives are: (1) charge these benefits exactly like all other benefits; (2) exempt from the charge all base-period employers; (3) exempt only the most recent employer; (4) exempt all base-period employers from whom the claimant separated under disqualifying circumstances.

Three principal factors influence the extent of noncharging.[9] The first is the law itself. The proportion of noncharged benefits will be the greater as the noncharging provisions apply to more situations, especially to more kinds of disqualifications, and to more employers—for example, to all base-period employers as well as to the most recent employer. The proportion will be the greater also as the disqualification provisions in the law provide for only a postponement of benefits rather than a requirement of intervening earnings or a cancellation of benefit credits. Noncharged benefits are likely to be especially numerous under provisions which allow benefits to be paid immediately in the case of a "potential" disqualification (see Chapter 2).

The second factor is the industrial pattern of the state and the consequent composition of the labor force. Some industries tend to have higher turnover rates than do others. Since high turnover rates lead to high disqualification rates, which in turn open the possibility of noncharged benefits, the proportion of such benefits will be higher in such industries.

The third factor is the extent of employer participation in the administrative process. The proportion of noncharged benefits will be the greater as employers understand the noncharging provisions and establish procedures to take advantage of the opportunities presented by such provisions. For this reason, the operation of service companies (Chapter 8), which are very alert to noncharging opportunities, tends to increase the proportion of noncharged benefits.

Noncharged benefits were first permitted by the Bureau of Employment Security in 1944, and by 1945 four states made provision for the noncharging of benefits in situations involving actual or potential disqualification.[10] By 1954, a decade later, noncharged benefits had reached the development shown in the following tabulation, which distributes states with noncharging provisions according to the percentage that their noncharged benefits were of their total benefits.[11] By 1954 the development seems to have stabilized somewhat; for the

8. Dependents' allowances are an exception to this general pattern. In the half-dozen states which pay but do not charge dependents' allowances, these noncharged benefits are nearly as large as those connected with disqualifications.

9. A fourth factor, of uncertain strength, is the tendency on the part of some agency personnel to decide difficult cases the easiest way—by paying benefits to the claimant but not charging the employer, and thus keeping everyone happy.

10. Maine, Minnesota, New Hampshire, West Virginia.

11. The data refer to benefits paid in the twelve months preceding the computation date used by the respective state. Data for 1954 are from *Labor Market and Employment*

picture is substantially the same another decade later (1966), except that the number of states in the bracket 20-29 percent had increased from four to ten.

	Noncharged Benefits As a Proportion of All Benefits			
	0%-9.9%	10%-19%	20%-29%	30% and more
43 states in 1954	20	16	4	3
47 states in 1966	20	14	10	3

In 1966 twenty states, having 55 percent of all covered workers, paid noncharged benefits that amounted to less than 10 percent of all benefits. That is, over 90 percent of all the benefits paid in those states were charged against some individual employer account.[12] In thirteen states, having 12 percent of all covered workers, noncharged benefits were 20 percent or more of all benefits. The three states with the highest proportions were South Carolina (47 percent), Hawaii (35 percent), and Montana (34 percent).

The term "experience rating" as applied to the states at the extremes of this array has obviously very different meanings. The possibility that experience rating will have any significant effects, good or bad, is evidently greater in states with a greater degree of experience rating and lesser in states with a lesser degree of experience rating.

Table 5-2 provides more illustrative detail in the ways in which the states have differed among themselves and over time in their use of the device of noncharged benefits. This table shows the experience of fifteen states for which such data were readily available during the decade 1957-66.[13] The historical changes reflected in the table illustrate most of the issues typically connected with the noncharging of benefits.

South Carolina has had an unusually high proportion of noncharged benefits since it first began the practice of noncharging in 1947. For the decade 1947-57 (not shown in the table) noncharged benefits averaged 25.9 percent of total benefits. The percentage kept climbing during the period shown in the table until almost half the benefits were noncharged. In later years (1967 through 1969) the percentage dropped somewhat, but still averaged about 38 percent.

Security (May 1956): 25. Data for 1966 are from a letter of the director of the Office of Actuarial and Financial Services, Bureau of Employment Security, September 26, 1969.

12. In eleven states (Colorado, District of Columbia, Illinois, Iowa, Louisiana, Michigan, New Jersey, New Hampshire, New York, North Dakota, and Wisconsin) the proportion of benefits charged was more than 95 percent.

13. The figures shown for 1966, the last year in the table, were still roughly valid in 1969, except that the South Carolina, Rhode Island, Maine, and California percentages had declined to 39.8, 15.6, 12.1, and 9.4 respectively, while Arizona, Georgia, and Oregon percentages had increased to 29.6, 17.5, and 10.9, respectively. There was virtually no change in the remaining states.

Table 5-2. Noncharged Benefits As Percent of Total Benefits, 1957 through 1966,[a] Selected States

State	1957	1958	1959	1960	1961	1962	1963	1964	1965	1966	Average 10 years
South Carolina	29.9	27.9	32.9	38.4	36.2	43.6	42.4	40.5	44.6	47.0	38.1
Arizona	22.8	21.1	23.4	32.5	22.0	24.9	22.7	22.4	22.4	25.8	23.9
Rhode Island[b,c]	—	—	—	—	—	—	—	—	19.7	20.8	20.3
Arkansas	14.5	14.1	17.3	18.0	20.2	21.3	d	20.1	20.8	22.0	18.7
Maine	18.8	21.8	18.0	25.3	21.4	12.8	10.7	10.9	11.7	15.1	17.7
Massachusetts[c]	10.9	12.8	13.8	16.8	18.9	19.3	19.9	19.4	19.6	18.7	17.4
California	18.4	22.3	28.3	17.7	13.2	13.7	14.2	15.2	14.1	12.1	16.0
West Virginia	14.8	11.7	14.6	14.8	13.5	14.0	12.5	14.1	14.8	14.9	13.8
Georgia	10.0	9.9	11.7	12.1	11.4	16.5	15.3	14.5	14.5	14.1	12.6
Oregon	13.3	6.1	7.3	7.3	7.9	7.0	6.9	6.7	6.4	6.0	7.1
Wisconsin	1.5	1.4	2.0	2.1	2.1	2.6	2.7	2.3	2.2	1.0	2.0
Ohio	0.8	0.6	1.4	0.7	0.4	0.8	0.9	2.7	5.8	5.8	1.4
District of Columbia[c]	1.4	1.2	1.3	1.3	1.0	1.5	1.5	1.9	1.6	1.5	1.4
New York	1.9	1.6	2.0	1.2	1.0	1.2	1.2	1.2	0.8	0.8	1.3
Michigan	0.4	0.3	0.4	0.5	0.3	0.6	0.7	0.8	0.9	0.0	0.4

Sources: Various publications of the Bureau of Employment Security, U.S. Department of Labor. Michigan and Wisconsin data furnished by respective states.

[a]The years represented are the twelve-month periods ending at "computation dates" in the respective years. Tax rates for the ensuing year are assigned on the basis of reserve ratios as of such computation dates, which vary from state to state, and from year to year for a given state.
[b]Experience rating was suspended in Rhode Island during most of this period.
[c]Noncharged benefits include dependents' allowances.
[d]Calendar year changed to fiscal year beginning 1963 – 64.

Benefits paid following a period of disqualification have always been the principle source of South Carolina's noncharged benefits. For example, in 1966, 34 percent of all the benefits paid in the state were benefits noncharged because paid following a period of disqualification for voluntarily quitting a job. The textile industry is by far the largest source of noncharged benefits in South Carolina. A special tabulation made by the state for the calendar year 1968 showed textiles accounting for 35 percent of all noncharged benefits. Over half (54.1 percent) of all benefits paid to textile workers were noncharged. The tax rate of the textile industry is usually somewhat below the state average, a reflection of the fact that over half the benefits in this industry are noncharged.[14]

Oregon, in 1947, made liberal provision for the noncharging of benefits. The noncharged benefits included benefits paid in the case of "potential" disqualifications (for example, to claimants who had left work voluntarily but with good cause) as well as benefits paid following a period of disqualification. Moreover, all base-period employers were automatically relieved of charges, as well as the employer from whom the separation occurred. During the decade 1947-56, more than one-third of all benefits in the state were noncharged, the proportion rising to 40 percent in 1953. Legislative changes in 1955 gradually reduced the proportion of noncharges to the much lower figures shown in Table 5-2. These changes were occasioned by considerations of solvency. Oregon's fund was in danger and a part of the explanation was seen to have been the drain represented by noncharged benefits which were not automatically replaced by the tax mechanism (Chapter 2). In 1967 the legislature again opened the door somewhat, and by 1969 the proportion had risen to 10.9 percent.

In Ohio noncharged benefits were a significant proportion of total benefits from 1949, when dependents' allowances began to be paid and were not charged, until 1955, when these benefits were made chargeable to individual employer accounts.[15] Thereafter noncharged benefits were negligible until 1963, when the law was amended to noncharge benefits paid to claimants who had quit their jobs. The proportion of noncharged benefits rose to 5.8 percent in 1965 and to 7.6 percent in 1968.

Wisconsin enacted a provision in 1945 permitting the payment of benefits to claimants who had quit either to take another job or because of compelling personal reasons. In 1951 the law was amended to provide that such benefits would not be charged to the account of the individual firm. In 1965 such benefits again began to be charged. In 1970 partial noncharging (only the first four benefit weeks are charged) was reinstituted in cases where the claimant quit

14. Tobacco firms resemble textile firms in having a high turnover rate; but they contribute very little to the total of noncharged benefits. South Carolina accumulates negative balances indefinitely, and many of the tobacco firms have such large negative balances that they see no likelihood of ever getting a tax rate below the maximum. Hence they do not bother even to request that benefits be noncharged.

15. In Massachusetts and Rhode Island, almost half the noncharged benefits consist of dependents' allowances.

to take another job. Such shifts back and forth in the provisions governing disqualifications and noncharging occur frequently among the states and reflect the tension and controversy that mark this part of the program.

In Arkansas, in 1951, noncharged benefits were 2.9 percent of total benefits.[16] By 1961 the proportion had grown to 20.2 percent. The principal change occurred in 1953 when benefits paid to certain classes of voluntary quits were made nonchargeable. The effect of this provision was felt fully for the first time in 1955, when the proportion of noncharged benefits was 13.2 percent, and continued to grow until it stabilized at a little over 20 percent. The proportion continued to average over 22 percent during the years 1967, 1968, 1969.

California formerly had substantial amounts of noncharged benefits, but in recent years has made less use of the device. A 1959 amendment eliminated a provision for the noncharging of benefits paid after eighteen weeks of benefits. The impact of this change is clear in the data. An amendment enacted in 1965, making it more difficult to draw benefits after a disqualification for voluntarily quitting a job, reduced the proportion of noncharged benefits still further to 9.4 percent in 1969. A decade earlier the proportion had been 28.3 percent.

California has watched its noncharged benefits very closely. In a series of studies,[17] noncharged benefits in the state have been analyzed in their relationship to tax rates, size of firm, and type of industry. These studies may be summed up in three propositions and illustrated for the fiscal year 1968.

(1) An inverse relationship exists between tax rates and noncharged ratios (Table 5-3). Firms with high tax rates tend to have relatively fewer noncharged benefits than do those with low tax rates. The smallest proportion of noncharged benefits (2.1 percent) was recorded for employers at the maximum tax rate.

For this correlation, there are probably two explanations, one economic and the other administrative. First, the high-tax firms tend to be characterized by the kind of unemployment that produces few noncharges. That is, most of their unemployment is the result of layoffs.[18] Second, high-tax firms, at least those taxed at the maximum rate, have less incentive to protest claims and carry through on the administrative procedures required to escape being charged with the benefits. In all probability, both factors are at work, and there is no way of measuring the extent of each one separately. The steadiness of the correlation would indicate, however, that the first factor is the main one. If the administrative factor were the principal cause, one would expect to find more irregularity in the correlation, because the degree of administrative concern varies unpredictably among firms.

16. For a detailed study of noncharged benefits in Arkansas, see [2, pp. 1247–64].
17. The studies appear as part of the series, Report 352A, #27, published by the California Department of Human Resources Development.
18. Some high-tax firms, however, may be like the tobacco firms of South Carolina described above. California, like South Carolina, accumulates negative balances indefinitely.

Table 5-3. CALIFORNIA: Percent of Regular Benefits Not Charged
during Fiscal Year 1968 to Employer Accounts
Active June 30, 1968, by 1969 Tax Rate

Tax rate[a]	Total regular benefits	Percent of benefits not charged
Total, all employers	$334,259,732	9.3
Rated employers	215,724,749	13.0
0.0	5,799,242	26.6
0.2	4,736,392	30.5
0.4	5,659,900	24.3
0.6	11,789,265	22.0
0.8	16,407,507	18.3
1.0	12,984,271	20.5
1.2	15,528,974	18.3
1.4	17,076,771	22.0
1.6	13,296,703	15.0
1.8	10,643,209	13.1
2.0	12,948,338	10.0
2.1	10,679,283	8.3
2.2	9,835,595	7.3
2.3	10,942,912	6.6
2.4	6,531,276	5.1
2.5	8,014,798	6.3
2.6	5,651,666	3.0
2.7	37,198,647	2.1
Negative reserve	32,642,167	1.8
Positive reserve	4,556,480	4.6
Unrated employers	116,052,273	2.5
Out of business after computation date[b]	2,482,710	4.5

Source: State of California, Department of Employment, Research and Statistics Department, Report 352A #27, Table 1, August 29, 1969.

[a]Excludes the balancing tax.
[b]Includes both rated and unrated employers.

(2) The noncharge ratio is also correlated with size of firm. This correlation is positive, the percentage increasing with size (Table 5-4, column 2). The smallest firms have the lowest proportion of noncharged benefits and the largest firms have the highest proportion. Here again the same two factors are probably at work and, again, the dominant factor is probably the economic one, as reflected in unemployment rates. It will be recalled that the largest firms tend to have below-average tax rates (see, for example, Table 4-10). However, the administrative factor may have somewhat more significance here. Certainly the larger firms generally have the greater expertise in the complex area of unemployment insurance administration.

Table 5-4. CALIFORNIA: Percent of Regular Benefits Not Charged during
Fiscal Year 1968 to Employer Accounts Active June 30, 1968,
by Size of 1967 Taxable Payroll

Size of taxable payroll	Total regular benefits	Percent of benefits not charged	Percent distribution of benefits not charged
	(1)	(2)	(3)
Total, all employers	$334,259,732	9.3	100.0
No taxable wages	257,368	12.0	0.1
$1- 4,999	5,504,383	3.9	0.7
5,000- 9,999	8,742,989	5.0	1.4
10,000- 24,999	21,565,038	5.4	3.8
25,000- 49,999	23,246,198	6.1	4.6
50,000- 99,999	29,641,525	6.2	5.9
100,000- 249,999	44,972,582	6.5	9.4
250,000- 499,999	31,800,134	7.2	7.4
500,000- 999,999	28,398,621	8.2	7.5
1,000,000- 2,499,999	33,946,915	9.1	9.9
2,500,000- 4,999,999	23,454,111	11.3	8.5
5,000,000- 9,999,999	23,360,043	11.4	8.6
10,000,000-24,999,999	26,134,072	13.9	11.7
25,000,000-49,999,999	12,620,983	16.3	6.6
50,000,000 and over	20,614,770	21.1	13.9

Source: State of California, Department of Employment, Research and Statistics Department, Report 352A #27, Table 3, August 29, 1969.

(3) According to these California data, there was considerable variation in the proportion of noncharges among industry divisions. (These industry tables are not shown.) Such variation would be expected, since there is considerable variation in unemployment rates, as well as considerable difference in average size of firm, among industries. Where the statewide proportion of benefits noncharged in 1968 was 9.3 percent, it was over 20 percent for many "steady" industries and less than 1 percent for many of the seasonal industries, such as the packing of fruits and vegetables and the canning of sea foods. Some of the latter may have resembled the South Carolina tobacco firms in not bothering to ask for noncharging.

Ineffectively Charged Benefits

The second and—in most states—the more important factor that explains why cost/tax ratios depart from unity is the extent of ineffectively charged benefits. The amount of revenue that can be obtained annually from any one firm is limited by the taxable base and, especially, by the maximum tax rate. When that amount is less then the benefits drawn by the employees of a given firm, the excess benefits may be charged to the account of the firm, but they will not be effective in producing corresponding revenue. In reserve-ratio states, so long as the firm has a positive reserve, its cost/tax ratio will remain less than unity (it will have taken out less than it contributed to the fund); but eventually, if the drain continues, its ratio will become greater than unity (it will have taken out more than it contributed) and its reserve account will become negative.

Thus data on negative accounts provide a measure of the extent of ineffectively charged benefits. Since ineffectively charged benefits comprise the principal limitation on experience rating, and since negative accounts most clearly mirror ineffectively charged benefits, data on such accounts are especially important in supplying answers to this chapter's two central questions: How much subsidizing occurs and who is subsidizing whom?

These data, which are available, of course, only in reserve-ratio states, are never complete.[19] It might seem that the condition of a firm's reserve account would provide a simple and clear measure of the extent to which the firm was or was not paying its way in the program and hence would provide a substitute for the cost/tax ratio. But a number of things can happen to reserve accounts that obscure the story they tell. For example: (1) Some benefits paid may never have been charged against any employer's account and thus never subtracted from anybody's reserve. Also (2), negative reserves may have been written back ("forgiven") in whole or in part—either annually as in New York and Ohio, or on occasion as in Michigan (1955–57) and California (1966). On the other hand (3), positive reserves may (in a few states) have been siphoned off from individual accounts into a Common Account. Also (4), some taxes may have been credited directly to a Common Account and thus never have been credited to any individual firm's account. Items (1) and (2) lead to an underestimate of negative accounts, while items (3) and (4) lead to an overestimate of negative accounts. Since in most states the first two items outweigh the other two, data on negative accounts should usually be interpreted "at the limit." They indicate that ineffectively charged benefits were at least this large.

The following review of negative accounts seeks to throw light on two groups of questions, the first purely quantitative, the other more qualitative: (1) How many firms are negative, and by how much are they negative? Also, what proportions of payrolls and benefits do they account for? (2) What kinds of firms are negative—what is their industry and size? With these two guides, the reader may more easily find his way through what otherwise might be a confusing melange of tables.

Extent of Ineffectively Charged Benefits

Some answers to the first question are provided by Table 5-5, which summarizes for a single year the major measures relating to firms with negative

19. The states were not required by Washington to report specifically on negative accounts until 1966, when a section for this purpose was added to the ES–204 Experience Rating Report.

balances. California may serve to illustrate the use of Table 5-5. Reading from the top down: About one-fifth (18 percent) of all firms in California were not paying their way. These seem to have been small firms, since their payrolls accounted for only 14.2 percent of all payrolls. Yet these negative firms accounted for over half of all the benefits charged in the state that year. In order to have made them pay their way in 1966, the state would have had to tax these firms at an average rate of 7.3 percent (instead of their actual average tax of 2.9 percent), with many of them assessed at rates well above that average. Of all the benefits charged in California that year, 28 percent were ineffectively charged, that is, were not matched by either the current contributions or the past contributions (reserves) of the relevant firms.[20] Over half (53.9 percent) of all the benefits charged to California's negative firms were ineffectively charged; that is, the contributions of these firms covered only 46.1 percent of the benefits charged to them. In order to pay their way, these negative firms would have had to pay an *additional* average tax of 3.9 percent. During this period, these negative firms drew out $2.17 for every dollar they contributed to the fund. Finally, 12.1 percent of the benefits paid by California in that period were not charged to any employer account. The combined items No. 9 and No. 5 lead to the conclusion that in California about 40.1 percent of all benefits were paid outside the experience-rating mechanism—12.1 percent that were not charged and 28 percent that were ineffectively charged.[21] (By this same measure—the sum of items 5 and 9—Michigan and Ohio have the highest degrees of experience rating, while Massachusetts and South Carolina have the lowest.)

Of the states in the table, New Jersey and California have the highest proportions of negative firms and payrolls. This is partly explainable by the absence of a write-off provision in these two states. As of the time represented by the table, New Jersey and California had written off few or none of their negative accounts.[22] South Carolina's very low proportion must be interpreted in conjunction with its very high proportion of noncharged benefits. When nearly half the total benefits are not charged against individual accounts it is to be expected that fewer individual accounts will show a negative balance. Michigan's low ratios for items 1 and 2 are the more impressive because Michigan (a) had no noncharged benefits, and (b) had not written off any negative balances since 1963. Michigan would seem to have a high degree of experience rating.

20. Since these were negative-balance firms, there could not have been, generally speaking, any reserves on which to draw.

21. The two figures are not strictly additive because the noncharged benefits are expressed as a percentage of benefits paid, while the ineffectively charged benefits are expressed as a percentage of benefits charged, which is a smaller quantity. Expressed as a percentage of benefits paid, item no. 5 for California would be 24.4 percent and the combined items would be 36.5 percent. This correction becomes the less significant as the proportion of noncharged benefits becomes the smaller. The correction is negligible, for example, in Michigan, New York, and Wisconsin.

22. As a one-time action, California wrote off *all* negative balances, effective June 1966. After that, negative balances began to accumulate again. New Jersey always retained at least the most recent ten years' experience.

Table 5–5. Significant Measures Relating to Negative-Balance Firms[a] for 1967 Rate Year, Selected States

Measure	California	Massachusetts	Michigan	New Jersey	New York[b]	Ohio	South Carolina	Wisconsin
1. Number of firms with negative balances as a percent of all firms.	18.0	16.2	5.4	30.2	14.9	11.3	3.3	11.9
2. Taxable payrolls of firms with negative balances as a percent of all taxable payrolls.	14.2	11.8	3.6	20.4	13.8	4.4	3.7	8.5
3. Benefits charged to negative-balance firms as a percent of benefits charged to all firms.	51.8	55.3	34.8		61.6	34.2	24.7	60.8
4. Benefits charged to negative-balance firms as a percent of their taxable payrolls.	7.3	5.9	7.1		8.0	4.9	2.0	7.0
5. Deficit[c] of negative-balance firms as a percent of all benefits charged to all firms.	28.0	24.3	12.7		33.1	4.8		25.1
6. Deficit[c] of negative-balance firms as a percent of all benefits charged to negative-balance firms.	53.9	44.0	36.6		53.7	14.0		41.3
7. Deficit[c] of negative-balance firms as a percent of their taxable payrolls.	3.9	2.6	2.6		4.3	0.7		2.9
8. Average cost/tax ratios of negative-balance firms.	217.1	178.6	157.6		216.0	116.3		170.4
9. Noncharged benefits as a percent of all benefits paid.	12.1	18.7	0.0	*	0.8	5.8	47.0	1.0

[a] Active firms.

[b] New York data represent sum of positive- and negative-balance firms.

[c] Deficit: excess of benefits charged to negative-balance firms over their contributions, including any subsidiary taxes.

Sources: Form ES-204, Experience Rating Report for 1967 rate year; New York: 1967 Unemployment Insurance Tax Rates, New York State Division of Employment (Albany, N.Y., April 1968).

*Less than 0.05 percent.

For all states except South Carolina, the proportions in item 2 of Table 5-5 are smaller than those in item 1, an indication that small firms account for a somewhat disproportionate share of the negative-balance firms (see also Table 5-9).

Item 3 shows how large a proportion of the benefit flow is attributable to negative firms and thus provides a direct measure of their relative importance. In New York, for example, although negative firms accounted for only 14.9 percent of all firms and 13.8 percent of all payrolls they accounted for 61.6 percent of all benefits. The proportions were roughly similar in Massachusetts, where 15.7 percent of all firms, with only 11.8 percent of all payrolls, accounted for 55.3 percent of all benefits; and in Michigan where 10.4 percent of all firms, with only 3.7 percent of all payrolls, accounted for 34.8 percent of all benefits. It would seem that in a prosperous period like 1967, the experience of the total program tends to be influenced greatly, even dominated, by the experience of negative firms. (This proposition holds expecially for high-cost industries, as illustrated in Table A-20.)

Data with respect to the first three items of Table 5-5, which provide a general view of deficit firms, are available for all reserve-ratio states and although not shown in the table may be summarized as follows. In these states, for the rate year 1968, negative firms made up only 10.6 percent of all firms, accounted for only 7.1 percent of all payrolls, but accounted for 40.6 percent of all benefits charged. In seven states, negative firms accounted for over half of all benefits charged.

It is important to note that the first three items of Table 5-5 provide no information on the taxes paid by these deficit firms and hence do not show the *extent* of their deficit. For such information it is necessary to use the data in items 5, 6, and 7. To illustrate the difference: In Wisconsin, benefits charged to negative firms were 60.8 percent of benefits charged to all firms (item 3), but the *deficit* of these firms amounted to only 25.1 percent of benefits charged to all firms (item 5). That is, one-quarter of all Wisconsin benefits in 1968 were ineffectively charged. Unfortunately, the data for items 5, 6, and 7 are not available for all states.

Industry Groups

Table 5-6 illustrates how industries differ in their experience with ineffectively charged benefits. In New Jersey, for example, 58.6 percent of construction firms were negative, as compared with 14.8 percent of firms in finance-insurance-real estate. In terms of taxable payrolls the differences were even greater: Where negative firms accounted for 54.8 percent of payrolls in construction, they accounted for only 3.9 percent of payrolls in finance-insurance-real estate. At the two-digit level (not shown in the table) the differences were even more marked. In Massachusetts, for example, negative firms accounted for 86.7 percent of the payrolls of "other general contractors," while they accounted for

Table 5-6. Negative-Balance Firms as Percent of All Firms, and Taxable Payrolls of Negative-Balance Firms as Percent of Taxable Payrolls of All Firms, by Industry Divisions, 1967[c], Selected States

Industry	Massachusetts			New Jersey		
	All firms	Negative-balance firms		All firms[a]	Negative-balance firms	
	Number (or amount)	Number (or amount)	Percent of all firms	Number (or amount)	Number (or amount)	Percent of all firms
	FIRMS					
All industry divisions	103,404	16,485	15.9	51,813	15,011	29.0
Agriculture, forestry, and fisheries	1,463	736	50.3	558	416	74.6
Mining	84	37	44.0	86	37	43.0
Contract construction	12,775	5,848	45.8	7,394	4,330	58.6
Manufacturing	9,996	1,633	16.3	10,061	3,528	35.1
Transportation, communication, and public utilities	4,071	680	16.7	2,517	586	23.3
Wholesale and retail trade	39,124	3,944	10.1	19,120	3,595	18.8
Finance, insurance, and real estate	8,220	574	7.0	3,103	460	14.8
Services	27,671	3,033	11.0	8,977	2,059	22.9
	TAXABLE PAYROLLS (in 000's)					
All industry divisions	$5,659,309	$623,263	11.0	$5,107,115	$910,866	17.8
Agriculture, forestry, and fisheries	28,014	13,524	48.3	14,222	8,457	59.5
Mining	4,442	2,246	50.6	9,613	4,895	50.9
Contract construction	384,844	213,720	55.5	345,215	189,029	54.8
Manufacturing	2,564,418	258,190	10.1	2,602,030	492,280	18.9
Transportation, communication, and public utilities	360,919	13,679	3.8	434,712	25,793	5.9
Wholesale and retail trade	1,277,838	66,760	5.2	1,032,941	103,072	10.0
Finance, insurance, and real estate	390,066	6,057	1.6	226,375	8,770	3.9
Services	648,768	49,088	7.6	442,078	78,620	17.8

Sources: Statistical tabulations published by the employment security agencies of the respective states, and supplementary data furnished by them as requested.

[a] All rated firms.
[b] All active firms.
[c] For Massachusetts, the firms were those rated for the calendar year 1968, and the taxable payroll was for the twelve months ending September 30, 1967; for New Jersey, the firms were those rated for the

only 0.3 percent of the payrolls in the electric and gas services industry. Within the manufacturing division, negative firms accounted for 51.3 percent of payrolls in apparel, but for only 0.9 percent of payrolls in chemicals.

Table A-20 is an extension of item 3 of Table 5-5, and shows how industries differ with respect to this item. In agriculture, mining, and construction, negative firms accounted for well over three-quarters of all benefit charges in the respective industries. The other industrial divisions held their accustomed relative positions: The proportions were lowest in finance-insurance-real estate, while trade reflected more "negative" experience than finance, but less than services. Table A-20 also provides some illustrative data for two states at the

	New York			Ohio			Wisconsin	
All firms	Negative-balance firms		All firms[b]	Negative-balance firms		All firms[a]	Negative-balance firms	
Number (or amount)	Number (or amount)	Percent of all firms	Number (or amount)	Number (or amount)	Percent of all firms	Number (or amount)	Number (or amount)	Percent of all firms
357,461	47,597	13.3	103,194	9.011	8.7	35,699	3,737	10.5
INA	INA		762	294	38.6	196	58	29.6
			923	192	20.8	176	100	56.8
27,096	10,601	39.1	14,929	4,227	28.3	4,759	1,693	35.6
39,261	10,674	27.2	12,277	658	5.4	5,227	404	7.7
11,347	1,441	12.7	3,635	313	8.6	1,573	170	10.8
126,147	12,317	9.8	43,193	2,093	4.8	15,785	641	4.1
38,476	1,910	5.0	6,574	261	4.0	2,154	56	2.6
112,186	10,374	9.2	20,901	973	4.7	5,817	374	6.4
7,008,543	2,062,547	12.1	$8,769,377	$261,855	3.0	$3,556,088	$255,894	7.2
INA	INA		15,923	3,966	24.9			
			63,207	4,413	7.0			
1,042,951	562,970	54.0	602,124	130,929	21.7			
6,405,239	909,010	14.2	4,790,302	78,286	1.6	INA	INA	
1,561,242	94,132	6.0	540,114	10,217	1.9			
3,872,819	217,151	5.6	1,750,315	18,424	1.1			
1,615,175	34,231	2.1	378,904	2,285	0.6			
2,484,254	240,994	9.7	628,488	13,334	2.1			

1967–68 fiscal year, and the taxable payroll was for the year 1966; for New York, the totals represent the sum of positive-balance and negative-balance firms for the year ending December 31, 1967, and the sum of their respective taxable payrolls for the twelve months ending September 30, 1967; for Ohio, the totals shown relate to employers "active for 1968" and their taxable payrolls for the year ending June 30, 1967; for Wisconsin, the employers are those rated for the calendar year 1968 and their taxable payrolls for the year ending June 30, 1967.

three-digit level. Thus, in construction, although negative firms accounted for relatively few benefits in electrical work, they accounted for nearly all benefits in painting-papering and masonry-plastering. In the apparel industry, negative firms accounted for even larger proportions of benefits, reaching 100 percent in the case of fur goods in Massachusetts.

Since a firm can be negative by a small or large amount, the previous data—on the proportions of firms and their payrolls that are negative, or the proportion of benefits charged to negative firms—cannot be used as a direct and adequate measure of the extent of experience rating. For this, it is necessary to have data on the extent to which firms are negative. Table 5-7, which is an extension of

Table 5-7. Deficit[a] of Negative-Balance Employers as Percent of Total Benefit Charges, All Rated Firms, for Selected Year,[b] by Industry Division and by Size of Taxable Payroll, Selected States

Industry division and size of taxable payroll	Massachusetts			Michigan			New York[c]		
	Benefit charges all firms 000's	Deficit of negative-balance firms		Benefit charges all firms 000's	Deficit of negative-balance firms		Benefit payments all firms 000's	Deficit of negative-balance firms	
		Amount 000's	Percent of benefit charges all firms		Amount 000's	Percent of benefit charges all firms		Amount 000's	Percent of benefit payments all firms
Totals	$72,517	$20,266	27.9	$60,244	$7,667	12.7	$294,202	$110,563	37.6
Industry division									
Agriculture, forestry, and fisheries	1,633	1,016	62.2	515	239	46.4	—	—	
Mining (including quarrying)	194	67	34.5	1,085	323	29.8	—	—	
Contract construction	16,676	7,926	47.5	13,555	3,576	26.4	54,301	30,521	56.2
Manufacturing	31,888	7,269	22.8	31,460	1,350	4.3	139,405	53,621	38.5
Apparel	7,695	3,699	48.1	456	51	11.2	52,553	31,565	60.1
Transportation, communication, and utilities	3,158	393	12.4	2,818	702	24.9	13,176	2,241	17.0

Wholesale and retail trade	10,748	1,744	16.2	6,207	682	11.0	41,648	9,916	23.8
Finance, insurance, and real estate	2,140	267	12.5	666	36	5.4	8,903	1,628	18.3
Services and miscellaneous	6,080	1,584	26.1	3,938	759	19.3	36,421	12,447	34.2
Size of taxable payroll									
Under $10,000	5,671	3,925	69.2	1,637	874	53.4	18,784	13,681	72.8
$10,000– 24,999	5,909	2,730	46.2	3,648	1,291	35.4	22,918	11,417	49.8
25,000– 49,999	6,206	2,429	39.1	4,178	1,090	26.1	26,892	11,760	43.7
50,000– 99,999	7,264	2,478	34.1	4,579	694	15.1	38,190	17,640	46.2
100,000– 249,999	11,057	3,368	30.5	7,037	1,327	18.9	57,267	24,926	43.5
250,000– 499,999	8,521	2,367	27.8	5,971	1,185	19.8	32,812	11,865	36.2
500,000– 999,999	7,004	1,315	18.8	4,836	482	10.0	23,309	7,602	32.6
1,000,000–2,499,999	7,714	1,377	17.9	7,094	666	9.4	22,588	5,105	22.6
2,500,000–4,999,999	3,665	163	4.4	3,366	58	1.7	16,445	5,433	33.0
5,000,000 and over	9,508	119	1.3	17,898	0	0	34,998	1,133	3.2

Sources: Massachusetts and Michigan: tabulations supplied by the employment security agency; New York: 1968 Unemployment Insurance Tax Rates, New York Division of Employment.

[a]Deficit: the excess of benefit charges over contributions, including emergency or subsidiary contributions.

[b]Massachusetts: computation year, October 1, 1966–September 30, 1967. Michigan: twelve months ending June 30, 1966 (for some employers), or December 31, 1966 (for others). New York: calendar year 1967.

[c]New York: (1) Although benefits paid are used instead of benefits charged, the difference is very small. (2) Data do not include lapsed accounts. (3) Agriculture, forestry and fisheries, and mining are included under "Services and miscellaneous."

item 5 of Table 5-5, exemplifies such data. This table shows the "deficit" (the excess of benefit charges over contributions) of negative firms and expresses this deficit as a percentage of all benefit charges. This percentage is a measure of the benefits that were ineffectively charged in the period shown. Thus, in New York 37.6 percent of all benefits were ineffectively charged and were outside the ambit of experience rating. In construction and apparel manufacturing, this ratio was over 50 percent while in transportation and finance it was under 20 percent. In Michigan the very small proportion (4.3 percent) for manufacturing is surprisingly low; it probably reflects, among other factors, a prosperous period for the auto industry. Of course, a key factor which affects all industry in Michigan is the unusually high maximum tax (6.6 percent) which is applicable in that state and which could result, apparently, in even construction paying most of its own costs.

Table A-22 is an extension of item 7 of Table 5-5 as applied to California. Because it shows the experience of only firms with the largest negative reserves, the table illustrates conditions "at the limit." It also illustrates the important difference between the deficit of a single year and cumulative deficits. Columns 2 and 3 show the deficits accumulated by these firms over their lifetime in the program. To clear their account, some of these industries would have had to pay a tax rate of more than 100 percent on their 1965 taxable wages. Agricultural services would have had to pay a 100 percent tax for almost two years before lifetime contributions would have equaled lifetime benefits.

In states which have the practice of writing off negative accounts, such a cumulative history is not available. In such states it is necessary to work with the annual deficit, such as is shown in columns 4 and 5. The annual experience is an unreliable guide to the cumulative total. Although column 3 reflects the experience of about thirty years, it is obviously not thirty times as large as column 5. Changes in benefit amounts and taxable wages, as well as periods of prosperity and depression, all affect the relationship between annual and cumulative ratios. This limitation should be kept in mind in any attempt to extrapolate annual figures, such as are contained in Table 5-7.

For any particular industry, it would be possible to construct a profile similar to that constructed for all industries in Table 5-5. By way of example, such a profile is presented in Table 5-8 for the construction industry in New York in 1967. This table shows the average figures for the industry as a whole and for two of its subgroups that differ widely. It is to be read in the same way as Table 5-5. Similar profiles could be drawn for other industries in other states, using the materials in the tables; and many states could draw upon additional materials to increase the detail of the profile for any given industry in their own systems.

Size Groups

Do negative-balance firms tend to be small or large firms? This question may be answered by looking at the problem from the various angles used in reviewing

Table 5-8. NEW YORK: Significant Measures Relating to Negative-Balance Firms[a]
in Selected Construction Industries, for 1967 Rate Year

Measure	Contract construction	Electrical work	Masonry and plastering
1. Number of firms with negative balances as a percent of all firms	41.6	–	–
2. Taxable payrolls of firms with negative balances as a percent of all taxable payrolls	58.5	3.4	79.3
3. Benefits charged to negative-balance firms as a percent of benefits charged to all firms	89.8	18.7	95.8
4. Benefits charged to negative-balance firms as a percent of their taxable payrolls	8.4	5.7	10.0
5. Deficit[b] of negative-balance firms as a percent of benefits charged to all firms	50.2	7.8	60.5
6. Deficit[b] of negative-balance firms as a percent of benefits charged to negative-balance firms	55.8	41.6	63.2
7. Deficit[b] of negative-balance firms as a percent of their taxable payrolls	4.7	2.4	6.3
8. Average cost/tax ratios of negative-balance firms	226.4	171.2	271.5

Source: New York State 1967 Unemployment Insurance Tax Rates, Department of Labor, Division of Employment.

[a]Data for all firms represent sum of positive- and negative-balance firms.

[b]Deficit: excess of benefits charged to negative-balance firms over their contributions, including estimated subsidiary tax.

the industrial characteristics of negative firms.[23] For the four states shown in Table 5-9, it is clear that the smaller firms are more liable to have negative balances than are the larger firms. Except for the largest firms, however, the difference in the experience of various sized firms is not very great.

Table A-21 brings out the correlation between size and the "importance" of negative firms. The smaller the sizegroup, the more it is dominated by the experience of the negative firms. In Massachusetts, for example: In the smallest sizegroups, negative firms accounted for 90.9 percent of all benefit charges, while in the next-to-largest group, the corresponding percentage was only 14.7, and in the largest group there were no negative firms at all.

Table 5-7 reinforces the conclusion that the problem of negative firms is more acute among the small firms than among the larger ones.[24] Not only are

23. The answer regarding size may be given more briefly than the answer regarding industry because size is a less important determinant than industry of cost-tax ratios.

24. If the program's solvency rather than its degree of experience rating were the point at issue, a different set of tables would have to be prepared, and these would show the small

Table 5-9. Negative-Balance Firms and Their Taxable Payrolls
As Percent of All Rated Firms and of Taxable Payrolls of Rated Firms,[a]
by Size of Firm, Selected States, 1967

FIRMS

Size of taxable payroll	Massachusetts[b]			New Jersey[b]			New York[c]			Ohio[b]		
	Number or amount in 000's	Negative-balance accounts	Percent of total	Number or amount in 000's	Negative-balance accounts	Percent of total	Number or amount in 000's	Negative-balance accounts	Percent of total	Number or amount in 000's	Negative-balance accounts	Percent of total
All size groups	103,404	16,485	15.9	51,813	15,011	29.0	357,461	47,597	13.3	86,409	5,763	6.7
Under $10,000	54,296	9,363	17.2	29,223	9,485	32.5	196,556	22,346	11.4	24,427	2,759	11.3
$10,000– 24,999	23,551	3,388	14.4	9,370	2,168	23.1	78,708	10,751	13.7	43,506	2,177	5.0
25,000– 49,999	11,407	1,604	14.1	6,143	1,500	24.4	38,012	5,711	15.0	8,920	393	4.4
50,000– 99,999	6,658	962	14.4	4,307	1,226	28.5	22,016	4,274	19.4	5,734	270	4.7
100,000– 249,999	4,523	736	16.3	1,459	399	27.3	14,305	3,246	22.7	1,865	95	5.1
250,000– 499,999	1,531	255	16.7	696	141	20.3	4,291	853	19.9	990	41	4.1
500,000– 999,999	805	116	14.4	614	92	15.0	1,943	260	13.4	967	28	2.9
1,000,000– 2,499,999	410	48	11.7				1,054	119	11.3			
2,500,000– 4,999,999	126	8	6.3				316	31	9.8			
5,000,000– 9,999,999	58	4	6.9				136	4	2.9			
10,000,000– 24,999,999	29	1	3.4				93	2	2.2			
25,000,000 and over	10	0	0				31	0	0			

TAXABLE PAYROLLS

All size groups	$5,659,309	$623,263	11.0	$5,107,115	$910,866	17.8	$17,008,543	$2,062,547	12.1	$8,668,599	$255,195	2.9
Under $10,000	228,323	36,227	15.9	341,566	95,368	27.9	804,681	95,202	11.8	142,220	13,161	9.3
$10,000- 24,999	372,416	53,388	14.3				1,219,089	167,030	13.7			
25,000- 49,999	400,365	56,210	14.0	331,336	76,604	23.1	1,314,544	199,773	15.2	984,599	47,253	4.8
50,000- 99,999	464,606	67,605	14.6	429,651	106,571	24.8	1,519,776	298,591	19.6	622,342	27,636	4.4
100,000- 249,999	693,318	115,388	16.6	665,152	192,284	28.9	2,178,702	491,842	22.6	877,755	42,875	4.9
250,000- 499,999	525,638	86,123	16.4	502,027	137,267	27.3	1,479,260	288,851	19.5	645,979	33,925	5.3
500,000- 999,999	555,281	79,979	14.4	485,874	96,370	19.8	1,340,294	176,587	13.2	687,464	26,996	3.9
1,000,000- 2,499,999	617,767	66,671	10.8	2,351,509	206,402	8.8	1,597,746	172,557	10.8	4,708,243	63,352	1.3
2,500,000- 4,999,999	431,831	24,072	5.6				1,104,501	110,033	10.0			
5,000,000- 9,999,999	386,010	26,955	7.0				955,844	30,102	3.1			
10,000,000-24,999,999	434,281	10,646	2.5				1,441,536	31,979	2.2			
25,000,000 and over	549,474	0	0				2,052,570	0	0			

Sources: Statistical tabulations published by the employment security agencies of the respective states and supplementary data furnished by them as requested.

[a] For Massachusetts, firms are those rated for the calendar year 1968, and taxable payrolls are for the twelve months ending September 30, 1967; for New Jersey, the firms are those rated for the 1967–68 fiscal year, and taxable payrolls are for the year 1966; for New York, the totals represent positive-balance plus negative-balance employers for the year ending December 31, 1967, and taxable payrolls for the twelve months ending September 30, 1967; for Ohio the totals are the number of employers rated for the calendar year 1968 and their taxable payrolls for the fiscal year ending June 30, 1967.

[b] All rated firms.

[c] Excludes firms with no taxable payrolls for year ending September 30, 1967.

more small firms negative but they are negative to a greater extent. In New York, for example, 72.8 percent of benefits charged to the smallest firms were ineffectively charged, while among the largest firms the corresponding figure was only 3.2 percent. Moreover, there was a fairly regular decline in this percentage as the size of the firm increased. These same general observations apply also to Massachusetts and Michigan.

Conclusions

In Chapter 5, the attempt has been made to illuminate more fully the relationship between the potential and actual degrees of experience rating. Chapter 5 has sought answers to two questions: (1) How close to balancing are benefits and taxes for the individual firm? That is, what degree of experience rating is there? (2) To the extent that benefits and taxes do not balance, who is subsidizing whom? Answers were sought from four sets of data, none of which was adequate in itself but each of which contributed something to the total picture. The four were cost/tax ratios, the operations of the Common Account, noncharged benefits, and ineffectively charged benefits.[25]

In general, it is clear that the system as a whole is very far from being completely experience-rated. The departures from experience rating are numerous and large. It is also clear that the degree of experience rating varies greatly among the states. States like Ohio and Michigan, for example, are marked by a much greater degree of experience rating than are states like Massachusetts and South Carolina. The allocative effect of experience rating is necessarily less in the latter states than in the former. All other effects of experience rating are probably also less.

The simplest, though not necessarily the most adequate, measure of departures from experience rating is the extent of negative balances. In most states, the number of negative firms is relatively small compared to the total number of firms, but typically they account for a large, sometimes the larger, part of all benefits paid, and their deficit (benefits minus contributions) is substantial. This deficit is subsidized by the contributions of the much greater number of positive firms. Because the positive firms so greatly outnumber the negative firms and have so much more of the covered payrolls, the burden of the subsidy is widely distributed and to that extent lessened for the individual firm. The chief

---

firm as less of a "problem" than the large firm. Although small firms may have a greater proportion of negative accounts than do large firms, the deficit of a single large firm may be more significant for solvancy than the deficits of a dozen, or a hundred, smaller firms.

25. It is not feasible to summarize effectively the numerous tables presented in the chapter. There is no substitute for a thorough, detailed study of these data. It is only by steeping oneself in the details of the tables that one can acquire a "feel" for the degree of experience rating in the system and a sense of the extent to which the present degree of experience rating may or may not be appropriate to an economy based primarily on the free market.

subsidizers are the firms whose cost rates are regularly lower than the minimum tax imposed by the state. Although most small firms are in this category, the absolute amount of subsidy they provide is small.[26] The principal regular subsidizers are the very large firms; but all firms contribute to the subsidy insofar as the interest earned by their unused contributions is credited to the general fund only, or a part of their contributions is credited to a Common Account, or they are required to build up "excessive" reserves.

Although it is clear that the system effects a substantial redistribution of taxes among firms, it is not equally clear to what extent this redistribution is of the insurance variety or the subsidy variety, as those terms are defined in Chapter 3 (p. 59). That is, it is not clear to what extent this redistribution is predictable or unpredictable. Some firms in the auto industry, for example, during the decade 1957-67 developed negative balances during several of those years, but eventually repaid the fund and built up substantial positive balances. Given the large, unforeseen fluctuations that can occur in this industry, these firms may quite possibly become negative again. This is the typical situation for which insurance is appropriate. During the same decade, however, in other industries some firms were negative, year after year, while other firms were paying into the fund more than they took out, year after year. The redistribution of funds between such firms would seem to be closer to the subsidy variety.

As a rough approximation, subject to many modifications according to differences among states and periods, it might be helpful to think of perhaps one-fifth of all firms covered by the program as regularly and predictably subsidized, while another fifth are regularly and predictably subsidizing. The remaining firms have somewhat less stable cost-tax relationships, and their experience comes closer to that covered by "insurance."

There is very little information on the cost/tax ratios of individual firms for periods longer than a single year. The states do not keep track of the cumulative cost-tax record of the individual firm. Indeed, even the firm itself usually does not know its own long-term cost/tax ratio except in the most general fashion.[27] However, some inferences can be drawn regarding the ratios of individual firms from two sources of related data. One source consists of data on the distribution of individual firms according as they have positive or negative account balances. Some firms have very large positive balances, while other firms have very large negative balances. In all probability, these two groups belong to different worlds of economic activities and regularly have the relationship to each other of subsidizer and subsidized.

26. The subsidy they contribute is also more likely to be temporary. Small firms very easily move from a positive to a negative status. In one or two years, a small firm may accumulate a negative balance larger than the accumulated subsidies that it provided during the previous decade.

27. In the course of this study a handful of large firms were asked for this information. In nearly all cases they had not previously assembled the information but had to make a special tabulation for this purpose.

Another source of data from which inferences may be made regarding the experience of individual firms are industry averages. Since the differences in cost/tax ratios between industrial groups are large and regular, it is probable that the differences stem from the natures of the economic activities involved. Since the individual firms which comprise the industries presumably share the economic nature of the industry, it may be inferred that the experiences of most of the individual firms comprising the industries differ in somewhat the same way as the industry averages do. It is in this sense that one may think of the industries of finance and retail trade, for example, as subsidizing the industries of construction and apparel manufacturing.

Actually, the low-cost firms in all industries subsidize the high-cost firms in all industries; but the proportion of low-cost and high-cost firms among the various industries vary in predictable patterns. Hence, although every industry includes low-cost and high-cost firms, the leaders of the various industries frequently see their interests in unemployment insurance as different from the interests of other industries. To adduce three of many possible examples: In Utah the retailers fought vigorously for years to increase the degree of experience rating in the state system because they were convinced they were subsidizing the mining industry and other high-cost industries [22, p. 124]. Or, again, in New York, where employers have an association that meets annually to discuss problems in unemployment insurance and to plan legislative strategy, the representatives of the construction and apparel industries choose not to attend such meetings. They do not attend because they see their interests in unemployment insurance as distinct from and even opposed to the interests of the other industries. Or, again, in Wisconsin. On one occasion the powerful Wisconsin unemployment insurance advisory council, composed of the major decision-makers among labor and management, made a unanimous recommendation to the legislature that the maximum unemployment insurance tax be raised from 4 percent to 4.6 percent. Although the recommendations of this council are regularly accepted by the legislature and enacted into law [22, Ch. 3], on this occasion the construction industry raised such a storm of opposition that the legislature declined to accept the agreed bill of the advisory council and fixed the maximum at 4.4 percent, instead of the recommended 4.6 percent.

To summarize. Chapter 3 developed the proposition that the allocative effect of experience rating was to be considered desirable unless in each specific instance there was positive proof to the contrary. Chapter 4 reached the dual conclusion that there was a considerable potential for experience rating (inasmuch as variations in benefit-cost rates were large and predictable) and that this potential was actualized to a significant degree (inasmuch as differences in tax rates were large enough to have some significance as an economic cost item). Chapter 5 has reached the conclusion that the potential for experience rating is still far from being fully realized and has shown that firms in some industries were regularly and predictably subsidizing firms in other industries.

To the extent that a state is characterized by large departures from experience rating, the effects of which on the allocation of resources have not been justified by specific evidence, the legislature may adopt one of three attitudes. First, it may decide that it does not accept the argument for the free market, as developed in Chapter 3, and therefore does not accept the argument's corollary that interventions in the market need to be justified by specific evidence of their desirability. Second, the legislature may accept the argument of the market, including the corollary regarding interventions, and, aware that existing interventions have not been justified by specific evidence, may amend the tax structure to move cost/tax ratios further toward unity (increase the degree of experience rating). Third, the legislature may agree with the argument for the market, may recognize the logic of the corollary regarding intervention, but may decide nevertheless not to make any substantial changes in the unemployment insurance tax structure. In the view of the legislature, the strain on practical politics resulting from an attempt to redistribute the unemployment insurance tax burden may not be worth the effort. If the program is meeting its essential financial obligations (is solvent), the legislature, having only limited time to find answers to an almost unlimited number of problems, may decide to follow one of the oldest of political guidelines and "let sleeping dogs lie." Unemployment insurance will probably not be the only operation in the state which is not completely logical by economic norms.

Quite possibly, the most frequent legislative attitude will be a combination of all three of the above. The legislature may not feel completely happy with the rigor of the argument developed in Chapter 3, especially in view of the large number of interventions that legislatures regularly make in the market. At the same time, it may feel not completely happy with the existing tax pattern, whereby low-wage firms in retailing, for example, may be subsidizing high-wage firms in construction. Finally, it may lack resources to investigate the actual effects of existing patterns and may feel reluctant to disturb the already established and accepted situation. In most cases, such a combination of attitudes would probably lead to a modest increase in the degree of experience rating by the adoption of one or more of the changes outlined toward the end of Chapter 13.

Is the existing degree of experience rating desirable? Should the degree be decreased or increased? Obviously, this question cannot begin to be answered until all the effects of experience rating have been examined. But with regard to this one effect, on the allocation of costs and resources, the answer would seem to be that the degree of experience rating should be increased—up to the point where it becomes *clear* that the allocation of resources is being affected undesirably.

Employer Participation in Administration I: *Opinion Survey*

The Issue

In the early years of the unemployment insurance program, little attention was paid to the possible effect of experience rating on employer participation in administration. Neither the Raushenbush-Rubinow debate in 1933 [16], [18] nor the Feldman-Lester debate in 1939 [9],[10] touched on the issue. The January 1936 issue of *Law and Contemporary Problems* was entirely devoted to unemployment compensation, but employer participation in administration was mentioned only once, in an article by Walter F. Dodd: "Where a specific employer's account is affected by a claim, as in Wisconsin and Utah, notice of a claim to the employer creates a sufficient adversary relation, and produces a contest, where the claim may be regarded as improper. Where there is a pooled fund, notice to the most recent employer will usually not create a contest even of an improper claim, and protection of a fund must be provided by some other means, if at all" [95, p. 109].

One of the earliest official recognitions of this effect of experience rating occurred in a 1940 report written largely by Paul A. Raushenbush for the Interstate Conference of Employment Security Agencies. "The advocates of experience rating suggest, finally, that it is needed to assure continuing employer interest in benefit administration, and to provide an 'adverse party' to contest improper claims" [31, p. 64]. Five years later, *The Yale Law Journal* devoted its December 1945 issue to unemployment compensation. Following upon seven years of experience in paying benefits, the articles showed increased interest in the problems of administration; but of the two articles that discussed experience rating, only one mentioned the issue of employer participation in administration. Almon R. Arnold still listed as functions of experience rating only the two of allocation and stabilization [60, p. 219]; but Emerson P. Schmidt added a third: "To stimulate an employer interest in the administration of the program" [78, p. 242]. Interest in this issue continued to develop as is illustrated by the difference between Eveline Burns's earlier [12, p. 166] and later [13, p. 169] treatments of this subject. At present, any serious discussion of experience rating is certain to deal with the subject explicitly (for example, [14, p. 331]).

An employer may participate in the administration of unemployment insurance in two ways: He may furnish facts. By appealing and arguing against decisions of the state agency he may also attempt to influence the interpretation of the law as applied to those facts.[1] In the main, the relevant facts pertain either to a job from which the claimant was separated (Was he laid off for lack of work? Did he quit? Was he discharged for misconduct?) or to a job to which he is referred or is referrable (Did he refuse suitable work? Is he available for work?)[2]

Sometimes the effect of an employer's participation is to disqualify a claimant from benefits, and sometimes its effect is merely to relieve the employer of benefit charges. (the second situation occurs when the state law provides for the noncharging of some benefits connected with actual or potential disqualifications.) The two effects are usually indistinguishable in the data, yet have very different significance. When experience rating is criticized for its effect on administration, the critic usually has in view the kind of employer participation which may affect the claimant's eligibility for benefits. The Massachusetts data analyzed in Chapter 7 are entirely of this latter sort.

Some critics of experience rating maintain that a satisfactory degree of employer participation is obtainable without it. In the first place, most claims require no employer participation at all (other than the furnishing of wage information). Most claims stem from layoff for lack of work. Since they thus involve no dispute, they require no employer participation.[3] Further, in that minority of cases where the claim stems from some other source, the word of the claimant will usually be a reliable guide as to the actual circumstances of his separation from employment. Finally, it is said, in that small proportion of cases where it seems advisable to secure a statement from the employer, the employer's cooperation may be counted on, apart from the financial incentive of experience rating. The effort required of the employer is minimal—to check a box or write a few words on a form—and can be elicited by no stronger incentive than the employer's own general disposition to conform to the law, the violation of which makes him liable to a fine and imprisonment. It was reasoning of this sort that led a recent study of experience rating to conclude: "Merit rating serves little policing function because it adds little to the employer's other strong motivations for reporting the reasons of termination and opposing unjustified claims" [96, p. 24].[4]

1. In this way he participates in the development of "administrative law" [22, p. 42].
2. The employer also, of course, supplies wage data, which are essential to the operation of an insurance system. But this obligation is the same, with or without experience rating, and is not relevant to the debate over the desirability of experience rating.
3. In many states, such as California, the employer is instructed that he need not reply at all to a notification of a claim filed when the claim stems from lack of work.
4. However, the study does not provide the evidence to support this particular conclusion. Designed primarily to investigate the possible effect of experience rating on employ-

Other critics of experience rating adopt the opposite position. So far from holding that experience rating has no significant effect on employer participation in administration, they maintain that it has a notable effect but an undesirable one. When the late Walter Reuther testified in 1965 before the Committee on Ways and Means, he expressed himself very strongly on this point:

> We know the pitiful results which experience rates have produced in the form of vicious disqualification provisions, unreasonably high earnings requirements, cancellation of benefit rights, and worst of all, the baseless unreasoning, devious contesting by employers of all claims which may adversely affect their tax rates. Every device imaginable is employed to beat down, wear out, and defeat the unemployed worker who has the temerity to file a claim for benefits. Trade associations encourage this process of contesting all claims. They point out that dollars are involved in a claim. And they say that no matter if the employer does know that the worker is entitled to benefits under the facts and the law, he should still contest the claim because that will delay things, cause the State agency to investigate and, maybe, cause the worker to give up the whole thing as an impossible fight to win [2, p. 1411].

When the Committee asked for the evidence to support this charge, Mr. Reuther said he would have no trouble assembling abundant evidence. Eventually, he submitted a statement which cited a situation in Ohio in the early 1950's, when some employers were challenging the availability of claimants across the board. (It was the same type of situation discussed below in the case of state B.) The statement also quoted from manuals that instructed employers how to control claims, and concluded:

"The original unemployment compensation conception assumed easy and informal administrative hearings and quick decisions without the need for lawyers, compensation experts, advisors, and actuaries. Over the years there has developed a harsh and abrasive maze of legalisms which has succeeded in undermining the purpose of the law. There is great need to reverse this ever-growing subversion of the basic philosophy of unemployment compensation"[2, p. 1423].

Mr. Reuther was speaking of employer protest at both the initial level of determination and at the later level of an appeal. In the following quotation another labor representative addresses himself specifically to the appeal process. For almost a decade (1951–59), New York required employers to deposit a sum of money whenever they filed an appeal. The purpose of this provision was to discourage unnecessary appeals. In arguing for the retention of this provision, the representative for labor said:

---

ment stabilization, the study and its materials shed little light on the desirability of employer participation in administration.

I heard talk this morning about the small percentage of employers that actually appeal and how insignificant this is. But I think the figure should be looked at in a different manner. Roughly, 1,500 to 2,000 workers each year have their unemployment benefits held up for periods of approximately two months, in the case of a referee hearing, and perhaps four months where the referee's decision is then taken to the appeal board. . . .

The statistics show that the vast majority of employer appeals are without merit. I cannot tell you how many of these appeals are filed capriciously or maliciously or in ignorance of the law. Undoubtedly some are. But the very fact remains that only one out of every five employer appeals to the referee's section are approved favorably to the employer, and only something like one in six at the Appeal Board level are approved favorably to the employer. The 1,500 to 2,000 workers I was talking about before are workers whose appeals, whose claims, were ultimately upheld by the referees or the Appeal Board and were ultimately granted their benefits [97, pp. 32-33].

In reply to these various allegations, the proponents of experience rating advance a number of counter arguments. First of all, the legal compulsion on the employer to provide potentially disqualifying information is minimal. The penalties for failing to provide such information are practically never applied.[5] The law is the more difficult to apply because the employer need not perform any positive action; he may merely omit an action. It is very difficult to prove that the omission was deliberate and was for the purpose of enabling a claimant to draw benefits illegally.

It is not true that separations from employment other than layoffs for lack of work are insignificant. During the period 1960-70, the number of quits in manufacturing exceeded the number of layoffs in five of those years. In 1970 the unemployment insurance agencies made about four million nonmonetary determinations.[6] Most of these were occasioned by a separation from employment for some reason other than lack of work and thus required that the employer supply information as to the facts in the case. In some states in some years, nonmonetary determinations are made on almost half of all initial claims. For particular firms, claims stemming from layoffs are regularly only a small part of all claims filed against the firm's account.[7]

---

5. Even the legal penalties for falsifying facts to *prevent* the payment of benefits are only occasionally applied. For this reason California in 1963 made such acts liable to an administrative penalty—one that the agency could impose without going to the courts.

6. A "nonmonetary determination" is one that involves an issue which may affect a claimant's eligibility for benefits.

7. For example, the records of one of the largest firms in New Jersey show that nearly 90 percent of the benefits charged to its account over a ten-year period were paid to employees who had retired, half of them voluntarily. See Chapter 8 for other examples of firms whose benefit charges reflect mainly separations other than layoffs for lack of work.

The process of participating effectively in nonmonetary determinations is not a simple one for the employer. It involves, first of all, the maintenance of records adequate for unemployment insurance purposes, and such records are usually more detailed than those required for other personnel needs.

"For many years the exact reason a worker left his employment had no special meaning and often no record was made, or if one was made, it would be in very general terms. However, because of Unemployment Compensation, the exact reason the worker left his employment now becomes of the utmost importance. This *exact reason* will be the deciding factor in determining whether or not the worker is eligible for benefits" [98, p. 13]. Effective claims control requires the employer to keep records that will enable him to distinguish between literally dozens of different kinds of separations and to prove the distinction if challenged. The burden of keeping such records is perhaps the chief obstacle to more effective employer participation in administration.

Effective claims control requires not merely adequate record keeping but also a knowledge of the unemployment insurance law. In large corporations this means the training of personnel in the complexities of the law. Ideally, the firm's technician responsible for claims control should know the unemployment insurance law as well as does the state unemployment insurance personnel. Not infrequently, large firms solve the training problem by hiring former state personnel. Some state associations of employers and a few large corporations have compiled manuals of instruction for the use of the technicians assigned to the task of handling unemployment insurance claims.[8] Next to seeing the technician actually at work, the reading of these manuals is probably the most direct way in which one not familiar with the subject can understand the proposition that to participate in the administration of unemployment insurance is not a simple task but one that requires adequate records, skilled personnel, and careful attention (that is, sufficient time). This proposition holds at every level of administration, but it acquires significance as a dispute over a claim mounts from the deputy to the referee to the board of review and finally to the courts.

The terms used to designate the personnel at the various levels of administrative decision differ among the states. For the purposes of this study, "deputy" refers to the state employee who makes the first determination in a disputed claim, "referee" refers to the state employee to whom this determination is next appealed, and "board of review" refers to the highest level of adjudication within the unemployment insurance system.

Even granted the need for experience rating to elicit effective employer participation, there remains the question of the desirability of such participation. The chief supporting argument here is usually drawn from the danger of claimant "abuse": "Claimants not really entitled to benefits represent only a small proportion of the total, but it is a proportion which will increase if such claimants are not challenged when they do apply" [101, p. 10]. Although there

---

8. For examples of these manuals, see [99] and [100].

is little statistical evidence on the actual (still less on the potential) extent of improper payments, judgments in this area are, nevertheless, probably the single most influential factor determining attitudes toward employer participation in administration.[9]

A related consideration is the moral hazard of unemployment insurance as it affects the employer himself. "Moral hazard" is that characteristic of insurance whereby the very availability of the insurance protection increases the incidence of the risk insured against. This "moral hazard" is not necessarily a form of immorality as understood in the customary sense, but as Mark Pauly explains, may be merely rational economic behavior: "Each individual may well recognize that excess use of medical care makes the premium he must pay rise. No individual will be motivated to restrain his own use, however, since the incremental benefit to him for excess use is great, while the additional cost of his use is largely spread over other insurance holders, and so he bears only a tiny fraction of the cost of his use. . . . Since the cost of the individual's excess usage is spread over all other purchases of that insurance, the individual is not prompted to restrain his usage of [medical] care" [103, pp. 534, 535]. Employers in certain situations are subject to such a moral hazard in unemployment insurance. They may be tempted to use unemployment benefits as a cheap, even costless, way of supplementing the wages they pay,[10] or of maintaining a convenient labor pool, or of just being a good fellow.[11] Although it would be easy to compile examples of these kinds of employer actions, there is no solid statistical basis for estimating the extent of the problem. All that can be said with certainty is that this moral hazard is lessened to the extent that experience rating causes each firm to bear the true actuarial cost of insuring its own workers (see also p. 239).

A final argument used to defend the desirability of employer participation in administration is based on the "proper" relationship to be maintained between labor and management. These two are the most powerful interest groups in the economy, and their relationship constitutes one of the most important social tensions in modern society. Hence unemployment insurance is to be evaluated partly for its effect on the relative bargaining power of labor and management.[12]

9. If an intensive study of this problem published two decades ago [102] is still relevant, the program is under constant pressure from attempts to gain benefits improperly, but the administrative walls of unemployment insurance, reinforced by experience rating, have been adequate to the task of resisting the onslaught.

10. Employers of seasonal labor, for example, sometimes explicitly mention in their advertisements the availability of unemployment benefits after the season closes. For another example, in 1970 in a large industrial state, the state manufacturers association sponsored a bill that would have lowered unemployment benefits by the amount of any private pension received. In the next few days, the executive director of the association received a score of protesting phone calls from members of the association, who said that they counted unemployment benefits as part of their pension plan.

11. Like the employer who would like to give unemployment compensation to his secretary as a wedding present.

12. It is perhaps for this reason that in the 1965 Hearings on Unemployment Insurance the then secretary of labor, Willard Wirtz, declined to commit himself on the issue of

Since this relationship is discussed in Chapter 9, it will not be further elaborated here. However, it should be recognized as one element in the evaluation of employer participation in administration.

In summary, the debate over employer participation in administration turns on two distinct though closely related questions: (1) What impact does experience rating have on employer participation? (2) Is employer participation desirable? Most of the materials in Chapters 6, 7, and 8 have some pertinence to both questions, although particular items will usually pertain more to the one than to the other. As usual, the materials do not suffice to provide exact answers to these qualitative questions but serve rather to delimit the areas within which the answers probably lie.

The 1969 Opinion Survey

Structure of the Survey

As a first step toward evaluating employer participation in the administrative process, a questionnaire was sent in 1969 to a representative sample of experienced deputies and referees.[13] These are the persons who are in constant contact with claimant and employer, serving as the bridge between them and arbitrating their disputes about claims—day after day, year after year. If any persons in the entire program have an opinion worth listening to, it would seem to be the deputies and referees. So this most knowledgeable group was asked the question: *Does employer participation in the administrative process help or hinder you in your job of carrying out the unemployment insurance law of your state?* All but one of the thirteen items in the questionnaire asked this central question in one form or another.[14] As stated in the instructions given to the respondents: "The purpose of this questionnaire is to learn to what extent and in what ways employer participation in the processing of disputed claims is a help or a hindrance to you in your task of carrying out the unemployment insurance law as you understand that law and its goals."

It was recognized that the replies of the deputies and referees would be colored to some extent by their individual personalities. The subjective elements would be modified in this group, however, by two circumstances. First, they were asked to base their opinions on the objective norm of the law they were administering. They were asked not whether they approved or disapproved of the law, but merely whether they were helped or hindered in their job of administering the law as given. Second, while there is room for differences in the interpretation of a given law, in the case of the deputies and referees the scope for such differences was limited by their professional training and by the constant supervision to which their interpretations were subjected. The restriction

employer participation in administration. He avoids the issue on page 352 and again on page 356 [2].

13. The meaning of these terms was defined earlier in the chapter.

14. The exception was Question 9, which falls outside the strict logic of the questionnaire.

of the questionnaire to respondents with five years' or more experience worked in this same direction. In five years' time, deputies or referees with extremely individualistic views would have become better trained or would have been weeded out. It is possible that these state personnel, better educated than the average claimant, tend to identify more readily with employer representatives than with claimants. However, in the many hearings I have attended, I have not observed any such general tendency among the referees.

With the cooperation of the federal Bureau of Employment Security and of the various states involved, the questionnaire was sent to deputies and referees in seventeen states: California, Maine, Massachusetts, Michigan, Mississippi, New York, Ohio,[15] Oregon, Pennsylvania, Texas, Utah, Virginia, Washington, Wisconsin, and states A, B, and C.[16]

These seventeen states included over 60 percent of all covered employees and were broadly representative in point of size, geographical location, and type of experience-rating plan. The sample included eight large states, six small states, and three average-sized states. It included five states from the east, four from the midwest, four from the far west, and four from the south. It also included the following experience-rating systems: reserve-ratio (9), benefit-ratio (4), benefit-wage-ratio (2), and payroll-variation (2).

The deputies and referees were instructed not to sign the questionnaire. Each returned his response directly to the Center for Social Studies in a stamped envelope provided for the purpose. As remarked above, the questionnaire was restricted to experienced deputies and referees, that is, to those with at least five years' experience. The questionnaire was sent to all such referees in the selected states, and to all such deputies in thirteen of the selected states. In the four largest states, however, the survey was limited to a sample of experienced deputies. The samples were large, ranging from one-fourth to one-half of all such deputies. In all, some 978 questionnaires were distributed, of which 893 (91 percent) were returned.[17] In nearly every respect, therefore, the sample has a high representative value. As an aid to the interpretation of the responses received in the questionnaire, I conducted follow-up interviews with deputies and referees in several states, specifically, California, Massachusetts, Michigan, Utah, and state B. In these interviews, I repeated the survey questions and probed for possible misunderstandings.

Scope of the Survey

To properly interpret the results of the survey, it is necessary to understand its underlying logic. Defenders of experience rating claim that it has a desirable

15. The chairman of the board of review in Ohio declined to permit the referees to participate in the survey; hence in this state the questionnaire was sent only to the deputies.
16. These three states participated in the survey, but preferred not to be identified.
17. Inflated to reflect the universe of the four states from which samples had been taken, the total number of returned questionnaires became 1,499. This is the number used in the tables.

effect, while critics charge that it has an undesirable effect on the administration of the program. The questionnaire cannot be used to prove either the claim or the counterclaim, but it could possibly be used to disprove one of them. The logic is simple: (1) The claim that experience rating has a desirable effect rests on two propositions: (a) Experience rating elicits employer participation in the administrative process, and (b) employer participation is good for the unemployment insurance program. (2) The counterclaim that experience rating has an undesirable effect also rests on two propositions: (a) Experience rating elicits employer participation in the administrative process, and (b) employer participation is bad for the program. For either the claim or the counterclaim to be true, both propositions must be true; hence, if either proposition is false, the claim or charge is false.

The questionnaire was not designed to test the first proposition, which was assumed to be true by both sides. (We attempt to test this first proposition in other ways in other parts of the study.) The questionnaire was designed to test the truth of only the second proposition: Is employer participation in administration good or bad for the program? The norm of "good" and "bad" was the extent to which employer participation helped or hindered the respondent to achieve the objectives of the law for whose administration he was responsible.

Strictly speaking, the questionnaire should have been directed only to that degree and kind of employer participation which was attributable to experience rating and excluded whatever employer participation would be present under even a uniform tax. Practically, however, this could not be done. None of the respondents was in a position to make such an exact distinction. However, they were answering out of a situation in which experience rating was actually operating, and the questionnaire provided them with the opportunity to reflect the prevalence or the absence of the chief abuses usually alleged to follow experience rating, such as the filing of "frivolous" protests. No more was expected of the questionnaire than that it would narrow the limits within which the answers lay and would enable one to conclude that the extent of undesirable effects associated with experience rating might be as great as X but could not be greater than was compatible with Y. The degree to which the reaction of the respondents was in general unfavorable to employer participation would set the X limit, and the extent to which their reaction was favorable would set the Y limit.

The thirteen questions shown in condensed form in Table 6-1 are given in their full form on pages 142 - 52. The answers received are shown *by state* in Table 6-2 and are summarized in Table 6-3 according as they were favorable or unfavorable to employer participation.

General Analysis

Before analyzing the responses to particular questions, it may be helpful to take a general view of the survey's results. In the tabulation presented below, answers to eight of the thirteen questions are coded as being generally favorable to employer participation, or unfavorable, or neutral. Five questions (numbers 4, 7, 8, 9, and 13) did not directly evaluate employer participation and hence did not lend themselves to inclusion in this summary.

Answers were classified as favorable, unfavorable, or neutral according to the code shown in Table 6-1. Responses that had any negative element at all were classified as unfavorable. The only responses that were classified as favorable were those that were clearly such. The remainder were classified as neutral. Thus, although of the neutral answers none could reasonably be considered unfavorable, some could reasonably have been classified as favorable. For example, in their answers to question 1, a sizable proportion (33.7 percent) of the respondents reported that employer participation had hindered them "moderately." Interviews with deputies disclosed that some respondents had extended

Table 6-1. Summary of Questions Asked of Deputies and Referees in 1969 Survey of Employer Participation in Administration

Questions (in condensed form)	Choice of answers[a]
1. a. Has it helped your work? How much?	$\bar{1}, \bar{2}$, or $\underline{3}$
b. Has it hindered your work? How much?	$\underline{1}, \underline{2}$, or $\bar{3}$
2. Would you desire more employer participation, or less:	
a. (Deputies) In protesting new claims?	$\bar{1}, 2$, or $\bar{3}$
b. (Deputies) In protesting additional claims?	$\bar{1}, 2$, or $\bar{3}$
c. (Referees) In appealing determinations?	$\bar{1}, 2$, or $\bar{3}$
3. Frivolous protests or appeals occur how often?	$\underline{1}, 2, 3, \bar{4}$, or $\bar{5}$
*4. Frivolous cases mostly from where?	1, 2, 3, or 4
5. Should an advance deposit discourage employer appeals?	$\underline{1}, \bar{2}$, or 3
6. Participation through a service company, acceptable?	$\bar{1}, \bar{2}$, or $\underline{3}$
*7. Participation lacking in which industries?	1 through 8
*8. Participation lacking in which manufacturing?	1 through 7
*9. Participation less if no experience rating? How much less?	1, 2, or 3
10. Inadequate employer help as to facts. How often?	$\underline{1}, \underline{2}, 3, \bar{4}$, or $\bar{5}$
11. Failure to appear at requested appeal hearings. How often?	$\underline{1}, 2$, or $\bar{3}$
12. Would you desire more or less or a different kind of employer participation?	Explain[b]
*13. Has participation changed over the years?	Explain

*Answers to these questions were not coded (favorable, unfavorable, or neutral) and are not included in Table 6-3.

[a]Classification code: Favorable=bar above; unfavorable=bar below; neutral=remainder.

[b]Classification code for Question 12: "More"=favorable; "less"=unfavorable; "different kind"=neutral.

Table 6-2. Percent Distribution of Answers Given in 1969 by Deputies and Referees[a] in Seventeen States to Selected Questions on Employer Participation in Administration, by State

Selected questions[b]		17 states combined	California	Maine	Massachusetts	Michigan	Mississippi	New York	Ohi
Totals— all respondents[e]		1,499	245	14	82	71	6	393	72
	Item								
(1) A	1	58.0	59.3	64.3	67.9	59.5	66.7	53.2	41.
	2	39.7	38.2	35.7	32.1	40.5	33.3	43.7	54.
	3	2.3	2.5	–	–	–	–	3.1	4.
(1) B	1	2.2	0.4	–	1.5	3.2	–	1.1	–
	2	33.7	28.8	35.7	32.4	41.9	20.0	31.8	42.
	3	64.1	70.8	64.3	66.1	54.9	80.0	67.1	57.
(2) A[f]	1	56.1	75.0	66.7	45.2	49.2	50.0	49.8	38.
	2	5.7	2.9	–	9.6	3.1	–	5.4	13.
	3	38.2	22.1	33.3	45.2	47.7	50.0	44.8	48.
(2) B[f]	1	55.6	77.6	72.7	65.8	61.3	50.0	42.7	37.
	2	9.8	3.0	–	6.8	4.8	–	11.0	18.
	3	34.6	19.4	27.3	27.4	33.9	50.0	46.3	43.
(2) C[f]	1	65.3	61.0	50.0	62.5	83.3	100.0	81.2	c
	2	8.3	14.6	–	12.5	–	–	–	c
	3	26.4	24.4	50.0	25.0	16.7	–	18.8	c
(3)	1	7.5	3.3	–	–	2.8	–	12.5	4.
	2	12.5	8.6	14.3	7.3	21.1	16.7	19.6	13.
	3	29.1	30.7	21.4	20.7	39.5	33.3	26.2	31.
	4	34.0	42.2	28.6	72.0	26.7	–	27.2	25.
	5	16.9	15.2	35.7	–	9.9	50.0	14.5	25.
(4)	1	44.7	44.7	50.0	42.6	45.8	83.3	43.0	33.
	2	22.3	20.4	35.8	25.6	25.7	16.7	19.8	13.
	3	26.3	24.2	7.1	28.1	17.1	–	34.0	48.
	4	6.7	10.7	7.1	3.7	11.4	–	3.2	4.
(5)	1	19.9	25.2	7.1	18.3	14.7	–	27.5	23.
	2	74.3	71.4	85.8	75.6	75.0	100.0	70.1	61.
	3	5.8	3.4	7.1	6.1	10.3	–	2.4	15.
(6)	1	25.5	17.6	35.7	23.2	18.5	33.3	38.2	31.
	2	50.4	66.5	64.3	56.0	60.0	50.0	33.0	42.
	3	24.1	15.9	–	20.8	21.5	16.7	28.8	26.
(9)	1	45.6	53.9	57.1	54.4	43.7	100.0	37.2	27.
	2	32.8	31.4	42.9	27.1	23.9	–	38.8	35.
	3	21.6	14.7	–	18.5	32.4	–	24.0	37.
(10)	1	3.2	2.5	7.1	1.2	5.6	16.7	3.1	2.
	2	9.4	9.1	7.1	7.5	22.5	–	10.7	12.
	3	36.2	31.8	21.5	49.4	40.9	–	41.0	30.
	4	27.3	33.5	14.3	–	18.3	50.0	25.5	37.
	5	23.9	23.1	50.0	41.9	12.7	33.3	19.7	16.
(11)[f]	1	8.3	9.8	–	12.5	–	–	–	c
	2	57.6	68.3	–	25.0	50.0	100.0	62.5	c
	3	34.1	21.9	100.0	62.5	50.0	–	37.5	c

[a]These are the combined answers of deputies and referees in each state. For the meaning of "deputy" and "referee," see Chapter 6.

[b]For the text of the questions, see Chapter 6.

[c]In Ohio, where referees did not participate, the responses were limited to deputies. Questions (2) and (11) apply only to referees.

Oregon	Pennsylvania	Texas	Utah	Virginia	Washington	Wisconsin	State A[d]	State B[d]	State C[d]
44	215	24	16	25	80	60	24	117	11
70.4	58.6	79.1	62.5	72.0	54.4	69.5	45.8	55.6	80.0
29.6	41.4	20.9	37.5	28.0	40.5	25.5	50.0	40.2	20.0
–	–	–	–	–	5.1	5.0	4.2	4.2	–
2.4	4.3	5.0	–	–	2.7	1.7	–	7.3	–
26.1	29.9	25.0	13.3	40.9	34.7	25.4	40.9	57.3	57.1
71.5	65.8	70.0	86.7	59.1	62.6	72.9	59.1	35.4	42.9
78.3	63.2	42.8	73.3	50.0	78.1	33.9	35.0	38.3	83.3
–	2.9	–	–	4.2	1.4	3.6	–	23.4	16.7
21.7	33.9	57.2	26.7	45.8	20.5	62.5	65.0	38.3	–
83.3	60.3	71.4	66.7	47.8	74.6	40.0	35.0	33.3	83.3
–	8.8	14.3	–	8.7	1.5	5.5	15.0	35.4	16.7
16.7	30.9	14.3	33.3	43.5	23.9	54.5	50.0	31.3	–
100.0	100.0	47.1	–	100.0	100.0	33.3	50.0	47.1	20.0
–	–	–	–	–	–	–	–	25.0	23.5	–
–	–	52.9	–	–	–	66.7	25.0	29.4	80.0
2.2	9.8	4.2	18.7	4.0	1.3	–	–	19.7	–
15.9	4.7	12.5	12.5	4.0	7.5	1.7	12.5	21.4	–
27.5	29.7	25.0	31.3	20.0	31.2	26.7	25.0	32.5	63.6
36.3	29.3	45.8	37.5	32.0	37.5	53.3	33.3	16.2	36.4
18.1	26.5	12.5	–	40.0	22.5	18.3	29.2	10.2	–
22.7	55.8	45.8	50.0	72.0	56.3	45.0	47.8	28.2	36.4
40.9	17.7	29.2	31.3	20.0	20.0	33.3	30.4	29.1	–
25.0	23.7	16.7	–	8.0	13.7	13.3	21.8	26.5	63.6
11.4	2.8	8.3	18.7	–	10.0	8.4	–	16.2	–
9.1	7.9	4.2	6.3	4.0	5.1	10.2	–	40.9	27.3
79.5	89.3	87.5	93.7	84.0	86.1	88.1	–	44.3	63.6
11.4	2.8	8.3	–	12.0	8.8	1.7	–	14.8	9.1
4.7	35.4	8.3	28.6	4.3	17.8	3.4	13.6	18.8	9.0
67.4	51.8	62.5	50.0	82.6	49.3	57.6	63.7	45.3	45.5
27.9	12.8	29.2	21.4	13.1	32.9	39.0	22.7	35.9	45.5
54.6	42.5	70.8	18.8	28.0	36.8	50.0	75.0	59.0	72.7
27.2	30.2	29.2	31.2	56.0	38.2	31.7	20.8	26.5	18.2
18.2	27.3	–	50.0	16.0	25.0	18.3	4.2	14.5	9.1
2.3	4.2	12.5	–	4.0	–	3.3	4.2	3.4	–
11.4	6.0	8.3	–	8.0	12.8	1.7	4.2	8.5	18.2
27.2	39.5	8.3	43.8	40.0	24.4	31.7	37.5	33.3	45.4
40.9	27.0	33.4	31.2	20.0	29.5	38.3	25.0	27.4	18.2
18.2	23.3	37.5	25.0	28.0	33.3	25.0	29.1	27.4	18.2
–	50.0	11.8	100.0	–	–	–	–	5.9	–
57.1	37.5	64.7	–	–	66.7	33.3	50.0	52.9	60.0
42.9	12.5	23.5	–	100.0	33.3	66.7	50.0	41.2	40.0

[d]States A, B, and C preferred not to be identified.

[e]Where some of the respondents failed to check any choice of a given question, the percent distribution has been based on the actual number of answers. For four of the larger states, the deputies whose opinions were requested were limited to a sample. The totals shown in the table represent inflated figures.

[f]Questions (2) A and (2) B were limited to deputies. Questions (2) C and (11) were limited to referees.

their definition of "hindered" to include situations where employers had failed to supply sufficient information on the forms they had submitted and thus had made it necessary for the deputy to write or phone them. The employer had simply scribbled, for example, "quit" or "discharged" on the form. What was really wanted in these cases was more, not less, employer participation. An additional indication of that is to be seen in the answers given to questions 2 and 12, where fewer than 10 percent and 5 percent, respectively, of the respondents said that they wanted less employer participation.

For another example, in question 12 respondents who said they wanted a "different kind" of employer participation nearly always explained, when interviewed, that they wanted the employer to be better informed on the law, to supply fuller details on quits and discharges, to bring "percipient" witnesses (those who could speak from first-hand knowledge) to hearings, and so forth. Since the "difference" they wanted really amounted to more effective employer participation, their responses might have been classified as favorable to employer participation; but actually they were classified as neutral. Thus, to the extent that there is bias in the classification code, it is in the direction of minimizing the favorable vote and maximizing the unfavorable vote.

Despite this bias, the general impact of the responses is clearly favorable to employer participation. Speaking out of a situation in which experience rating was operative, an overwhelming majority of these respondents nevertheless considered employer participation as helpful to their task of administering the unemployment insurance law. The 13,067 answers received from 1,499 respondents showed the following distribution:

	Percent
Favorable to employer participation	74.0
Unfavorable to employer participation	15.0
Neutral	11.0

It should be noted that these percentages do not refer to employer actions nor to the number of respondents, but only to the number of responses.[18] It would not be correct, for example, to say that 15 percent of employer actions were judged unfavorably, nor that 15 percent of the respondents passed an unfavorable judgment on employers. The correct statement is that 15 percent of all the answers received represented an unfavorable judgment. When presented with the opportunity to disapprove of employer actions, the deputies and referees did so 15 percent of the time. On the other hand, when presented with the opportunity to express approval of employer actions, they did so 74 percent of the time.

18. In the calculation of average distributions for the survey as a whole, and for the respective states, all responses were treated as having equal importance, because no practical scheme could be devised for assigning weights. This limitation should be kept in mind in interpreting the averages.

In the judgment of the program's deputies and referees, the gains from employer participation clearly outweighed the losses. If this judgment is correct, and if the original assumption is also correct—that experience rating promotes employer participation—then it would seem that the effect of experience rating on administration, as experience rating was operative at the time of the questionnaire, should be entered on the plus side when making up the balance sheet of its desirable and undesirable effects.

As may be seen from Table 6-3, the sample was marked by a strong central tendency among the states. All but six states returned favorable verdicts that fell

Table 6-3. Percent Distribution of Answers Given in 1969
by Deputies and Referees in Seventeen States,
Indicating Favorable, Unfavorable, and Neutral Opinion
of Employer Participation in Administration

State	Favorable to employer participation	Unfavorable to employer participation	Neutral
Average distribution—17 states	74.0	15.0	11.0
California	76.3	11.9	11.8
Maine	86.3	8.1	5.6
Massachusetts	77.3	11.5	11.2
Michigan	72.1	15.3	12.6
Mississippi	83.0	7.5	9.5
New York	71.2	17.4	11.4
Ohio	69.8	18.8	11.4
Oregon	79.7	10.8	9.5
Pennsylvania	79.7	10.3	10.0
Texas	74.8	12.4	12.8
Utah	82.3	7.8	9.9
Virginia	80.8	9.6	9.6
Washington	79.7	11.2	9.1
Wisconsin	80.2	11.0	8.8
State A	74.3	13.9	11.8
State B	55.3	32.6	12.1
State C	63.8	16.0	20.2

Note: For key to how answers were classified, see Table 6-1.

within the (rounded) 70-80 percent bracket, and all but seven states returned unfavorable verdicts that fell within the (rounded) 10-15 percent bracket. State B showed the lowest proportion of favorable answers (55.3 percent), while Maine had the highest proportion (86.3 percent).

Among the seventeen states cooperating in the study were three (Mississippi, Oregon, Texas) operating under a straight benefit-ratio experience-rating plan.[19]

19. One of these, Texas, had changed from a benefit-wage-ratio plan to a benefit-ratio plan two years before the survey was made.

Favorable answers from each of these states averaged higher than those coming from the nine reserve-ratio states. This was also true of Pennsylvania, whose formula is described as a "benefit-ratio plan that uses the reserve ratio as one of its factors." The two states (Washington and Utah) using the payroll-decline plan also showed favorable percentages well above the seventeen-state average.

It will be noted that the states varied widely in the distribution between "unfavorable" answers and those classified as "neutral." In the case of state C, for example, although it produced a favorable rating significantly below average, it produced an unfavorable rating that was just about average; the explanation lay in the unusually high proportion of answers coded "neutral." Here, especially, interviews with the respondents might have resulted in a reduction of the "neutral" figure, with a corresponding increase in the "favorable" category.

The only states whose ratio of unfavorable answers was noticeably higher than the average of 15 percent were Ohio (18.8 percent) and state B (32.6 percent). The combined answers of these two states made up about one-fourth of all the unfavorable responses. The current Ohio situation was not investigated, but it was once similar to that in state B described below. The memory of that past situation may be part of the explanation for Ohio's present responses, which were submitted by long-term employees.

State B. The higher proportion of unfavorable comments in state B stemmed from the practice of some firms of frequently appealing cases on the ground of nonavailability for work. This practice, which began to develop about 1960, was facilitated in state B by four circumstances: (1) The state furnished each employer a current listing of claimants whose benefits were being charged against that employer. (2) This notice of liability for charges was considered a "determination" made by the state, and as such it could be appealed. (3) The employer's simple statement that in his judgment the claimant was unavailable was sufficient to halt the payment of benefits until a hearing had been held on the appeal. (4) A court decision in the early years of the program had placed the burden of proof of availability on the claimant.

Somewhat similar practices once existed in Ohio and Massachusetts. In Ohio the practice began to develop about 1951–52 and was based on the same four circumstances listed above for state B. In 1963 Ohio amended its law to provide that the charge-back notice furnished by the state did not constitute a "determination" that could be appealed; that any employer who challenged a claimant's continued eligibility must support the challenge with "specific facts"; and that the failure of a claimant to appear at the hearing held on an employer's appeal did not of itself preclude a decision in the claimant's favor. Thereafter the practice, which had been restricted to one service company and a handful of individual firms, virtually disappeared.

In Massachusetts a similar practice began about 1957, when one service company (the same one as in Ohio) and a few individual firms began to challenge nearly all claims automatically on the basis of nonavailability, even when the immediate cause of the unemployment was a layoff for lack of work. At first, the state handled these protests as it did all others. That is, if it decided that the claimant was eligible it sent the protesting employer a notice to that effect. This notice could then be appealed, and as a matter of fact such notices were appealed in large numbers. The number of disputed claims and appeals accumulated to a point where they threatened to disrupt the administrative process. The state thereupon made an administrative ruling that an allegation of claimant unavailability, if unaccompanied by positive evidence of such unavailability, would not lead to a nonmonetary determination and would not provide the basis for an appeal.[20] Thereafter the practice disappeared. Thus Massachusetts accomplished by an administrative ruling what Ohio accomplished by a legislative amendment.

In state B, also, the practice was largely confined to one service company (not the same one as in Ohio and Massachusetts) and a half-dozen individual firms. In practically all cases, the firms involved were marked by high turnover rates. Interviews with the service company and with two of the firms elicited statements that they used the practice on a selective basis. They appealed only those kinds of claims which experience had demonstrated to be doubtful. An agency check on the "win" record of these firms in this kind of appeal supported their statements: The proportion of nonavailability appeals won by these appellants was about the same as the average of wins in other types of appeals by these firms and by firms generally.

The deputies and referees who criticized the practice did so on two scores. The first was the inevitable delay that occurred in the payment of benefits, even when the appeal was lost and the claim was upheld. This delay could easily amount to a month or more. The second was the possibility that the claimant would not appear at the hearing held on the appeal—perhaps because by that time he was again employed and could not take time off from his new job—and would therefore probably lose the case, since he would not have proved his availability. The agency made some provision for this contingency by allowing the claimant to come to the office on a Saturday and put his testimony on a tape. The agency also followed a liberal policy in accepting proof of availability. Usually the claimant needed only to indicate that he had applied for some work at two or three firms in the recent past. Nonetheless, there were some claimants who never responded to the notice of the hearing, but simply abandoned their claims. Whether this abandonment of the claim stemmed from an unwillingness

20. Regulation No. 30-2 (8)a reads: "A timely return by a most recent employing unit or other person of a notice of claim filed with a statement merely questioning the claimant's eligibility under the provisions of Section 24(b) of this chapter shall nevertheless bar such employing unit or other person from being a party to further proceedings relating to the allowance of the claim unless such statement so furnished is supported by factual information."

to risk a current job by taking time off for the hearing, or was an admission of nonavailability, or was a reflection of the fear and uncertainty with which some uneducated persons view the judicial process, could not be ascertained.

Other service companies and other individual firms in state B disapproved of this practice of appealing on the basis of nonavailability. They felt that the practice gave employers generally a bad image. In defense, the employers who followed the practice said that the nonavailability of claimants was more of a problem for them than for the average firm, and cited their record (their disqualification ratio) as proof that they were not appealing cases indiscriminately.

A 1971 decision of the U.S. Supreme Court in what has become known as the "*Java* case" [104] forbade the suspension of benefit payments during the interval between an employer's appeal and the state's decision on the appeal. While it is too early at present writing (1971) to discern the exact impact of the Java case on the various state laws, the practice under discussion here will be at least greatly diminished and probably will be virtually eliminated.

Questions and Answers

The following section shows the specific questions asked of the respondents, along with their answers to each question. The answers appear as a percentage distribution of seventeen-state totals for deputies, for referees, and for all respondents combined. Unless otherwise specified, comments refer to the combined responses of deputies and referees. (For individual states, these combined answers are shown in Table 6-2.)

Question (1) *You may have found that to some degree employer participation has helped you in your task of administering the unemployment insurance law but that, to some degree, also, it has hindered you. Indicate the statement in each list below which describes your experience.*

	Deputies	Referees	Combined
A. Helped:			
1. Greatly	57.1	66.7	58.0
2. Moderately	40.9	28.4	39.7
3. Insignificantly	2.0	4.9	2.3
B. Hindered:			
1. Greatly	2.1	2.5	2.2
2. Moderately	35.2	19.2	33.7
3. Insignificantly	62.7	78.3	64.1

Question (2) *Would your experience lead you to desire more, or less, or the same degree of employer participation in each of the following:*

	Deputies	Referees*
A. In protesting new claims:		
1. More	56.1	
2. Less	5.7	
3. Same	38.2	
B. In protesting additional initial claims:		
1. More	55.6	
2. Less	9.8	
3. Same	34.6	

Question (2)C. *Would your experience lead you to desire more, or less or the same degree of employer participation in appealing determinations?*

	Deputies	Referees
1. More		65.3
2. Less		8.3
3. Same		26.4

*Deputies answered (2)A and B. Referees answered (2)C.

Question (1) invites the respondents to express themselves in the most general fashion with respect to employer participation. In answering, most respondents chose the extreme favorable positions "helped greatly" (58 percent) and "hindered insignificantly" (64.1 percent). A miniscule proportion chose the extreme unfavorable positions, "helped insignificantly' (2.3 percent) and "hindered greatly" (2.2 percent).

Questions (1) and (2) are closely related. It was to be expected, therefore, that, overall, respondents who had been helped greatly or moderately by employer participation would represent about the same proportions as those who wanted more or about the same degree of employer participation as they were currently experiencing. The relatively few who indicated that they had been "hindered greatly" by employer participation were matched by the relatively few who desired less of it. Thus the answers to these two general questions lean heavily on the side of favoring employer participation.

The responses show considerable variation as between one state and another (Table 6-2). The differences are especially notable in the distribution between "helped greatly" and "helped moderately" and also the distribution between "hindered moderately" and "hindered insignificantly." Since the terms "greatly," "moderately," and "insignificantly" were purposely left without definition, it was not to be expected that all respondents would have had the same meaning in mind when they selected the item to be checked. Hence, in viewing the percent distributions for the respective states, it is helpful to view the two major items in combination as well as separately.

In each of the seventeen states, 95 percent of the respondents had been helped either greatly or moderately by the employer participation they had experienced. Similarly, in sixteen states (state B being the exception), 95 percent or more indicated that hindrance attributable to employer participation had been "moderate" or "insignificant."

Generally speaking, the referees regarded employer participation more favorably than did the deputies. The referees tended to cluster even more than the deputies at the two extreme positions: "helped greatly" (66.7 percent) and "hindered insignificantly" (78.3 percent). Again, the notable exception was state B, where the corresponding referee percentages were only 29.4 and 58.3. In that state, where 6.1 percent of the deputies responded "hindered greatly," 16.7 percent of the referees returned this answer. The explanation of the difference probably lies in the nature of the practice which was causing the friction. This practice, discussed above, affected appeals more than it did first-stage protests.

In both of the states in the sample that did not have a charge-back experience-rating system (Utah and Washington) greater-than-average percentages said they wanted more employer participation (question 2, Table 6-2). It is relevant to note that the frequency of employer appeals in both these states is below the national average (see Table 8-7)).

Question (3) *Where the employer has protested [appealed] a claim which you find, nevertheless, to be an allowable claim, how often is the protest [appeal] completely unfounded and, in the legal sense, frivolous?*

	Deputies	Referees	Combined
1. Very often (say in 15%-20% of such disputed claims) [appeals]	7.8	5.6	7.5
2. Often (say in 10%-15% of such disputed claims) [appeals]	12.4	13.2	12.5
3. Sometimes (say in 5%-10% of such disputed claims) [appeals]	28.6	33.3	29.1
4. Seldom (say in less than 5% of such disputed claims) [appeals]	34.3	30.6	34.0
5. Rarely (say in less than 2% of such disputed claims) [appeals]	16.9	17.3	16.9

Question (4) *To the extent that employers have entered such unfounded protests [appeals], have these instances been*

	Deputies	Referees	Combined
1. Scattered among employers generally?	44.5	46.1	44.7
2. Confined to isolated firms?	21.6	29.1	22.3
3. More prevalent among firms which employ a service company?	26.9	20.6	26.3
4. More prevalent among firms in a particular industry? Specify.	7.0	4.2	6.7

Question (5) *In a few states, employers have been required to post a sum of money with each first-stage or second-stage appeal they file. The purpose would seem to be to discourage the filing of unfounded appeals. Do you believe your state should have such a provision?*

	Deputies	Referees	Combined
1. Yes	19.8	20.9	19.9
2. No.	74.7	70.5	74.3
3. Don't know	5.5	8.6	5.8

Questions (3), (4), and (5) all have a bearing on the allegation that employer participation often represents an attempt to deprive a claimant of benefits to which he is obviously entitled, or to harass him in one way or another, by filing "frivolous" (unfounded) objections to the allowance of his claim.

The meaning of "frivolous" was intentionally left general, so as to give the fullest opportunity for any expression of dissatisfaction. Interviews revealed that deputies and referees commonly did not restrict the term to malicious actions, but also included protests and appeals filed in ignorance of the law—that is, protests and appeals that were objectively, though not necessarily subjectively, frivolous.[21]

In the interpretation of the replies to question (3), there may again be some guidance in the related answer from question (12). For example, in New York, where 32.1 percent said that frivolous claims occurred very often or often (question [3]), only 1.2 percent said that they wanted less employer participation (question [12]). Hence, one would be inclined to judge that whatever the interpretation of that 32.1 percent is, the state probably did not have a serious problem in this area. By contrast, in state B, where we know there was a

---

21. The situation mentioned most frequently was the following: A claimant files for benefits but is disqualified, and no benefit year is set up. The claimant requalifies and a benefit year is established. At this point the employer is notified. Out of ignorance he then protests the claim—but uselessly, since the original disqualification has been purged. Some states could remedy this situation by improving the forms they send to employers.

problem, 44.9 percent of the respondents in question (12) voted for less employer participation.

Question (3) raised the problem of "frivolous" employer objections in terms of their relation to all claims protested or appealed by the employer. This would be the only basis available to these respondents, since they did not come in contact with claims which were not disputed. As a measure, however, of the extent and importance of "frivolous" employer objections, a more appropriate base would be the entire population of claimants. The central question is: What proportion of *all* claimants are affected by frivolous objections raised by employers?

This proportion may be estimated for Massachusetts with the aid of data drawn from Chapter 7. These data show that Massachusetts employers tend to dispute about 9 percent of all initial claims. In the opinion of most of the respondents from that state (92.7 percent), frivolous objections accounted for less than 10 percent of the total objections raised by employers; most respondents felt that they accounted for less than 5 percent. When these percents are applied to the total initial claims filed, frivolous protests, even broadly defined, apparently affect less than 1 percent of all claimants. This conclusion is supported by additional data presented in Chapter 7.

About 45 percent of the respondents believed that frivolous protests (to the extent that they occurred) were scattered among employers generally; 22 percent believed them to be confined to isolated firms. About one-quarter of the deputies were of the opinion that unfounded protests were more prevalent where a service company was involved. Relatively fewer of the referees indicated that opinion—perhaps because the service company, which is usually well informed with respect to the technicalities of the law and is in business to make a profit, will seldom initiate the expensive appeals process unless it has some grounds for hoping for a favorable decision. A full discussion of service companies is to be found in Chapter 8.

In answers to question (5), nearly three-quarters (74.3 percent) said that they would not like their state to have a provision requiring employers to post a sum of money with each appeal filed. Where nationally (seventeen-state average) only 19.9 percent expressed approval of such a provision, in state B the proportion was 40.9 percent. Neither in state B nor nationally was there a significant difference between deputies and referees in their answers to this question.

Of the states in the sample, only three had had any experience with such a provision. Pennsylvania operated under such a provision during the brief period 1949–51 and New York during the longer period 1951–59. State A had enacted the provision some years earlier and it was still in effect at the time the survey was made.[22]

---

22. The respondents from state A were asked whether they thought that the provision had accomplished its intended purpose (presumably the discouragement of needless em-

Question (6) *Where the employer does not participate directly, is his participation through a service company an acceptable substitute?*

	Deputies	Referees	Combined
1. Yes, just as good	27.1	11.8	25.5
2. Better than no participation	49.4	59.0	50.4
3. No	23.5	29.2	24.1

In their answers to this question, about one-quarter (25.5 percent) definitely approved of service companies, while another quarter (24.1 percent) definitely did not. Thus, at least three-quarters of the respondents gave a guarded vote of approval to service companies; but three-quarters, also, preferred to deal directly with employers.[23] In the interviews, the most frequent reason advanced for preferring direct employer participation was the inconvenience and loss of time involved in dealing with an intermediary. This objection was especially likely to be voiced when the service company was at a considerable distance, sometimes clear across the country.

The interviews also revealed that the third choice presented by this question was misunderstood by some of the respondents. The third choice was supposed to mean: "If I had to choose between no employer participation at all, or participation through a service company, I should prefer no participation at all." But some understood it to mean simply that participation through a service company was not as good as participation by the employer himself. In other words, they understood the third choice as a denial of the first choice only and not, as it was intended to be, a denial also of the second choice.[24] Such respondents should probably have checked the second choice. Hence the significance of the "no" answers to this question is clouded.[25]

The referees viewed participation through a service company less favorably than did the deputies. Only 11.8 percent of the referees considered service companies "just as good." However, 70.8 percent of the referees found service companies at least an acceptable substitute.

---

ployer appeals), and 95 percent of them answered "yes." Their answer to this question was consistent with their answer to Question (3), where more than 62 percent of them expressed the opinion that unfounded protests and appeals occurred "seldom" or "rarely" in state A, as compared with 50.9 percent for the average state in the survey.

23. A special compilation was made of the answers received from the deputies and referees of four states (California, New York, Ohio, and Pennsylvania) in which service companies were most numerous and active. The respondents in these states would have had more than average experience with such companies. The general impression conveyed by this more significant part of the sample was about the same, or perhaps a little more favorable, than that conveyed by the seventeen-state averages.

24. For example, see the responses of the referees in state C, discussed below.

25. In the compilation of Table 6–3, however, these answers were taken at their face value and all were coded "unfavorable," in accordance with the conservative bias explained earlier.

Question (7) *Employer participation is much less in some industries than in others. Check any industries in which, in your experience, employer participation is notably lacking—relative to the claim load from that industry.*

1. Agriculture, forestry, fishing
2. Mining
3. Construction
4. Transportation, communications, public utilities
5. Wholesale and retail trade
6. Finance, insurance, real estate
7. Services
8. Manufacturing

Question (8) *This is a contunuation of the previous question. Check any of these subdivisions of manufacturing in which, in your experience, employer participation is notably lacking—relative to the claim load from that industry.*

1. Primary metals
2. Lumber and wood products except furniture
3. Textiles
4. Apparel
5. Printing and publishing
6. Leather products'
7. Other (specify)

These two questions had been included in the questionnaires for the purpose of pin-pointing industries in which employer participation in administration had been noticeably lacking. However, interviews revealed that the respondents had only a general idea of the respective claim loads coming from the various industries, hence, their answers were at best only vague impressions of the situations they were describing. Very many did not even attempt to answer this question. For this reason it was decided to omit the percentage distributions of the replies to this question lest there be conveyed a false impression of mathematical accuracy.

Well over half of the respondents mentioned the construction industry as one in which there was a dearth of employer participation. No other industry was mentioned nearly as often, but among the more frequently mentioned were agriculture, services, lumber and wood products, and apparel manufacturing. In his answer to Question (12) one respondent commented: "Some employers in apparel manufacturing will not protest claims and risk having sewing machine operators leave them to work for another manufacturer."

In interviews, deputies observed that in the construction industry the great majority of separations were layoffs, that referrals to jobs were controlled by the unions rather than by the employment service, that wages were very much higher than benefits, and that many construction firms were paying the maximum tax rate. The first three characteristics reduced either the need or the opportunity for employer participation and the fourth reduced employer motivation to participate. In interviews the deputies stressed the first three factors much more than the fourth. However, they were aware that in some situations the fourth factor was also operative. (See the history of company C in Chapter 8.)

Question (9) *In your judgment, if the unemployment insurance tax rate were uniform instead of experience-rated, would employers file fewer objections [appeals]?*

	Deputies	Referees	Combined
1. Many fewer	42.8	72.2	45.6
2. Somewhat fewer	33.7	24.3	32.8
3. No significant difference	23.5	3.5	21.6

Answers to this question are matters of conjecture to a greater extent than are answers to the other questions. But because the respondents were in such close and constant touch with employers—day after day, year after year—it seemed worth while to ask their opinion on employer motivation.[26] A little less than half (45.6 percent) of all the respondents thought that experience rating had a considerable effect on employer participation. But there was a marked difference between the answers of the deputies and those of the referees. Where 42.8 percent of the deputies thought that without experience rating employers would file "many fewer" protests, 72.2 percent of the referees were of this opinion. The difference is plausible: To file an appeal entails much more effort and expense than to make the original protest and hence it requires more motivation.

Only about one-fifth (21.6 percent) of all respondents felt that experience rating has no significant effect. Here again there was a marked difference between deputies and referees: this was the opinion of 23.5 percent of the deputies but only 3.5 percent of the referees.

One would have expected all respondents to have given this answer—that a uniform tax would make no significant difference—in the two states (Utah and Washington) that did not have a chargeback system of experience rating. In these states an employer's tax rate was not directly influenced by his protests of appeals, and hence an employer's participation in administration would remain essentially the same under the uniform tax system as under such an experience-rating system. But in these two states, instead of the expected 100 percent, only 50 percent in Utah and 25 percent in Washington chose number 3. It is possible

---

26. Note that the question is phrased in quantitative terms only and does not attempt to distinguish between desirable and undesirable forms of employer participation.

that the question was misunderstood by some of the respondents. Interviews with a sample of deputies in Utah disclosed that some of the respondents assumed that "experience rating" in the context of this question meant a charge-back system and they answered in terms of that assumption rather than in terms of the system actually operative in their own state. It was not possible to check the Washington responses by holding similar interviews.

In Ohio 37.2 percent of the deputies answered "no significant difference." This was the highest proportion returned by any state, except Utah. An analysis of the respondents constituting this 37.2 percent showed that none was from a large office, but that otherwise they did not seem to differ from their fellows.

However, their answer here was inconsistent with the answer some of them gave to Question (12). For example, one of them remarked that "employers who use a service company seem to participate the most" and several others were emphatic in their wish for less participation by service companies. Since such firms owe their existence entirely to experience rating, these answers would seem to imply a recognition of the relationship between participation and experience rating. One of these respondents complained that employers do not appear at the hearings of claimant appeals if their rate is not affected, while another noted regretfully that employers were becoming too aware of the relationship between their protesting activity and their tax rates. Both comments, while reflecting opposite values, recognized the relationship between participation and tax rates. If answers showing such inconsistencies were removed from the total, the average in Ohio would closely approximate the national average of 23.5 percent.

Many respondents added comments, in Question (12), on the relationship between experience rating and employer participation. According to a Wisconsin deputy: "Employers participate by reporting only to the extent required by law, and it is abruptly pointed out by employers that reporting to government agencies is not a part of the business which is likely to produce a profit, but is a cost item for which the employer gets no return." A New York referee observed: "Employers in seasonal industries, such as apparel and construction, whose tax rate already is at the highest level allowed under law, often do not bother to show up at hearings." Some of the older respondents recalled the reconversion period of 1945–47, when unemployment benefits were available for the returning veterans under the Servicemen's Readjustment Act, whose costs were borne entirely by the federal government out of general revenues. Employers participated relatively little in the administration of this program: they often failed to send in any separation information at all; what reports they did submit were often late and incomplete; when urged to pay more attention to these claims, employers tended to reply that it was not their responsibility.[27]

27. Lack of employer participation in administration may be one reason why the proportion of improper payments was notably higher in the veterans' program of readjustment allowances than in the regular unemployment insurance program [102, passim].

Question (10) *It may happen that the employer involved in a dispute makes it difficult for you to ascertain all the relevant facts. In your experience, how often does this occur?*

	Deputies	Referees	Combined
1. Very often (say in 15%–20% of all disputes)	3.3	2.8	3.2
2. Often (say in 10%–15% of all disputes)	9.9	5.6	9.4
3. Sometimes (say in 5%–10% of all disputes)	38.1	17.4	36.2
4. Seldom (say in less than 5% of all disputes)	27.1	29.2	27.3
5. Rarely (say in less than 2% of all disputes)	21.6	45.0	23.9

This question is a cousin to Question (3) and inquires after another, milder, form of obstruction. Like Question (3), this is not a sharply focused inquiry. It was purposely left vague so as to leave the maximum opening for the expression of any dissatisfaction. About half (51.2 percent) of all respondents reported that this form of obstruction occurred "seldom" or "rarely." About three-quarters (74.2 percent) of the referees gave this answer as contrasted with 48.7 percent of the deputies. Only 12.6 percent reported that this occurred "very often" or "often." (The answer, "very often" was returned by 3.3 percent of the deputies and 2.8 percent of the referees.) Interviews revealed that some of the respondents gave a wide interpretation to "makes it difficult for you." They included even situations of nonparticipation—as when the employer would reply, when contacted over the telephone, that he was too busy to be bothered. Although it is doubtful that such respondents were opposed to employer participation, in accord with the bias explained earlier, their answers were coded "unfavorable" in Table 6–3.

Question (11) *Employers sometimes appeal a determination and then fail to appear at the hearing. In your experience, how often does this occur?*

	Deputies	Referees	Combined
1. Frequently		8.3	
2. Occasionally		57.6	
3. Rarely		34.1	

This question, answered only by referees, was directed to a particular form of irresponsible employer behavior. (For a fuller discussion of this, probably the most objectionable practice connected with employer participation in administration, see Chapter 8, pages 202-3). Only 8.3 percent of the respondents answered "frequently" and these were concentrated in five states (Table 6-2). On the other hand, 34.1 percent chose the other extreme position of "rarely," and these were scattered over all but two states. Because they were not defined in any way, for example by percentages, the three choices cannot be assigned exact meanings. They convey information only about general attitudes. However, for a few of the states included in the sample it is possible to connect some scattered data with these expressed attitudes. The data are given in Chapter 8, in the end of the discussion of employer appeals.

Question (12) *In general would your experience during this five-year period lead you to desire more, or less, or a different kind of employer participation? (Explain)*

Question (13) *In your total experience, have there been any changes in employer participation over the years? (Explain)*

These two questions were of the essay type and allowed the respondent a maximum degree of freedom. As a result, although the answers to these questions were very interesting, they were more difficult to summarize.

In Question (12), only 4.8 percent of all respondents expressed a wish for less employer participation, and even this low proportion chiefly reflected the answers of one state (state B), where the proportion was 44.9 percent. On the other hand, over half (57.5 percent) wanted more employer participation,[28] while 15.1 percent generally expressed their satisfaction with the existing situation.

The most frequently expressed desires for changes in employer participation were that employers would provide more detailed information in their original protests, that they would appear at the hearings initiated by claimants, and that they would bring to all hearings, whether initiated by themselves or by claimants, "percipient witnesses" that is, those persons who could give first-hand testimony regarding the issues involved in the appeal. The following quotations, the first from a referee and the second from a deputy, are typical.

> The timekeeper, payroll clerk or personnel manager with hearsay testimony is a poor substitue for the lead-man, foreman, superintendent—or fellow employee—who saw and heard and took part in what happened that culminated with the filing of the claim and the appeal.
>
> Current method of participation is satisfactory to accomplish desired purposes. However, terse one-word, or one-phrase replies to claims filed,

---

28. This proportion was 73 percent in Utah and 81 percent in Washington, states which did not have a charge-back experience-rating system.

such as "Fired," "Quit," "Fired for misconduct," "Unable to do job," and like replies require time-consuming correspondence or unnecessary toll telephone calls to determine facts of case. I should like to see more detailed information provided, including, if discharged, (1) why, (2) specific employer rules violated, (3) whether or not claimant had prior warnings, (4) if violation were other than an isolated single instance. In the case of voluntary quitting, employers should provide information from their records, if available, as to reasons why claimant quit, if known. In addition it would make my task of arriving at a fair and impartial decision easier if employers would indicate the supporting evidence they have in their files, i.e., voluntary quit on medical advice of Dr. A. B. Blank (address). Did not request available sick leave in lieu of quitting.

It is a not uncommon practice of some firms and service companies to supply a minimum amount of information in making the initial protest because in most cases no more is needed. If the protest is overruled and the employer decides to appeal, he then begins to prepare his case in earnest. The wish expressed by many deputies and referees that the employer would supply more adequate information at the very beginning may be helped on to fulfillment in the 1971 *Java* decision of the U.S. Supreme Court [104]. Since, according to that decision, a claimant's benefits are no longer suspended by an employer's appeal, the employer is under a new incentive to try to win his case before the deputy, rather than wait until it comes before the referee.

One frequently repeated complaint of deputies was that employers often did not appear at hearings of appeals initiated by claimants. The referee had to balance testimony given under oath (the claimant's) against hearsay evidence (the employer's).[29] The result was sometimes a reversal of the deputy. Referees who were interviewed about this complaint of the deputies said that reversals sometimes did occur in this way, especially where the decision depended on the exact details of the quit or discharge, but they added that usually the referee was guided by the testimony gathered previously by the deputy and would so question the claimant at the hearing as to ascertain the true state of affairs, even in the absence of the employer. However, the referees expressed the wish even more frequently than did the deputies that the employer would attend the hearings on claimant appeals.[30]

A deputy from Pennsylvania voiced a common complaint when he said: "In many cases employers desire that benefits be denied but do not want the claimant to think that their information had anything to do with the disqualification." A Virginia deputy added the explanation: "It would be helpful if the

29. In most states the hearing is de novo, and the referee's decision is made on the basis only of evidence submitted at the hearing.
30. Since claimant appeals are much more numerous than employer appeals (Table 8-7), appearances at such hearings would represent a sizable burden, especially for the small employer. The assumption of this task is one of the main selling points of service companies.

employer would give the worker the real reason for terminating the worker. In some cases this situation proves to be a real problem. For example, the worker is told 'Don't need you any more,' but the employer tells the deputy 'Fired for drinking on job.'" Some of the referees remarked that if employers would give the full story at the time of the original determination, many appeals could be avoided.

In answer to Question (13), about one-quarter (26.4 percent) of all respondents reported no significant changes, while 1.7 percent—nearly all of them in one state, (state B)—thought a change for the worse had occurred. The rest (about 72 percent) felt that employer participation had increased and improved. Among these latter were 17.7 percent who mentioned a growth in employer awareness of experience rating and 12.2 percent who reported a marked growth in service companies. This general picture of increased and improved employer participation was somewhat more evident in the answers of the referees than in those of the deputies. A Michigan referee summed up the historical change thus: "Younger personnel or labor-relations representatives are more alert, better educated, less contentious, prone to present pertinent original records for inspection by a referee, with copies available for substitution as exhibits, and less apt to state 'the law is not fair' or 'the employer doesn't have a chance.' They are cooperative in arranging for presence of witnesses who have personal knowledge of incidents that resulted in discharge etc., and less apt to take the position that the employer's statements should not be doubted or questioned."

In their answers to the open-end Questions (12) and (13), many respondents commented on the inherent dilemma of the situation. They were convinced that to elicit adequate employer participation it is necessary to employ the tax incentive, but they also perceived that some of the participation elicited by this method was of an undesirable nature. They recognized that to increase employer participation by means of experience rating is to increase both the desirable and the undesirable forms of participation. According to a California referee: "Employer participation results primarily from experience rating interest. Often because of this there is an attempt to confuse or to hide the true facts. I don't know how to achieve better participation. If experience rating were not present, then there would be less interest and less participation." However, in balancing the gains and losses of increased employer participation through experience rating, the great majority of them chose increased employer participation. Typical is the following comment of a New York referee. "As an original proposition I could doubt the overriding value of employer participation; its existence, at least *a priori*, could convert the hearing process into a purely adversay proceeding between claimant and the employer, with the referee looking on as an arbiter. *My experience does not lend extensive support to this possibility.* I have come to value employer participation as an adjunct to a claims investigation which is all too frequently lacking in depth." It is clear that in general the deputies and referees of the country do not see "too much" employer participation as a major problem. They desire to maintain at least as much employer participation as there has been in the past; moreover, the increase in employer participation that has marked the recent past is viewed by them as a good development which they would like to see prolonged into the future.

Differences in Answers by Size of Office

When answers were classified by the size of office from which they came, the smaller offices showed more approval of employer participation than did the larger offices. This difference was small but consistent. Thus 58.4 percent of the smaller offices reported that employer participation had helped them greatly, as compared with 56.3 percent in the large offices. Where 3.1 percent in the large offices reported that employer participation had hindered them greatly, only 1.9 percent gave this answer in the small offices. Where 64.8 percent in the large offices were opposed to charging the employer an appeal fee (Question [5]) in the smaller offices this figure was 77.4 percent. In Question (12), where 11.9 percent of the respondents in the large offices wanted less employer participation, only 2.8 percent returned this answer in the small offices. The answers to the other questions showed a similar pattern.

It may be that the deputies and referees in the small offices are known by the employers personally and are influenced by them. Against this possibility is a generally recognized situation that it is more difficult to disqualify a claimant in a small town than in a large city. The desire of the smaller offices for more employer participation may reflect an often repeated statement of the deputies that employers in small towns, hesitant to incur the odium of their neighbors, wish the local office to take the whole initiative in imposing a disqualification.

Employer
Participation in
Administration II:
Massachusetts
Experience

Introduction

This chapter is concerned with the same two fundamental questions that occupied Chapter 6: (1) What is the extent of employer participation in the administrative process? (2) Is this participation desirable? To avoid getting lost amid the multifarious details of the chapter, the reader may find it helpful to recall at each point in the discussion that all the data in the chapter are intended to illumine one or the other of these two questions. The data are usually presented in the form of a participation ratio, which shows the proportion of claims challenged by the employer and thus measures the extent of employer activity, or in the form of a disqualification ratio, which shows the proportion of employer challenges confirmed by the judgment of the state and thus throws some light on the desirability of employer activity.

The basic materials of the chapter consist of data supplied by the Massachusetts Division of Employment Security, showing Massachusetts *nonmonetary determinations made on initial claims.* According to the federal Bureau of Employment security "a nonmonetary determination occurs when a decision is made by the initial authority that the facts relative to an issue do or do not require the denial of benefits." The nonmonetary determination is thus distinguished from a monetary determination, which looks to whether the claimant has worked (enough) in covered employment. It is also thus distinguished from a separate chargeability ruling, which looks to whether the employer's reserve account is to be charged with whatever benefits are paid. Such separate chargeability rulings most often relate to a base-period employer who is not the separating employer. To judge from some of the data in Chapter 8, employer activity that affects only chargeability is a large part, sometimes almost a half, of total employer activity connected with claims control. The omission of this activity must be kept in mind when using Massachusetts nonmonetary data as a measure of the extent of employer participation in the program.

The materials are further restricted to nonmonetary determinations on *initial* claims. An initial claim is the first claim filed at the beginning of a period of unemployment; it declares the claimant's entrance into unemployment status. Claims subsequent to the initial claim are termed "continued" claims. These are excluded because employer challenges are confined, for the most part, to initial claims.[1]

There were several reasons for the selection of Massachusetts as the source of nonmonetary data. Besides being conveniently near, the Massachusetts Division of Employment Security was most cooperative in providing special tabulations for this analysis. Furthermore, Massachusetts classifies its nonmonetary data in a unique way. It shows nonmonetary determinations according as they were occasioned by a challenge from the employer alone, or from the state alone, or from both employer and state. This distinction is particularly useful for the purpose of relating nonmonetary determinations to employer activity and thus to experience rating.

Because this distinction is used throughout the chapter, it may be advisable to explain the terms more fully and to show their interrelationship by a diagram. "Employer alone": These are situations in which the state agency has not seen anything questionable in a claim prior to receiving information from the employer. "State alone": These are situations in which the employer has not raised an issue, but the information furnished by the claimant has caused the claims-taker to raise a question regarding the claimant's eligibility. "State and employer jointly": These are situations in which the employer and the state agency have both raised an eligibility question, with respect to the same claim, independently of each other. In the diagram below the illustrative numbers are taken from Table 7-1 and refer to nonmonetary determinations; with the substitution of other numbers, the diagram would apply equally well to most of the other tables in the chapter.

Nonmonetary Determinations Occasioned by State and/or Employer (497,308)

State total: 445,768		
State alone (245,920)	State and employer jointly (199,848)	Employer alone (51,540)
	Employer total: 251,388	

Massachusetts, an industrial state containing about 3.5 percent of covered employment nationwide, has several characteristics that favor a degree of employer participation somewhat above the average. Besides being a reserve-ratio

1. If employer challenges are compared with all the claims employers might challenge, the employer "participation ratio" shrinks to the vanishing point. In Massachusetts in 1967, for example, nonmonetary determinations occasioned by employers were only 0.2 percent of all claims filed.

state, it is a request-reporting state. That is, it requests wage data from the employer at the time a new claim is filed. The employer is asked to supply separation information at the same time and on the same form as that on which he supplies wage data. Since the legal pressure to provide wage data is much greater than to provide separation data, the employer is more likely to provide the latter when it is combined, as it is in Massachusetts, with the former. Furthermore, Massachusetts has various provisions for the noncharging of benefits paid after a disqualification period has elapsed. In recent years such noncharges have been about 10 percent of all benefits paid. To the individual employer, the noncharging of benefits has the appearance of the most complete of disqualifications and may thus provide a considerable incentive to report possible disqualifying information. These characteristics provide some offset to the relatively high proportion of ineffectively charged benefits in the Massachusetts system (see Table 5–5, item 5).

This chapter makes use of two bodies of data, both referring to nonmonetary determinations on initial claims. The first is a set of five-year totals (1963–67), while the other is a small sample drawn from the fourth quarter of 1967. The sample brings within the reach of analysis certain aspects of nonmonetary data that are not available in the five-year totals. The chapter also includes some data on employer appeals.

Massachusetts was one of the states that participated in the opinion survey analyzed in Chapter 6. The answers given by Massachusetts deputies and referees can thus be identified in Table 6–2. The data analyzed in the present chapter enable one to form some judgment of what the Massachusetts employer activity was like that gave rise to the opinions expressed in the survey. Since the answers of Massachusetts were generally close to the national averages, there is some reason for considering the participation of Massachusetts employers in the administrative process as fairly typical.

The legal obligation of employers to furnish possibly disqualifying information is spelled out in Section 38(b) of the Massachusetts Employment Security Law as follows:

Notice of a claim so filed shall be given promptly by the director or his authorized representative to the most recent employing unit of the claimant and to such other persons as the director may prescribe. If such employing unit or person has reason to believe there has been misrepresentation or has other reasons which *might* affect the allowance of said claim . . . it or he shall return the said notice . . . in accordance with the procedure prescribed by the director. Failure to return said notice and information within the time provided in this section or prescribed by the director shall bar the employing unit or other person from being a party to further proceedings relating to the allowance of the claim, and failure knowingly to return it within such time shall subject the employing unit to the penalties provided in section forty-seven. [Italics supplied.]

Nonmonetary Determinations in Massachusetts, 1963-67

Participation Ratios

A nonmonetary determination is an official answer to a question raised by someone about the eligibility of a claimant. The question may have been raised initially by the employer, or by the state in the person of its claimstaker, or by both. The answer to the question is normally supplied by a deputy in the form of a nonmonetary determination. In this context, a "participation ratio" is a measure of the extent to which the employer was active in raising the questions that occasioned the nonmonetary determinations. The ratio is obtained by comparing the number of times the employer has questioned an initial claim with the total of initial claims or with the total of nonmonetary determinations. In the latter ratio there is implicit a comparison with the activity of the state in questioning claims.

By helping to define the limits of employer participation in administration, these ratios help to define the limits of any effects, desirable or undesirable, that experience rating may have had on administration. Any desirable effects on adequate policing and any undesirable effects on claimant harassment are contained within these limits.

Table 7-1 provides a five-year history of nonmonetary determinations classified according to the person who questioned the claim and thus occasioned the determination. (In all the tables of this chapter, the term "Division" refers to employees of the Massachusetts Division of Employment Security.) Of the 2,755,935 initial claims filed during this five-year period, nonmonetary determinations were made on 497,308, or 18 percent.[2] About half of these determinations (251,388) were occasioned by an employer-raised question. The employer's contribution to the administrative task of identifying doubtful claims was thus limited to about 9 percent of all initial claims. As shown in item 7, the Massachusetts Division of Employment Security also questioned the claimant's eligibility in most (199,848) of these cases, even before it received the employer's information. Hence the employer's unique contribution to the task of identifying doubtful claims was limited to the 51,540 nonmonetary determinations occasioned by the employer alone (item 4). These represent only 10.4 percent of all nonmonetary determinations, 1.9 percent of all initial claims, and perhaps about 0.2 percent of all claims (see footnote 1).

As compared with the employer, the Division played a much greater role in the job of identifying doubtful claims. Twice as many nonmonetary determinations were occasioned by the Division as by employers (items 3 and 5). Indepen-

---

2. It should be recalled that discussion here is entirely in terms of initial claims. Although nonmonetary determinations are also made on continued claims, the employer usually participates in only a tiny fraction of these.

Table 7-1. MASSACHUSETTS: Nonmonetary Determinations[a]
Occasioned by Employer and Division, as Percent of All Initial Claims
and of All Nonmonetary Determinations, Five-Year Totals, 1963-67

		Percent
(1) Initial claims	2,755,935	
(2) All nonmonetary determinations (4+6+7)	497,308	= 18.0 of (1)
(3) All nonmonetary determinations occasioned by employer (4+7)	251,388	= 9.1 of (1)
		= 50.5 of (2)
(4) Nonmonetary determinations occasioned by employer alone	51,540	= 10.4 of (2)
(5) All nonmonetary determinations occasioned by division (6+7)	445,768	= 16.2 of (1)
		= 89.6 of (2)
(6) Nonmonetary determinations occasioned by division alone	245,920	= 49.5 of (2)
(7) Nonmonetary determinations occasioned by employer and division jointly	199,848	= 40.2 of (2)
		= 7.3 of (1)

Source: Unpublished tabulations made available by the Massachusetts Division of Employment Security.

[a]As explained in the text, these data are limited to nonmonetary determinations made on *initial* claims.

dently of any information obtained from the employer, the division was active in identifying 89.6 percent of all the questionable claims (item 5). Thus for the purpose of identifying doubtful claims, the Division was able to obtain adequate information from the claimant himself in nine-tenths of the cases. It is probable, however, that information obtained from claimants would become less adequate if employers ceased to exercise the kind of initiative represented by item 3, and if this change became generally known.[3] As Taulman Miller once observed: "Although employer interest is not a substitute for the development of high standards of administration, it may be helpful in attaining them" [36, p. 30].

Should the employer have been more active than he was? For example, should he have challenged some of the 245,920 claims (item 6) which the Division was alone in questioning? Any answer to this question must take cognizance of the fact that a significant proportion of these nonmonetary determinations probably arose from nonseparation issues, about which the separating employer generally has little knowledge. For example, in the Massachusetts sample analyzed later in this chapter, of all the monetary determinations occasioned by the Division alone, about 40 percent arose from nonseparation issues.

3. According to the Internal Revenue Service, our tax system relies on "voluntary compliance." But the system clearly works better when the IRS knows how much a taxpayer has earned, and he knows it knows. Compliance is much lower when the IRS lacks such independent verification. For example, in 1963, the first year the IRS got information on the payment of interest, returns with interest income leaped 45 percent.

Disqualification Ratios

To the extent that the Division upholds an employer in his protest and disqualifies the claimant, a presumption is established that the protest was justified. On the contrary, where the protest is not upheld, a question may arise whether the emplyer did not delay the payment of the claim unnecessarily. Hence disqualification ratios (the percent that disqualifications are of nonmonetary determinations) are pertinent to the task of setting limits within which the charge of claimant harassment might or might not be true. Table 7-2 shows disqualification ratios for the employer, and ratios calculated in analogous fashion for the Division.[4]

A preliminary word may be in order on the interpretation of these disqualification ratios. As noted above, the Massachusetts law requires the employer to report any reason "which *might* affect the allowance of the claim." In practice, if the reason for separation is anything other than lack of work, it will occasion a nonmonetary determination. The employer may recognize that the claim is probably valid—for example, it is one that stems from an involuntary quit or from a voluntary quit with good cause—and he may have no intention of protesting the claim; yet he is required to take an action (report the circumstances of the separation) that usually occasions a nonmonetary determination. Thus a degree of ambiguity attaches to disqualification ratios when used as a measure of the proportion of "challenges" that are "justified." It would be incorrect to conclude that the complementary ratio, the proportion of nonmonetary determinations that did not result in disqualifications, represented the proportion of "challenges" that were "unjustified."

This same ambiguity is present to an even greater degree in the nonmonetary determinations that are occasioned by the Division's action. In order to keep the processing of claims moving swiftly, the Division employs a coarse screening device at the outset. The Division employee who takes the claim and makes the first judgment on the eligibility of the claimant sorts out those claims, the great majority, where the claimant has said nothing to make the claimstaker doubt the validity of the claim and moves them along without interruption. But where the claimant's statement has raised some shadow of doubt, the claimstaker puts these aside for a second, closer look by a deputy. This second look counts as a nonmonetary determination. When, as happens more often than not, this second look—aided by more information from the claimant and perhaps, by this time, information also from the employer—suffices to establish the validity of the claim, the Division's "disqualification ratio" is lowered. The true nature of such nonmonetary determinations is revealed in Table 7-4, which shows that 60.8 percent of the nonmonetary determinations occasioned by the Division alone

---

4. The deputy receives questions regarding the eligibility of claimants from two sources—the employer and the claimstaker. The questions from both sources are answered in the same way—through a nonmonetary determination made by a deputy. This is the basic similarity in the process which founds the analogy.

Table 7-2. MASSACHUSETTS: Disqualifications Resulting from
Nonmonetary Determinations[a] Occasioned by Employer and by Division,
Five-Year Totals, 1963-67

		Percent
(1) All nonmonetary determinations	497,308	
(2) Disqualifications resulting from all nonmonetary determinations (6+10+12)	200,119	= 40.2 of (1)
(3) All nonmonetary determinations occasioned by employer	251,388	
(4) Disqualifications resulting from all nonmonetary determinations occasioned by employer (6+12)	125,440	= 49.9 of (3) = 62.7 of (2)
(5) Nonmonetary determinations occasioned by employer alone	51,540	
(6) Disqualifications resulting from nonmonetary determinations occasioned by employer alone	24,150	= 46.9 of (5) = 19.3 of (4) = 12.1 of (2)
(7) All nonmonetary determinations occasioned by division	445,768	
(8) Disqualifications resulting from all nonmonetary determinations occasioned by division (10+12)	175,969	= 39.5 of (7) = 87.9 of (2)
(9) Nonmonetary determinations occasioned by division alone	245,920	
(10) Disqualifications resulting from nonmonetary determinations occasioned by division alone	74,679	= 30.4 of (9) = 37.3 of (2)
(11) Nonmonetary determinations occasioned by both division and employer jointly	199,848	
(12) Disqualifications resulting from nonmonetary determinations occasioned by division and employer jointly	101,290	= 50.7 of (11) = 50.6 of (2)

Source: Unpublished tabulations made available by the Massachusetts Division of Employment Security.

[a]As explained in the text, these data are limited to nonmonetary determinations made on *initial* claims.

were settled in favor of the claimant *without any delay* in the payment of the claim.

Table 7-2 reveals the same preeminence of the Division as was evident in Table 7-1. Of the total disqualifications assessed during this period (200,119), the employers were the occasion of 125,440, while the Division was the occasion of 175,969. Thus the Division was the occasion of 50,000 more disqualifications than were employers. The employer was initially active in 62.7 percent of all disqualifications (item 4), while the Division was initially active in 87.9 percent (item 8). It is against this background that the relative importance of the Division and the employer to the total task of claims control must be assessed. Only 12.1 percent of the total number of disqualifications (item 6) could be attributed uniquely to employer intervention in the administrative process.

However, at the disqualification stage, the employer does more than merely raise a question. He also supplies information that goes far to determine the answer. In an unknown proportion of cases, including some occasioned by the Division alone, a disqualification resulted only because of the employer's contribution of adequate information.

As items 3 and 4 of the table indicate, of the 251,388 employer "challenges," about half (49.9 percent) resulted in the disqualification of the claimant and in this sense were justified. Whether this ratio is to be considered acceptable will depend on more fundamental norms which are outside the scope of this study,[5] but it is relevant to note, first, that the Division's disqualification ratio was even lower (39.5 percent)[6] and, second (as explained before), not all nonmonetary determinations occasioned by the employer represent genuine "protests" nor do all cause a delay in the payment of benefits. In the complex world of unemployment insurance it is often not possible to determine the exact nature of the claimant's relation to the labor market except by an examination of the circumstances. But this very examination constitutes a nonmonetary determination which gets into the denominator of the fraction and helps produce a low disqualification ratio.

Of the 497,308 challenged claims, 297,189 (item 1 minus item 2) proved to be valid claims. These questioned but valid claims are the measure of possible inconvenience caused to claimants. Of these questioned but valid claims, the employer participated in questioning 125,948 (item 3 minus item 4). On the reasonable assumption that where the Division joined the employer in questioning the claimant's eligibility, the challenge was probably not completely groundless (frivolous, in the legal sense), then the outside scope of what could possibly be termed employer "harassment" is limited to those valid claims which the employer alone questioned. This number is 27,390 (item 5 minus item 6) and equals 1 percent of all initial claims. It is not likely that all or even a large proportion of the 27,390 questioned claims represented deliberate attempts to frustrate the purpose of the law. Some of the questions would have been raised through ignorance of the law; some would have arisen from objectively border-

5. The norms are likely to reflect primarily one's judgements on (1) the amount of potential "abuse" in the program and (2) the "proper" relationship of unemployment insurance to the relative bargaining power of labor and management.

6. Over 60 percent of the nonmonetary determinations occasioned by the Division involved nonseparation issues, for which the Division's disqualification ratio was only 19.8 percent. Its disqualification ratio for separation issues was 43.1 percent, not very different from the employers' ratio of 49.9 percent.

line cases, where the determination might have gone either way; and some finally would not have been "challenges" at all but, as explained above, would have arisen simply from the requirement of the law that the employer give the reason for the separation. The extent of genuine "harassment," therefore, must have been something much less than 1 percent of initial claims. Thus, the Massachusetts statistics bear out the answers of the Massachusetts respondents in the opinion survey as to the infrequency of frivolous protests.

Employer Appeals

As indicated earlier, of the 251,388 nonmonetary determinations occasioned by the employer, 125,948 (50.1 percent) were favorable to the claimant. Of this number of determinations favorable to the claimant, the employer elected to appeal 5,243 (4.2 percent). Of these lower-authority appeals, he lost 3,240 or 61.8 percent. Of these adverse decisions he elected to appeal 1,491 (46.0 percent) to a higher authority. Thus he was ten times as likely to appeal from the referee to the Board as he was to appeal from the deputy to the referee: 46.0 percent versus 4.1 percent. This illustrates the point made in Chapter 8 that an employer appeal is a much more definite indication of an employer "protest" than is a nonmonetary determination occasioned by an employer. Of the appeals to the higher authority, he lost 996, or 66.8 percent.

To look at the other side of the coin, disqualifications resulting from employer initiative in questioning claims may be summarized in round figures as follows. About 250,000 employer protests resulted in about 125,000 disqualifications; about 5,000 employer appeals to the lower authority resulted in about 2,000 additional disqualifications; and about 1,500 appeals to the higher authority resulted in another 500 disqualifications.

Where the "win ratio" of the employer had been 49.9 percent at the level of the initial determination, it was only 38.2 percent at the level of the lower-appeal authority, and 33.2 percent at the level of the higher-appeal authority. The lower ratios at the appeal level are the less significant for the issue of claimant harassment because they affect fewer claimants, but are the more significant because the delay to the claimant's benefits is much greater at the appeal level than at the initial determination level.

Massachusetts Sample of Nonmonetary Determinations

This section continues the exploration begun in the preceding section, asking the same questions but attempting to provide more detailed answers. The analysis here is directed to a sample rather than to the entire population of nonmonetary determinations. The sample consisted of 867 nonmonetary determinations on initial claims drawn at random from 18,640 such determinations made by the Massachusetts Division of Employment Security in the fourth quarter of 1967. The 867 claims in the sample were distributed by issue and by outcome as follows:

	Number	Percent of grand total	Percent distribution
Total separation issues	600	69.2	100.0
Determined valid	343	39.6	57.2
Determined invalid	257	29.6	42.8
Total other issues	267	30.8	100.0
Determined valid	203	23.4	76.0
Determined invalid	64	7.4	24.0
Grand total (all issues)	867	100.0	

Voluntary quit (305) and *misconduct* (229) cases accounted for 89.0 percent of the 600 total of separation issues. *Availability* (187) cases accounted for 70.0 percent of the 267 total of "other" issues.

The analysis of the sample has a number of advantages over the analysis of the entire population. In the first place, it allows for a separate analysis of new and additional claims. It also allows for a separate analysis of nomonetary determinations relating only to separation issues. Third, it allows for a measure of the actual delay accompanying employer protests. Finally, it permits correlation of employer activity with industry, size of firm, and exployer tax rates.

As may be seen in Table 7–3, the participation and disqualification ratios of the samples are generally similar to those of the five-year total, as shown in tables 7–1 and 7–2. The sample differs from the five-year total chiefly in showing a somewhat lower disqualification ratio: 37.0 percent in the sample as against 40.2 percent in the five-year total. This same difference appears in the disqualification ratios of both the employer alone and of the Division alone. In

Table 7–3. Massachusetts Sample:[a] Nonmonetary Determinations and Resulting Disqualifications, by Source of Challenge

Source of challenge	Total nonmonetary determinations		Resulting disqualifications	
	Number	Percent of total	Number	Percent of column 1
	(1)	(2)	(3)	(4)
All sources	867	100.0	321	37.0
Employer alone	111	12.8	45	40.5
Employer and Division	366	42.2	163	44.5
Employer total	477	55.0	208	43.6
Division alone	390	45.0	113	29.0
Division total	756	87.2	276	36.5

Source: Unpublished tabulations made available by the Massachusetts Division of Employment Security.

[a]Sample drawn from all nonmonetary determinations made on initial claims in the fourth quarter of 1967.

other words, both the employer and the Division had a somewhat better (higher) disqualification record generally than the sample would indicate. The reader may be helped by noting that the analysis of the sample proceeds in terms of three principal groups: the total number of determinations (867); the determinations involving the employer (477); and the disqualifications on separation issues (257).

New and Additional Claims

A "new" claim is the first claim to be filed starting the individual's benefit year. If this claim series is interrrupted, for example by employment, and then is renewed later in the same benefit year by another spell of unemployment, the first claim in the renewed series is called an "additional" claim. Of the 867 disputed claims in the sample, 620 were new claims and 247 were additional claims. Employers were involved in 62.6 percent of the disputes relating to new claims, but they were involved in only 36.0 percent of those relating to additional claims.

Three possible explanations related to experience rating suggest themselves for the lesser degree of employer activity relating to additional claims. First, in a request-reporting state like Massachusetts, the state's request for separation information is on the same form as its request for wage information. Since the employer is under considerable legal pressure to furnish the wage information, he is more likely to submit both kinds of information when he is asked for them together than when he is asked only for the separation information, where the legal pressure to comply is much less. An additional claim, however, does not require wage information, since the benefit year was established by the preceding new claim. With respect to an additional claim an employer is asked only for separation information. If the employer simply ignores the state's request for separation information, and if the claimant has said nothing to arouse a suspicion of ineligibility, the state will normally take no further steps, but simply assume that the employer has nothing to report. This may be one reason for the lesser degree of employer participation on the occasion of an additional claim.

A second reason may be the employer's chargeability. The most recent employer of a worker filing an additional claim is, in many cases, not a base-period employer for purposes of the claimant's current base year, which had already been established when the earlier (new) claim was filed, and he will not be chargeable for payments during the current benefit year. Such an employer has a lesser immediate financial incentive to participate in the administrative process.

If he fully understood the intricacies of the unemployment insurance law—as few employers do—he would, nevertheless, notify the state of any possibly disqualifying circumstance connected with the additional claim. This same claimant may later establish a new benefit year in which this employer *is* a base-period employer. At that time he will be charged with benefits, even though the claimant may have left him under disqualifying circumstances, because he neglected so to inform the state *at the time* the additional claim was filed. In interviews, deputies have commented on the propensity of employers to neglect the additional claim because they are not *at that time* chargeable, and the employer's later futile dismay when he does become chargeable.

Finally, additional claims are somewhat more likely than initial claims to arise from layoffs in the seasonal industries. Since layoffs provide no basis for an employer protest, fewer such protests are likely to be made on additional claims. Furthermore, many employers in the seasonal industries, in which additional claims are most common, are already paying the maximum tax rate because of recurring heavy layoffs during the slack seasons. Such employers have a lesser financial incentive to participate in the administrative process. This reason may greatly strengthen the action of the other two reasons mentioned above.

Delayed Benefits

A major objection urged against employer participation in administration is the delay caused in the payment of benefits to eligible claimants. This objection obviously refers only to those claims that are ultimately held to be valid. Of the 867 disputed claims in the sample, 546 were determined to be valid. Of the 546 challenged claimants who were determined eligible, 501 actually drew benefits. The other 45 had dropped out of the claims line without having signed a claim for a compensable week. (They may have dropped out of claimant status for any number of reasons, such as reemployment, relocation, illness, death.) The total number, therefore, of claimants whose benefits could have been delayed because their claim was challenged is 501. Table 7-4 shows the distribution of these 501 claims according to the source of the challenge and the number of weeks their benefits were delayed.

As may be seen, the period of delay tended to be shorter when the Division alone questioned the claim and the employer was not involved. This is so because when the employer is not an interested party the Division may begin the payment of benefits as soon as it arrives at a determination in favor of the claimant. When the employer is an interested party benefits may not be paid until the expiration of the statutory period allowed for a possible employer appeal. In Massachusetts in 1967 this period was seven days from the day the claim notice was sent to the employer.

A large number of these challenged claimants—220, or 43.9 percent—experienced no delay at all. This percentage was 60.8 for the Division alone, 46.9 for the Division total, and 25.9 for the employer total. Thus, it may not be assumed that all nonmonetary determinations cause some delay in the payment of benefits.

On the assumption that where the Division also questioned a claim the employer was probably not guilty of claimant harassment, the potential for such harassment would seem to be limited to the 57 cases where the employer had been the sole challenger. Since 12 of these 57 had caused no delay at all, the

Table 7-4. Massachusetts Sample:[a] Nonmonetary Determinations
and Resulting Delay in Payment of Benefits

| Source of challenge | Beneficiaries | | Weeks' delay in receipt of check for earliest compensable week for which it was payable | | | | | | | | |
| | | | No delay | | 1 | | 2 | | 3-5 | | Over 5 | |
	Number	Percent	Number	Percent	Number	Percent	Number	Percent	Number	Percent	Number	Percent
All sources	501	100	220	43.9	134	26.7	77	15.4	54	10.8	16	3.2
Employer alone	57	100	12	21.0	15	26.3	16	28.1	13	22.8	1	1.8
Employer and division	186	100	51	27.4	60	32.3	41	22.0	21	11.3	13	7.0
Employer total	243	100	63	25.9	75	30.9	57	23.4	34	14.0	14	5.8
Division alone	258	100	157	60.8	59	22.9	20	7.8	20	7.8	2	0.7
Division total	444	100	208	46.9	119	26.8	61	13.7	41	9.2	15	3.4

Source: Unpublished tabulations made available by the Massachusetts Division of Employment Security.

aSample drawn from all nonmonetary determinations made on initial claims in the fourth quarter of 1967.

potential is further narrowed to the remaining 45. These 45 cases of challenged but valid claims represent 9.4 percent of all (477) nonmonetary determinations occasioned by the employer (Table 7-3), and 0.8 percent of all the initial claims (about 5,700) which the employer might have questioned in the fourth quarter of 1967. As a percentage of all claims in the quarter (initial plus continued claims) the proportion was minute.

As usual, the Division played a larger role in the administrative process than did the employer. There were 243 eligible claimants whose claims had been questioned by the employer; they experienced a total of about 400 claimant weeks of delay. There were 444 eligible claimants whose claims had been questioned by the Division; they experienced a total of about 500 claimant weeks of delay.

Delays can be especially long when the employer exercises his right to *appeal*. Of the 243 sample beneficiaries whose claims had been challenged by the employer, 15 were delayed in receiving their checks because of employer appeals at the referee level. Eight of these 15 beneficiaries were delayed more than 5 weeks. The possibility of a delay in benefits caused by an employer appeal seems to have been effectively eliminated by the 1971 decision of the U.S. Supreme Court in the Java case ([104] and see Chapter 8.)

Employer Challenges by Tax Rates[7]

Of the 867 nonmonetary determinations that make up the sample, 477 were occasioned by employer action. Of these 477, 17 were occasioned by employers at the minimum tax rate and 32 were occasioned by employers at the maximum tax rate. Of the 17 determinations, 11 resulted in disqualifications, for a disqualification ratio of 64.7 percent. Of the 32 determinations, 11 also resulted in disqualifications, for a disqualification ratio of 34.4 percent. Thus the disqualification ratio of employers at the minimum tax rate was twice as good (high) as that of employers at the maximum tax rate.

It may be that employers at the minimum tax rates are more knowledgeable in affairs of unemployment insurance than other employers. However, it may also be that the kind of unemployment characteristic of minimum-tax employers leads to disqualification more frequently than the kind of unemployment that is characteristic of maximum rate employers.

The sample of 867 nonmonetary determinations included 257 determinations on separation issues which resulted in the disqualification of the claimant. As Table 7-5 shows, the employer participated (questioned the initial claim) in only 191 of these cases. In the remaining 66 cases (25.7 percent of the total) the claimant had been disqualified by the Division without the most recent em-

7. For lack of an appropriate base, it is not possible to calculate *participation* ratios by tax rates. The same limitation applies to the discussion in the following section of participation ratios by industry. Hence in these two sections, the analysis is concerned only with disqualification ratios.

Table 7-5. Massachusetts Sample:[a] Disqualifications on Separation Issues
with and without Employer Participation,[b] by Employer Tax Rate

1967 Tax rate of most recent employer	All disqualifications	Disqualifications with employer participation	Disqualifications without employer participation
Totals	257	191	66
All rates	100.0	100.0	100.0
0.7	5.5	5.2	6.1
0.9-2.7	56.4	64.4	33.3
2.9-3.5	38.1	30.4	60.6

Source: Unpublished tabulations made available by the Massachusetts Division of Employment Security.

[a]Sample drawn from all nonmonetary determinations made on initial claims in the fourth quarter of 1967.

[b]The employer "participated" if he questioned the initial claim and thus occasioned the nonmonetary determination which resulted in a disqualification.

ployer having notified the Division of the disqualifying situation.[8] Since these 66 disqualifications turned on separation issues, in which the employer is normally involved, and since they actually led to disqualification of the claimant, they evidently point to a lack of even the minimal employer participation that might have been expected.

When these 66 cases—of employers who should have participated but did not—are distributed by tax rates, it is seen that a disproportionate number of these nonparticipating employers fall in the very high tax rates. It would seem that employers with tax rates above 2.7 percent were twice as likely to be nonparticipating as were employers between the minimum and maximum tax rates. This disparity may indicate that an employer is less interested in policing claims when he has little prospect of obtaining a reduction in his tax rate—particularly if his industry is one where, from the viewpoint of available labor supply, there is some advantage to him in allowing the claimant to draw benefits despite disqualifying circumstances which often cannot be discovered by the Division without the employer's cooperation.

This attitude is the more likely to be found when the employer is subject to the maximum tax rate regularly, year after year. A tabulation of Massachusetts employers who had been subject to the employment security law throughout the nine-year period 1960-68 (Table 4-9) showed that 12 percent (8,164) had been taxed at the maximum rate for five years or more of that period, and that more than one-quarter (2,215) of these had paid the maximum rate during the entire nine-year period.

8. The employer was probably contacted by the Division and asked for information after the Division had questioned the claim, but the employer himself had raised no question.

The situation at the minimum tax rate is interesting. Insofar as there is a difference, it suggests that employers at the minimum tax rate, like those at the maximum tax rate, are less likely to participate, even in separation issues that lead to disqualification. A possible explanation is that if an employer's normal cost rate is well below the minimum tax rate, he has as little incentive to control claims as does the employer whose normal cost rate is well above the maximum tax rate. Both are in the "zone of indifference."

Employer Challenges by Industry[9]

Of the 447 nonmonetary determinations occasioned by employer challenges, 43.6 percent had resulted in disqualifications. By industry divisions, this disqualification ratio varied between one-third and one-half.

Industry division	Percent of employer challenges resulting in disqualification
All industries	43.6
Services	33.9
Finance, insurance, and real estate	38.7
Construction	41.2
Wholesale and retail trade	44.1
Manufacturing	46.0
Transportation, communication, and utilities	50.0

On the assumption that a low disqualification ratio means a high proportion of "unnecessarily" challenged claims, services would seem to have the worst record. In this division, which covers a wide variety of activities, 66.1 percent of employer challenges were not supported by the Division's determination. The division of transportation, communication, and utilities had the best record, finding half of its challenges supported by the state.

Are these industrial differences stable differences? It is not possible to give a firm answer. These data reflect the experience of only one-quarter, and the various industries differ considerably among themselves in their experience with claims at different times of the year. Hence it is not possible to generalize from this small sample. It is illustrative rather than representative.[10]

As indicated earlier (Table 7-5), the sample included 257 determinations which had disqualified the claimant on a *separation issue*, and in 66 of these

9. See footnote 7.
10. Similar disqualification ratios were computed, though they are not shown, for thirty of the larger industrial groups (two-digit classifications), and these revealed much greater variation. The disqualification ratios varied from 16.7 percent for leather and leather products to 63.6 percent for machinery.

disqualifications the employer had not challenged the claim. The 66 cases of nonpartiticipation represented 25.7 percent of the 257 disqualifications on separation issues. This proportion varied from 5.6 percent for the division comprising transportation, communication, and utilities, to 30.5 percent for the trade division. Thus the division of transportation, communication, and utilities was marked by two signs of effective claims control—the highest disqualification ratio and the lowest nonparticipation ratio.

Employer Challenges by Size of Firm

Of the 867 nonmonetary determinations that make up the sample, 477 were occasioned by employer action. This section examines the participation ratios and disqualification ratios of these 477 employer challenges as they are related to the size of the firm making the protest. A comparison of the distribution in column 4 with that in column 2 of Table 7-6 seems to indicate that the smaller firms are underrepresented and the larger firms are overrepresented in the number of nonmonetary determinations occasioned by employers. For example, the firms with less than 20 employees accounted for 22.4 percent of all covered employees but for only 15.8 percent of all employer-occasioned nonmonetary determinations. For firms with over 1,000 employees, these proportions were reversed: large firms accounted for only 18.9 percent of covered employees but for 24.6 percent of nonmonetary determinations. This is compatible with the generally accepted opinion that the larger firms are more knowledgeable about unemployment insurance and participate more actively in administration. Many of the deputies and referees in the opinion survey made this observation.

Column 6 of the table indicates that not only do smaller employers challenge fewer claims, but they also are upheld in fewer of those they do challenge. The two smallest groups (those with less than 10 employees) show a combined disqualification rate of 26.1 as contrasted with the average rate of 43.6. This also is compatible with the widely held opinion—and one expressed by a number of deputies and referees in the opinion survey—that the smaller employer acts more frequently than does the larger firm through ignorance of the law or through emotion.

The disqualification ratio of the largest firms (those with 1,000 or more employees) was 39.8 percent. While this was greater than that of the smallest firms, it was still below the average of 43.6 percent. The very largest firms, those with more than 20,000 employees, had a disqualification ratio of 34.3 percent (not shown in the table).

If the below average record of the smallest firms is explained by ignorance and emotion, what is the explanation of the record of the largest firms? Did some of these firms have a policy of challenging claims on inadequate grounds? One reason for venturing an affirmative answer might be the higher-than-average participation ratio of the larger employers: although making up only 18.9 percent of the covered population, they accounted for 24.6 percent of all employer

Table 7-6. Massachusetts Sample:[a] Nonmonetary Determinations Occasioned by Employer and Resulting Disqualifications, by Size of Firm

Size of firm (Number of employees)	Covered employees in private employment in March, 1968		Sample nonmonetary determinations in which employer was involved					
	Number	Percent of total	Number	Percent of total	Effect on claimant			
					Disqualified		Not disqualified	
					Number	Percent	Number	Percent
	(1)	(2)	(3)	(4)	(5)	(6)	(7)	(8)
All firms	1,655,169	100.0	477	100.0	208	43.6	269	56.4
0– 3	81,674	4.9	17	3.6	5	29.4	12	70.6
4– 9	144,733	8.8	29	6.1	7	24.1	22	75.9
10– 19	144,438	8.7	29	6.1	14	48.3	15	51.7
20– 49	222,097	13.4	60	12.6	28	46.7	32	53.3
50– 99	192,113	11.6	48	10.1	28	58.3	20	41.7
100–249	249,019	15.0	82	17.2	43	52.4	39	47.6
250–499	167,145	10.1	51	10.7	18	35.3	33	64.7
500–999	142,488	8.6	43	9.0	18	41.9	25	58.1
1,000 or more	311,462	18.9	118	24.6	47	39.8	71	60.2

Source: Unpublished tabulations made available by the Massachusetts Division of Employment Security.

[a]Sample drawn from all nonmonetary determinations made on initial claims in the fourth quarter of 1967.

challenges. Thus in Massachusetts the largest firms were more apt to challenge claims and less apt to have their challenge upheld. That a low disqualification rate is not necessarily characteristic of the large firm, however, is illustrated in the firms described in Chapter 8.

As indicated earlier (see Table 7-5), employer participation had been notably lacking in 66 out of 257 disqualifications on separation issues, where employer participation was most to be expected. This lack of participation varied considerably by size of firm, with the smallest firms accounting for a disproportionate number of the 66 cases of employer nonparticipation. Firms with less than 20 employees made up 27.3 percent of the 66 nonparticipating employers, but only 13.6 percent of the 191 participating employers. This disproportion is compatible with the other finding, that small firms tend to have low participation and disqualification ratios, and probably stems from the same root—lack of knowledge and interest. The largest firms did not show the opposite relationship, as might have been expected, but are represented in about equal proportions among the participating and nonparticipating employers.

Conclusions

In an attempt to shed additional light on the extent and desirability of employer participation in the administrative process, the experience of one state, Massachusetts, was subjected to more detailed analysis. Massachusetts is a reserve-ratio state, a request-reporting state, and a state which noncharges a significant amount of benefits paid after a disqualification period. Since all three of these characteristics tend to encourage employer efforts at claims control, it is likely that the effects, desirable and undesirable, of employer participation in Massachusetts should be at least as sizable and visible as in most states.

Extent of Employer Participation

The first task in claims control is to identify those claims that require a second look and might have to be disqualified. In this task of instigating a nonmonetry determination, the state clearly played the major role. Of all the nonmonetary determinations made, the employer participated in (occasioned) only 50.5 percent, while the Massachusetts Division of Employment Security participated in (occasioned) 89.6 percent. Thus the state was completely dependent on the employer to identify questionable claims in only 10.4 percent of all the claims questioned. This ratio marked one limit of the employer's importance in the initial stage of the administrative process, where questionable claims must be identified.

However, if employers cease to exercise the kind of initiative represented by their 50.5 percent, and if this change became generally known, the information obtainable from claimants might gradually become less adequate. Indeed, it is possible that the actions of some claimstakers and deputies might also be affected. Further, although a state agency may be able to raise an eligibility question independently of the employer, it frequently cannot find the correct answer except through the employer.

In the Massachusetts sample data sixty-six cases were identified which involved a separation issue that led to a disqualification, and which the employer, nevertheless, had not brought to the attention of the Division. These cases clearly reflect the absence of even minimal employer participation. Employers at the maximum tax and small-sized employers accounted for more than their share of the sixty-six negligent employers.

Employer participation did not extend far beyond the actions of questioning claims and supplying information at the initial stage. Massachusetts employers made relatively little effort to change the Division's initial interpretation of the law as applied to the information they had submitted. When the Division rejected an employer protest and ruled favorably to the claimant, the employer usually accepted the determination. Massachusetts employers appealed only 4.2 percent of such determinations at the referee level, and only 1.2 percent at the level of the Board of Review. However, as explained in Chapter 8, the impact of employer appeals extends much further than their small number might seem to indicate.

Desirability of Employer Participation

On the assumption that the employer was "justified" in challenging a claim when the Division joined with him in this action, or when the Division upheld the employer by assessing a disqualification, the limit of "unjustified" employer activity would be set by items 5 and 6 in Table 7-2. In the five-year period 1963-67, Massachusetts employers questioned 27,390 initial claims (item 5 minus item 6) which were not also questioned by the Division and which did not result in disqualification. This was equal to 1 percent of all initial claims. Since it is not likely that all or even a large proportion of the 27,390 challenged claims represented deliberate attempts to frustrate the purpose of the law, the outside extent of possible "harassment" would have been something much less than 1 percent of all initial claims. Thus the Massachusetts statistics bear out the answers of the Massachusetts respondents in the opinion survey as to the infrequency of frivolous protests.

A major objection urged against employer participation in administration is the delay caused in the payment of benefits to claimants who are ultimately found to be eligible. In the Massachusetts sample, of the 501 such cases, the employer was the sole cause in 57, or 11.4 percent (Table 7-4). Since 12 of these 57 cases had caused no delay at all, the potential for unjustifiable delay is narrowed to the remaining 45. These 45 cases of valid claims challenged solely by the employer represent 9.4 percent of all the nonmonetary determinations occasioned by the employer, slightly less than 1 percent of all initial claims, and much less than 1 percent of all claims. Since the *Java* decision [104] this source of benefits delay has been removed completely.

Small employers and employers at the highest tax rates tended to have the poorest record in the matter of filing protests that were not supported by the Division. That is, they tended to have the lowest disqualification ratios. To the extent that the size of firm and the tax rate were correlated, the chief factor of explanation might be the size of the firm. Because small employers tend to be less knowledgeable, they also tend to protest claims that a larger employer recognizes as valid under the law.

Employer Participation in Administration III:
Individual Firms And Service Companies

This chapter is concerned with the same issues that occupied the preceding two chapters—the impact of experience rating on employer participation in the administration of unemployment insurance and the desirability of such participation. This chapter presents examples of employer participation "at the limit," that is, examples of firms that participated in administration most fully. Here if anywhere the effects of experience rating, desirable and undesirable, should be most visible.[1] The details contained in these examples should also contribute to a better understanding of what "employer participation" is in the concrete. Some of the examples relate to individual firms which control their own claims, while others relate to "service companies" which perform this task for client firms.

Individual Firms

North American Rockwell Corporation[2]

Although no one firm makes use of all possible techniques of claims control, the system in use at the California divisions of North American Rockwell (NR) is probably as adequate as any. Further, the results of this effort at claims control have been recorded in considerable detail and are published. For these reasons the system of NR, which began to operate in 1947, is chosen as our first example of claims control "at the limit." Our description is limited to the company's operations in California.

The company, which is engaged in aerospace, electronics, nuclear energy, and space systems manufacturing and research and is subject to considerable fluctuations in employment, was for some years the largest firm in the state. When I visited the corporation in 1969 it had five divisions in California, each of which had multiple facilities. The unemployment insurance activity of the company

---

1. This procedure does not serve to illumine another important question: How active is the average employer? To answer this question it would be necessary to study a representative sample of firms. But since the task of ascertaining actual administrative practices involves intensive, time-consuming field work, to investigate the large number of firms needed to comprise a representative sample would be a major research project in itself.
2. North American Aviation, Inc., merged with the Rockwell Corporation in 1967.

was centralized in one unit that consisted of a supervisor and four highly trained technicians. The following is a brief description of the unit's procedures.

Notices of claims filed are sent by the state to the individual plants from which the claimants came. These plants take no action on the notices, but forward them to the central unit, which assumes entire control of the process from that point on. This unit supplies all essential information to the state, mails all required forms, and decides which claims to protest. The corporation's reasons for centralizing claims control, rather than assigning the task to the individual units, were generally similar to those listed in Appendix G.

In California the employer is expected to return the form giving separation information only when the reason for separation may possibly be disqualifying. Otherwise, the employer is free to disregard the notice of claim filed. Silence on the part of the employer is thus ambiguous. He may be telling the state that he thinks the claimant is eligible, or he may be simply ignoring the notice of the claim—either because he is too busy to be bothered or because he wishes the claim to be paid, though the circumstances may be disqualifying.[3]

Table 8-1 shows the operations of the company's unemployment insurance unit at the level of the first determination of the claim during the period 1955-70. Column 1 shows the growth of the company through 1964 and then its subsequent decline; in 1970 its monthly employment was less than half the peak figure. The next three columns show the claims that arose out of this employment history and the proportion of claims that the company protested. Column 7 shows the proportion of protested claims decided in favor of the company.

In general, the table reflects a large and effective operation. On the average, 37.5 percent of all claims were protested and 82.3 percent of these protests were upheld. The operations of the unemployment insurance unit responded sensitively to the underlying economic realities: the proportions of claims protested varied directly with the company's fortunes. The unusually high percentages of claims protested in 1955 and 1956 reflect a period when employment was building up rapidly. Separations from employment were mostly discharges for misconduct or voluntary quits without good cause, and hence nearly all claims were protestable. Layoffs began in 1957, but the company was still able to offer laid-off employees transfers to suitable work in other divisions and, hence, was in a position to successfully protest claims arising out of the layoffs. In 1958, however, when layoffs were very heavy and alternative suitable work was not available, the percentage of claims protested dropped to 26.9. During the extraordinarily heavy layoffs of 1969-70 the percentage of claims protested dropped still further to 10.5. This impression of a reasonable and responsible policy on the part of the unemployment insurance unit is confirmed by a win ratio that was above 75 percent in all but one year.

3. In the latter case, the employer is legally bound to reply to the notice of claim filed, but in practice he may safely ignore it. Except in cases of wholesale collusion, the states do not attempt to penalize employers for failing to report possibly disqualifying circumstances.

Table 8-1. North American Rockwell: [a]
Claims Protested at Initial Determination, 1955-70

Fiscal year	Monthly employ-ment	All claims	Claims protested		No determina-tion issued[b]	Determinations favorable to employer	
			Number	Percent of all claims		Number	Percent of all determina-tions[c]
(1)	(2)	(3)	(4)		(5)	(6)	(7)
1955	46,136	2,773	2,263	81.6	216	1,893	92.5
1956	53,369	2,052	1,727	84.2	309	1,300	91.6
1957	49,722	2,668	2,012	75.4	359	1,468	89.8
1958	42,269	13,440	3,617	26.9	471	2,713	86.2
1959	50,717	4,599	1,457	31.7	234	1,009	82.5
1960	56,474	6,138	2,421	39.4	270	1,618	75.2
1961	67,630	6,679	3,594	53.8	341	2,457	75.5
1962	80,074	7,102	3,903	55.0	405	2,503	72.0
1963	87,949	10,419	5,305	50.9	596	3,609	76.5
1964	89,282	10,922	4,813	44.1	521	3,683	86.0
1965	85,262	10,956	4,671	42.6	591	3,502	86.0
1966	75,622	7,234	3,084	42.6	425	2,302	86.6
1967	74,168	7,220	2,846	39.4	316	2,137	84.5
1968	68,314	7,290	2,576	35.3	278	1,919	83.5
1969	54,920	11,879	2,419	20.4	222	1,751	79.7
1970	40,253	18,173	1,910	10.5	119	1,490	83.2
1955-70	1,022,161	129,544	48,618	37.5	5,673	35,354	82.3

Source: Data supplied by North American Rockwell.

[a] Aerospace and Systems Group.

[b] These are claims where the claimant received no benefits either because he had insufficient wage credits or because he did not report back to the local office after filing his initial claim.

[c] All determinations equal Column 3 minus Column 5.

The unsuccessful protests caused some delay in the eventual payment of benefits to the claimant, but the delay was less in California than it would have been in most other states because California begins the payment of benefits immediately upon a favorable determination and does not wait until the period has elapsed during which the employer may appeal the original determination.

Of the successful protests, a significant number affected only the employer's chargeability, and not the claimants eligibility. Such protests occur when the company is only a base-period employer and not the separating employer. Column 3 contains an unknown but certainly sizable proportion of protests the only effect of which was to exempt the company from being charged with the benefits that were paid. The analysis of a sample of claims for 1968 and for 1970 showed that in these two years about one-third of all protests affected only the company's chargeability. It is noteworthy that when the company was the base-period employer only and not the separating employer it tended to protest a higher proportion of claims. Thus, in 1968, claims in which the company was the base-period employer only accounted for 18 percent of all claims, but this 18 percent of claims accounted for 30.2 percent of the company's protests. The corresponding figures for 1970 were 14 percent and 36.7 percent (see similar data in Table 8-5).

The central unemployment insurance unit also has the responsibility of representing the company when claims are appealed. The state's initial determination on a benefit claim may be appealed either by the claimant or the employer, at either the referee or the board level. After the state has set a date for the hearing of the appeal, the unemployment insurance unit makes the necessary preparations, which usually involve gathering more detailed information and presenting it in a more formal fashion than was needed for the determination at the initial level. Photostats of essential documents are prepared, affidavits are secured, and arrangements are made to have present at the hearing witnesses who can speak from first-hand knowledge ("percipient witnesses"). At the hearing itself, one of the staff of the unemployment insurance unit represents the company. (For the special significance of employer activity on the appeal level, see the analysis of the appeal function given later in the chapter.)

Table 8-2 shows the operations of the unemployment insurance unit with respect to appeals. During the period 1955-70 the company lost 7,591 of the protests it filed at the deputy level.[4] Of these the company appealed 1,683 or 22.1 percent, to the referee. Of these appealed claims, the company won 1,140, for a win record of 67.7 percent. In view of their precedent-setting character,[5] such a number of successful appeals must be recognized as a significant effect of employer participation. The high win ratio probably indicates also that the unit was avoiding "frivolous" appeals. Finally the unit never defaulted (failed to appear) at hearings on appeals in which the company was the appellant.[6]

The claimant appealed many more determinations than did the employer, but won fewer of them. The claimant was upheld only 15 percent of the time before the referee. His low win ratio is probably attributable to two causes—on the one hand, emotion and lack of understanding of what the law provides, and on the other, lack of ability to present his case effectively. In 545 of the 3,020 claimant appeals (18 percent), the claimant failed to appear at the hearing. No information is available on the causes of these failures to appear.

At the appeal board level, the number of appeals was much smaller and the win ratios were lower, especially for the claimant. Over the entire period, the

4. This is the difference between column 3 and the sum of columns 5 and 6 in Table 8-1.

5. Only a few decisions are precedent-setting in the strict legal sense that they must be followed; but all decisions on appealed cases have something of this character insofar as they are likely to influence the future decisions of deputies as they find their past decisions overturned or upheld.

6. A 1963 unpublished California study of attendance at appeals before the referee found that employers and claimants both had the same record: when they were the appellants they failed to appear at hearings 19 percent of the time. This full-time NR unit thus had a much better record than the average employer.

Table 8–2. North American Rockwell: Appeals Decided Favorably to Employer, 1955–70

	Appeals to referee						Appeals to board						All appeals		
	Employer appeals			Claimant appeals			Employer appeals			Claimant appeals					
		Favorable to employer			Favorable to employer			Favorable to employer			Favorable to employer				Favorable to employer	
Fiscal year	Total	Number	Percent	Total	Number	Percent	Total	Number	Percent	Total	Number	Percent	Total	Number	Percent
	(1)	(2)	(3)	(4)	(5)	(6)	(7)	(8)	(9)	(10)	(11)	(12)	(13)	(14)	(15)
1955	59	46	78.0	90	70	77.8	15	7	46.7	10	9	90.0	174	132	75.9
1956	24	21	87.5	91	82	90.1	2	0	0.0	13	12	92.3	130	115	88.5
1957	12	9	75.0	85	68	80.0	6	1	16.7	13	13	100.0	116	91	78.4
1958	23	16	69.6	147	121	82.3	13	5	38.5	12	11	91.7	195	153	78.5
1959	34	26	76.5	92	78	84.8	12	1	8.3	17	13	76.5	155	118	76.1
1960	40	32	80.0	105	89	84.8	12	4	33.3	13	11	84.6	170	136	80.0
1961	120	81	67.5	167	141	84.4	35	15	42.9	26	23	88.5	348	260	74.7
1962	83	61	73.5	196	167	85.2	23	11	47.8	27	25	92.6	329	264	80.2
1963	107	72	67.3	229	180	78.6	27	11	40.7	30	27	90.0	393	290	73.8
1964	188	111	59.0	242	208	86.0	40	15	37.5	35	33	94.3	505	367	72.7
1965	190	122	64.2	209	198	94.7	27	17	63.0	46	41	89.1	472	378	80.1
1966	158	100	63.3	282	235	83.3	21	7	33.3	50	43	86.0	511	385	75.3
1967	169	112	66.3	294	233	79.3	22	8	36.4	72	67	93.1	557	420	75.4
1968	142	92	64.8	256	227	88.7	7	6	85.7	44	41	93.2	449	366	81.5
1969	251	175	69.7	363	319	87.9	24	19	79.2	91	86	94.5	729	599	82.2
1970	83	64	77.1	172	150	87.2	10	9	90.0	43	42	97.7	308	265	86.0
1955–70	1,683	1,140	67.7	3,020	2,566	85.0	296	136	45.9	542	497	91.7	5,541	4,339	78.3

Source: Data supplied by North American Rockwell.

employer won 45.9 percent of his appeals to the board and the claimant won 8.3 percent.

The 1,276 successful employer appeals (the sum of columns 2 and 8 in Table 8-2) constitute the clearest measure of the effect of experience rating, for most of these appeals would not have been filed except for experience rating, and many of them probably influenced decisions on subsequent claims. The 3,063 claimant appeals decided in favor of the employer (the sum of columns 5 and 11) constitute an additional but less clear measure of the effect of experience rating. This measure is less clear because many of these appeals might have been decided in the same way even if the employer had not attended the hearing.

Table 8-3, column 6, presents a birds-eye view of the claims control function as it might appear to the finance officer of a corporation. During the decade

Table 8-3. North American Rockwell: Sources of Benefit Charges and Amounts of Estimated Savings,[a] 1960-70

Fiscal year	Total benefit charges	Charges due to layoffs		Charges due to other causes		Estimated savings[a]
		Amount	Percent of total	Amount	Percent of total	
	(1)	(2)	(3)	(4)	(5)	(6)
1960	$ 1,032,319	$ 783,590	75.9	$ 248,729	24.1	$ 497,344
1961	1,195,229	679,084	56.8	516,145	43.2	860,684
1962	958,853	324,590	34.0	634,263	66.0	742,848
1963	1,691,837	852,483	50.4	839,354	49.6	1,281,280
1964	2,360,128	1,421,663	60.0	938,465	40.0	1,622,390
1965	3,525,006	2,649,712	75.2	875,294	24.8	1,800,270
1966	1,688,928	1,228,090	72.7	460,838	27.3	989,100
1967	2,632,284	2,230,535	84.7	401,749	15.3	1,316,791
1968	2,061,427	1,676,558	81.3	384,869	18.7	907,145
1969	6,308,350	5,933,532	94.1	374,818	5.9	1,338,576
1970	10,467,512	10,186,248	97.3	281,264	2.7	1,033,340
1960-70	$33,921,873	$27,966,085	82.4	$5,955,788	17.6	$12,389,768

Source: Data supplied by North American Rockwell.

[a]Savings resulting from all decisions—by deputy, referee, and appeals board—finally favorable to the employer. Estimate based on average benefit charge per qualified claimant.

1960-70, the company received thousands of favorable decisions, (Tables 8-1 and 8-2). If these decisions had gone the other way, and if the claimants involved had drawn the average amount of benefits actually paid to NR claimants in the respective years, the company would have been charged with an additional $12,389,768 (Table 8-3). In evaluating this "saving" of the company, three important qualifications must be borne in mind.

First, the amounts indicated were not saved directly and immediately. The direct and immediate effect was to increase the firm's reserve over what it would have been without these favorable decisions. Eventually an increased reserve will lower a firm's tax rate. Given the operation of the "natural tax rate" (Appendix B), a firm like NR, whose tax rate was usually between the maximum and minimum rates, will actually save, other things being equal, the amount of any benefits that might have been charged to its account and were not.

Second, perhaps one-third of this amount represents a saving to the employer, but not to the unemployment insurance state fund. At least in 1968 and 1970, as mentioned above, a third or more of all protests had the effect not of denying benefits but only of freeing the company of charges for benefits paid.[7] From the viewpoint of the individual firm, the $12 million is a proper measurement of the "saving" attributable to and justifying the existence of a specialized unemployment insurance unit. From the viewpoint of the state fund, only part of that amount represents the effect of experience rating in diminishing benefit flows.

Third, of the remaining "saving" some proportion represented disqualifications that would have been made by the state even if the employer had provided only minimal cooperation or no cooperation at all—as illustrated in Chapter 7. But this latter qualification must itself be qualified as regards employer appeals. Here the result is entirely attributable to employer activity and the results at the appeal level may have repercussions on large areas of claims for years after the appealed case has been decided. In other words, some later state activity may be ultimately explainable in terms of earlier employer activity. These three qualifications should be kept in mind when evaluating any saving said to result from employer participation in administration.

Table 8-3 shows that except in one year (1962), layoffs were the major source of valid claims against the company. The sum of columns 4 and 6 represents the economic significance of claims arising from "other causes" than layoffs. Column 4 measures the costs incurred and column 6 measures the costs averted in connection with "other causes." In all years, the charges averted were larger than the charges incurred. The two combined are a measure of the area of *potentially* useful employer participation in administration. Until the exceptional year of 1970, this area (columns 4 and 6) comprised usually about half of the total area of claims activity (columns 1 and 6). In other words, about half of all claims required employer attention and participation.

The proportion of benefits due to "other causes" (column 5) varied from 66.0 percent in 1962 to 2.7 percent in 1970. The variance reflects the same realistic adjustment in underlying economic forces as does the changing proportion of claims protested (column 4 of Table 8-1). The activities of the unemployment insurance unit clearly took cognizance of the changing realities of the market.

The actual records of the unemployment insurance unit are much more detailed than Table 8-3 suggests. For example, the records of the unit show the

7. Even this advantage was only temporary for a company like NR. These noncharged benefits had to be funded eventually by contributions (the subsidiary tax and interest earnings) paid by subsidizing companies like NR.

costs in column 4 distributed into eighteen classes, according to the situation which occasioned the claim. Arranged roughly in the descending order of the size of benefit charges, the eighteen classes of cost (other than layoffs) were as follows:

Discharges or Permitted Resignations	Untimely Answer to Claim Notice
Retirements	Unsatisfactory Probationary Employee
Forced Medical Leave	Medical Restrictions
Other Employment	Child Care
Join Husband	Dissatisfied with Job or Shift
Personal Reasons or Personal Illness	Maternity Leaves
Overstayed Leave or Absent 5 Days	Military Service
Transportation Difficulties	School (Summer Employees)
Illness in Family	Employer Misstatement

This list of possible sources of claims illustrates the complexity of the employment relationship and the consequent complexity of the task of controlling claims.

The relative importance of many of the sources of charges varied significantly over time. For example, the amount of unemployment benefits paid in connection with maternity leaves diminished greatly after 1963, when the company changed its policy and allowed pregnant employees to work until a doctor certified that they were unable to work.[8] These benefits were $192,717 in 1963, but only $3,653 in 1965, and $1,170 in 1969. In the same period of time, unemployment benefits connected with retirements grew from $57,158 in 1963 to $128,100 in 1969.

The records of the unemployment insurance unit cross-classify all these eighteen sources of charges by each major operation of the company. Thus, on a single sheet of paper it is possible to see for a year the hundred or more separate springs contributing to the final, companywide flow of benefits that determines the company's tax rate. This pinpointing of the sources of benefit charges probably had some of the effect of internal experience rating. Directors of personnel at both corporate and plant levels were made aware of the exact size and nature of the unemployment problem. Such a detailed, concentrated report on separations from employment would seem to be serviceable as a management tool.

Several conclusions are reasonably clear from the experience of NR. First, this company considered claims control important; for it set up a staff of five highly trained people. Second, this interest in claims control stemmed largely from experience rating. In all probability, if the company were faced with a uniform tax rate it would sooner or later disband the cental claims unit and allow each operation to handle its own claims. As a result, there would probably be fewer claims protested, the protests would be made less accurately, and

---

8. Previously the company would not permit the employee to work beyond the sixth month of pregnancy. This change in company policy was brought about (not easily) by the central unemployment insurance unit.

appeals activity would practically disappear. Third, if one may judge from the company's high win ratio at the levels of both initial protests and later appeals, the participation of this firm in the administrative process probably helped in the attainment of the objectives of the law. This conclusion was strengthened by interviews conducted with some of the deputies in the state local offices with whom the company's unemployment insurance unit frequently dealt. The deputies reported that the members of the firm's unemployment insurance unit seemed to be concerned only to bring out all the facts and to see that the law was properly administered. There were several instances where the firm supplied incorrect information, tending to disqualify a claimant. In California such an employer action is punishable by an administrative penalty.[9] In each instance the state decided after investigation that the incorrect information had stemmed from an error and not a deliberate attempt to deceive.

To complete the picture of NR it may be noted that the company has been a subsidizing employer in California. Over the entire period in which it has been covered by the program (1936 through 1970) the company has contributed more than twice as much as its employees have drawn out.[10] As of the end of the fiscal year 1970, the company had a reserve sufficient to pay benefits at the highest annual rate in its history for over seven years without making any further contributions. Even at the end of the extraordinary year 1970, after the firm's employment had dropped by more than one-fourth, its reserve was sufficient to carry the burden of four more such extraordinary years without the firm making any further contributions.

On the east coast, The Raytheon Company resembles NR in having most of its operations concentrated in one state. The largest firm in Massachusetts, Raytheon also has centralized unemployment insurance claims control. The following table illustrates its experience with claims control in recent years:

	1967	1968	1969
1. Initial claims filed	2,044	2,616	3,249
2. Protests filed	442	860	681
3. Protests upheld	352	678	503
4. Participation ratio (2 ÷ 1)	21.6%	32.8%	20.9%
5. Disqualification ratio (3 ÷ 2)	79.6%	78.8%	73.8%

9. About 800 such penalties are assessed each year. One much publicized case (not relating to NR) illustrates the difficulty of maintaining claims control in a large corporation. The foreman in a local plant discharged a young employee for inefficiency. Because the young man was a recently returned veteran and the son of a long-term employee in the same shop, the foreman agreed to call it a quit—for the sake of the young man's employment record— on the termination report. Neither the foreman nor the employee was aware of the implications of this action for unemployment benefits. When the employee filed for benefits, the unemployment insurance unit, working from the termination report, routinely protested the claim. Eventually the full story came out (primarily because of a public outcry raised by the young man's mother) and the firm was fined $600.

10. This calculation excludes from "contributions" all subsidiary taxes which were credited to the Common Account, and excludes from "benefits" all noncharged benefits.

Examples of other firms with centralized claims control could be adduced, but they would tell much the same story.

Ford Motor Company

Centralized claims control was facilitated in NR because so large a proportion of its operations was concentrated in one state. Other large corporations with a wide diversity of operations scattered over many states typically settle for a less centralized system of claims control. The Ford Motor Company provides one of the best examples of a widespread firm which decentralizes administration, yet maintains close contact with all its various parts. Briefly, the central unit in Detroit operates through the following controls:

1) A succinct statement of the *general policies* to be followed in unemployment insurance is supplied to each of the company's operations.

2) Detailed *manuals of procedures* are prepared for use in the four states in which the company has most of its manufacturing operations. Each manual varies according to the provisions of the state law to which it applies. (The preparation and maintenance of even a single manual is a laborious task; hence the limitation on their number.)

3) *Quarterly reports* are submitted to the central unemployment insurance unit by each operation. These reports are very detailed. They show the nature of the separations which gave rise to the claims, the proportions of claims protested and appealed, and the proportion of wins and losses.

4) *Conferences* are held annually in five regions for all those who have unemployment insurance as their responsibility in connection with personnel or taxation or plant management. These conferences last for a day and a half and are held away from the plants.[11]

5) *Field audits*, unannounced, are made from time to time by one of the staff of the central unemployment insurance unit. The audit covers all aspects of unemployment insurance operations in a given plant for a given period of time. At the end of the audit, a report is prepared and sent to the interested parties.

6) *Frequent informal contacts* are made with local operations as these latter write or phone the central unit about their local problems. These calls for assistance are the more numerous because of the close relationships established through the conferences described above.

During the period 1954–68, the Ford Motor Company also made use of internal experience rating (see Chapter 12), an indirect means of control probably as effective as all the other controls combined. During this period, the

---

Excluded also from contributions are the substantial amounts of interest earned by reserves. Noncharged benefits were a small amount compared to the sum of subsidiary taxes and interest earnings.

11. The similar meetings held by the General Motors Corporation antedate those of Ford and go back to the early 1950's. The corporation's central unemployment insurance unit maintains a complete record of the proceedings of these meetings, which thus constitute a "library" of all major unemployment insurance problems. This "library" is said to be very useful to the administrators of unemployment insurance in the General Motors plants.

Ford Motor Company must have had one of the most complete systems of claims control of any widespread corporation in the country.

Other Companies

The wide geographical dispersal of operations does not in itself preclude centralized claims control. Retail chains like Sears Roebuck & Co., Montgomery Ward, and J. C. Penney, for example, have had centralized controls in at least several regions (each region including a number of states) where operations were more concentrated, while permitting local control in regions where operations were more sparsely scattered. An even clearer example is the Walgreen Company, which directly administered all unemployment insurance operations out of its Chicago headquarters. This central unemployment insurance unit received and handled the notices of claims filed against the company in any state. The system was so centralized that it operated automatically even in states like Utah, where benefits were not charged against the account of the individual employer.[12] Despite its very high rate of turnover, the Walgreen Company in most states has had a low tax rate. A part of its low rate was probably due to its close control of claims, which included the practive of referring claimants to open jobs in other stores in the same area. This practice had the twofold advantage of lessening benefit charges and retaining experienced employees. Although obviously desirable for general personnel reasons, the practice was in fact inaugurated and maintained under pressure from the unemployment insurance unit.

The General Electric Company exemplifies the large company with very little central claims control. Outside of an unemployment insurance specialist at the central headquarters, who is available to assist the local operations when problems arise, there is no effort to exert central control of claims. The company does, however, provide all operating units with policy guides for handling unemployment insurance problems. The American Telephone and Telegraph Company does not even have an unemployment insurance specialist at headquarters. My impression is that most large corporations resemble General Electric and American Telephone and Telegraph, rather than NR or Ford or Walgreen, in their degree of claims control.

Small firms. I have the impression, also that most small firms pay little attention to claims control. Not understanding the complexities of the law, and not having enough claims volume to justify the assignment of the task to a specialist, they dispatch what they consider to be their legal duties with the least possible expenditure of time and attention.

The typical small firm is probably exemplified by *Company D*, a supplier of food services with about 400 employees. A study made under my supervision of the firm's unemployment insurance experience [91] revealed an almost com-

---

12. Deputies whom I interviewed in Utah were aware that the Walgreen participation in administration, stemming out of the Chicago central office, was different from that of most other firms.

plete lack of effective claims controls. Separations that were clearly protestable had not been, as a matter of fact, protested. Also, while the firm was receiving regular notices from the unemployment insurance office that former employees who were listed as reemployable workers were drawing benefits, the firm was hiring new employees for exactly the same kind of work. The study estimated that by proper claims control the firm could have reduced its unemployment insurance taxes for the three-year period, 1961–63, by about $30,000. Since in two of these years the firm's unemployment insurance taxes were larger than its after-tax profits, there was sufficient financial motivation for installing a more effective system of claims control. But in fact, the firm was not aware of the possibility of this substantial saving. In this it probably typified most small firms.

The task of adjudicating a disputed claim is a complex one if justice is to be done to both parties under the law. The law itself is complex, and many diverse facts are needed before the deputy can make a proper judgment in applying the law. Frequently several different kinds of evidence are needed—attendance records, the exact wording of the firm's regulations, an eye-witness account of an argument or fight, payroll records on wage rates, an exact technical description of a job, proof of the number of warnings given, proof that a genuine job offer was made, and so forth. In the opinion survey described in Chapter 6, several deputies commented that the small employer often replies to a phone call asking for further information by saying: "I don't have time to find out what you want to know. Do the best you can with what you have."[13]

In large firms, the persons immediately in charge of day-to-day operations, like foremen, tend to resemble the small employer in their attitude toward paper work. For example, they tend to supply a minimum amount of information with regard to a separated employee. Yet such persons are the key to an efficient claims-control program. A manual prepared for New York employers makes the following recommendation: "Having line-supervision initiate the controls procedure is probably the most critical aspect of a smooth-running system. Once such personnel are exposed to the experiences of appearing at a hearing as a witness (or even as an observer) and learn the value of good information, they are usually far less reluctant to submit the reports and undertake the face-to-face conversations required for pre-building a good case" [99, p. 15]. All large corporations have training sessions for line-supervision personnel. Some corporations arrange for the company's unemployment insurance administrator to participate in these sessions and explain the requirements of effective claims control.

Trends in Employer Participation

Next to a detailed knowledge of how the mass of employers currently participate in administration, a knowledge that is beyond our reach, it would be most

13. Then if the deputy grants the claim, the employer may get angry. Sometimes he appeals the determination and at the hearing brings out the full, documented facts, which

desirable to know what the trend is in employer participation. The trend during the past two decades has clearly been in the direction of increased participation. The chorus of agreement on this point among the deputies and referees of the opinion survey is confirmed by such developments as the establishment of central unemployment insurance units in large firms and the growth of service companies to handle the unemployment insurance chores of smaller firms. For better or for worse, employers have been undertaking to play a more active role in the program. By way of illustration, there follow three brief histories of firms that have moved from a passive to an active posture with respect to claims control. The histories are followed by a listing of the principal factors which seem to underlie and explain the trend.

Company A. This company is in the oil industry, and like most other firms in that industry, has always had a tax rate below the state average. A sharp rise in the company's rate in the late 1940's drew its attention to unemployment insurance and triggered an investigation which revealed that the company was doing practically nothing in the area of claims control. Only two claims had been protested by the company (a very large company) in the entire preceding year. After the investigation, responsibility for claims control in company A was shifted from the personnel department to the tax department, which by 1950 had a thorough-going claims control program in operation. When I reviewed the work of this unit in 1969, it had three full-time employees and in addition occasionally used company attorneys to attend the hearings on appeals. The operations of the unit are shown in Table 8–4 for the period 1959 through 1969. During this period the company protested 72.5 percent of all claims received, and won 69.8 percent of those it protested.[14] The high proportion of claims protested and the high proportion of protests won indicate clearly that there was a wide potential for claims control even in a company like this, whose tax rate was much below the state average. The period covered by the table contrasts sharply with the period preceding the establishment of the unemployment insurance unit, when only two claims were protested by the entire company in the course of a year.

The savings resulting from the work of the unit during the period covered by the table were estimated at over four million dollars (column 7). These savings are to be interpreted according to the norms and distinctions explained above in the discussion of the savings shown by the NR unit. Although this observation may not be repeated, it applies to all the other instances described later of "savings" resulting from claims control.

---

cause the referee to reverse the deputy. The *Java* decision [104], however, provides an additional incentive for the employer to present his full case to the deputy.

14. Some of the claims came to the company as base-period employer only, and the protest affected only the firm's chargeability. Others came to the company as separating employer and the protests affected the claimant's eligibility for benefits. The relative proportions of these two kinds of protests in the data are not known.

Table 8-4. Company A: Claims Protested by Employer As a
Proportion of Claims Filed and Results of Protests, 1959-69

Fiscal year ending	Index of annual taxable payroll (1959=100)	Claims filed	Claims protested		Favorable rulings received		Estimated savings[a]
			Number	As percent of claims filed	Number	As percent of claims protested	
(1)	(2)	(3)	(4)		(5)	(6)	(7)
1959	100	1,784	1,224	68.6	823	67.2	$ 157,398
1960	99	2,531	1,725	68.2	1,224	71.0	246,615
1961 ⎫ 1962 ⎭	106	4,777	3,273	68.5	2,373	72.5	747,508
1963	117	2,617	1,945	74.3	1,361	70.0	443,657
1964	120	2,628	1,933	73.6	1,313	67.9	412,976
1965	121	2,621	1,933	73.8	1,205	62.3	414,840
1966	160	2,120	1,593	75.1	902	56.6	318,334
1967	161	2,557	1,952	76.3	1,499	76.8	492,950
1968	162	1,949	1,410	72.3	1,104	78.3	343,903
1969	163	2,578	1,978	76.7	1,441	72.9	561,703
1959-69		26,162	18,966	72.5	13,245	69.8	$4,139,884

Source: Data furnished by Company A.

[a]Savings estimated as the product of Column 5 and the average benefit charge per claim.

The claims unit kept a record of the benefit cost attributable to each separate operation of the company. This record also showed the reason for the separation that led to each claim resulting in benefits. Distributed as it was to all the operations, this record had something of the effect of internal experience rating: it made each operation aware of its share in the company's total cost.

The benefit-cost rate (benefits charged as a percent of covered payrolls) of company A averaged 0.61 for the period 1942-50 (nine years) and averaged 0.35 for the period 1951-69 (nineteen years). Thus, in the period following the establishment of closer claims control, the company's benefit-cost rate was almost halved. As usual, it is impossible to say how much of this decrease was due to closer claims control and how much to other factors. However, the extent of the activity revealed in Table 8-4 makes it highly probable that improved claims control was one of the factors leading to the lower cost rate.

As would be expected, company A was a subsidizing firm. In addition to making substantial contributions to the fund in the form of subsidiary taxes and interest earned on its reserve, none of which was credited to its account, company A had what was clearly an excessive reserve. By the end of 1969 its reserve was sufficient to pay benefits for twenty-eight years at the highest annual rate in the history of the company, even if the company made no further contributions to the fund.

Company B. A subsidiary of the American Telephone and Telegraph Company, company B had over 90,000 employees in 1969, of whom about one-third were telephone operators, another one-third were repair and installation men, and the rest were engineers, auditors, clerks, etc. Marked by very high turnover, the company has to hire over 20,000 new people each year in order to maintain an average work force of about 90,000.

The parent corporation leaves responsibility for claims control entirely to each subsidiary. During its first two decades of coverage under the unemployment insurance law, company B followed a permissive policy with respect to claims. Concerned with its image as a public servant, the company avoided protesting claims which were controversial. If, for example, an employee had to be dismissed for theft or drunkenness or insubordination the company would report the separation to the state under the vague description of "no longer useful to the company." Whatever decision the state made on this vague information was accepted: the company never appealed. About 1959, a couple of cases of spectacular abuse, plus a strike, plus some internal organizational changes, brought about a change of policy and a decision to exercise more control over claims. The impetus for the change seems to have come from the legal department, which had long been unhappy over the previous policy.

The new procedures were put into operation gradually in one area after another. Progress was slow because procedures had to be developed and personnel trained, and there was still no central unemployment insurance unit. In 1962, in connection with another companywide reorganization, a central unemployment insurance unit was established and was gradually expanded. In 1970 when I reviewed the work of the unit it consisted of a supervisor and three assistants. At that time, the system of claims control was firmly established in one of the three territories into which the state was divided, was fairly well advanced in the second, but was only beginning in the third. The slow pace of the development is a reflection of the difficulty of establishing claims control in a large corporation.

The central unit's procedures for controlling claims were generally similar to those described for NR. The unit kept detailed records which showed the sources of all claims—by location,[15] as well as by the type of separation that led to the claim. From these records the finance and personnel managers of the company could see at a glance the cost of the unemployment benefits stemming from the company's various activities and from its personnel policies. Since the company's total unemployment insurance taxes were substantial—several millions of dollars—even small reductions in the company's tax rate could mean sizable savings in dollars. Since these records were circulated widely in the company, they probably served some of the functions of internal experience rating.

In addition to preparing a detailed claims control manual for use in the field, the central unemployment insurance unit prepared a ten-page explanation of unemployment insurance for use by the company's internal auditors. In the

15. The records showed the experience of each territory, of each geographical area into which a territory was divided, and of each operating department (traffic, commercial, accounting, plant, engineering) in an area.

company's "Outline of Internal Auditing Procedures" the auditors are told: "It is the auditor's responsibility, through periodic review, to determine whether claims are thoroughly and properly investigated, disputed when appropriate, and whether the necessary supporting records are maintained." The auditor is also told that "responsibility for the entire scope of unemployment claim processing is interdepartmental" and he is instructed to review the cooperation of the legal, the tax, and the personnel departments.

Very little of the company's high turnover rate represented layoffs. As a result, in most years over half of the claimants were disqualified for benefits. The potential area for claims control therefore was wide. With the advent of closer claims control, the benefit-cost rate of the company declined and remained low. However, so many other economic factors were at work simultaneously that it is impossible to isolate and measure the effect of the single factor of claims control.

The central unemployment insurance unit has a general policy of reviewing the eligibility of claimants who have remained in benefit status for five weeks or more. The unit is aware of these claimants, because the state notifies employers on a weekly basis of benefits charged to their account. Where the condition of the labor market seems to justify the action, the central unit writes to the appropriate state local office and requests that it review the eligibility of the claimant. These letters are not appeals and of themselves have no direct effect on the claimant's eligibility for benefits. They thus differ in this vital respect from employer protests on the issue of availability in state B, as described in Chapter 6.

If the company's records show that the claimant is a desirable employee, the unemployment insurance unit can often arrange a job offer. A specific offer of a job is mailed to the claimant over the signature of the supervisor of employment, and a copy of the letter is sent to the state local office. A couple of hundred such job offers might be made in the course of an average year, with perhaps fifty resulting rehires. The rehires represented a double benefit to the company— the acquisition of experienced personnel as well as the saving of unemployment benefit charges. The job offers resulted also in many disqualifications. Since the company lists all its job openings with the employment service, the state might have made these same job offers without the company's action; but the rehires and disqualifications resulting from the job offers did not, as a matter of fact, occur until the company acted.

To complete the picture, it may be noted that company B was a "subsidizing" firm. During the period 1959 through 1970, the company's employees drew out in benefits only 25 percent of what the company had contributed to the state fund. As of 1970, the company's reserve was large enough to pay benefits for twenty years at the highest annual rate in the company's experience, even if the company made no further contributions. The company's reserve is exclusive, as usual, of the additional contributions made by the company in the form of subsidiary taxes credited to the Common Account and the substantial interest earned by the company's unused previous contributions.

Company C. From 1959 through 1965 this company, one of the largest construction firms in the United States, paid the maximum tax rate of 2.7 percent in the state in which it had most of its operations, and it would have paid an even higher rate if the maximum had been higher. In some years it would have paid over 4 percent.

In 1964 the state was seriously considering an increase in the maximum tax rate. Company C's financial vice-president, realizing that an increase in the maximum tax would mean greatly increased costs for his company, made a study of the company's unemployment insurance experience during the fiscal year ending September 30, 1964. The purpose of the study was "to determine the effect upon our future state unemployment tax rate if we developed a more active program [of claims control] and to determine if our personnel records are accurate and complete regarding terminations.[16]

The study revealed that staff in the personnel department had been making inadequate use of what termination reports were available and that staff in the field had been making inaccurate termination reports. The company had protested 7 percent of the benefit wages charged against its account, whereas on the basis of information available in its own files (its termination reports) it should have protested 22 percent.[17] Clerks had been putting "ROF" (reduction of force) on the form going back to the state without even consulting the termination reports, which in many instances indicated that the claimant had quit or had been discharged for cause. The personnel records for still another 7 percent of the charges were "so incomplete or missing that we were unable to conclude whether or not they should have been protested." Finally, the study examined a sample of termination reports and found that over one-quarter of them were incorrectly marked "ROF" when the real reason for the separation had been something else.

As a result of the findings of this study and in connection with a general reorganization of the company required by its considerable growth over the preceding decade, in 1965–66 a specialized unemployment insurance unit was established which gradually set up procedures to maintain closer claims control. At the same time, the company was reorganizing its personnel department so as to diminish the amount of unnecessary turnover.

At the time of my visit to the company, in 1970, the unit had not been summarizing the results of its activities. For the purpose of this study, however, the unit did make the two-year summary shown in Table 8–5. In 1969 the company protested 38.6 percent of all claims and received a favorable decision on 92.0 percent of its protests. In 1970 the corresponding percentages were 32.4 percent and 90.5 percent. Thus, in the two years combined, over one-third of all claims merited the company's attention. Evidently, even in the construction

16. Internal company memorandum, July 13, 1965.
17. Since at that time the state used the benefit-wage-ratio system, the study was in terms of benefit wages charged against the firm's account. For a description of this system, see Appendix B.

Table 8-5. Company C: Claims Successfully Protested
by Employer 1969, 1970

Fiscal year	Claims received			Percent protested			Percent of protests won		
	Total	As base period employer only	As sepa-rating employer	Total	As base period employer only	As sepa-rating employer	Total	As base period employer only	As sepa-rating employer
1969	1,129	520	609	38.6	48.7	30.0	92.0	96.8	85.2
1970	2,611	1,069	1,542	32.4	46.5	22.6	90.5	90.5	90.5

Source: Data received from Company C.

business there can be substantial numbers of separations that are not layoffs and hence provide a potential area for claims control. Evidently, also, to judge by its win ratio the unit did not protest claims needlessly.[18]

In the opinion survey, the deputies and referees noted that construction firms participated relatively little in administration. Those who were interviewed advanced the probable explanation that in this industry nearly all separations were layoffs and hence provided no basis for protest. To the extent that company C's experience is typical (it may not be) it casts some doubt on the validity of this reason, at least as a general explanation. It leaves some room for the alternative explanation that since a disproportionate number of firms in this industry are at the maximum tax rate, they have no financial incentive to protest. Also according to service companies which have construction firms as clients, employers in this industry, under union pressure, sometimes instruct the service company not to protest certain types of claims.

The data of Table 8-5 throw additional light on the usually hidden difference between claims involving only the employer's chargeability (when the employer is only a base-period employer) and the claimant's eligibility (when the employer is the separating employer). As in the case of NR, the claims involving only the employer's chargeability were almost as numerous as claims of the other type. Like NR, company C tended to protest a greater percentage of the claims that involved only its chargeability.

Table 8-6 shows the company's benefit-wage ratio from 1957 through 1967. The sharp drop in the ratio after 1965, when the new policy of claims control was in full operation, was partly the result of the increase in taxable wages, but was also partly the result of the decrease in the amount of benefit wages charged against the company's account.[19] How much of the latter charge was the result

18. Originally, in the first flush of instituting a new system of control, the unit seems to have proceeded too rigorously and mechanically, with consequent needless inconvenience to claimants. Becoming aware of the situation, the state took the not uncommon step of contacting informally top management in the company, which promptly instituted remedial action. Thereafter the state seems to have had no complaint.

19. Also, the benefit wages charged in 1967 reflect only the first three-quarters of that year. A new system, the benefit-radio system, took effect on October 1.

Table 8-6. Company C: Taxable Wages, Benefit Wages Charged, and
Benefit-Wage Ratio,[a] 1957-67

Three years ending	Taxable wages	Benefit wages charged	Benefit-wage ratio[a]
1957	$ 35,252,124	$ 3,860,115	11.0
1958	42,479,951	5,018,365	11.8
1959	42,551,053	7,393,887	17.4
1960	44,651,846	8,191,271	18.3
1961	51,338,253	7,409,122	14.4
1962	62,973,473	9,027,782	14.3
1963	67,109,384	12,570,105	18.7
1964	66,220,646	12,298,727	18.6
1965	69,362,220	10,100,636	14.6
1966	82,607,095	6,470,104	7.8
1967	$102,054,511	$ 4,890,669	4.8

Source: Data received from Company C.

[a]Benefit wages charged as percent of taxable wages.

of the company's prosperity, as reflected in the growth in taxable wages, and how much was the result of closer claims control is impossible to say. However, there would seem to be a solid probability that the new policy of claims control has exerted a significant effect.

The period following 1967 is not directly comparable with the earlier period because the tax system was changed—from the benefit-wage ratio to the benefit-ratio system—effective October 1, 1967. Under the new system, company C paid a tax rate of 0.2 percent of taxable wages in 1968 and 0.1 percent (the minimum) in 1969. These are remarkably low rates for a firm engaged in heavy contract construction, an industry generally marked by cost rates and tax rates far above the average (see, for example, Tables A-5, A-6, and A-7). Although the main causes of this happy condition were probably the state's and the company's prosperity, along with the change in the tax system, such very low rates could hardly have been attained if claims control had remained as loose as it had been before 1964.

Factors Affecting Trends

The three examples given above of firms that changed from a loose to a strict form of claims administration include a manufacturing firm, a service firm, and a construction firm. In one case the initiative for the change came from the tax department of the corporation, in another it came from the legal department, while in the third it came from the finance department. In all cases, the change had its chief impact on the personnel department.

Other examples could be given of the trend toward closer claims control; but they would not add up to a representative sample, and no point would be served in merely multiplying examples. It might contribute to a wider view, however, to survey the factors that may explain the general trend toward increased employer participation. Some of these factors relate to the state unemployment insurance system and some to the individual firm.

State provisions. (1) The degree of sensitivity in the experience-rating system is probably one factor. Employer participation is likely to be the greater the closer the system comes to allocating taxes in proportion to benefit-cost rates and the clearer this relationship is to the employer. The reserve-ratio system probably elicits the most employer participation, while the annual payroll-decline system certainly elicits the least. The long-term trend in the program has been toward more sensitive experience-rating systems (Table A-1). (2) Disqualification provisions. The financial saving represented by a disqualification and hence the incentive for employer participation in administration is the greater as the disqualification provisions are the stricter. The general trend has been toward stricter disqualifications. (3) Noncharging provisions. As explained before, from the viewpoint of the individual employer, the effect of the noncharging of benefits is like the most complete of disqualifications. The incentive to protest a claim is greatest under a noncharging provision. Again, the trend has been toward more such provisions. The realization that all employers must eventually pay for these noncharged benefits in no way diminishes the incentive of the individual employer to protest claims. As long as noncharging provisions are in the law, the individual employer can only gain by taking advantage of them and only lose by neglecting to take advantage of them. Moreover, the employer usually finds it easier to get a favorable decision when only his chargeability and not the claimant's eligibility is at issue.

Characteristics of the firm. (4) Tax level. The higher their tax rates, the more attention firms give to the unemployment insurance program and to the possibility of achieving some tax savings through claims control (except, of course, where the firm's cost rate is well above the state's maximum tax rate). For this reason, service agencies tend to avoid states with low average tax rates and to proliferate in states with high tax rates. The generally high unemployment of the 1950's and the consequent higher unemployment insurance taxes marked the beginning of a new interest in unemployment insurance for many firms.

(5) Size of firm. The large firms can afford to assign one or more persons to specialize in unemployment insurance matters. In administration, as in production, specialization leads to increased efficiency. The growth of company C, for example, was one of the factors leading to the establishment of a central unemployment insurance unit.

(6) Finally, the extent of employer organization and the level of employer education is a factor. Some states run periodic workshops for employers to instruct them in the unemployment insurance program. California has been especially active in this respect. In other states, employer organizations themselves

have organized workshops for this purpose. In some states (New York and Michigan, for example), employers also have a statewide organization concerned solely with unemployment insurance problems. Within firms, central unemployment insurance units play a crucial role in the educational process (see the example of the Ford Motor Company, above).

Not included in the above list of favoring factors are chance events, such as occasioned the establishment of a central unemployment insurance unit in a large retail chain. By mistake, the tax manager received the notice of a determination awarding benefits to a claimant on the ground that the company paid "substandard" wages. The tax manager directed that the determination be appealed and himself attended the hearing. At the hearing the referee commented on the unusual event: someone from this firm present at an appeals hearing. The tax manager returned from the appeal, which was eventually decided in favor of the company, and proceeded to set up a central unemployment insurance unit.

Although the result of all these various factors has been an increase in the degree of participation in unemployment insurance administration for many firms, it probably remains true that the average employer still does not understand unemployment insurance and does not participate in its administration beyond the absolute minimum required by the law. The average firm probably resembles the three companies A, B, and C in their early periods, before they began to give serious attention to claims control. Even if the trend toward increased employer participation should continue, the attitude of the average firm is not likely to change notably—certainly not in the short run and probably not in the long run.

Employer Participation in Appeals

Employer activity at the appeals level offers what is probably the clearest reflection of the effect of experience rating. Participation in the appeal process, whether the appellant be the employer or the claimant, involves a cost for the employer in terms of time and effort much greater than that required to participate at the level of the initial determination. For effective participation in an appeal, the employer must make a much more careful preparation of the evidence he plans to submit, such as affidavits and copies of essential documents, and he must attend the hearing. Not infrequently it is necessary to take highly paid supervisory personnel from their regular work in order to have them testify at the hearing. For these reasons, employer activity at the appeal level is the most sensitive measure of employer interest in administration. Only very interested employers will undertake the bother and cost of appealing claims or of attending the hearings on claimant appeals.[20]

20. There is another difference between employer activity at the appeals level and at the level of the initial determination. The employer "protest" at the level of the initial determination may affect only the employer's chargeability, whereas the employer appeal—or the employer's opposition to a claimant appeal—practically always affects the claimant's eligibil-

The importance of appeals is not to be measured by their relatively small number. Decisions on appealed cases often set precedents that may affect subsequent decisions for long periods of time. Decisions on appeals constitute a very extensive body of administrative law which approaches in its significance the law itself. While it may be arguable whether experience rating has a significant effect on legislation (Chapter 9), there can be no doubt that experience rating influences administrative law. It is clear that experience rating increases employer participation in the appeal process and equally clear that employer activity at the appeal level has an impact on administrative law.

Some light on the desirability or undesirability of employer appeal activity is provided by two ratios. The first is the relative frequency of appeals, as measured by the ratio of appeals to new spells of unemployment. The other is the proportion of appeals won by employers. What is the "proper" size of these ratios? The answer to that question depends partly—indeed largely—on what one conceives to be the "proper" balance of power between labor and management, an issue which is discussed in Chapter 9. Here it suffices to note that a difference in view on the more fundamental issue permits very different conclusions to be drawn from the same data. For example, when Mississippi was debating the adoption of experience rating (1948), the complete absence of employer appeals in the state was described by the chief opponent of the proposal as a desirable situation that would be spoiled by experience rating, while the proponents of experience rating were pointing to the same fact as proof that experience rating was needed. Thus, again, when Pennsylvania amended its law (1949) to require employers to deposit a fee for the privilege of appealing a claim, employer appeals had been amounting to only 10 percent of all appeals, and employers had been winning over half of the appeals they filed. Likewise, when New York adopted a similar provision in 1951, employers were accounting for only 1.5 percent of all appeals filed. Since the purpose of the provision was to discourage employer participation, these ratios were evidently deemed too high.[21] But however one is inclined to judge a given ratio, as being good or bad, there is need to know what the ratio is in order to know how good or how bad the actual situation is.

Table 8-7 shows a decade of appeals experience for the country as a whole and for twelve states which include over half of all covered workers and exemplify a wide variety of employer participation. Claimant appeals are also shown, because they provide a measure of comparison and because the larger part of employer activity at the appeals level consists of attending hearings on claimant appeals.[22]

---

ity as well. Thus employer activity on the appeals level is not obscured by the ambiguity attaching to employer "protests" at the level of the initial determination.

21. The same fundamental difference appears in the Railroad Unemployment Insurance program, where employers have no right to appeal any determination on claims. This limitation is considered desirable by labor, undersirable by management.

22. It should be noted that the data of Table 8-7 are in terms of appeals *decisions*. Appeals that were filed but never came to a decision are not included in the data. Such

Table 8-7. Lower Authority Appeals Experience for Nation and for Selected States,[a] Average for Period 1961-69

State	Decisions on appeals as percent of estimated new spells of unemployment, compared with 52-state average			Percent of decisions in favor appellant, compared with 52-state average		
	Clearly below average	About average	Clearly above average	Clearly below average	About average	Clearly above average
Employer appeals						
52-state average		0.26			41.9	
California		0.34				46.7
Connecticut	0.17					52.8
Illinois			1.41			46.4
Massachusetts	0.19				38.6	
Michigan[b]	0.19			26.1		
New York	0.07			22.0		
Ohio[b]	0.19				42.5	
Pennsylvania	0.18			25.2		
Rhode Island[c]	*					
Utah	*					
Washington	0.05					52.4
Wisconsin		0.27			39.0	
Claimant appeals						
52-state average		1.62			27.3	
California	1.15					35.1
Connecticut		1.81				30.0
Illinois			2.19		25.1	
Massachusetts		1.50		19.6		
Michigan[b]	0.68					37.5
New York			2.14		27.7	
Ohio[b]	0.95				24.0	
Pennsylvania		1.70		20.9		
Rhode Island[c]	0.78					33.1
Utah	0.44			18.4		
Washington	0.61					38.2
Wisconsin	0.90				24.6	

Sources: 1961-1963, Statistical Supplement, Labor Market and Employment Security; 1964-1969, Unemployment Insurance Statistics, both published by U.S. Department of Labor, Bureau of Employment Security, Washington, D.C.

*Less than 0.01 percent.
[a]The twelve selected states included 54.1 percent of all covered workers in 1969.
[b]An appeal may be taken only from a redetermination. This provision tends to decrease the number of appeals.
[c]Includes decisions rendered by Rhode Island's Board of Review (higher authority).

The national averages show that employer appeals tend to be only about one-sixth as numerous as claimant appeals, but almost twice as successful. For every one thousand opportunities that might possibly have given rise to an appeal (determinations on claimant eligibility on the occasion of a new spell of unemployment)[23] employers actually appealed 2.6 times. If none of the decisions on these appeals had been favorable to the appellant, this would have been the outside measure of possibly "frivolous" appeals whose only effect was to delay the payment of benefits. Since the employer appeals were successful 41.9 percent of the time, this outside limit is reduced to about 1.5 out of every 1,000 opportunities. Since not all unsuccessful employer appeals may be considered frivolous, the actual number of employer appeals that could reasonable be called unnecessary by any widely accepted norm is something much less than 1.5 out of every 1,000 opportunities. This general finding is in agreement with the more detailed analysis made of the sample of Massachusetts employers (Chapter 7) and with the findings of the opinion survey (Chapter 6)

The win ratio (41.9 percent) of employers nationally is lower than that of the companies with unemployment insurance specialists, such as those described above, or of the service companies discussed below. This illustrates the general principle that the more professional the appellant, the fewer the number of unsuccessful and of unnecessary appeals. The large corporations, with their full-time experts, and the professional service companies make better judgments than does the average employer on what claims should be appealed. The average employer usually has less knowledge and exhibits more emotion than his more professional counterparts. For this reason some deputies and referees said they would rather deal with a service company than with the average small employer. If the experience of the larger firms and of service companies were subtracted from the employer data of the table, the win ration of employers would be more like the win ratio of claimants.[24]

---

appeals are of two sorts, chiefly: appeals that were withdrawn and appeals in which the appellant defaulted (failed to appear at the hearing). If such appeals were included in the base, the win ratios of all appellants, both employer and claimant, would be somewhat lower than those shown in the table. However, data on withdrawn and defaulted appeals are not regularly available. (For samples of such data, see later in this chapter.)

23. The use of new spells of unemployment as the base against which to measure employer appeals assumes that employers protest and appeal only on the occasion of the first claim. Actually, employers may and sometimes do protest the later, or the "continued," claim. However, except in a few states, such protests are insignificant in number and their inclusion would not noticeably affect the numerator of our ratio, while the addition of all continued claims to the denominator would reduce the percentages to the vanishing point. If the data had been available, it would have been useful to construct another table showing the ratio of appeals to nonmonetary determinations made in favor of the claimant. While not as useful as a measure of the outside limit of employer "harassment," it would have been more useful as a measure of the extent of employer interest in administration.

24. Both the average employer and the claimant sometimes lose a case because they lack the sophistication to present it effectively. This possibility is the more serious in the case of the claimant, both because claimant appeals are the more numerous and because the entire

Comparisons between states must be made with great circumspection because it is usually not possible to determine which of several factors explains a given difference between states. However, a few observations may usefully be made. Rhode Island, Utah, and Washington produced practically no employer appeals during the period shown by the table, and the reason is probably to be found in the slight degree of experience rating that marked those three states. Utah and Washington operated under the payroll-decline system, which does not charge benefits against the account of the individual firm and hence offers the employer no direct financial incentive to undertake the costly step of appealing claims.[25] In Utah even the largest firms could not recall, when interviewed, that they had ever appealed a decision of the agency.[26] In some years, Utah held more appeal hearings for other states (on interstate claims) than it held for itself. In Washington a disproportionate number of the few employer appeals came from one very large company, which because of its size felt an obligation to supply leadership to the employer community. In Rhode Island experience rating was suspended for the first half of the period covered by the table (see Table A-2); furthermore, employer appeals have been discouraged since 1958 by a requirement that an employer appellant pay a $20 fee, which the state retains unless the employer wins his appeal.

In Illinois both employer and claimant tended to appeal more frequently than the national average. Despite the frequency of his appeals, the Illinois employer had a higher win ratio than the national average. In New York the behavior of the claimant is almost identical with that of the claimant in Illinois, but the New York employer presents quite a different picture. He rarely appeals (the claimant accounts for 97 percent of all appeals), and his win ratio is far below the national average. An inquiry addressed to the New York agency and to some New York employers turned up no clear explanation of the low ratios in that state. California and New York show almost exactly opposite patterns for employers and claimants: where the one is high, the other is low, and vice versa. In Wisconsin, the home of experience rating, employer appeal experience was about at the national average. Except for California and Illinois, the large industrial states are below average in the proportion of claims appealed by employers. It is tempting to speculate on the reasons for this; but it would be pure speculation.

---

system was established to serve the claimant. However, I have found in attending claimant appeals that the referee in charge of the hearing usually tries to protect the claimant from his own inadequacies.

25. Previous to July 1, 1964, Mississippi operated under a payroll-decline system. During the two-year period, July 1, 1962 through June 30, 1964, employers filed twenty appeals. Effective July 1, 1964, Mississippi changed to the benefit-ratio system, which charges benefits directly to the account of the individual employer. During the two-year period, July 1, 1964 through June 30, 1966, employers filed 374 appeals, an increase of almost 2,000 percent. Of the 374 appeals, 98 affected the claimant's eligibility and 276 affected only the employer's chargeability [105].

26. One firm did recall appealing an agency decision to *deny* a class of claims. The firm had worked out a relationship between its retirement program and unemployment benefits which the agency's denials were upsetting. A compromise was worked out with the agency.

The 1971 *Java* decision of the U.S. Supreme Court [104], requiring that benefit payments be continued while an employer's appeal is pending, is likely to have different effects on employer propensity to appeal, depending on what is done about the disputed benefits in cases where the employer wins. The claimant may be required to repay the benefits or he may be allowed to retain them; in the latter case, the benefits may be charged against the employer's account or they may be noncharged. If such benefits are noncharged, the employer's incentive to appeal a claim will probably be unaffected.

Since claimant appeals make up five-sixths of the total, the chief opportunity for employer participation on the appeal level is in attending hearings on claimant appeals. What scattered data are available indicate that employers attend claimant appeals less than one-third of the time. Such attendance is important because, as many deputies and referees observed in the opinion survey, the testimony presented under oath (the claimant's) usually outweighs (other things being equal) the absent employer's testimony, which is not presented under oath. One of the principal selling points of the service companies is their offer to undertake the chore of attending hearings on claimant appeals.

Employer appeals may discourage claimants from pursuing their just claims. For example, the claimant may be working again by the time the appeal is heard and may be unwilling or unable to take time off from work to attend the hearing. Although some states try to provide against this possibility by offering to take the claimant's testimony whenever he can present it, even on a Saturday, the possibility remains. Deputies and referees who were interviewed thought that instances of such discouragement were infrequent; but no data were available to verify this opinion.

When an employer appeals a claim and then fails to be present at the hearing on his appeal, he is said to be in default. How widespread is this practice, probably the most objectionable feature of employer participation in administration?[27] There are no regularly published data on the extent of the practice, and the scattered examples given below may be used safely only to indicate vague limits within which the actual averages probably lie. Based on small sample studies made at various times, and quite possibly reflecting somewhat different definitions, the following percentages indicate the proportion of all employer appeals that were defaulted:

California	(1963)	18.5 percent
Massachusetts	(1967)	10.1

27. Claimant defaults on appeals filed by claimants also occur. Relatively more numerous than employer defaults, claimant defaults may be costly for the firm. An employer may carefully prepare for a scheduled hearing on a claimant appeal, may take time from his business to be present at the hearing, and may even bring other personnel with him as witnesses, only to find that the appellant has defaulted. Here, however, we are concerned only with employer defaults.

Illinois	(1970)	5.3
Michigan	(1971)	4.0
New York	(1971)	19.0
Ohio	(1971)	7.4
Wisconsin	(1971)	7.1

An employer may default for a variety of reasons: because he is out of town on the day of the hearing, or is ill, or is especially busy; or because a key witness is ill, or away, or especially busy; or because he has decided he has no case and neglects to withdraw his appeal; or because he has filed the appeal originally only because he wished to harass the claimant. Without information on the relative importance of these various explanations it is impossible properly to evaluate the significance of defaulted employer appeals. It is pertinent to observe however, that since the 1971 decision of the U.S. Supreme Court in *Java* [104] the chief objectionable feature of defaulted appeals—the delay caused in the payment of benefits—has been removed. In the future (unless Congress should change the social security law) the claimant will continue to receive his benefits during the interval separating the state's initial favorable decision and the hearing of the employer's appeal.

Service Companies

Instead of attempting to control their own unemployment insurance claims, some firms delegate the task to another company which specializes in providing this service. Companies of this sort, which are here called "service companies," have developed from various roots. In the early days of the program the most usual root was an existing firm which had been providing industrial services and which simply extended the scope of its activities to include the new program of unemployment insurance. In many cases this new activity grew to be the major activity. Later firms were established with this activity as their sole purpose. Very little capital is required to begin one of these firms. Knowledge of unemployment insurance, contacts with possible clients, and some management ability are the only essentials. The founder of a new firm is frequently either a former employee of another service company or a former employee of a state employment insurance agency.

Background. Little information is available on the history of these service companies. Apparently they developed slowly until after World War II, and the total development still represents a small industry. The chief development took place in the 1950's and 1960's and was very uneven among the states. California probably has the largest number of service companies. In 1969 there were 60 such firms operating in the state and representing 12,150 client firms.[28] The

---

28. In 1963 there had been 44 service companies representing 9,726 client firms.

largest service company had nearly 5,000 clients, ten companies had 400 or more clients, and a dozen companies had only 1 or 2 clients.[29] In Pennsylvania, in 1968, approximately 2,500 firms were represented by service companies.

Service companies find a congenial climate in states with the following characteristics: (1) a relatively high unemployment insurance tax. The higher the unemployment insurance tax, the more interested are corporate finance officers in suggestions on how to control the tax. The high unemployment insurance taxes of California are one of the reasons for the proliferation of service companies in that state. (2) A relatively high degree of experience rating in the tax system. The more closely taxes follow experience the greater is the likelihood that claims control will lower taxes for a particular employer. States like Washington and Utah have little attraction for a service company. The slight development of service companies in Illinois is probably due to the benefit-wage-ratio system of that state, along with its relatively low average unemployment rate. (3) Relatively strict disqualification provisions. The stricter the disqualification provisions the more scope there is for the claims control provided by the service companies. (4) Noncharging provisions. As explained before, from the viewpoint of the individual firm looking at its own tax rate, the noncharging of benefits is like the most complete of disqualifications. Since it is much easier to win a protest that affects only the chargeability of the employer than to win one that affects the eligibility of the claimant, noncharging provisions provide the service company with opportunities for numerous easy victories. The interest of the service companies in promoting noncharging provisions sometimes puts them on the side of labor and opposed to the rest of the employer community. Thus it has happened that service companies were urging more liberal noncharging provisions in the state legislature at the same time that the employer organizations in the state were trying to eliminate noncharging provisions already in existence.

Nature. Service companies differ considerably in the services they offer, in the fees they charge, and in the titles under which they operate. They differ also in the reputation they have among the deputies and referees' with whom they deal. Moreover, the same service company will operate differently in various states, depending on the provisions of the unemployment insurance law in each state and on the preferences of the individual regional manager.

It is convenient to view the services offered as falling into two groups—those that directly affect unemployment insurance costs and "other." The first of the direct services is aid in responding appropriately to the state's notice that a claim has been filed. Most service companies themselves perform this first crucial task in claims control. But there are some that merely supervise this task, which is

29. In itself, the number of clients is not a reliable measure of relative size. One large client firm might be the equivalent of a score of smaller firms. A better measure would be the amount of covered payroll, and the best measure would be the number of covered employees. But such data are not available.

actually performed by the client firm. In the usual case, the service company requests the state to send all correspondence relating to the claim directly to them. Most states honor this request, but some insist on dealing directly only with the client firm, which must then transmit to the service company all materials it receives from the state. Service companies operating under both procedures say that the difference is not major.

The other direct service relates to appeals, whether filed by the employer or by the claimant. Service companies are not inclined to make useless appeals. Because the appeal process is time-consuming, it is costly and tends to lessen the profitability of an account. As a result, established service companies appeal relatively few determinations and their win ratio tends to be high. There have been service companies, especially new ones "on the make," which have for a time appealed claims indiscriminately; but, as several referees remarked in the opinion survey, such companies do not stay in business very long unless they learn to act more responsibly.

Most appeals are filed by claimants, and most employers are unwilling to take the time to attend the hearings on these appeals. Service companies, on the other hand, are more faithful in attending such hearings. Indeed, they make this service one of their major selling points in dealing with prospective clients.

In addition to these direct aids to claims control, the service company may perform several other functions. The better service companies have sufficiently broad experience in management to advise their clients, especially the smaller firms, on personnel practices that should characterize the well-run firm. The service company may also help its clients set up an adequate record-keeping system, which is the basis of claims control. If the client is a multi-plant or multi-store operation, the service company will often offer to conduct training sessions for the managers and personnel directors of the various plants and stores. I have come across instances where the service company was the active agent in arranging transfers of the about-to-be-laid off employees of one client to the payroll of another client.

The service company typically audits the periodic statements of benefit charges received from the state.[30] It checks to see that the claimant whose benefits are charged against the firm was really an employee of the firm, that he had earned sufficient wages to be eligible for benefits, that the total amount of benefits charged is correct, that the firm has not been charged more than its proportional share of the total, and that none of the benefits should have been "noncharged." The service company is sometimes asked by its larger clients to estimate next year's tax rate, because the client has started to put together its budget and cannot wait until it receives official notification from the state. The service company is also sometimes expected to advise its client on whether to make a voluntary contribution so as to lower its tax rate for the coming year.

---

30. The states differ greatly in the amount of detail they furnish in these statements.

The service company usually makes some kind of annual report to its clients. The information provided in these reports varies greatly. Depending partly on what the client is willing to pay for,[31] the report may be a paragraph in a letter or a fifty-page bound document. Some of these reports are as complete as any of those mentioned in connection with central unemployment insurance units.

One very full report which is before me as I write shows the total number of claims filed against the client's account and the sources of these claims—that is, the operating unit from which the claimant came and the reason for the claimant's separation from employment.[32] The report also shows the proportion of claims that were successfully protested and the proportion that resulted in a charge against the client's account. These latter are shown by the name of each claimant and the total amount of benefits drawn by the claimant.

The report points out the relationship between claims and particular policies of the client firm regarding vacations, leaves of absence, pensions, and pregnancies. The report also identifies the claims that were charged against the employer's account because the manager of plant X was unable to supply sufficiently definite evidence on the characteristics of a separation, or because the personnel director of plant Y failed to inform the service company that a claim had been filed or had forwarded the required information too late to be admissible under the state law. The report also indicates the claims that were paid because someone in the firm had requested that the claim not be protested. On other occasions, the report has also highlighted loose personnel policies that led to excessive claims, such as the wholesale hiring and firing of temporary employees. Such detailed reports become management tools whose potential significance is much greater than the specific unemployment insurance experience it describes.

The report contained the following statistics, which are given here simply to fill out the example. Of 264 claims, the service company successfully protested 70 percent. Of 23 appeals, it received a favorable decision in 16. The resulting savings for the client were estimated at $180,000. Allowed claims resulted in charges against the client's account totaling $50,000, of which only $23,000 represented separations due to lack of work. In 14 of the allowed claims, representing several thousands of dollars of charges, the client was at fault in some way, usually by failing to notify the service company in time to file a protest. In 2 of the 14 cases, the client had instructed the service company "Do not protest."

Operations. The typical client is a medium-sized firm whose tax rate is between the minimum and the maximum. Small firms do not have enough claims to warrant the fee charged by the service company, while the largest firms have

31. But I have come across service companies that supplied their clients with a much more detailed and useful report than did other companies charging a higher fee.
32. The client was a large manufacturing firm with many separate plants.

such a volume of claims as to warrant establishing a specialized unemployment insurance unit of their own. Nevertheless, the service companies do have clients among the largest corporations in the country. Such a corporation may have a medium-sized plant or two in a state far removed from the corporation's central office; headquarters may decide that the most efficient way to handle the claims of these plants is to hire a service company. Or the client may be a corporation with a chain of retail stores. The total number of employees working in all these stores may be sufficient to justify a (nearly) full-time unemployment insurance administrator, but if the chain operates in a large number of states, such an administrator may find claims control very difficult, especially in handling appeals. He may find himself required to appear at appeal hearings in several different states on the same day. Chains that do not wish to rely on the individual store may turn this task over to a service company.[33]

The typical client of the service company is at neither the maximum tax rate nor the minimum tax rate. The service company's primary selling point is its promise to lower the client's tax, and the probability of fulfilling this promise is least when the client is at the maximum or the minimum rate. The client at the maximum tax rate may have so much unemployment that no amount of claims control can bring him below the maximum. The firm at the minimum tax rate (if the state minimum is above zero) may have so little unemployment that even very careless claims control may have no impact on his tax rate. Nevertheless, the service companies have picked up some clients who were at maximum and minimum tax rates at the time they signed the contract. These may have been firms that were at the margin of dropping below the maximum rate or at the margin of rising above the minimum rate. Or, they may have been firms that simply wanted to get rid of the chore of handling their own unemployment insurance claims. The service companies claim that, quite apart from the possibility that they may lower the client's tax rate, they can perform more cheaply than can the firm itself the minimum administrative tasks required by the law.[34]

In trying to sell its services to the large multiplant corporation that permits each plant to handle its own unemployment insurance claims, the service company argues for the advantages of centralization, using some of the same reasons that apply to the establishment of a central unemployment insurance unit in a large corporation, namely, that at the local level the required knowledge and motivation will often be lacking. Local personnel usually do not acquire an adequate knowledge of the complexities of unemployment insurance because they must also master a multitude of other duties, most of them more important

33. Other chains, however, neither rely on the individual store nor hire a service company, but set up their own centralized administrative unit. The Walgreen Company is one of these. Sears, Roebuck and Montgomery Ward use centralized administration in some regions but not in others.

34. In a letter to the author, one national retail chain denied this claim emphatically: "A contract offered us by one service company would have cost us $50,000 in each large state. We spend less than $2,000 to do the job ourselves in these same states."

than unemployment insurance administration. Adequate motivation is also frequently lacking, so that the local personnel do not use even the limited knowledge they have. The local plant manager in a large corporation that does not use internal experience rating is in a position almost identical with that of a firm in a state which uses a uniform tax. Both have only an indirect and slight financial interest in the cost of the benefits drawn by its employees. When the local plant manager becomes very busy, the first task to be skimped or omitted is likely to be unemployment insurance claims control. No one will know if he gives this chore little or no attention, nor does diminished attention make any measurable difference in his profits. The availability of "costless" unemployment insurance benefits may tempt the local plant manager to use them as a wage supplement, and they may permit the local personnel director to follow careless procedures in hiring and firing. This is the "moral hazard" arising naturally from any system of unemployment benefits that is not experience-rated.

What the service company (like the central claims unit) undertakes to do is to supply adequate knowledge and motivation. It also undertakes to keep the finance department aware of practices in the personnel and production departments that increase unemployment insurance costs. Without a central unemployment insurance unit or a service company, the finance department usually does not have access to this information. If the prospective client agrees, but argues that it would be better to train one or more of its own employees to perform this task, the service company points out that promotion, or some other form of turnover, may remove the trained employee from his post and bring an inexperienced person in his place; whereas, if the firm hires the service company, training costs are eliminated and stability is assured.

Evaluation. An evaluation of service companies in relation to experience rating must turn on the usual two questions: Does experience rating encourage employer participation? Is such employer participation desirable?

The answer to the first question is clearly affirmative. Indeed, the service company is probably the clearest proof that experience rating affects employer participation in the administrative process. Without experience rating there would be no service company; for the principal selling point of the service company is the possibility that by claims control the firm's tax rate may be lowered.

If experience rating does encourage employer participation through the service companies, is this effect desirable? In the opinion survey analyzed in Chapter 6, responses to the questions relating specifically to service companies were clearly negative in about one-quarter of the cases. The other three-quarters found such companies at least tolerable. Some of the deputies and referees said they even preferred to deal with service companies rather than with the average employer because the service company was more "professional" (more knowledgeable and less emotional). Also the service company simplified the work of the deputy in cases involving large plants, where the relevant information had to be gathered together from several sources.

Nevertheless, there was a significant proportion of respondents in the questionnaire who expressed a definite dislike of service companies. The commonest objection was that the interjection of the service company between the state and the employer slowed the administrative process and increased the delay in getting benefits into the hands of claimants who ultimately were declared eligible. The objection was also voiced that service companies tend to be too mercenary in their approach, protesting claims needlessly or fighting over them too legalistically. Certainly the service company is more open to the temptation to emphasize the tax saving consideration at the expense of all other considerations, since tax saving is its prime motive in operation.

The service company frequently wears a double face. In describing itself to its client firms, it tends to present itself as the relentless policeman of the system. But in its actual dealings with the deputies and referees it usually shows prudent moderation, recognizing that its long-term effectiveness depends on keeping their respect. It also recognizes that it must avoid actions that run counter to the general policies of the client firm in the area of employee relationships. Some firms are unwilling to hire service companies precisely because they fear to admit an "outsider" to this delicate area. Aware of this objection, the larger and better established service companies try to adapt their procedures to their clients' general policies. For example, many service companies do not appeal any claim until the client has approved the action.

The service company is probably best understood as the equivalent of the central unemployment insurance unit of a large corporation. The two perform about the same functions, show about the same motivations, and have about the same relations with the deputies and referees. The main difference between them is in their relationship to the firm. The central unit is an insider; the service company is an outsider. Although each relationship has its advantages and disadvantages, that of insider usually is preferable. Because of the ease of entry into this industry, there is always the danger that unqualified practitioners will set up shop and under the pressure of competition adopt undesirable procedures. Although such a company is not likely to grow, or even to stay in existence, so long as it does operate it can do much harm to the program.

General conclusions that might be drawn from the preceding three chapters regarding the participation of employers in the administrative process are most conveniently left to the final section of this study, where the effects of experience rating on administration can be seen in relation to other effects of experience rating.

9

Employer
Participation in
Legislation

Nature of the Issue

Does experience rating have a desirable or an undesirable effect on legislation? The anwer to this question probably carries the most weight of all in the final judgment on experience rating. Certainly, this issue is the chief source of opposition to experience rating. If there were no fault to find with experience rating on the score of its effect on legislation, opposition on the whole might be relatively light. It is probable that the effects of experience rating on the allocation of resources and on administration, for example, are feared primarily because these initial effects are expected to have undesirable secondary effects on legislation.

Recently, while talking with a high official in the Department of Labor, who has been a critic of experience rating for many years, I asked him: "If experience rating had no undesirable effect on legislation, would you still be opposed to it?" He considered the question thoughtfully for some time and then said: "That is certainly my principal objection to experience rating. If the system had no undersirable effects in this area, other criticisms I might have would be minor."

The effect of experience rating on legislation is sometimes criticized for two reasons that are specious and misleading. One involves the issue of solvency, the other the issue of interstate competition. It may be well to dispose of these two at the outset so as to clear the ground for adequate treatment of the main issue.

Solvency

Experience rating is said to lessen the total amount of funds available for benefits and thus to bring about restrictive legislation. This possible effect of experience rating has been a concern of labor since the beginning. In a 1939 article in the *American Federationist*, which still remains labor's fullest treatment of experience rating, the American Federation of Labor asked: "What effects can we predict from merit rating?" and answered, "First, a menace to adequate benefits [because] the average of contributions will fall below the 2.7 percent of the payrolls which has been set up as the standard contribution" [28, p. 50]. Twenty years later, in 1959, labor's spokesman told the assembled administrators of unemployment insurance:

The heart of the problem with experience rating—and the reason organized labor would like to at least modify its effect—is that it results in inadequate financing which in turn leads to inadequate benefits.

For example, in thirteen states last year, large numbers of experience-rated employers made no contribution whatsoever to the compensation fund. What this means, quite naturally, is that next year, when the organized labor movements of these states again try to get better laws and more equitable benefits, the employers will point to the low reserve balance in the state fund and say: "We can't afford it." Certainly they can't afford it—because during all the fat years of prosperity—when they should have been building the fund—they were slipping out on their responsibility through the escape hatch of experience rating.

Thus it is that—in state after state—benefits are geared not to the level of the worker's need—but to the level of income that the fund receives—a level perpetually kept inadequate by a gimmick that has no valid place in a system of social insurance [106, p. 39].

Thirty years after the 1939 article, another piece in the *American Federationist* manifests the same concern. Experience rating is condemned because it has "deprived the system of needed income by permitting the application of grossly inadequate tax rates to a constantly dwindling tax base" [30, p. 17].

Essentially this issue was discussed in Chapter 2 in its relationship to fund solvency. The basic observations made there apply here also. Experience rating does not in itself determine the size of the fund or the size of the total tax burden, but only how the tax burden is to be distributed. The forces which tend to limit the size of the reserve would be operative under a uniform tax as well as under experience rating, and, except for temporary periods, the size of the reserve would probably be roughly the same under experience rating or under a uniform tax. As explained earlier (pp. 31 - 34), it is misleading to compare the "standard" tax of 2.7 percent with the actual average tax under experience rating and conclude: "This is the amount of money lost to the program because of experience rating." It is certain that as the individual states found that a tax of 2.7 percent on all employers was bringing in more money than the states wanted to spend on unemployment benefits, they would have demanded and obtained some way of lowering the total tax, whether it was to be distributed uniformly among all employers or was to be experience-rated. Even under a uniform tax, the states would have been faced with the choice between liberalizing benefits or lowering taxes. Moreover, even with the same benefit provisions, some states would have needed to impose much lower taxes than other states. The McCormack amendment, passed by the House in 1939, (see p. 13), pointed the direction in which the program was destined to develop in the absence of experience rating. The states would have been permitted to reduce taxes on some other basis than the experience of the individual employer.

The other assumption involved in this criticism of experience rating—that the amount of money available determines the liberality of the program—has more substance, but also needs qualification. While the size of the available reserves does have implications for legislation, the relationship is not simple or inevitable. Some states with above-average reserves are below average in the liberality of their benefit and disqualification structures. At times some states have had reserves sufficient to pay benefits at their past average rate for a quarter of a century, even if they never collected another dollar in taxes. As of the end of 1967, ten states had reserves sufficient to pay benefits for three or more years at their highest annual rate in the preceding decade [BES No. U-198-R, U.S. Department of Labor]. Virtually all of these states were below average in liberality. Obviously, it was not lack of available funds that kept such states from further liberalizing their programs. Dangerously low reserves certainly do act as a brake on liberalization. For example, in the restructuring of the Pennsylvania unemployment insurance law in 1960, the condition of the fund was a significant factor in the elimination of uniform duration and the addition of certain disqualifications. The point here, however, is that the condition of a state's fund is not the result of experience rating as such.

Interstate Competition

A second line of argument, much used but having little substance, runs from experience rating through interstate competition to legislation. Experience rating is alleged to intensify the competition among states for the location of firms, and this competition is said to limit the liberality of unemployment insurance provisions. Walter Reuther voiced the typical objection against experience rating on this score when he said:

> It is, however, important to recognize that because of experience rating the threat of interstate competition in tax rates has again entered into the unemployment program. Today, the basic reasons for the failure of the States to increase benefits to adequate levels are the same reasons which prevented States from enacting State unemployment insurance laws prior to the passage of the Federal tax offset provisions in 1935. Increased benefits in one State would increase costs and to increase costs would mean that the employers of that State would have to pay more into the State unemployment reserve fund [2, p. 1410].

To travel expeditiously through the tangled underbrush that has grown up around this issue, it may be advisable to establish three propositions, like direction markers, and make our way carefully from one to the other.

1) Unemployment insurance taxes are not a significant factor influencing the location of firms. Of all the alleged effects of experience rating, this is the least likely. Every careful analysis has reached the conclusion that unemployment insurance tax differentials are not large enough to have a measurable influence on the location of firms.[1] In the course of the 1965 hearings on HR 8282, the leading spokesmen for government (Secretary of Labor Willard Wirtz [2, p. 114]), for labor (George Meany [2, p. 832]), and for management (John Post

---

1. See especially [107], [108], and [2, pp. 596-617]. The article by Zecca [107] is a particularly useful survey of the literature on the subject.

[2, pp. 596-617]), expressed their agreement with this proposition. Post's presentation was especially detailed and factual.

Although the alleged effect of unemployment insurance taxes[2] on the location of firms may be more fear than fact, the fear may have been influential in some circumstances. Certainly the lobbyists for management have appealed repeatedly to this effect, as have also the lobbyists for labor. Management and labor are both apt to turn the argument to suit their particular purposes. Management, when it is before Congress and fending off proposals for federal standards, minimizes or denies the alleged effect; but when it is before a state legislature fending off a proposal to raise benefits it recoils in fear from the alleged effect. Labor pursues the exact opposite course, giving the alleged effect maximum stress when asking Congress for federal standards and muting it when asking a state legislature for some liberalization of the program. Probably the chief effect of these representations of labor and management is to deter states from taxing high-cost firms fully.

The great and continuing differences between the states with respect to unemployment insurance tax rates and program liberality are a strong argument against assigning a dominant influence to interstate competition. If such competition were a significant operative force, it should tend to reduce state programs to a common level. But as a matter of fact, the state unemployment insurance programs differ greatly. It is a common occurrence for individual states to depart from the pattern of other states, even those nearby. For example, interstate competition did not prevent Wisconsin from raising its maximum benefit to $56 when that of its neighbor, Minnesota, was only $38. Although these two states adjoin each other and are in competition industrially, Wisconsin was not stopped by the fear that it might lose firms to Minnesota. As a matter of fact, Minnesota later acted to narrow the gap and raised its own maximum benefit. It is worth noting that interstate competition gives rise not only to fear but also to emulation. Many a proposal to liberalize one state's program has been bolstered by an appeal to the record of a neighboring state which was doing better by its unemployed. My own impression, based on over twenty years of observation, is that this emulation has considerable force. John R. Commons relied on it as one of the major mechanisms of social reform. To encourage such interstate rivalry in the provision of more adequate unemployment benefits, the Wisconsin agency has for years distributed a one-page table showing at a glance which states were leading or lagging in their maximum basic benefits.

The alleged effect of unemployment insurance tax differentials on the liberality of unemployment insurance provisions frequently takes the form expressed by the spokesman for the Department of Commerce, Andrew F. Brimmer, in the

2. Sometimes this allegation takes a somewhat more subtle form. Unemployment insurance influences the location of firms, it is said, not only or even primarily because of the tax involved, but because its provisions, especially those governing disqualifications, are looked upon as indicators of the kind of labor/management "climate ' a new firm might expect to find in the state.

1965 Hearings: "In general, it seems that states which offer somewhat less liberal benefits tend to have lower tax rates, and this would tend to offer a cost advantage to firms in those states" [2, p. 215]. In this connection, there may be some interest in Appendix Table A-23, which shows the degree of correlation that existed in 1967 between tax rates and the four chief measures of program liberality. As may be seen, two of the correlations (columns 3 and 4) were close enough to be statistically significant,[3] while the other two were not. Reflecting, as it does, only one year of experience, this table is obviously more illustrative than representative. It suffices, however, to sound a note of caution with respect to Brimmer's "In general . . . ." The heterogeneous relationships illustrated in the table are a reminder of the heterogeneity of the causes at work in the unemployment insurance program.

2) Interstate competition arises, not from experience rating but from the existence of separate, financially independent state programs. Because the states vary widely in their experience with unemployment, and also because they have the freedom to set their own benefit standards, their costs—and therefore their taxes—will vary widely. Whether the tax be uniform or experience-rated within each state, so long as there are separate state programs the average tax rates of the individual states will differ significantly. Hence interstate competition would be as operative under a system in which the tax was uniform within each state as under a system in which the tax was experience-rated within each state. Since interstate competition does not stem from experience rating—except in the historical, accidental sense already explained in Chapter 2 and earlier in this chapter—it is not relevant to the issue under discussion, namely, the legislative effects attributable to experience rating as such. The central issue raised by interstate competition is not experience rating, but federal benefit standards accompanied by federal subsidies.

3) If experience rating has any effect on interstate competition based on unemployment insurance tax differentials, it is to lessen the degree of such competition. In the absence of experience rating, a firm would still be faced with tax differentials between states, as just explained. A firm would know that to locate in state A would mean paying a tax of 2 percent, while locating in state B would involve a tax of only 1 percent. Such interstate differentials would be the principal concern of a firm as regards unemployment insurance. Under experience rating, such interstate differentials carry less weight because they are not the principal determinant of a firm's unemployment insurance cost. The principal determinant under experience rating is the firm's own unemployment pattern, which will follow the firm no matter in what state it chooses to locate.[4] Hence the interstate differentials will mean less to a firm under experience rating than under a uniform tax.

3. However, the correlation in column 4 is subject to the serious limitation described in footnote b of Table A-23.
4. As was shown in Chapter 4, large and regular differences in benefit-cost rates tend to be associated with the various industries.

In leaving this topic it may be worth noting that if federal benefit standards were introduced, tax differentials between states would not disappear and might even become greater. If every state had to meet the same benefit standards, a state which regularly had twice as high an unemployment rate as another would have to levy twice as high a tax, all else being equal. Experience rating could play a useful role in mitigating any interstate competition (for industry) that would remain under federal standards.

Employer Participation in Legislation

Apart from the two preceding issues, which are largely spurious, there is a third line of criticism which does raise a genuine issue relating to experience rating. Experience rating is said to increase the interest of the individual employer in unemployment insurance and thus cause him to take a more active part in shaping the legislative provisions of the program, especially the provisions that regulate disqualifications. Like the issue of employer participation in administration, this issue of employer participation in legislation received little attention in the early literature of experience rating, although it became prominent later. Perhaps the earliest recognition of this precise issue occurs in the Unanimous Report of the 1940 Interstate Conference Committee on Experience Rating: "It is further[5] argued that experience rating will make it much harder to obtain the enactment of liberalizing changes in State laws, because employers will tend to oppose adequate benefit provisions more strenuously in order to protect their individual accounts or experience records from heavier benefit charges. . . . Experience rating would represent a major threat to the sound development of unemployment compensation, in case the foregoing objections should prove to be well-founded or in any substantial measure true" [31, pp. 63, 64].

The issue began to be raised repeatedly and strongly during the war years, which saw two simultaneous developments: (1) With the demand for labor greatly exceeding its supply, a trend set in toward stricter disqualification provisions. (2) With state reserve funds growing far beyond expectations, a trend set in to adopt experience rating, which was the only available method of lowering taxes. From this time on, the charge was frequently made that experience rating was causing the changes in disqualification provisions. For example, a long, thorough article in the Social Security Bulletin for January 1944 documented the growth in the severity of disqualifications and linked the trend to experience rating [51]. A committee of the states established to study disqualifications offered a rebuttal of this charge in 1944 [109], but the debate has continued on to the present time. The review of twenty years of unemployment insurance published by the Bureau of Employment Security in 1955 contained a balanced critique in which experience rating was identified as one of many influences determining the nature of disqualifications [110, p. 41]. Walter Reuther's 1965

---

5. The report had just discussed the issue of solvency, which was recognized as distinct from the "further" issue of employer participation in legislation.

statement exemplifies labor's current criticism of experience rating on this score: "We know the pitiful results which experience rates have produced in the form of vicious disqualification provisions, unreasonably high earnings requirements, cancellation of benefit rights. . ." [2, p. 1411].

The effect of experience rating on unemployment insurance legislation, like its effect on administration, is to be judged in the light of two propositions: (1) Experience rating causes employers to participate more effectively in the legislative process. (2) This participation is [un] desirable. The following analysis considers these two propositions in order.

Extent of Employer Participation

Multiple Causality

Two preliminary observations may be helpful. First, there is no doubt that employers participate in state unemployment insurance legislation in a major way. In some states, employers channel their participation through formal advisory councils [22] while in others they operate through their associations and lobbyists; but in all states they are much more active in unemployment insurance than in other programs of social insurance and social assistance. One reason may be that unemployment insurance touches more closely than do the other programs on sensitive areas of labor/management tension.

Both the critics and the defenders of experience rating tend to assume, rather than attempt to prove, that experience rating is a major cause of effective employer participation in the legislative process. (In this respect, the legislative issue is similar to the administrative issue previously discussed.) Proof is not offered, probably because it is so difficult to obtain. Since experience rating is only one part of the multiple and complex causality that underlies the final legislative product, it is normally impossible to isolate and measure its distinctive effect. Among the other causal roots of unemployment insurance legislation at least three merit mention.

One important factor is the political party that happens to be in power in a particular state at a particular time. The goals of either labor or management will receive more sympathetic consideration under one regime than under another. In Ohio, for example, changes in the general political climate have produced notable swings in the tenor of unemployment insurance legislation [22, p. 241]. Much the same can be said about unemployment insurance developments in Pennsylvania and other states. Currently (1971), Hawaii is the only state to meet all proposed federal standards regarding benefits and disqualifications, and yet the reserve-ratio experience rating plan of Hawaii is not significantly different from that of the other states. Obviously forces other than experience rating are at work.

In the early years of the program (1943), there were eight states which still had a uniform tax, and these eight had disqualification provisions clearly more liberal than those of the states which had adopted experience rating [51, p. 14]. In six[6] of the eight states, the absence of experience rating and the absence of severe disqualifications need not have been causally related, for both could have stemmed from a common root. Where labor was strong enough politically to keep out experience rating, it was probably strong enough to keep out severe disqualifications also. In at least the remaining two states (Louisiana and Mississippi) however, this explanation seems improbable. In their cases, the absence of experience rating may indeed have been the explanation of the absence of severe disqualifications.[7]

Events and personalities, separately or in combination, comprise a second group of factors that are obviously important determinants of unemployment insurance legislation. In periods of heavy unemployment, the amount and duration of benefits are likely to increase while disqualification provisions are likely to be relaxed. Contrariwise, during periods of prosperity and a tight labor market, while benefits are not likely to be reduced, disqualifications are very likely to be tightened. The clearest example of such a development was the period covered by World War II, when every warm body was in demand and there was scant understanding or sympathy for the payment of benefits to persons who were unemployed.

In their disqualification provisions, the state laws are like the restless sea. Practically all exhibit a pattern of constant tinkering with these provisions. A disqualification may be taken out of the law in one session of the legislature, restored in the following session, and removed again in the third. In the meantime, the experience-rating structure may have remained unchanged. Even a personal experience may move a key legislator to demand a change in a particular disqualification, either liberalizing it or making it more strict. The continuous operation of such evanescent causes changes the program in ways that quite escape the would-be historian and make it difficult, if not impossible, to isolate the effect of some one factor like experience rating.[8]

A third influential factor in legislation that usually has no relationship to experience rating is the political practice of "package" bargaining. The reference here is not to the bargaining between labor and management over a package of unemployment insurance provisions, where a tightening of a disqualification

6. Alaska, Montana, New York, Rhode Island, Utah, Washington.
7. The causal relation is the more plausible, because at that early date employer interest and knowledge were minimal, even in states with experience rating.
8. A striking illustration of the uncertainties that can attach to the legislative process is given in [22, pp. 158–59], which describes how in Illinois in 1953 the agreed bill on unemployment insurance, formally approved by the responsible leaders of labor and management and unanimously passed by both houses of the legislature came to vetoed in the Governor's office. Another illustration would be the story, if there were space to recount it here, of how Colorado in 1959 became the first continential state to cover the employees of all nonprofit organizations. This extremely controversial provision was adopted without the slightest ripple of controversy because practically no one in or out of the legislature was aware of what was happening.

provision may be traded for an increase in benefits, but to logrolling, strictly so-called, where a favorable vote in one area is traded for a favorable vote in another, completely unrelated, area. To cite one of countless similar situations:

> The crucial decision not to raise the maximum benefit was made outside the council and in a sense outside the unemployment compensation program. The governor was insistent that something would have to be given to labor to balance a reduction in corporation taxes which had been given to employers, and employers said that they would prefer to see an increase of benefits in workmen's compensation rather than in unemployment compensation. The legislature accordingly increased the maximum benefit in workmen's compensation while leaving unemployment compensation unchanged, with the result that for the first time in the history of the two programs the maximum benefit was not the same for both. A bill which also increased benefits in unemployment compensation had been passed by the House but had been killed in the Senate. Labor was told by the Senate that if it fought for the unemployment compensation increase it would lose the workmen's compensation increase as well. Labor accepted this as a fact and subsided [22, pp. 303-4].

On another occasion in this same state employers were given to understand that if they wanted to get a certain unemployment compensation amendment they would have to drop their opposition to a beer tax which the governor wanted. Instances of political trading of this sort across the borders of distinct programs abound in legislative history. The log jam of bills at the end of a legislative session, when the clock is covered to allow the legislature to complete its business, is not simply the result of poor scheduling. It reflects the unwillingness of legislators to give their favorable vote to any one bill until they have seen what the total package looks like. Some of the crucial trades are made at this last stage of the legislative process.

The multiple causality underlying legislation in unemployment insurance, and of course the qualitative nature of the problem, make it quite unrealistic to look for a mathematical proof of a relationship, or the absence of a relationship, between legislative provisions and types or degrees of experience rating. The best that can be done to illumine this obscure area is to seek out the seasoned judgments of persons with long experience in the legislative arena.

Opinion Survey

Analyzed below are four reasons for thinking that experience rating has influenced employers to participate more effectively in the legislative process and four reasons for thinking the contrary. About forty-five experienced persons in the ranks of management, government, and labor were asked to evaluate these "affirmative" and "negative" arguments. The respondents included a couple of dozen persons from management, a dozen from government, and a half-dozen from labor.[9] The sample was not intended to be representative. The basis for the

9. They represented the following states: California, Illinois, Massachusetts, Michigan, New York, Ohio, Pennsylvania, Rhode Island, South Carolina, Texas, Virginia, Washington, Wisconsin. These thirteen states accounted for about 60 percent of all covered employment.

selection of respondents was simply their extensive experience in the area under discussion. Since the questionnaire did not deal with value judgments (is employer activity desirable?) but only with a factual situation (how do employers go about seeking to influence legislation?) the sample was weighted heavily with employer respondents, who would be the ones most intimately acquainted with employer legislative activity and employer motivation. The respondents were given the following instructions:

> It has been said that because of experience rating, employers work more effectively than they otherwise would in determining the content of benefit and disqualification provisions. This increased employer effectiveness in the field of legislation is viewed by some as helpful and by others as harmful to the program; but please note carefully that this difference of opinion is *not* the issue here. All that is at issue here is a matter of fact: *Does experience rating cause employers to work more effectively in determining the content of benefit and disqualification provisions?* Several reasons have been alleged for answering in the affirmative and several for anwering in the negative. Which of these reasons do you consider valid, and which do you consider invalid? And who wins the debate, the affirmative or the negaive?

It should be noted that the questionnaire was restricted to benefit and disqualification provisions. This limitation permitted concentration on those legislative areas which are most in dispute; but it should be recognized that employers are interested and active in other areas as well, especially those of coverage, eligibility, and tax rates.

Affirmative Arguments

A-1. *Experience rating results in the development of more specialized unemployment insurance experts among employers, at least in the large firms. These specialists enable employers to operate more effectively on the legislative level.*

This argument met with general acceptance. However, four respondents (all from management) qualified their agreement substantially. Of the four, two were legislative representatives with long experience who tended to confine the question to what happens in the legislature itself. One said: "The best lobbyists we have on unemployment insurance legislation are experts in lobbying, *not* in unemployment insurance. I will agree that the experts are useful in pinpointing effects of particular legislation which might go unnoticed by others; but when it comes to contacting legislators and working with them, we usually leave this to their constituents and to the professionals—the lobbyists." Another spoke from a background of experience in California, where decisionmaking was highly centralized and technical experts played a less direct part in the legislative process than they did in some other states.[10] The dissenters were making the point that

10. In California employers are accustomed to a division of labor, whereby a particular legislative area becomes the primary responsibility of a particular employer organization. Unemployment insurance, for example, during most of the program's history was the primary responsibility of the California Retailers Association.

technical considerations are not the only, or even the most important, factors determining unemployment insurance legislation.

It would be a fair summation of the opinion of this group of experienced respondents to say that the impact of the employer specialists in unemployment insurance varies from state to state and from time to time, is rarely major, but is usually significant. One of the clearest examples of significant participation in the legislative process on the part of employer specialists occurred in the early 1950's, when a number of large states in the midwest and on the east coast amended their laws to adopt quite similar changes in their benefit and tax formulas. The similarity was largely due to a small group of employer specialists who worked with employer organizations in those states, helping them to analyze their problems and work out solutions.[11]

Experience rating undoubtedly accounts for the existence of employer specialists. Experience rating also accounts for the existence of service companies, but these latter only exceptionally play an important part in formulating employer legislative objectives. In at least one state, where they are numerous, the other employer groups have made it clear to the service companies that they are not to exercise any independent legislative activity.

Illinois provides an example of a legislative process into which the unemployment insurance experts were explicitly incorporated. The entire process had seven steps,[12] starting from the employers' social security committees and working up through the Joint Technical Committee, to the Joint Executive Committee, to the Board of Unemployment Compensation Advisors.

> On paper the process looks cumbersome. In practice it was simplified by the fact that the same few key people were active at each step. Thus, the employer representatives [the specialists] who comprised the "second row" at the council meetings were the same ones who started the work in the social security committees, took the resulting recommendations to the Joint Technical Committee meeting, accompanied their principals to the Joint Executive Committee meeting, and were on hand to explain and defend the recommendations when they reached their final destination in the advisory council meeting [22, p. 146].[13]

A-2. *Experience rating elicits the interest of individual employers in specific aspects of the unemployment insurance law, for example in the eligibility and disqualification provisions. This interest leads to more proposals for specific changes in the law.*

This argument, which emphasizes the specific nature of the activity elicited by experience rating, was also widely accepted. However, some observed that it

---

11. One has to see the legislative process in action to realize how helpless an interest group can be in a technical program like unemployment insurance, if it has no one to turn to for expert advice. This is where labor frequently is weak. Labor representatives often have to depend on personnel in the state agency for technical guidance.

12. For a description of the seven steps see [22, pp. 145–46].

13. Employer members of the federal advisory council on employment security also used the device of the "second row" of technical experts at council meetings [22, p. 377].

was not a major issue; others remarked that it was only a matter of degree—even under a uniform tax employers would make specific demands. All agreed that it applied chiefly to disqualification provisions.

The practice of noncharging benefits in connection with actual or potential disqualifications (see Chapter 2) is one of the clearest indications of a relationship between experience rating and legislation. "As an alternative to measures distorting the disqualification provisions of state laws, the Social Security Board suggested to the states at the end of 1944 that provisions might be adopted eliminating all charges to employers' experience rating records for benefits paid to unemployed workers under certain circumstances" [60, p. 238]. As shown in Chapter 5, the states have made considerable use of this escape from experience rating, and usually for the reason just mentioned—as an alterntive to stricter disqualification provisions. In state after state, a package deal was made: an amended disqualification provision favoring claimants was combined with a noncharging provision favoring employers. In the light of the history of noncharging provisions, there can be little doubt that experience rating does affect legislation, at least in the area of disqualifications.[14]

A-3 *Because of experience rating, employers become personally interested in unemployment insurance. When bills affecting unemployment insurance are before the legislature, individual employers are more likely to take the trouble to contact their representatives in the legislature and even to appear at the hearings. This direct participation by individual employers impresses legislators more than would the same actions taken by the professional representatives of employer organizations.*

This argument, which emphasizes the *personal* involvement of the employer, especially in hearings before the legislature, won acceptance from all but four of the respondents. (The four dissenters were from management.) One respondent, who formerly had been a state senator, assigned considerable weight to this argument. A number of other experienced respondents observed, however, that employers only occasionally made such appearances and that only rarely were such appearances really important. One respondent of much experience observed: "I think companies break down into those who participate in legislative activities and those who do not. Those who do, generally participate on many fronts, including unemployment insurance." The implication seemed to be that they would probably participate in unemployment insurance even without experience rating.

A-4. *To the extent that experience rating raises the costs to some employers above that which they would have under a uniform tax system, they are under greater economic pressure to favor restrictive legislation.*

N-4. *To the extent that experience rating lowers the costs to some employers below that which they would have under a uniform tax system, they are under less economic pressure to favor restrictive legislation.*

14. When employers oppose the spread of noncharging, it is usually on the ground of its effect on administration. Occasionally they also object on the ground of its long-run effect

The fourth affirmative argument and the fourth negative argument are opposite sides of the same coin and may be conveniently discussed together. The respondents generally felt that there was some validity to both sides of this argument, but they accorded more weight to the affirmative side. They thought that employers who had higher-than-average tax rates (short of the maximum rate) might be more active under experience rating than they would be under a uniform tax in opposing legislation that would increase their costs. Also, legislators might lend a more attentive ear to protesting employers who were paying a tax rate of 3 or 4 percent, as might be the case under experience rating, than they would if the highest tax anyone was paying was 1 or 2 percent, as might be the case in some states under a uniform tax. This may be one of the reasons why all states place a ceiling on the maximum tax.[15] Although such a ceiling limits the effectiveness of experience rating in allocating resources according to true costs, the limitation is accepted in order to avoid possible undesirable effects on legislation.

On the other hand, many respondents pointed out that the highest-cost employers—those at the maximum tax rate—were sometimes the least active, rather than the most active, in opposing liberalizing legislation in the areas of benefits and disqualifications. Chronically deficit employers have no clear financial incentive to oppose an increase of benefits or a liberalization of disqualifications. In fact, if they are using unemployment benefits to supplement wages or to maintain a surplus labor force, they may actually favor such liberalizing amendments.

The full import of this argument may be more easily grasped in terms of the table below, which illustrates how various groups of employers might view the cost aspects of any given legislative amendment designed to increase benefits or liberalize disqualifications.[16] The table shows under which tax system, uniform or experience-rated, an employer would see himself incurring the greater cost as the result of such an amendment. The answers given do not purport to show how his costs would actually be affected, but only how he would expect them to be affected. Presumably his financial incentive to oppose a given legislative pro-

---

on legislation; this more sophisticated objection has been heard somewhat oftener in recent years.

15. Several readers of the preliminary manuscript felt constrained to comment at this point that there were other reasons for limiting the maximum benefit. These other reasons are reducible to the inability (presumed or proved) of some firms to carry a higher tax and hence properly belong to a discussion of the allocation effect of experience rating. One reader, an employer legislative representative, added the comment: "Secondarily, but important from the legislative angle, the ceiling on the maximum tax helps keep the employer group together." This comment is relevant to negative argument no. 3.

16. As was pointed out previously, the discussion is limited to benefits and disqualifications because these are the areas where controversy is sharpest and the legislative impact of experience rating is chiefly criticized. It should be noted, however, that employers might show a different pattern of reaction to legislation that affected their tax rates directly—for example, an increase in the minimum or maximum tax rates or an increase in the taxable wage base.

posal will be in some proportion to the increase in his cost as he sees it. Neither does the table purport to show under which system a given employer would be better off in general. Obviously, employers with above-average costs would be better off under a uniform tax, while employers with below-average costs would be better off under experience rating.[17] The table merely shows under which tax system a given employer would see himself incurring the greater cost if the law were amended to increase benefits or liberalize disqualifications.

To an employer whose long-term tax rate under experience rating would be:	*The cost of increasing benefits or liberalizing disqualifications would appear greater under a tax system which was:*
A. At the minimum	Uniform
B. Above the minimum but below the state average	Uniform
C. Above the state average but below the maximum	Experience-rated
D. At the maximum	Uniform

Under a uniform tax system, class D employers would pay the average increase in taxes produced by a benefit liberalization, but they would pay none of such increase under experience rating because they would have been already paying the maximum. Hence they should have less reason to oppose such a liberalization under experience rating than under a uniform tax. Indeed, as several of the respondents noted, they might welcome such a liberalization as a costless way of supplementing wages or maintaining a surplus work force. The same logic holds for some of the employers in class A, namely, those whose long-term cost rate is well below the minimum tax rate. These employers also are in a "zone of indifference" to increased benefit costs.

The other employers in class A, as well as all employers in class B, would anticipate some increase in their costs under experience rating, but the increase would be less than under a uniform tax. Under experience rating, they would pay for only their under-average share of the increased costs, while under a uniform tax they would pay the average share, which would include part of the above-average costs of other employers.

Only class C employers would see the proposed liberalization as more costly for them under an experience-rated system than under a uniform tax system. Under a uniform tax, part of the increased costs attributable to the employees of

17. This, on the assumption that no other changes in the program accompanied the change in the tax system.

class C employers would be borne by class A and class B employers, whereas under an experience-rated system, class C employers would have to meet all or, at least, more—of their own above-average costs. The proportion of class C employers varies from state to state and from time to time. On the average, perhaps about one-third of all employers are class C employers.

According to this logic, a proposal to effect a given liberalization in benefits or disqualifications would represent a greater cost to more employers under a uniform system of taxation than under experience rating. Hence, if costs were the only factor influencing the attitude of employers, there should be more employers opposing a given liberalization under a uniform tax than under experience rating.[18]

Does this logic work in fact? At the extremes—among the class A and class D employers—it clearly does in many cases. It is not uncommon to find that banks and construction companies, for example, are relatively indifferent—for opposite reasons—to unemployment insurance legislation, even when amendments are proposed that would increase the state average tax. Nearly all professional legislative representatives of employers report this kind of behavior. The logic is probably less operative for class B and class C employers, who usually do not understand the mechanism of the unemployment insurance tax well enough, or do not reflect on it enough, to be influenced by the logic involved.

Negative Arguments

N-1. *Employers as a group would have the same general legislative goals under a uniform tax as under experience rating. The professional representatives of employers would have an interest in controlling costs and therefore an interest in benefit and disqualification provisions.*

Less than half of all the respondents expressed general agreement with this argument. Of those who did agree many felt it necessary to qualify their answers by such observations as: employers might have the same general goals, but they would differ with regard to many specifics; they might have the same general goals, but they would not be nearly so active in pursuing them; the argument has a germ of truth in it, but not much more; the argument may be true in the abstract, but it does not work out this way; and so forth. One employer respondent said: "Their interest would be strictly *pro forma*. The difference in the degree of incentive would be so great as to be in fact a difference in kind. I remember quite clearly the intensive efforts we made over a number of years to interest employers in public assistance programs and our total lack of success." One respondent with long experience remarked that the interest of the professional representatives of employer organizations derived in large part from the

18. A simpler, though less adequate, summary of the situation might be: Under a uniform tax all employers have a financial reason to oppose a liberalizing amendment; under experience rating some employers (in class A and class D) have no financial reason to be in opposition.

interest of the individual members of those organizations. Since the individual members would be less interested under a uniform tax system, the professional representative of the organizations would probably also show less interest—in actual practice.

N-2. *Disqualification provisions in unemployment insurance are closely related to personnel policy and industrial discipline. Hence, even apart from tax considerations, employers would continue to be interested in the content of disqualification provisions.*

This argument is a continuation of the previous argument, but applies specifically to disqualification provisions. The respondents were about evenly divided in their judgment, almost as many considering it invalid as considered it valid. Of those who expressed agreement, many qualified their answers. "Employers might be interested," said one, "but they would lack the incentive for serious action." Some respondents expressed disagreement with the argument because they incorrectly understood it to mean that disqualification provisions were penalties which employers used to enforce discipline. Those who agreed with it understood it to mean that employers would feel an inconsistency in setting up industrial rules on the one hand and providing benefits to violators on the other.[19] This feeling of inconsistency and irritation would tend to funnel up to the legislative level. This situation would be present, they thought, at least to some degree even under a uniform tax system. One very experienced labor respondent disagreed with the argument and observed: "Many personnel officers tell employees that they don't fit in and instruct them to 'go and get your unemployment.' When the employee claims benefits, the employer then protests. Except in a few cases, this is not deliberate nastiness, but a recognition of the fact that good personnel practice would usually favor quits without good cause as relieving the employer of an unsatisfactory employee." Except for experience rating, he thought, employers would often gladly avail themselves of unemployment benefits as a method of easing the departure of an undesirable employee and would favor very liberal disqualification provisions.

N-3. *In the pursuit of their goals under a uniform tax system, employers would be more effective than under experience rating because they would be more united. Experience rating splits the ranks of employers, dividing them into high-cost and low-cost employers, whose interests are often opposed. Under a uniform tax, more employers would have common interests and would thus present a more united front before the legislature. This increased unity would offset any decrease in individual employer interest as a factor affecting legislation.*

Only about 15 percent of the respondents agreed with this argument. Among employers the proportion who agreed was only about 10 percent. Most of those

---

19. At least one large corporation makes this explicit point in the unemployment insurance policy statement provided to its plant supervisors.

who agreed that employers would be more unified under a uniform tax went on to deny that employers would therefore be more effective. They did not believe that the increased unity would offset the decrease in activity.

Those who disagreed gave various reasons. Many noted that the extent of division between employers depended on the issue involved. On the issues of benefits and disqualifications there was relatively little division. On these issues high-cost employers differed from low-cost employers under an experience-rating system only by showing less interest. The chief division among employers arose from the issue of where to set the minimum and maximum tax rates. Chapter 5 provides several examples of such a division.

Under a uniform tax system employers can be deeply divided over experience rating itself. Thus in the state of Washington for a full decade (1959–69) the main issue dividing employers was whether to have a more meaningful system of experience rating than that provided by payroll variations. By taking advantage of this split among employers, labor was able to keep a chargeback system of experience rating off the legislative books, but only at the cost of accepting less liberal benefits. The subsidizing employers, by far the majority, so resented the size of the subsidy they were forced to provide that they blocked most proposals to liberalize the program. The maximum benefit amount in Washington did not change during the whole decade, while it was rising in all other states in the nation. In 1970 it rose from $42 to $70, when labor finally accepted a more effective experience-rating system.

Such an impasse, most dramatically exemplified in Washington's experience, would always be a threat under a uniform tax system. The subsidizing firms, resenting their enforced role, would be more inclined to oppose program liberalizations. In a large industrial state not long ago (1970), I was at luncheon with four persons: the principal lobbyists for labor and management, the legislative liaison person from the governor's office, and the legislative liaison person from the state unemployment insurance agency. All four were in agreement that under a uniform tax system the subsidizing firms, which in that state included the most influential firms, would show more opposition to program liberalization.[20]

In some circumstances, experience rating may be a force permitting the enactment of more liberal legislation. In the first place, there are some disputed, marginal uses of unemployment benefits which are likely to find more general acceptance if the employers involved are bearing the costs involved. For example, should seasonal unemployment be compensated? This has been a disputed issue from the beginning of the program and is still being debated.[21] From time to time states have excluded seasonal firms from coverage or have applied

20. For examples of this kind of opposition see [22, chapters on California, New York, Pennsylvania, Rhode Island, Utah].

21. [111, pp. 82–96]. See also a forthcoming monograph on this issue by Merrill Murray to be published by the W. E. Upjohn Institute for Employment Research.

special disqualifications to claimants coming from seasonal firms. To the extent that experience rating allocates the cost of seasonal benefits to the responsible firms, opposition to the payment of such benefits is diminished among the nonseasonal employers, who are by far in the majority. For another example, some firms work unemployment benefits into their pension policy and expect pensioners to exhaust their unemployment benefit rights. This practice is likely to arouse less criticism if the firms involved bear the cost of the unemployment benefits paid to their retired employees.

Second, if experience rating causes employers to participate more actively in administration and thus to keep the program more free of "abuse," the way is cleared to get more liberal provisions from the legislature. This was a major reason given by two long-term state unemployment insurance directors for favoring experience rating on balance. As noted later, the public sees "abuse" as the chief defect of the present unemployment insurance system. Granted that the public is often misinformed, as long as this attitude exists, whatever improves administration may improve the prospects of more liberal legislation.

Market Mentality

The most important line of causality leading from experience rating to employer participation in legislation may be more subtle than any developed in the eight arguments above. Experience rating may inculcate a certain attitude of mind among employers whereby the "social" aspect of social insurance is minimized and the "insurance" aspect is emphasized. Experience rating obviously accepts the values of the competitive market and its operation reinforces them. This interrelationship may have a crucial significance for unemployment insurance legislation.

The market mentality engendered by experience rating shows itself most clearly in the area of disqualification provisions, where the chief controversies arise.[22] Should unemployment benefits be paid to someone who quit his job for a compelling personal reason? Or who was forced to retire? Or who quit to take another job, which proved temporary? Or who refused a job far below his capacity? Or who was dismissed for inefficiency? Or who was dismissed for a minor infraction of rules? To these and to many similar questions, the market mentality congenial to experience rating might return a negative answer, while the needs of society might require an affirmative response.

Experience rating rests on the principle that the employer is to be charged only for that unemployment for which he is in some sense responsible. As indicated in Chapter 3, the term "responsible" may be given a narrower or a wider

22. Typical of the criticism directed against experience rating on this score is the following, taken from a UAW–CIO publication: "The merit rating incentive has led employers to write into the laws outrageously restrictive disqualification provisions—legal fishhooks, barbed wire and booby traps—under which many thousands of workers are denied benefits each year on the flimsiest of excuses" [112, Question 29].

meaning and the market mentality tends to choose the narrower interpretation. Throughout the history of the program there has been a tug-of-war in the legislatures and in the courts over the scope to be assigned to employer responsibility. An excellent review of court cases turning on this issue is provied in a 1945 article entitled, "Employer Fault vs. General Welfare as the Basis of Unemployment Compensation" [113]. The author, Earle V. Simrell, was at that time the assistant general counsel of the Federal Security Agency.

One of the most intersting of these early decisions was delivered in Wisconsin, "the Mount Sinai of Experience Rating," as the author remarks. This was the 1941 decision of the Wisconsin Supreme Court in *Boynton Cab Company* vs. *Neubeck*. A taxicab driver was discharged after having had three accidents during eight weeks of employment. When he was granted unemployment benefits by the Wisconsin agency, of which Paul A. Raushenbush was then director, the company protested on the ground that the employee's unemployment was caused by his own actions and was not attributable to any employer fault. The case eventually reached the Supreme Court of the state.

In its brief defending its award of benefits, the Wisconsin Commission argued: " 'Experience rating' was certainly not designed for the purpose of allowing employers to restrict and sabotage the efficient operation of the primary purpose of any unemployment compensation law, namely, the payment of benefits to out-of-work employees. Nothing could strike the cause of experience rating a more grievous blow than to have it prostituted to this purpose" [113, p. 187]. The Wisconsin Advisory Committee on Unemployment Compensation and the Wisconsin Manufacturers Association filed briefs in support of the Commission's decision. The advisory committee, which was made up of the leaders of labor and management in the state, argued:

> Unemployment compensation is not a penalty imposed on the employer because of fault on his part, but rather is an involuntary contribution for the relief of unemployment attendant upon his operations. . . . The last man hired and first laid off is the inefficient fellow, the one who does not pay a profit when business is poor, the one who is prone to make mistakes. If compensation is denied to him, because the employer selects him for discharge on account of those qualities, then the statute will defeat its own purpose, by withholding benefits from those who need them most. [113, pp. 187–88]

The Wisconsin Supreme Court, in an opinion largely reflecting these briefs, affirmed the Commission's award of benefits.

The case illustrates the tendency of experience rating to engender the kind of protest raised by the taxicab company, but at the same time it demonstrates that employer responsibility need not be thus narrowly interpreted, but can be understood to cover any unemployment "attendant upon [not necessarily caused by] the employer's operations." The same leaders among Wisconsin employers who fought for experience rating fought for the payment of benefits in this case lest experience rating be "prostituted."

Wisconsin and Utah have operated through very efficient advisory councils, whose agreed bills have for all practical purpose determined the unemployment insurance law in their respective states [22, Chapters 3 and 5]. Both states have been leaders in unemployment insurance matters and have shown themselves to be progressive, imaginative, and innovative. As a result, both states have developed an unemployment insurance program clearly above average in adequacy and efficiency. But they have differed in the degrees to which they have adopted experience rating and in the quality of their disqualification provisions. Wisconsin has had a greater degree of experience rating than Utah and has had stricter disqualifications. Both differences would seem to reflect a greater acceptance of the market mentality on the part of Wisconsin.

Yet Wisconsin itself has vacillated between a greater and a lesser acceptance of the market mentality.[23] To take one example: Originally Wisconsin disqualified claimants who had quit their jobs for reasons not attributable to the employer, that is, for personal reasons. Recognizing that this strictness could sometimes have undesirable social consequences, the Advisory Council approved and the legislature passed, a 1945 amendment to the law allowing benefits to claimants who left their jobs for "compelling personal reasons." Six years later, in 1951, the law was amended to provide that these benefits would be noncharged. The market mentality is not at ease with the charging of unemployment benefits when the unemployment is not attributable to the market. But then, fourteen years later (1965), the Advisory Council and the legislature had second thoughts and reverted essentially to the pre-1951 law. In 1969 third thoughts split the charges by charging the first few benefit weeks and noncharging the rest. This legislative see-saw, which is typical of all the states in the matter of disqualification provisions, may be very significant. It may indicate that at least as regards unemployment insurance there is a rough balance between the individualistic market forces and the social welfare forces.

For over thirty years there has been operating, side by side with the experience-rated state programs, a substantial program that has never been experience rated—Railroad Unemployment Insurance. The similarities and differences between these two systems shed considerable light on the alleged effects of experience rating. The history of legislative developments in the railroad program is particularly enlightening. The details are to be found in Appendix E, especially under the headings "Solvency" and "Legislation."

Desirability of Employer Participation

On the assumption that experience rating does stimulate employer participation in the legislative process, and on the further assumption that this increased activity has an impact on the provisions of the law, especially the disqualification provisions, the crucial question arises: Is this effect desirable? In attempting

---

23. As remarked earlier, practically all states have a record of tinkering constantly with their disqualification provisions—making them now less strict, now more strict.

to evaluate the desirability of employer participation in administration, an objective norm was available in the unemployment insurance law. "Desirability" could be given a meaningful definition in terms of whether employer participation helped or hindered in the attainment of the objectives of the law. But here the issue is the desirability of the law itself. What norms are available for evaluating whatever effect experience rating may have on the law?

At this level, the only available norms are the systems of social values, only once removed from the absolute values of philosophy and theology, upon which each society builds its social structures. Although it is beyond the scope of this study to pass judgment on the competing value systems of our society, some purpose may be served by reviewing the relationships between unemployment insurance and the more relevant of these basic values. If such a review does not provide answers, it may at least clarify the nature of the questions requiring answers.

On the positive side, there is the widely accepted principle that the individual should be free of legal restraints in choosing and changing his way of making a living. If unemployment benefits widen the scope of this freedom, that is in accord with legislative intent. There is also the widely accepted principle that welfare programs (programs established to aid persons in difficulty) should be interpreted liberally. In judging claimant eligibility, the law should give the claimant the benefit of the doubt. Thus the burden of proof is on whoever would make the disqualification provisions more strict. This preferred position of the claimant leads to the conclusion that, in the absence of positive proof to the contrary, the effect of experience rating on disqualification provisions is undesirable. (When such provisions are in fact tightened, it is usually in response to the presentation of claimed evidence for specific abuses.)

On the negative side, it is necessary to take cognizance of two other values, namely, those expressed in the public's attitudes toward benefit "abuse" and toward the "proper" balance of power between labor and management. Both attitudes need to be considered in the broad context of social evolution.

In 1944 Eveline M. Burns presented to the American Economic Association a paper in which she delineated a possible evolutuionary law of growth underlying all social security programs, including unemployment insurance. In her paper Professor Burns identified three stages of social insurance evolution. The stages differed from one another in a number of ways, but in general each succeeding stage emphasized individual responsibility less and social responsibility more. Professor Burns placed the United States of that period in Stage II and judged that we were in movement toward Stage III. The market mentality and experience rating are more congenial to Stage I and Stage II than they are to Stage III. Twenty years later, in 1964, the same author discussed the same theme before the Industrial Relations Research Association and concluded that although the United States had not yet arrived at Stage III, we had moved perceptibly closer to it.

To have some chance of success, concrete proposals for unemployment insurance must be in accord with the stage of development in the underlying structure of social values. To misjudge this basic value structure is to invite failure. The CIO in Ohio made this mistake, for example, in 1955 when, having failed to obtain from the Ohio legislature the unemployment insurance liberalizations that the CIO judged necessary, it took its case to the people of Ohio by way of an initiative petition [22, p. 241]. The initiative petition lost by a margin of almost two to one and thus weakened rather than strengthened the likelihood of liberalization.

Polls taken in the United States have uniformly found that the general populace was at best lukewarm toward unemployment benefits and was under the impression that many claimants abuse the program. In 1970 the Canadian government carried out an extensive survey of public opinion regarding unemployment benefits. The survey found widespread ignorance regarding the program and a general impression of claimant abuse.[24] For example, when asked to rank in the order of priority seven changes that should be made in the unemployment insurance provisions, by far the most frequently mentioned desirable change was "Reduce the possibilities for people to cheat." Thus, where 44 percent of the respondents mentioned the need to increase the amount of the benefit, and 54 percent mentioned the need to extend coverage, 65 percent mentioned the need to reduce the possibilities for cheating [115, p. 8].[25]

The 1970-71 proposal of the Nixon administration to guarantee a minimum income for every family is clearly an important stride in the direction of Stage III. However, the proposal does not mean the abandonment of the market as the major mechanism for the allocation of resources. The market mentality is still the dominant mentality of our economy. In its review of the complex and deep-rooted welfare problems to which the Nixion proposal was addressed, *Time* offered this concluding observation:

> Despite the growing notion of welfare by right, the "work ethic" is not dead for either the poor or non-poor; a stigma still attaches to the jobless, just as a "P" was once pinned to paupers in Philadelphia. The force of the concept comes through clearly in the view of Nicholas Kisburg, legislative director of the Teamsters Union Joint Council 16 and a self-made man.

24. "The principal classes of abuses are, of course, well known. They include among others: drawing of benefits by married women that have withdrawn from the labour force; drawing of benefits by retired persons that receive pensions but are not seeking gainful employment; the failure of individuals to disclose their earnings during periods of partial employment; the failure of claimants to indicate their nonavailability for employment; and, employers and employees acting in consort and providing improper information concerning reasons for termination" [114, p. 55].

25. In 1971 the U.S. Department of Labor inaugurated a program of instruction in unemployment insurance designed for use in high schools. Such a program may eventually remove misconceptions currently held by the public regarding unemployment insurance. At present, public mistrust of the program is a factor of some importance, and it may remain so for some time to come.

Despite his seventh-grade education, he now gives courses in labor and politics at Fordham University. "I'm a strong believer in the Protestant ethic," he says. "Work and discipline are necessary. One reason why blue-collar guys hate welfare so much is that they feel, psychologically, that it threatens them. Working, bringing home the check each week, is one way of establishing their supremacy to themselves and their families. Work is the one thing they have. When they see a guy getting a check for doing nothing, they go crazy" [116, p. 18].

A 1968 Gallup poll which questioned people on the proposal to provide a guaranteed annual income up to $3,200 per year for every family showed that a majority of Americans opposed such a plan. Even the families with lower incomes ($5,000 or less per year) did not favor the guaranteed annual income proposal. However, the respondents overwhelmingly supported a plan that would guarantee each family enough *work* to provide this amount of money.

One of the assigned discussants of Professor Burns's 1964 paper was Professor Margaret Gordon, who observed that while significant movement had occurred toward Stage III in other social security programs, especially in the old-age program, relatively little movement in this direction had occurred in unemployment insurance. Professor Gordon's observation is a reminder that unemployment insurance tends to travel its own road and to be somewhat different, set apart from the other members of the social security family. One reason for the distinctive position of unemployment insurance in the social security scheme is that it is more closely intertwined than the other programs in the competitive market process and comes closer to being an integral part of the industrial machine. Unemployment insurance pays benefits to potential workers—rather than to widows, children, the aged, the sick, the disabled—and this, besides raising problems of maintaining initiative, affects the bargaining power of labor. It affects the bargaining power of labor by affecting the main brake on the use of that power—unemployment. Unemployment benefits diminish, as they are intended to, the pressures on the unemployed to take other, less desirable jobs. Unemployment benefits also diminish a social pressure that tends to limit strikes, namely, the dissatisfaction of those thrown out of work by the strikes of others. Workers thus indirectly unemployed because of strikes are eligible for unemployment benefits.[26]

Thus, where the other social security programs operate like Red Cross units behind the lines, unemployment insurance operates somewhat like a troop unit at the front and has implications for the general economic issues of wages,

---

26. The states differ in the norms they use to decide whether a claimant is directly or indirectly unemployed becuase of a strike, and hence whether he is disqualified or eligible for unemployment benefits. As of 1971, eight states (California, Delaware, Kentucky, New York, North Carolina, Ohio, Utah, Wisconsin) did not attempt to distinguish between strikers and those unemployed because of a strike and hence disqualified many claimants who would be paid in other states. In New York this effect was offset by a provision to pay benefits to strikers after seven weeks of a strike disqualification.

industrial discipline, productivity, and inflation. A symbol of this industrial character of unemployment insurance, and to some extent a result of it, is to be seen in the fact that unemployment insurance is not housed with the other federal social security programs in the Department of Health, Education, and Welfare, but dwells alone in the Department of Labor.

To understand why unemployment insurance is so closely linked with the competitive market, it is necessary to understand the relationship between unemployment—more exactly, the possiblility of unemployment—and the allocation of resources. In general, there are two ways of allocating resources—through a planned economy backed by the power of government or through the competitive market. The market always operates in conjunction with the possibility for unemployment.[27] If all owners of all resources (capital and labor) were assured of receiving whatever price they chose to name for the use of their resources— that is, were assured that their resources would never be unemployed—complete economic chaos would be the result. The only way out of the chaos would be to call upon the coercive power of government, which would have to set all prices and wages. There would then no longer be a free society as we understand the term. The equivalent of unemployment would then be some kind of legal or political penalty. For example, under the new (1971) Cuban labor law, enacted to control a growing problem of labor absenteeism, all able-bodied males of working age, except students, are faced with two years at forced labor if they refuse to take jobs. A fifteen-day absence from work draws a similar penalty [117, p. 1].[28]

Unemployment benefits are, of course, inescapably related to the choices just described. Imagine a situation in which everyone was assured of unemployment benefits that equaled one hundred percent of his wages, for as long a period of time as he chose to claim them, and under eligibility conditions set by himself. Such an unemployment benefit scheme would so change the meaning and function of "unemployment" as to disrupt the economy. Aid to the unemployed can never be completely segregated from the larger social issue of the use of the market to allocate resources.

Rubinow is one of the few writers who has explicitly adverted to the characteristic of unemployment insurance that sets it apart from other social security programs, namely, its close relationship to the market situation and the way it affects the balance of power between labor and management.

> While theoretically at least, the proper measures for meeting the economic problems of accident, disease, and old age have been discovered and to a great extent applied, the situation is very complex in one branch of

---

27. The unusual tenacity displayed by the force of inflation in recent years, even during a period of recession, may indicate that management or labor or both have found themselves some relatively efficient shelters from the threat of the unemployment of their resources.

28. For a recent view of the function of unemployment, even in a socialistic country, see [118]. See also footnote 5 of Chapter 10.

social insurance, which, as the most learned theorists of social insurance admit, is the pivotal point by which the entire structure of social insurance is to be judged—and that is unemployment insurance. For many years the problem of unemployment insurance baffled the best efforts, and was by many considered insolvable. Not only the vastness of the problem, but also the difficulty of differentiating between voluntary and involuntary unemployment, the very great danger of simulation, and finally *the very close connection of the question of unemployment and the entire matter of the struggle between the employer and labor, and the grave problems raised by state intervention in the struggle*—all this made the possibility of state insurance of unemployment a very doubtful one [119, pp. 23 and 24, emphasis supplied].

Employers do not directly determine the substance of unemployment insurance legislation, but participate in the legislative process by attempting to persuade legislators and judges. The issue here is the desirability of this attempt at legislative and judicial persuasion. When Sir William Beveridge produced his "cradle to grave" social security plan for postwar Britain, he deliberated long over the employer payroll tax as a possible source of revenue. Although he explained all the disadvantages of such a tax, he nevertheless recommended its use. His chief reason seems to have been that thus employers would be induced to participate more actively in the program [120, p. 109]. According to Eveline Burns, Beveridge saw employer participation as a guard against excessive liberalization of the program [121, p. 209].

One of the principal spokesmen for management, Stanley Rector, rested the case for experience rating largely on this principle of a balance of interests: "In a democratic society, attempting as it does to resolve its problems through the expression and interplay of different and frequently conflicting forces, it seems pre-eminently in point, wherever possible, to provide effective 'checks and balances.' Our constitutional framers built on this premise. . . . When all is said and done, it is perhaps the main contribution of experience rating to provide effective 'checks and balances' in the field of unemployment compensation" [127, pp. 348-49]. In his extensive treatment of experience rating, prepared for the Kansas state legislature, Professor Taulman A. Miller recognized the relation of the payroll tax to "a reasonable balance of interest" and concluded: "With strong interest groups involved in employment security programs, changes develop through what might be termed legislation by negotiation. If there is a reasonable balance in the strength and influence of opposing viewpoints, and a willingness to recognize social and economic necessity, the public interest may be served effectively" [36, p. 37].

The year 1970 saw Congress take the significant step of further limiting the discretion of state legislatures in the area of disqualifications. The states may no longer make full use of the most severe form of penalty, the cancellation of benefits or benefit rights. This, along with the growth of noncharging provisions, may represent movement toward Burns's Stage III. Is this the beginning of a profound change, an avalanche? Probably not. Changes in the future are likely to come as did most changes in the past—slowly, by small degrees.

Summary

Does experience rating cause employers to work more effectively in the area of unemployment insurance legislation? Because experience rating is only one of many factors influencing unemployment insurance legislation, it is not possible to give a statistically demonstrated answer to this question. But the weight of seasoned opinion seems to be on the affirmative side. Because of experience rating, employer participation in the legislative process is probably more effective, from the employer's point of view.

There is little doubt that experience rating stimulates employer interest, especially in the disqualification provisions. The increased employer interest is manifest in employers generally, but shows itself most clearly in the development of unemployment insurance specialists in the larger companies. While neither the rank-and-file employers nor the unemployment insurance specialists usually influence legislation directly, they do influence employer organizations and thus influence the professional representatives of those organizations—the lobbyists. Also on occasion the specialists work directly with the lobbyists and with key legislators.

The generally affirmative answer just given needs to be qualified, however, by two related observations. First, under a uniform tax system all employers would have a financial incentive to oppose liberalizations of benefits or of disqualifications, whereas under experience rating some employers would have either no such incentive at all or at least a lesser incentive than under a uniform tax system. Second, under a uniform tax, the subsidizing firms, which are in the majority, would be contributing a greater subsidy to the high-cost firms than they would under experience rating. As a result they would be less willing to agree to liberalization of the program. At the limit, the subsidizing firms might attempt to block all liberalizations until some degree of experience rating was introduced.

To judge the desirability of the effects of experience rating one must have norms. At this level the norms are basic social values. Evaluation will especially depend on one's acceptance of the preferred position to be accorded the claimant, on one's opinion of the danger of claimant "abuse" of benefits, and still more on one's view of the "proper" balance of power that should characterize labor/management relationships—basic issues that are beyond the scope of the present study.

10.

Stabilization
of
Employment

Introduction

Society's first concern with unemployment must always be its prevention. Unemployment is a disease of the body economic and like any disease should be prevented or cured if at all possible. Only that unemployment which cannot be prevented or cured should be treated with the palliative of unemployment benefits. In its positive form, unemployment prevention is called employment stabilization. Although more generally used, the term "stabilization" is also more open to misunderstanding. In a growing population, employment must grow, not stabilize in the literal sense. In this context, employment stabilization really means unemployment prevention.

Experience rating is related to the goal of unemployment prevention in three ways. One way is through its countercyclical effect, discussed in Chapter 11. Another way is through its impact on the allocation of resources. This effect was touched on in Chapter 3, but perhaps should be made more explicit here. To the extent that unemployment insurance increases the expenses of firms with unavoidably high benefit-cost rates, it represents a force making for lessened activity on the part of such firms.[1] To the extent that firms with high unemployment rates represent a smaller part of the total mix than they otherwise would, the average unemployment rate of the total economy will tend to be lower—assuming that the workers not hired by the irregular firms will eventually be hired by the more regular firms. Both of these effects are independent of the employer's ability to control unemployment.

The third way in which experience rating may influence the level of unemployment is dependent on management's ability to control unemployment. Experience rating may provide an incentive for the individual employer to manage his business so as to avoid causing unemployment. It is this "management" effect of experience rating which is the subject matter of the present chapter, as it was the subject matter of most discussions of experience rating in the past.

Good management was accorded great prominence in a movement which flourished in New England during the first three decades of the present century.

1. When the cost of a product increases, other things remaining unchanged, a smaller quantity of the product will tend to be demanded and supplied.

Known as the "New Emphasis" and fostered by a group of progressive business-men, the movement was based on two principles. First, unemployment is not inevitable, but like any disease is to some extent controllable. This was the gospel which Louis D. Brandeis preached tirelessly to his business friends and to government. In a 1911 speech entitled, "The Road to Social Efficiency" he said: "Some irregularity in employment is doubtless inevitable, but in the main irregu-larity is remediable. . . . Irregularity of employment is to my mind the greatest industrial waste and one of the main causes of social demoralization" [17, pp. 107, 118]. In 1914 Brandeis told the U.S. Commission on Industrial Rela-tions that "Industry has been allowed to develop chaotically, mainly because we have accepted irregularity of employment as if it was something inevitable" [7, p. 29].

According to the second guiding principle of the New Emphasis, the physi-cian most competent to cure the disease of unemployment was the businessman. If businessmen would only apply their managerial skills to the problem of unem-ployment, it could be brought under some control. This proposition drew considerable support from the parallel movement of "Scientific Management," which had begun to flourish in the industrial northeast shortly after the turn of the century.

The American Association for Labor Legislation, founded in 1906, played a leading role in this campaign against unemployment and eventually formulated a four-point "Practical Program for the Prevention of Unemployment," which called for the establishment of a system of public employment exchange offices, a program of public works to counteract cyclical fluctuations, the regularization of employment by individual employers, and a system of unemployment insur-ance. Unemployment Insurance was regarded by some of its early advocates as primarily a method of preventing unemployment—by making it expensive for the employer, who would thus be pressured to apply his managerial skills to the task of avoiding unemployment.[2] The position of Paul A. Raushenbush was more balanced, as may be seen in pp. 8, 52.

The 1929-33 economic cataclysm and the political responses of the New Deal swept away most of the old landmarks. From being a vague possibility for a few states, unemployment benefits became an actuality for the nation from 1935 on. The prevention of unemployment, which once was the most respect-able justification for this "socialistic" program, was now generally dismissed as a faulty foundation for a truly adequate program. Those who had been the "pro-gressives" leading the battle against unemployment found themselves bypassed by the rush of events. They had to struggle to maintain some community interest in the goal of unemployment prevention. The struggle took the form of the dispute over experience rating, as narrated in Chapter 1.

2. For a strong statement of the prevention theory see two articles written by John R. Commons in 1921-22. The first appeared in the *Survey*, (Vol. 47, October 1, 1921); the other, in *American Labor Legislation Review* (March 1922).

President Roosevelt, in his early 1935 message to Congress transmitting the report of his Committee on Economic Security, said: "An unemployment compensation system should be constructed in such a way as to afford every practicable aid and incentive toward the larger purpose of employment stabilization." Congress responded by permitting any state to provide for experience rating, and most of the states took advantage of the permission from the start (Table A-1). The typical state unemployment insurance law includes in its statement of public policy that one of the objectives of the law is the prevention of unemployment, or the stabilization of employment.[3]

To some, this objective remained the primary goal of unemployment insurance. In the 1940 debate over experience rating, the representative of the National Association of Manufacturers (NAM) declared that "the underlying principle of this legislation is the prevention of unemployment, not the compensation of it" (see p. 54). At least as late as 1952, this still seemed to be the position of the NAM [123, p. 7]. When I interviewed the members of the Wisconsin Unemployment Compensation Advisory Council, in 1950, the leading employer member insisted that the chief objective of unemployment insurance was to provide an incentive for employers to stabilize employment. Although one still encounters this point of view on occasion, it has been almost universally replaced by the view that the primary objective of unemployment insurance is to maintain part of the income of the unemployed person [124, p. 2]. Indeed, the pendulum has swung to the other extreme. Perhaps in reaction to the earlier exaggerated claims, the stabilization objective of unemployment insurance is likely to be dismissed as "negligible" or "unimportant."

Although employment stabilization is no longer considered to be the primary objective of unemployment insurance, it is still frequently spoken of as the primary, almost the sole, objective of experience rating. The early emphasis on this objective, as described in Chapters 1 and 3, has continued down through much of the literature dealing with experience rating. Textbooks on labor economics typically reduce the debate over experience rating to this one issue.[4] This study seeks to restore balance to the debate.

The Issue

It is claimed for experience rating that it influences management in two ways. First it limits any tendency of unemployment benefits to *increase* managerial

3. Currently (1971), of the thirty-six states whose laws contain a declaration of "public policy," thirty-two include an explicit statement that one of the objectives of the program is the prevention of unemployment or the stabilization of employment.
4. For example, Florence Peterson says: "Experience rating is based on the theory that unemployment is largely within the control of individual employers" [125, p. 794]. Lloyd G. Reynolds describes the "logic of experience rating" in similar terms [126, p. 377]. Melvin W. Reder declares: "The case for experience rating rests on the proposition that unemployment can be reduced materially by proper output planning by individual firms" [127, p. 476]. Turnbull, Williams, and Cheit endorse the idea that the "primary purpose of

carelessness and thus to increase unemployment. Without experience rating, unemployment benefits may appear to an employer as a fixed, not a variable, cost. Thus viewed, the availability of benefits may induce the employer to accept more unemployment than he would if there were no unemployment benefits at all. This is the "moral hazard" described above (p. 131).[5] It is instructive to note that when Sir William Beveridge came to review the performance of the British system of unemployment benefits after its first two decades of operation he showed considerable concern over this hazard. After raising the question of "Where the real dangers of today's unemployment insurance scheme lie and do not lie," he gave the answer:

> Those dangers, in a sentence, lie not so much in the risk of demoralizing recipients of relief, so that they do not look for work, as in the risk of demoralizing governments, employers and trade unions, so that they take less thought for the prevention of unemployment. . . . The fear of causing unemployment may vanish from the minds of trade-union negotiators and open the way to excessive rigidity of wages and so to the creation of unemployment. Industries practising casual engagement or perpetual short time may settle down to batten on the taxation of other industries or of the general public in place of reforming their ways. [71, p. 43]

The hazard can take many forms, from simple carelessness in hiring (for example, laying off employees in one department while hiring employees with similar skills in another department) to the planned use of unemployment benefits to maintain an excessively large labor pool (for example, hiring large numbers of workers during peak periods and providing partial employment with unemployment benefits for everybody during the rest of the year). A leading employer specialist in unemployment insurance, Russell L. Hibbard of the General Motors Corporation provided examples of this hazard in a paper presented to the Industrial Relations Research Association in 1959 [131, pp. 105-6]. Through its allocation of cost, experience rating exercises some restraint on these practices. Experience rating was indeed one remedy suggested by Beveridge: "A yet more drastic plan would be to make each employer individually liable to the unemployment fund for the whole or a proportion of the benefit paid by the fund to any workman formerly employed by him, the liability being fixed either on the last employer or on a succession of employers, in proportion

---

experience rating" is to stabilize employment [128, p. 407], while Daugherty and Parrish [129] advocate elimination of experience rating, chiefly for the reason that the individual firm cannot by itself achieve employment regularization.

5. Although the Soviet Union does not have a system of employment benefits, its method of allocating manpower encourages managers to hoard manpower with a consequent serious reduction in labor productivity. In the "Shchekino experiment," the number of workers in the plant was reduced by 870, labor productivity was trebled, and output was 10 percent above target. In October of 1969 the Central Committee announced a policy of applying the principles of this experiment more widely and of providing financial incentives for managers to dismiss superfluous personnel [130].

to the workman's length of service with each" [21, p. 411]. If firms nevertheless make use of such practices, experience rating at least assures that more of the resulting costs will be borne by the responsible firms.

Experience rating may not only prevent an increase in unemployment, it may, more positively, motivate employers to lessen the amount of unemployment usually connected with their business. The evidence of this effect is provided primarily by three studies that have been made of representative samples of firms operating under experience rating. The first two studies (of Wisconsin and Indiana employers) are the more thorough, but they are old; the third study (of Connecticut employers) is recent, but is less thorough.

Three Representative Samples

Wisconsin Sample

During the period July 1937–July 1938, Charles A. Myers interviewed a sample of 247 Wisconsin employers to ascertain "whether the Act had encouraged any stabilization efforts" [61, p. 709].[6] This sample, which was 3 percent of the approximately 8,000 employer accounts in the state, included 34 percent of all the workers subject to the Act and was representative in its distribution of firms by size, industry, and tax rate. Wherever possible (in two-thirds of the cases), Myers checked statements made in the interviews against statistics of employment, man-hours, and labor turnover. He used as his admittedly imperfect definition of "stabilization" the following: "The maintenance of a labor force of approximately the same size for approximately the same number of hours per week over a particular period" [61, p. 711].[7]

The investigation was subject to limitations. First of all, when Myers conducted his interviews in 1937–38, experience rating was not yet generally applicable. In 1938 the number of firms with reduced rates was only 114, as compared with 2,863 the following year. Reduced rates were a possibility rather than an actuality when the firms were interviewed. It is questionable how many employers are accustomed to think a year or more ahead as regards the effect of a new and unfamiliar program. Second, to measure accurately the impact of the tax on a firm's personnel and production policies, one would probably have to live within the firm for weeks or months at a time and make use of elaborate statistical procedures. Myers warns the reader of "the impossibility of covering the field thoroughly in one year" [61, p. 709] and explains the limitation of his method: "But no refined statistical studies were made, the analysis being con-

6. The "Act" was the Wisconsin Unemployment Reserves and Compensation Act, which became law on January 29, 1932. Wisconsin employers became liable for taxes beginning July 1, 1934, and Wisconsin workers became eligible for benefits after July 1, 1936. Experience rating, however, did not apply generally until 1939.

7. The definition was intended chiefly to exclude all extreme work-spreading. But it also excluded, for example, the dovetailing of employment between two or more firms, which is a form of genuine employment stabilization.

fined to a visual inspection of the amplitude of the plotted curves. When the movement of the curves was noticeably more regular after benefit liability began, this was presumptive evidence of stabilization. . . . The final estimates of the degrees of stabilization accomplished under the Act by the firms interviewed are rough only because no more precise method of evaluation was acceptable" [61, pp. 711-12].

Table 10-1 shows the extent to which the sample firms had attempted to stabilize employment under the impetus of expected future experience rating. About three-fifths of the firms (61.1 percent) showed some response to the Act. A group of 10.9 percent had achieved an "appreciable" degree of stabilization; while another group of 15 percent had achieved "some" degree of stabilization.

Table 10-1. WISCONSIN: Classification of Firms Interviewed during 1937-38,
According to Degree of Stabilization Achieved
As a Result of Efforts Induced by the Act[a]

Group Class	Degree of stabilization	Number of firms	Percent
I.	1. Appreciable—and as a direct result of Act	27	10.9
II.	2. Some—but efforts began before Act for other reasons	12	4.9
	3. Some—but success limited by difficulties	25	10.1
	Subtotal: 2,3	37	15.0
	Subtotal: 1-3	64	25.9
III.	4. Negligible—had attempted before Act for other reasons	44	17.8
	5. Negligible—largely unsuccessful or little attempted	39	15.8
	6. Negligible—Act ignored for the most part	4	1.6
	Subtotal: 4-6	87	35.2
	Subtotal: 1-6	151	61.1
IV.	7. None—had stabilized before Act	24	9.7
	8. None—business naturally stable	20	8.1
	9. None—difficult or impossible	39	15.8
	10. None—Act ignored	13	5.3
	Subtotal: 7-10	96	38.9
	Grand total: 1-10	247	100.0

Source: [61, p. 711]

[a]Wisconsin's Unemployment Reserves and Compensation Act became law on January 29, 1932, and went into operation on July 1, 1934. Benefits became payable July 1, 1936.

A third group of 35.2 percent had achieved a degree of stabilization characterized as "negligible." The classifications "appreciable," "some," and "negligible"
are not defined, but represent rough estimates made by Myers.[8]

The firms having a record of "appreciable" stabilization (class 1) included
22.7 percent of all the employees in the sample, while the firms in classes 2 and
3 included another 16.2 percent. Thus, the 25.9 percent of the firms which had
achieved some significant degree of stabilization accounted for 38.9 percent of
all the employees in all the sample firms [132, p. 77].

About two-fifths (38.9 percent) of the sample firms (classes 7-10) were not
influenced at all by the Act. Among these were 17.8 percent (classes 7 and 8)
which had stabilized before the program was enacted or which were naturally
stable. Thus only 21.1 percent of all firms (classes 9 and 10) that might have
been affected were not affected.

The interviews repeatedly mentioned the psychological as distinguished from
the financial impact of unemployment insurance. The two following quotations
are typical of many others:

> The costs of fluctuating employment are so great that the additional cost
> placed on us by the Act is actually relatively unimportant. But the Act is
> of importance psychologically. It has caused a lot of supervisors (foremen)
> to think more seriously about the problem of regularity of employment
> [61, p. 716].

> I could talk control of production to foremen until doomsday and not
> have an argument as potent and strong as the unemployment compensa-
> tion law, which is costing us money. I have tried to point out overhead and
> labor turnover costs associated with irregular operation, but it makes no
> impression on foremen because it is too general and they are thinking only
> of themselves and their department. But benefits paid out of their depart-
> ment impresses them. The responsibility is placed directly upon them, so
> now each one tries to do his best to regularize the work in his department
> and keep down benefit payments in it [132, pp. 80-81].

Firms in classes 3, 5, and 9, comprising 41.7 percent of all the firms in the
sample, were faced with above-average difficulty in the task of stabilization.
Myers gives examples of firms faced with fluctuating demand or dependent upon
seasonal supplies of raw materials. "Frequently, also, employers were restricted
in transfer and work spreading by the seniority provisions of union agreements"
[61, p. 717].

Because the twenty-seven firms which had achieved "appreciable" stabilization
represented the effect of the Act "at the limit," Myers provided numerous detailed examples of the steps taken by this group. To illustrate:

8. To illustrate his norm of "negligible" Myers uses the Kimberly–Clark Corporation, of
which he reports: "The main tangible thing done as a result of the Act was the establishment of a central clearing house for all employees in the Fox River Valley Mills. Before one
mill lays a man off, it contacts this office and a place is sought for him in one of the other

[Cudahy Meat Packing Company.] Formerly a considerable amount of casual labor, taken at random each morning from the crowd at the gates, was used for as little as an hour or two in such work as loading hides, unloading paper boxes, shoveling snow, etc. Under the Act this would eventually have been costly in benefits, and consequently steps were taken to eliminate it. A "utility crew" of about 18 men was organized to move from one part of the plant to another, performing these odd jobs. Steady work was thus given to members of the crew, but, of course casual laborers in the city received less work. Large groups of men waiting outside the plant each morning is a thing of the past [132, p. 23].

[Schuster Department Store.] Before benefit liability began there were nearly a thousand people on the extra list, or just about twice as many as would be needed at any one time. Each department had its own extras and there was little transfer between them. A study of the problem, induced by the Act, resulted in a reduction of the list by half, leaving about 500 who would then be employed more steadily. There was no greater volume of work for the extras as a group, but each of those remaining was assured of more regular work than any had received before. A further step along this same line, which was partly prompted by the Act, was to discontinue the "padding" of the estimated number of extra employees required for store-wide sales events. It was formerly the practice to be over-optimistic as to how many extras were needed, and consequently more were sometimes hired than were necessary [132, p. 41].

A distribution of the 1939 tax rates of 244 of the sample firms[9] is shown in Table 10-2, along with a similar distribution of tax rates for all Wisconsin employers. (High-tax firms seem to have been overrepresented in the sample and low-tax firms to have been underrrepresented.) After analyzing the characteristics of the sample firms in order to determine why they had the tax rates

Table 10-2. WISCONSIN: 1939 Contribution Rates for All Employers and Estimates for Employers Interviewed in 1937-38

Rate (percent)	All employers	Percent of total	Employers interviewed	Percent
0	390	5.4	5	2.2
1	2,473	34.0	99	40.5
2.7	3,725	51.3	78	31.9
3.2	676	9.3	62	25.4
	7,264	100.0	244	100.0

Source: [61, p. 720]

mills in that region. As noted earlier, this was done before the Act more or less informally; now it has been centralized and done more extensively" [132, p. 63].

9. Three of the 247 firms were excluded from this tabulation because one was a subsidiary of another, and two were out of business at the time the 1939 tax rates were assigned.

shown in the table, Myers concluded that most of the low rates went to firms that were naturally stable, rather than to firms which had made special efforts to prevent unemployment. He noted, however, that "An important minority of firms in industries where stabilization was considered difficult or impossible qualified for reduced contribution rates" [61, p. 721]. Although he recognized that part of this variation within an industry was traceable to differences in the nature of the economic activity being performed, he concluded: "But the interviews in 1937–38 gave ample evidence that comparable firms may differ in their stabilization attitude, policies, and success. Certainly, some of the reduced rates went to employers who genuinely earned them, and increased rates went to those who neglected to make use of their opportunities" [132, p. 139].

Other Effects. In his study of the sample firms, Myers encountered several practices which were either doubtfully desirable or clearly undesirable. Among the former was the practice of contracting out to another firm that part of a job which is especially irregular; by so doing, firm A may stabilize its employment record at the expense of firm B. This is not necessarily an undersirable practice. If firm B accepts the contracted work, presumably it finds the work worth while despite the unemployment benefit costs that go with it. The responsibility for stabilizing or bearing the cost of instability then rests on firm B. (The relationship between the two firms is essentially similar to that between the two divisions of General Motors described in Chapter 12.)

A second practice was that of work-spreading, which is encouraged under experience rating. About half of the sample firms reported making more use of work-spreading after the Act than before. Some forms of work-spreading were "part of a well-rounded stabilization program" or were practiced "because union agreements required it." But about 12 percent of the sample firms had employed, at some time or other, the most extreme form of work-spreading in which the employees earned just enough wages to disqualify them for unemployment benefits. Myers does not say whether these were large or small firms. If they were like the 15 percent of the firms described below, which made extreme use of probationary employees, only a small percentage of employees were affected.

A third practice was hiring for the probationary service period only. The Act then provided that an employee would not be eligible for benefits from a particular employer until he had been employed for four weeks. "Taking advantage of this, 15 percent of the firms interviewed have hired unskilled laborers for such jobs as unloading cars of material, loading scrap, shoveling snow, etc., being careful to lay them off before the end of four weeks and hiring a new set the next time" [61, p. 715]. These were small firms, however, and included less than 1 percent of the workers in the sample firms. (Under current state laws, this practice is no longer feasible.)

Conclusions. There are two reasons for thinking that this Wisconsin study represents the "limiting case" and that the impact of unemployment insurance on employment stabilization was about as great here as could be expected anywhere. First, Wisconsin at that time used the individual-reserves system, which provides the maximum employer incentive. Second, in Wisconsin at that time unemployment benefits had been in the public eye to an extraordinary extent. The 1932 enactment of the Wisconsin Unemployment Compensation Law had preceded the national law by three years and had been accompanied by a controversy remarkable for the interest it generated nationwide. In the period just preceding the Myers study, there were few issues in Wisconsin which rivaled unemployment benefits in point of publicity.

On the other hand, the 1937-38 interviews occurred a year or more before experience rating became fully effective in Wisconsin. If the interviews had been held in late 1939, for example, the impact of experience rating might have been found to have been somewhat greater.[10] As it was, about 25 percent of the firms (accounting for about 40 percent of the employees) were affected by the Act to some significant degree. In Myers's summation: "Although the stabilization accomplishments under the Wisconsin Law are not as great as those foreseen by earlier proponents, they are worthwhile and tangible" [61, p. 722].

Indiana Sample

In 1941-42 Taulman A. Miller conducted a series of interviews with a representative sample of 238 Indiana employers, who accounted for over one-third of all covered employment, to ascertain the influence of experience rating on their efforts to stabilize employment.[11] "Stabilization" was considered to mean "the inauguration of policies designed to reduce the degree of employment fluctuation within a plant and provide greater regularity of employment for its workers" [90, p. 159]. At the time of the survey, Indiana, like Wisconsin, had an individual reserve system of experience rating; but Indiana's experience rates were in full effect from 1940 on.

As shown in Table 10-3, the answers of the 238 firms were classified into five groups. Except for the 37 firms in Group I, this classification was made

---

10. Until the interruption of the war, employer interest in employment stabilization continued to grow in Wisconsin after the Myers' interviews. In 1940, for example, about 1,000 management representatives attended an all-day "Conference on Steadier Jobs" held in Milwaukee. Also, between January 1940 and August 1942, the Employment Stabilization Service, established by the Minnesota American Legion Foundation, sent out weekly bulletins to thousands of employers discussing experience rating and describing concretely how specific employers in various industries had succeeded in providing steadier jobs.

11. The full account of this survey is contained in Taulman A. Miller, "Economic Effects on the Experience Rating Provisions of the Indiana Employment Security Act, 1942" (Doctoral Dissertation, Yale University, 1942). The survey is summarized in [90], from which the materials in this section are taken.

Table 10-3. INDIANA: Classification of Firms Interviewed during 1941-42,
According to the Extent of Their Attempts to Stabilize Employment

Group	Extent of stabilization attempts	Number of firms	Percent of total
I.	Some efforts as a *direct* result of experience rating	37	15.5
II.	None as a *direct* result of experience rating. Some inaugurated before the Indiana Act, or for other reasons, but continued and intensified under the Act	35	14.7
III.	None. Efforts not necessary because of natural stability of the firm	38	16.0
IV.	None. Stabilization deemed impossible	83	34.9
V.	None. Little or no attention paid to experience rating	45	18.9
	Total	238	100.0

Source: [11, p. 159]

entirely on the basis of the statements of the employers themselves, without verification. Group I of the table includes firms which had established completely new stabilization programs, as well as those which had added to existing programs. Group II includes employers who reported they had been stimulated by experience rating to continue or intensify programs previously established. The remaining three groups reported no attempts to stabilize employment as the result of experience rating. Groups III and IV indicated their (opposite) reasons for not making such attempts. Group V offered no specific reason and exhibited little knowledge of the program or understanding of experience rating.

The picture that emerges from the table may be summarized as follows. Approximately 15 percent of the firms had begun to make some efforts at employment stabilization; another 15 percent had continued and increased stabilization policies previously instituted; about 70 percent reported that experience rating had had no effect on their efforts to stabilize. This 70 percent is very similar to the 74.1 percent of the Wisconsin firms which had achieved little or no stabilization under the stimulus of experience rating.

Miller attempted to evaluate the efforts reported by the thirty-seven firms in Group I. He used as his basic test the extent to which employment fluctuations in the plant diminished after unemployment insurance was inaugurated. He was able to get what he considered clear proof of significant success in only twelve of the thirty-seven cases. Miller judged that in seventeen of the remaining cases "the degree of success was negligible" and that in eight cases the available information was inadequate for a reliable judgment. In making this evaluation, he tried to take into account the generally rising level of employment in the period 1941-42, which would have increased stabilization apart from any new managerial efforts. On the other hand, he recognized that the pressures of the developing war economy would have lessened the significance of any costs connected with experience rating and would have distracted the attention of managers from the problem of stabilization.

Miller explored the possible effect of experience rating on "benefit avoidance," especially in the form of extreme work-spreading, and concluded: "The extent of such policies in Indiana was less than the extent of genuine stabilization efforts. . . . In Indiana, benefit avoidance has not been sufficiently widespread through 1941 nor of such a nature as to equal the modest stabilization efforts" [90, pp. 163–64].

Miller, like Myers, was not in a position to measure with any exactness the proportion of unemployment that was within the control of the employer. Like Myers, however, he was convinced that controllable unemployment was a minor proportion of the total. Writing against the background of a period in which exaggerated expectations had been entertained of the degree of stabilization that could or would be affected by experience rating, Miller argued vigorously that "the effectiveness of these programs [of stabilization] would seem to be limited to some minor reduction in the amount of frictional unemployment; and, regardless of motivation, their aggregate influence upon the stability of employment in general, or even within a state, does not seem likely to be of major significance" [90, p. 157].

Connecticut Sample

In 1968 the Connecticut Employment Security Division made a study [96] of the effects of experience rating in Connecticut, including the effect on employment stabilization. The study relied primarily on a questionnaire. In addition, 140 employers were interviewed; but for some unstated reason the results of these interviews proved unusable and were not published. The questionnaire was mailed to a representative sample of 5,000 of the state's 30,000 employers. Returns were received from 3,526, a response rate of 64 percent. The response rate of employers at the minimum tax rate was 66 percent, while for employers at the maximum tax rate it was only 58 percent.

The key questions dealing with employment stabilization were no. 6 and no. 7. These are reproduced below with the answers returned to them. Question no. 6 dealt with the broad issue of employment policies, while question no. 7 confined itself to layoffs. In question no. 7, since a single respondent could give more than one answer, the total of answers exceeds the total of respondents.

6. How much does your unemployment contribution rate, viewed in relation to the costs of doing business, influence your employment policies? (Check one.)

A. It is a major factor	101
B. It is an important factor	392
C. It influences employment policies moderately	461
D. It influences employment policies very little	528
E. It does not influence employment policies	1,890
No answer	154

7. When faced with a lay-off, which of the following factors do you consider? Number those which you *use* starting with 1 for the most important, 2 for the next important, etc. Leave blank if not considered.

	Order of Importance						
	1	2	3	4	5	6	7
A. Production requirements	997	554	243	83	20	3	2
B. Retention of skilled workers	906	837	289	55	17	0	0
C. Shorter workweek	111	171	311	337	223	84	4
D. Unemployment Compensation Tax	38	56	124	253	452	211	2
E. Availability of labor	189	295	564	346	143	33	1
F. Union contract requirements	224	154	119	113	62	224	5
G. Other (specify)	72	13	4	6	2	3	30
No answer 972							

In answering question no. 6, 954 respondents (27 percent) said that the unemployment insurance tax influenced their employment policy at least moderately (A, B, C). Thus, 73 percent reported that the unemployment insurance rate had little or no influence on thier employment policies. This compares closely with the 74 percent of Wisconsin employers and the 70 percent of Indiana employers who reported that unemployment insurance had a negligible effect or no effect at all.

Question no. 7 asks the respondents to rank the unemployment insurance tax among a number of other factors which might enter into the employer's decision whether to lay off workers. The unemployment insurance tax was mentioned as a factor by 1,136 (32 percent) of the respondents. (This is the sum of the answers on line D.) The unemployment insurance tax was rated among the first four factors by only 471 (13 percent) of the respondents.

In question no. 6, the 954 respondents who answered that unemployment insurance influenced their employment policies at least moderately (answers A, B, C) were identified for special study. In question no. 7, only 469 (49 percent) of this subgroup mentioned the unemployment insurance tax as one of the factors they considered when faced with a possible layoff. This raises some question about the consistency of the answers of the other 485 (51 percent), who answered in question no. 6 that unemployment insurance influenced their employment policy at least moderately. The explanation may stem partly from the broader scope of question no. 6, and partly from the larger number who did not answer question no. 7. The number (972) not answering question no. 7 was six times as large as the number (154) not answering question no. 6.

When all respondents to question no. 6 were classified by size of firm and industry, it was clear that large firms and manufacturing firms were more likely than the average firm to be influenced by their unemployment insurance tax rates in setting their employment policies [96, p. 50].

Of the 3,526 firms in the Connecticut survey, 751 were at the maximum tax rate. A special tabulation of these respondents, made at my request, showed that their answers were not markedly different from the answers of the sample as a whole. For example, in question no. 6, 23.1 percent of the 751 employers at the maximum tax rate said that the tax influenced their employment policies at least moderately. The corresponding percentage for all employers was 27.1 percent.[12]

It should be remembered that these data reflect what the employers *said* they did. In all probability, the answers exaggerate the actual impact of the unemployment insurance tax. Exaggeration is likely to be especially pronounced in those firms where the questionnaire was answered by the finance officer in the firm rather than by the plant manager or the personnel manager. The man who actually makes the decisions on employment policy is likely to think like the finance officer (in terms of tax costs) only when the company makes use of internal experience rating.

Although the Connecticut study raised the issue of possible "distortions in employment policies" caused by experience rating [96, p. 16], it was not able to add much light. In the questionnaire itself only one part of one question was even distantly related to this topic. Part F of question no. 8 asked the respondent if he ever "retained the full work force for reduced hours per week during periods of declining sales." In reply, 5 percent of the employers said "frequently" and 15.8 percent said "occasionally" [96, p. 34]. No information was provided by which to judge whether this was a desirable form of adjustment or a "distortion." The Connecticut report concluded that "distortions" in employment policies were probably "quite rare because the costs of such employment manipulation normally outweigh the advantages gained in merit rating. Further, such practices are strongly opposed by unions in collective bargaining, both through negotiation of specific contractual provisions and through grievances and arbitration" [96, pp. 16-17].

According to the Connecticut survey, there was a general lack of understanding of the program on the part of employers:

> One central feature of the study should be underlined at the outset. The Council did not set out to study how well employers understood merit rating and various elements of the law which directly relate to it. The Council, perhaps naively, assumed that most employers understood at least the elementary facts and principles of merit rating. This assumption was demonstrated to be wholly unjustified. The responses to the questionnaires and the interviews indicated that many employers, perhaps more than half, had no understanding of the system or their relation to it. For example, some believed that they had a favorable rating when they were in fact paying the maximum, many had distorted ideas of what made their rates go up and down, and most had no understanding of the reporting systems and the Employment Security Division's administrative procedures. The employer's lack of understanding affects practically every part of the system. [96, pp. 4-5].

12. It is interesting to note that when these maximum-tax employers were asked—in question no. 4—whether all employers should pay the same tax rate, 54 percent answered "No." Thus, the majority of these maximum-tax employers expressed themselves in favor of experience rating, even though their costs would be less under a uniform tax.

This sweeping generalization seems overly emphatic; more evidence than the survey was capable of producing would seem to be required to establish the proposition that "most" employers had "no" understanding of the program. Moreover, even if the proposition were true, it would have to be qualified by the observation that knowledge of the program is greater among the larger firms and that the larger firms include the majority of covered employees. However, the emphasis on employer ignorance may be more justified in Connecticut than in most states because of Connecticut's singular system of experience rating. (See description of the system of compensable separations, Appendix B.)

Where the Wisconsin results may reflect the maximum of employer activity, the Connecticut results, on the contrary, may reflect the minimum. First of all, where the range of tax rates in Wisconsin was 0 to 3.2, in Connecticut the range was 0.9 to 2.7. Second, where Wisconsin used the individual-reserve system of experience rating, Connecticut used the system of compensable separations, which is much less sensitive and less understandable to employers. Third, since the Connecticut law provided for the noncharging of benefits in connection with all the major disqualifications, the impact of experience rating may have been lessened by a significant amount of noncharged benefits. In Wisconsin, at the time of the survey, all benefits were charged.

A major limitation of the Connecticut study was its reliance on a questionnaire. Myers (like Miller) used interviews whose results he checked against statistics; but, even so, he felt obliged to confess "the impossibility of covering the field thoroughly in one year" [61, p. 709]. The Connecticut study also states that it does not "pretend to be exhaustive or definitive. In many respects it can claim to be little more than preliminary" [96, p. 3]. The chairman of the State Advisory Council on Employment Security, under whose direction the survey was made, further developed this statement as follows:

> Our study is certainly not definitive, though our experience in making it indicates the nearly impossible task of making a definitive study. I suspect that in order to make a study which would avoid the uncertainties which we found and give one an increased confidence in the reliability of the results would require that one have research assistants actually live within industrial enterprises of various sizes and types for periods of weeks or months, making in-depth interviews in the meantime in order to find out how and why people actually do what they do inside the business structure. In addition, the study would have to be made repeatedly during various stages of the business cycle to determine whether reactions are different in different stages of the cycle [133, p. 3].

If this is an accurate appraisal of the situation—and I believe it is—it leads to a conclusion of caution that applies to all three studies. It means that we do not have, and are not likely soon to have, a clear and detailed view of the relationship between experience rating and employment stabilization. Here, perhaps even more than elsewhere, we must be content to narrow the limits within which the answers probably lie.

Analysis

The findings of the three studies are in general agreement. On the assumption that they present a picture which is approximately accurate, it is natural to ask why the effect of experience rating on employment stabilization is that small and why it is that large. In other words, what are the limits and what is the potential of the stabilization effect of experience rating?

Limits of Stabilization

Most unemployment insurance costs are not within the control of the individual firm. This is the chief limitation on the extent to which experience rating may be expected to provide an incentive for the stabilization of employment. Most layoffs are occasioned by economic forces outside the individual employer's control, such as cyclical fluctuations, shifts (seasonal or secular) in consumer demand, changes in the technology of production, and seasonal fluctuations in the supply of raw materials. The regular differences in benefit-cost rates between the various industries (Chapter 4) are traceable primarily not to differences in managerial skills, but to differences in the natures of economic activities. Furthermore, the actual amount of benefits drawn by a separated worker will depend largely on the duration of his unemployment, and this is likely to be beyond the control of the employer, except to the extent that he can give hiring preference to former employees drawing benefits.

Additional limitations on the employer's control over his costs are technical in nature. All experience-rating systems have provisions which modify, to a greater or lesser degree, the direct correspondence between an employer's experience and his tax rate. As a result, the cost-tax ratios of most employers depart from unity, the incentives provided by experience rating are correspondingly impaired, and the tie between the stabilization efforts of an employer and his benefit costs is weakened.

The above limitations stem from factors (economic and political) which are not under the control of the individual employer. But even when unemployment insurance costs are completely under the employer's control, they will provide an inadequate incentive if the costs of stabilization are considered to be greater than any resulting savings from lowered unemployment insurance taxes. The size of the incentive required to influence production and personnel policies is exceeded only by that required to influence the location of a firm. Thus a tax saving that might be sufficient to induce an employer to participate in administration might not be sufficient to induce him to change personnel or production policies as a means to employment stabilization.

To cite two of many examples, a large California retailer was accustomed to hire a number of temporary employees twice each year to write and affix price tags to articles of merchandise. Laid off, these temporary employees regularly claimed unemployment benefits. The central headquarters of a major corporation in New York had the same experience with temporary employees hired to do annual financial reports. Both companies were sufficiently concerned about the resulting unemployment insurance costs to make a study of alternative procedures that would obviate the need for hiring these temporary employees. In both cases the costs of stabilization were judged to be greater than the unemployment insurance costs, and no change was made.

In the case of the New York corporation, the decision may have been influenced by the fact that the headquarters unit was not paying its own way in unemployment insurance. A "joint account" arrangement (see Appendix C) allowed the headquarters unit, a legally separate entity, to share the very low unemployment insurance tax rate of another division of the corporation in the same city. In both cases, the decision may have been influenced also by a failure to recognize that the cost of hiring temporary employees such as these is measured by the benefits they draw spread over the hours they work, as explained below.

The size of this incentive could, of course, be increased by raising the maximum tax rate. There is little doubt that if the construction industry had a greater financial incentive, it could achieve a greater degree of stabilization than characterizes it currently.[13] A recommendation for "heavier contributions by employers in seasonal industries" was made by Myers and Swerdloff in their article on "Seasonality and Construction" [134, p. 8]. What Herbert Hoover said in 1924 is much more true today, when great advances have been made in techniques and materials that permit work in all kinds of weather: "Custom, not climate, is mainly responsible for seasonable idleness in the construction industries" [135, p. 11].

Potential for Stabilization

Not all unemployment is beyond the control of the individual firm and not all stabilization policies are too costly. There remain areas within which the personnel and production policies adopted by management make for a lesser amount of unemployment and cost. Although the cost calculations of the two companies mentioned above eventuated in a decision not to stabilize, it is significant that the firms made the calculations. Potentially, at least, the tax was a significant factor. Other firms making similar calculations in different circumstances might reach decisions to modify their policies.

What is the unemployment insurance cost of a given personnel or production policy? How is it calculated? The method varies with the different systems of experience rating, but is basically simple in the most prevalent form, the reserve-ratio system. For all employers, except those who are at the maximum and expect to remain there indefinitely, the following is a simple, workable rule:

---

13. This is not to say that the industry *should* have been so taxed. Other considerations are involved besides supplying employers with an incentive to stabilize employment. The point here is that the stabilization effect of experience rating can be made very significant if desired.

Every benefit dollar charged against firm A's account will have to be replaced by a firm A tax dollar.[14]

This simple relationship may be obscured by the complexity of the mechanism involved and by the time-lag between the action which caused the tax increase and the tax increase itself. But the employer need not be able to calculate the exact impact of a given benefit payment on his reserve ratio and the consequent eventual impact on his tax rate. It is enough if he recognizes the operation of the basic rule expressed above. In some states, like New York and Wisconsin, employers receive weekly statements of the charges made against their reserve accounts. These statements are regarded by employers, quite accurately, as a record of their "nonworking payroll."

Thus the true cost to a firm of hiring a temporary employee is the sum of the wages plus the unemployment benefits paid to the employee. If, for example, a worker received $800 in wages and then drew $400 in unemployment benefits, his true cost to the firm would be $1,200. Calculated on a per-hour basis, the employee would have been paid at time-and-a-half rates.[15]

Obviously, the major limitation on this kind of calculation is the uncertainty attaching to the total amount of benefits that the laid-off employee will draw. If the amount is anything less than the maximum for which the worker is eligible, the true cost of his layoff is uncertain. Depending on the pattern established by past experience, the employer will probably use either the total benefits for which the employee is eligible or the average amount of benefits drawn by all the firm's separated employees. The shortest-term employees are likely to be the most costly.

The chief significance of the unemployment insurance tax is to be sought in its relationship, not to total operating costs, but to profits. Businessmen tend to think of this tax as "coming off the top of profits." In many instances, the dollar amount represented by the unemployment insurance tax is a significant proportion of profits. At my request, six large firms in durable manufacturing calculated the proportion that their unemployment taxes were of profits (after taxes) for the decade 1960–70. Their proportions ranged from 3 to 7 percent. No company would consider negligible a cost that lowered its profits by 3 or 7 percent. Applied to profits of many millions of dollars, these percentages represent large absolute sums. In the case of the food service company mentioned earlier, the unemployment insurance tax was sometimes larger than profits. In most years, 20 percent or more of all businesses end the year without a net profit.

Besides its direct financial impact, experience rating has the psychological effect of focusing attention on employment stabilization. The other gains from stabilized employment are generally greater than any possible gain from a

14. See the "natural tax rate," Appendix B.
15. Depending on the state law and on the length of time worked, the ratio between wages and benefit rights based on those wages varies greatly (from 25 percent to 100 percent) but averages about one-third or more for most states.

lowered unemployment insurance tax. Employment stabilization can bring gains, for example, in decreased training costs, decreased spoilage, increased productivity, even an improved image as a good place to work. But these gains tend to be less visible and calculable. They can easily be overlooked, especially if responsibility for them is diffused, but the unemployment insurance tax is a cost for which the employer must write a check and which is directly traceable to one cause—unemployment. All three studies emphasize this aspect of experience rating, as does the following quotation from Marion B. Folsom, whose experience with unemployment benefits has been unusually broad and deep.[16] Talking to the administrators of the state employment security agencies, Folsom said:

> Some people discussing this problem who haven't had much experience in business say that a one or two per cent saving in payroll is not sufficient incentive and that there is a greater incentive already because of the many benefits a company can get from stable employment. I think they would change their attitude if they worked in the industry a few years. Companies are always trying to find ways of making a definite saving of this type, especially of taxes. The other benefits they get from stabilization of employment are indefinite, intangible, but here is something you can put your finger on that is very definite. The head of the company will soon ask "Isn't there something we can do to cut down this payroll tax? Can't we do what those other companies are doing?" [29, p. 61].

The sharply focused stimulus provided by experience rating is the more critical where responsibility for unemployment is the more diffuse. Large firms operate through separate departments, such as finance, accounting, sales, production, and personnel. The stabilization of employment is a function of all these departments, but is the specific obligation of none of them. If the firm does not use internal experience rating, the unemployment insurance tax appears to each department like a fixed cost. And each department is open to the moral hazard of using unemployment benefits as a costless way of achieving its own objectives more easily. The finance officer, who does see unemployment benefits as a variable cost, usually lacks the operating opportunity to control this cost directly. However, he can use the unemployment insurance tax as a kind of window onto the possibility that policies pursued in the sales or production or personnel departments are resulting in an unnecessary amount of unemployment. Looking through this window, top management is in a position at least to ask searching questions.

But there is more to it than that. In large firms unemployment insurance is frequently made the responsibility of some one person. This person may serve as a bridge between the finance officer and the operating departments with respect to unemployment costs. The need for such a bridge is indicated in the following quotation from a letter written by the director of the Connecticut study:

16. He was treasurer of the Eastman Kodak Company, which had introduced an unemployment benefit program for its own employees before the Social Security Act was passed.

What our study does suggest is that those who know the advantages of merit rating and what it offers to the firm, have no practical control in most situations over the way the layoffs are made or the way in which the reports are filed. The accountants and the comptrollers think in terms of merit rating; the foremen, the production managers and, indeed, those in the personnel department who are directly involved have little or no sensitivity to merit rating. In simplest terms, the right hand doesn't know what the left hand is doing [133, p. 3] (see also [96, pp. 8–9]).

Depending on his ability and prestige in the firm's hierarchy—and this varies a great deal among firms—the unemployment insurance specialist is in a position to help unite the left and right hands. Like the finance officer, the unemployment insurance specialist sees the unemployment insurance tax as a variable cost, and he usually has the expertise and the time to track this cost to its various sources. Some of these specialists prepare monthly and annual reports which show the source of every unemployment benefit by operating unit within the company and by reason for the separation.[17] Such reports are potential management tools. The unemployment insurance specialist who assembles such reports is the direct result of experience rating, without which he would not exist.

Examples of Stabilization

This generalized description of the potential for employment stabilization may be made more concrete by examples. While such examples cannot, of course, claim to be representative of employers generally, they serve as a reminder that a potential for employment stabilization exists and that unemployment insurance can in some circumstances help to actualize that potential.

In the larger firms, which account for the majority of covered workers, it very easily happens that workers are being hired in one part of the corporation while workers with similar skills are being laid off in another, or that former employees are being paid unemployment benefits while new employees are being hired for jobs that the former employees could very well fill. I came across a number of instances where under the direct stimulus of experience rating a company modified its personnel policy so as to avoid this pattern as far as possible. Although the major gain was probably the retention of trained personnel, yet as a matter of fact the new policy was not inaugurated except under the prodding of the unemployment insurance specialist or service company, which used the unemployment insurance costs as a catalyst of action.

Chapter 8 provided several illustrations of this relationship—for example, the Walgreen Company and company B. It will be recalled that the change in the

---

A member of the influential Senate Advisory Committee on Social Security in 1939, he was later Secretary of the United States Department of Health, Education and Welfare.

17. For examples of such reports see in Chapter 8 the descriptions of North American Rockwell, Ford, company A, company C. As noted in the chapter, the service company often performs this same function for its clients.

policy regarding pregnancies at North American Rockwell was traceable chiefly to the influence of the unemployment insurance unit. When company C set about to lower its tax rate, one of the steps it took was to centralize personnel policies sufficiently to facilitate the shifting of employees from a job that was ending to a job that was about to begin. The company had the more latitude in this respect because it did not work through a union hiring hall. Under the combined impact of unemployment insurance and SUB (Supplemental Unemployment Benefits), the Ford Motor Company in Detroit set up an enlarged "clearing house" for open jobs and available employees.

I came across a number of instances where firms about to lay off skilled employees had telephoned a neighboring firm to see if it was in the market for such employees. I have seen such transfers actually occur in the steel industry, the auto industry, and in a couple of foundries. In each case the stimulus came from unemployment insurance tax considerations, and in several cases the actual negotiators were the persons in charge of their respective companies' unemployment insurance units. I have also come across a number of instances where a firm was contemplating a change in production (or in location) that would involve layoffs, and the person responsible for unemployment insurance was asked for an estimate of the resulting unemployment benefit cost. This cost was never the decisive factor, but it was sufficiently important to be asked for and to be included in the factors considered.

A service company in a midwestern state told me it had over a hundred laundries as clients. When they became clients in the 1950's, they were practically all at the maximum tax rate. In 1970 they all had below-average tax rates and many were in the minimum rate. In the interval they had improved their wage scales and hiring practices so as to greatly diminish turnover. The incentive of a diminished unemployment insurance tax was not the chief factor, but it was one of the steadily operating factors favoring the change.

In the late 1950's a large New York manufacturing company began to give serious attention to its pattern of fluctuating employment and succeeded in achieving a greater degree of stabilization. In retrospect the personnel director of the company gave a significant share of the credit to the unemployment compensation benefit administrator.

> Bormon, who was our U.C. Benefit Administrator, had one great quality in abundance and that quality was enthusiasm. When he saw the staggering sums that were being paid by our Division each week on U.C. he turned his energies to doing something about it. Bormon talked with everyone in the Division who would listen to him about the apparent waste. He was well armed with unemployment insurance cost statistics, and continually needled the General Manager, the Works Manager, the Personnel Director, and the Production Manager to do something about it. He would not take "no" for an answer. Bormon did not on his own get our stabilization program into being but he did help provide the spark, and his example

shows what any good Unemployment Compensation Administrator can do to trigger this activity [136].

Another official of the same company summed up the results of the stabilization campaign as follows:

We had averaged 1246 layoffs each year for the years 1957, 1958 and 1959. In 1962, we had 46 layoffs and in 1963, we had none. I fully realize that the good economic climate of 1962 and 1963 helped us in our stabilization. I am positive, however, that without a stabilization program which looked plant-wide rather than by product or department, we would have had in these past two years in the area of 400 to 600 layoffs. In addition to actual dollar savings from Unemployment Insurance, scrap, medical expenses, grievance time, fringe costs, there have been real benefits which cannot be measured in dollars. The morale of employees has improved. Our reputation as a stable employer has resulted in a far greater number of applicants for each job. In 1963, we reached a point of 23 applicants for each job opening, an all time high, giving us the best selection opportunity we have seen in years. These are a few of the benefits which have resulted [136].

The following is one of many stabilization efforts described in a publication produced by unemployment insurance specialists and addressed to New York employers:"Within the concept of a flexible labor pool, one company completely retrained surplus, semi-skilled, female assemblers for clerical positions, where a shortage existed. The costs of retraining were considerably less than the $1,300 in unemployment insurance benefits each laid-off employee could have been expected to draw against the company account" [99, p. 27].

In Massachusetts the General Electric Company publishes an unemployment insurance bulletin which goes to all the company's plants. In 1969, the May 6 bulletin reminded plant managers: "Once again, we caution you that with the vacation period coming up shortly, those people who are not eligible for the total vacation period may receive unemployment benefits if you close your plant. As you know, judicious handling of vacation benefits was one of the factors that helped us over the hump last year and earned us a sizable tax decrease." A later bulletin (July 14) announced: "We were pleased to note the communication put out by the Armament Plant in Springfield, regarding work for short-service employees during the vacation period. This type of cooperative effort shows strong desire to help earn rate reduction." Presumably, both parties profited from such an arrangement—the company from a decrease in unemployment benefit costs, and the short-service employers from an increase in income.

In the Railroad Unemployment Insurance system, contributions are not experience-rated (see Appendix E). As seen by the individual company in the short run, unemployment benefits are a fixed cost not significantly affected by the extent to which any one company dips into the pooled funds. In their study of employment fluctuations in this industry, William Haber and his coauthors reach the conclusion that the individual railroad companies would be more concerned to avoid unnecessary and violent fluctuations in employment if each had to stand the cost of its own employment policy [137, p. 116-26, 228, 230-31].

Examples of this sort could be multiplied almost without end.[18] But no lengthening of the list would lead to a reliable estimate of their quantitative importance. Such managerial attempts to lessen frictional unemployment certainly do not constitute anything like a major determinant of the level of unemployment in the economy. Still, some opportunity to lessen frictional unemployment seems to pervade a large part of the economy, and it would be a rash judgement to write off the opportunity as negligible.

Undesirable Stabilization

Faced with a pattern of fluctuating workloads, an employer can adjust in one of three ways: (1) He may hire temporary workers for peakloads and lay them off thereafter. (2) He may take measures to lessen the degree of fluctuation in the workload. (3) He may maintain a constant number of employees who work full-time or overtime during the busy season and work short-time during the slack season. Experience rating tends to move an employer away from policy #1 toward policy #2 or alternatively toward policy #3. A question then arises whether policy #3 is preferable to the original policy #1.

Policy #3 involves the issue of work-spreading. Experience rating has been charged with causing employers to spread work, both not enough and too much. That is, experience rating is said to be a bar to desirable work-spreading and a stimulus to undesirable work-spreading.

In the early years, the charge was frequently made that experience rating acted as a bar to desirable work-spreading. The fear was expressed that experience rating would stablize unemployment and result in a hard core of unemployables. The objection seemed to rest on a "block of labor" theory and assumed that there was less work to be done than there were workers to do it. This was an understandable judgment in the light of the prolonged mass unemployment of the 1930's. One of the strongest statements of this position came from the New York Unemployment Insurance State Advisory Council:

> Essentially, therefore, stabilization does not mean increased employment, Rather it means that whatever employment there exists will be the more heavily concentrated in that group who are fortunate enough to have jobs now, with a corresponding decrease in employment opportunities for those not so favorably situated. . . .
> We know full well the evil which is irregularity of employment. And yet, is it not a lesser evil than the segregation of our working people into two classes, one steadily employed and the other steadily unemployed? Even a

18. Two early and extensive collections of such examples are [138] and [139].

slight amount of work coming at irregular intervals and uncertain in its duration is better than no work at all [140, p. 5].

This position was adopted as its own by the signers of the Majority Report of the 1940 Interstate Conference Committee on Experience Rating [33, p. 45]. Other writers on the subject were making the same point at about this same time.[19]

When the issue was debated at the 1940 meeting of the Interstate Conference of Employment Security Agencies, Paul A. Raushenbusch Replied to this objection against experience rating as follows:

> It seems to me very strange, to say the least, to suggest that we ought to have less stable employment, that we ought to have as much instability as possible for millions of our workers in order to give a few short-time jobs to those who do not now have a regular connection with industry. That does not seem to me to be a constructive solution.
>
> Let me put it to you State administrators, specifically to those who stress "hard core" problems and therefore attack incentives for stabilization,—how do you run your own agencies? You have your people on a salaried basis the year round so far as practicable, and use temporary help as little as possible, don't you? Even if your various civil service and merit systems would permit, would you consider for one moment laying off all your workers every three months, in order to hire others, in order to help the hard core of unemployment, by turning people over every three months? If you did that you would make a real contribution, according to some of the people who say the experience rating is going to have devastating effects by making jobs steadier. If you have 100 people now, and you lay them off every three months, you might need 125 or 150 to do the same job. It would be very inefficient, so we all recognize that we would not practice it in our own enterprise, and that if we did we could not defend it.
>
> My thought is that a far better long-run hope for solving the problem of the hard core of unemployment is for private industry to continue working on the problem of producing more efficiently and employing its people more steadily. Those two are closely related, because anyone can tell you that if and to the extent that greater stability can be achieved, to that extent you are also going to have lower production cost, and steadier purchasing power, and more jobs, and the whole economy will gain by that [29, pp. 92–93].

A related though distinct objection sees experience rating as lowering total employment by making seasonal employment too expensive. This is one of the main objections to experience rating, for example, voiced by Joe Davis, President of the AFL -CIO in Washington state, where the highly seasonal industries of lumbering, fishing, and canning provide a significant proportion of total employment. Such an objection is probably more valid when fluctuations in employment stem from seasonal variations in the supply of raw materials. When the

19. See, for examples [10, p. 38], [141, p. 6], [142, p. 101], [32, p. 106].

fluctuations stem from arbitrary changes in demand, intervention in the market is harder to justify.

Some persons seem to argue that concerns operating with peak loads of labor are beneficent and should be encouraged. In asserting that experience rating would hamper employment they ask, for example, why a department store with fluctuating personnel requirements should be penalized for taking on special Christmas employees. The fallacies in this question will be more apparent if it is put in another way. If consumers insist upon concentrating their purchases within a two months' period, with consequent dismissal of workers after the rush is over should not the consumers be charged for part of the compensation cost resulting from the temporary work caused by their capricious buying habits, and could not the stores take further steps to spread the buying season over a longer period [9, p. 21]?

Another alleged undesirable effect of experience rating is the possibility that it may hinder programs that aim at the training and placement of marginal workers, as in the Manpower Administration contract programs. Such workers pose a greater-than-average risk for the employer because they are more likely to become unemployed and draw benefits. Under experience rating, these benefits are charged to the employer's account and thus become an additional reason for the employer not to take them on in the first place. This is, indeed, a possible difficulty. If it should prove to be an actual difficulty (thus far, none of the studies made of the manpower programs has raised this issue) it might be met by a provision to noncharge any benefits paid to such workers.

Experience rating is also critical on the opposite score, that it results in too much work-spreading. At the extreme, an employer may so divide the available work that everyone earns just enough to make him ineligible for unemployment benefits. The three studies described above—Wisconsin, Indiana, Connecticut—mention this practice but do not give any actual examples. They conclude that instances of this kind of "benefit evasion" are rare compared to instances of genuine stabilization.

This kind of work-spreading, which results in a minimum payout of unemployment benefits, is less frequent also than that form of work-spreading which keeps a large work force attached to a firm by alternating full weeks of work with full weeks of benefits. Textile and shoe firms in Rhode Island and Massachusetts, for example, have used the latter technique for years. The director of the Massachusetts Division of Employment Security once said to the owner of a textile firm, "You would not follow this pattern if the maximum unemployment insurance tax rate were higher." The owner calmly replied, "Probably not."

Conclusions

The New Emphasis was a good emphasis. The Brandeis principle, that unemployment is to some extent preventable, was sound. As a matter of fact, we have learned to prevent much unemployment. Although reliable data on unemployment rates are not available until after World War II, what statistics we do have indicate that the average level of unemployment has been lower after the war than it was before. For the period 1890-1930, the best estimates of average unemployment cluster around a rate of 10 percent.[20] For the postwar period 1947-70, the average unemployment rate has been less than half that.

Most of this gain has probably come from other causes, especially from the improved monetary and fiscal policies of government; but some also has resulted from better business management. There is a literally endless list of examples to show that good management on the part of the individual firm can in some circumstances lessen unemployment. This managerial effort to control unemployment is like the struggle against any endemic disease—constant progress is possible, for there is always more to be done. For example, the Ford Motor Company recently (1971) announced that the downtime needed for model changeover will be lessened this year and in the future. For another example, a half-dozen studies of the construction industry are currently in progress aiming at, among other things, a lessened seasonal fluctuation in that troubled industry. In this unending struggle to lessen unemployment, unemployment benefits can be a hindrance or a help.

In themselves, unemployment benefits tend to be a hindrance to employment stabilization. Their availability constitutes a "moral hazard" for the employer, inviting him to accept more unemployment than he otherwise would. Experience rating turns this hindrance into a help, giving the employer an incentive to avoid unemployment. While the unemployment insurance tax is not usually the main consideration moving a firm to attempt employment stabilization, neither is the tax a negligible factor. Belonging to that category of small costs which every business seeks to minimize in its effort to improve efficiency, the tax functions as an added reason for avoiding unemployment.

In addition to this direct financial incentive, experience rating has the psychological effects of sharply focussing management's attention on the costs of unemployment. The unemployment insurance tax, experience-rated, is thus a minor but constant pressure working throughout the economy, punishing (mildly) businessmen who become careless or who are simply inefficient. The net effect of experience rating on employment stabilization is to be counted a plus. If this were the system's only effect, it would constitute a solid though minor reason for having experience rating.

20. For a convenient listing of the major estimates for the early period, see [7, pp. 24-25].

11

Timing
of the Tax

Although the payment of benefits in the unemployment insurance program is clearly countercyclical in its timing pattern, there is some question about the timing pattern of the payment of taxes. Given a set of eligibility and benefit provisions, given also an anticipated average rate of unemployment over a business cycle, a state unemployment insurance system can expect to have to raise a total amount of taxes sufficient to pay the covenanted benefits over that period of time. The state has some freedom, however, in the way it goes about accumulating this total tax amount. The required taxes may be levied according to one of three timing patterns. First, taxes may be levied as they are needed, so that higher taxes are imposed in years when the benefit drain is greater. Second, roughly the same tax may be levied each year. This stable, level-premium tax would be the average tax needed over a complete business cycle. Third, a countercyclical pattern may be followed, whereby lower taxes are levied in years when the benefit drain is greater, leaving the deficit to be made up by higher taxes in the years when the benefit drain is less.

There seems to be general agreement that if it can be done without interfering with the attainment of other objectives, it is desirable to follow a countercyclical timing pattern. Without inquiring into the validity of the economic theory underlying it, the present chapter accepts this agreed-upon goal and asks whether experience rating helps or hinders its attainment.

There is a "macro" and a "micro" aspect to the issue, depending on whether the reference is to the economy as a whole or to employers taken singly. Most of the literature dealing with the timing pattern of the unemployment insurance tax discusses the issue on the macro level and stems from those whose main interest is not unemployment insurance but something else, for example, public finance or the business cycle. Although at least as important, the micro aspect of the issue has been generally overlooked. This chapter discusses first the macro aspect of the issue, then the micro aspect.

Macro Effect

The effect of experience rating on the business cycle is both small and uncertain. For both reasons, this effect is not a major issue in the social debate over the desirability of experience rating. The issue needs to be discussed, however, if only to clarify it and remove certain misunderstandings.

The unemployment insurance tax is a very small part of the total economy it is said to influence. It never amounts to more than a fraction of a percent of the gross national product. Even when the more relevant comparison is made—between changes in the unemployment insurance tax and changes in the total economy—the ratio still remains very small. During the four cycles that marked the period 1945–64, changes in unemployment insurance taxes averaged only about 1 percent of the corresponding changes in national income [143, p. 203].[1]

Actually, the relevant quantity is smaller even than this. The relevant quantity is the *difference* in the tax that would be paid at a given time under an experience-rated tax and that which would be paid under a uniform variable tax.[2] Since there is no experience under a uniform variable tax to which to refer, we can only speculate on the size of the difference, but in all probability it would be small. The amount of the taxes to be raised and their timing would probably be very similar under either a uniform variable tax or under experience rating. The difference between experience rating and a uniform variable tax relates not to the amount of the total tax nor to its timing, but only to its distribution among taxpayers. One would not expect this difference to have a perceptible impact on the business cycle. (This expectation is supported by the findings of the Palomba study discussed below.)

The effect of experience rating on the average unemployment insurance tax and hence on the business cycle is not only small; it is also uncertain. It is uncertain, in the first place, partly because it is small. The measurement of the impact of so small a quantity as a change in the unemployment insurance tax on so large a quantity as the gross national product must necessarily be something less than certain. The effect of experience rating is uncertain also because there are causes other than experience rating that affect variations in umployment insurance taxes. Among other causes are the political forces mentioned in the chapter on legislation. It may happen, for example, that a sizable reserve fund will enable "politics" in the narrow sense to dictate an ad hoc lowering of the unemployment insurance tax rate at the same time that benefits are increased. This is a policy that pleases all sides and leaves for tomorrow—and perhaps for another administration—the unpleasant task of rebuilding depleted reserves. There is no reason to think that politics would work differently under a uniform variable tax.

In another situation, politics may dictate not the squandering of a needed reserve, but the avoidance of an "excessive" reserve. The accumulation of addi-

---

1. The larger countercyclical impact of the unemployment insurance program is on the *benefit* side. Changes in benefits are larger and more concentrated than changes in taxes and offset a larger proportion of changes in the national income [143, p. 198].

2. Uniform as between employers, variable over time. As explained in Chapters 1 and 2, this is the only reasonable alternative to an experience-rated tax.

tional reserves may be feared as an invitation to demands for more liberal benefit provisions. This has always been a potent political consideration, helping to dictate the size of the fund and hence the behavior of the average tax rate.

There is also an element of uncertainty in the underlying business cycle theory, especially as regards the "proper" behavior of the tax on the upswing. The statistical studies of the countercyclical impact of the unemployment insurance tax define as "stabilizing" a change in the unemployment insurance tax similar in direction to a change in the economy. Thus the tax is considered to be stabilizing if it declines when the economy declines and rises when the economy rises. While there is general agreement on the desirability of a stabilizing effect on the downswing, there is considerable uncertainty as to when such stabilization becomes desirable on the upswing. It is hardly desirable to stabilize employment at the low level which characterizes the trough of a cycle or the early stage of recovery. For this reason, as explained later, what happens on the downswing is more important than what happens on the upswing.

History of the Issue

Countercyclical financing shared in the interest generated by the general goal of employment stabilization. The desirability of so timing the unemployment insurance tax as to counterbalance the business cycle was strongly stressed in 1940 by the Interstate Conference of Employment Security Agencies' committee on experience rating. The "Unanimous Report" of the committee, authored by Paul A. Raushenbush, urged the practical adoption of this objective. The report also recognized that the objective had a micro aspect as well:

> The importance of building up substantial reserves, especially in good years, can hardly be over-emphasized . . . substantial reserves should be built up during the fat years, to help finance benefit payments during the lean years. . . . Ideally it would probably be desirable under any experience-rating system to make effective in the relatively good years the increased contribution rates which are normally apt to result from adverse experience during bad years. . . .

> This would also hold true as to individual employers, who could better afford to pay a slightly higher rate during periods of expanding payroll, and a slightly lower rate during periods when their payroll is declining [42, p. VI-8].

Addressing the 1942 annual meeting of the Interstate Conference, Ewan Clague, representing the Bureau of Employment Security, added the federal endorsement of this objective: "The ideal would be if the system worked so that the employer in bad times achieved the lower rates he had earned in good times, while conversely he suffered in good times for the unemployment experience he had during bad times" [42, p. VI-8].

Experience rating has been criticized frequently for working contrary to the goal of countercyclical financing. In 1945, for example, Charles Myers wrote:

"Variations in contribution rates and revenues for payment of benefits are exactly the opposite of the variations in social security contributions suggested as desirable over the cycle by the British White Paper on *Employment Policy*" [62, p. 352]. Professor Albert G. Hart wrote in 1948: "But grafted onto the process is a destabilizer—merit rating. In many states, a separate reserve account is kept for each employer, and benefits to workers whose unemployment is attributed to him are charged against this account. The larger the employer's reserve becomes, relative to his payroll, the more his contribution rates are reduced. Hence heavy unemployment, draining the reserves, leads to an increase in contribution rates—which tends to make unemployment worse" [144, pp. 475-76]. The influential 1949 Senate Advisory Council on Social Security stated in its report: "The tendency for the rate of unemployment contributions to rise as employment decreases can have serious consequences for the economy" [42, V-7]. In 1954 Arthur Larson, then undersecretary of labor, remarked that the desirable objective of countercyclical financing was "almost the direct opposite of the way in which experience rating has been operating in our experience, for contributions go up when unemployment goes up" [145, p. 158]. Richard Lester seems to agree with this criticism in his 1962 work, when he ends his discussion of "cyclical fluctuation" with the statement: "To summarize, tax rates may have an adverse cyclical effect because their variation is influenced by experience rating. . . ." [63, p. 71].

Studies of Macro Effect

The validity of this line of criticism was examined in a number of statistical studies made during the 1950's and 1960's. In the light of these studies it has become quite clear that this particular criticism has little foundation in actual experience. Up to the present, at least, the unemployment insurance tax system, experience-rated as it has been, has generally operated countercyclically.

Five of these studies are summarized below. Essentially, each study examined the relationship between changes in the economy and changes in the unemployment insurance tax. As shown in the following table, the studies used a variety of measures of cyclical change and two different measures of tax change. Some of the studies used annual data, while others used quarterly data. Because of the abnormal nature of the war period, all the studies limited their investigation to

Study	Period covered	Type of data used	Measure of cyclical change	Measure of tax change
Andrews and Miller (1954)	1946-51	annual	unemployment rate	tax rate
Spivey (1958)	1946-55	annual	benefit payments	tax rate
Raphaelson (1966)	1948-61	annual	total wages	taxes
Rejda (1966)	1945-64	quarterly	national income	taxes
Palomba (1966)	1948-64	quarterly	gross national product	taxes

the postwar period. The results of four of these studies are summarized in Table 11-1. Spivey's results are not included because they could not be fitted into the format of the table. (Where the other studies analyzed program totals, Spivey analyzed each state separately.)

In Table 11-1, "S" stands for a stabilizing change, while "D" stands for a destabilizing change. A change is considered to be stabilizing when it is in the same direction as a change in the economy; it is considered to be destabilizing when it is in the opposite direction. As explained earlier, there is uncertainty about the stage in the upswing at which an increase in the tax becomes desirable, but there is general agreement on the desirability of a decline in the tax as soon as possible on the downswing. For this reason, interest centers chiefly on what occurs during the downswing. In a statistical study of the behavior of the tax, the main question to be answered is, "Did the tax fall, or at least not rise, during the downswing?" In any event, it may be taken for granted that if the tax does decline on the downswing, it must rise sooner or later on the upswing.

Andrews and Miller [146]. The earliest of these studies was that made by William H. Andrews and Taulman A. Miller in 1954. In point of clarity of exposition, cogency of analysis, and balance of judgment, this first study is one of the best. These authors had an intimate knowledge of the program from within, an advantage that shows at every turn. Despite the paucity of data with which they had to work at that early date, their expository analysis is useful even today.

In their study, Andrews and Miller compared annual changes in the (national) average tax rate with annual changes in the (national) insured unemployment rate during the period 1946 to 1951 for all experience-rating states combined. During this period, there was only one downswing, that of 1949. The tax rate effective in this year was higher than in the year before and by definition was therefore destabilizing. However, the rise was so small, (from 1.24 to 1.31) as to be negligible. (The tax rose in twenty-seven states, while declining in twenty-four states.) Moreover, the average tax rate of the reserve-ratio states declined in 1949 and was therefore stabilizing. In general, when the states were classified into groups according to the type of experience-rating plan in effect, the reserve-ratio states were found to exhibit a better timing pattern than that of the system as a whole.

The authors qualify their findings by pointing out that "some of the changes were small, and that no effort was made to distinguish between changes arising out of normal operations of experience rating and those due to statutory change or other extraneous factors" [146, p. 206]. However, they conclude that experience rating "is surely less in conflict with fiscal measures designed to promote economic stability than has been assumed by most economists who have dealt

Table 11-1. Summary of Four Studies[a] of the Stabilizing (S) and
Destabilizing (D) Effects of Unemployment Insurance Taxes

Calendar year	Andrews and Miller Effect	Raphaelson[b] Effect	Rejda Period of upswing or downswing	Rejda Effect	Palomba Business cycle	Palomba Effect
1946	S		1945-IV ⎫			
1947	S		⎬ Upswing	S		
1948	D	S	1948-IV ⎭		1948-IV ⎫	
1949	D	D	1948-IV ⎱ 1949-IV ⎰ Downswing	S		
1950	S	S	1949-IV ⎫			
1951	S	S	⎬ Upswing	S	⎬ I	S
1952		S				
1953		S	1953-III ⎭		1953-II ⎭	
1954		S	1953-III ⎱ 1954-III ⎰ Downswing	S	1953-II ⎫	
1955	D		1954-III ⎫		⎬ II	S
1956		S	⎬ Upswing	S		
1957	D		1957-III ⎭		1957-III ⎭	
1958	D		1957-III ⎱ 1958-II ⎰ Downswing	S	1957-III ⎫	
1959	S		1958-II ⎫ Upswing	S	⎬ III	S
1960	S		1960-II ⎭		1960-II ⎭	
1961	S		1960-II ⎱ 1961-I ⎰ Downswing	S	1960-II ⎫	
1962			1961-I ⎫		⎬ IV	S
1963			⎬ Upswing	S		
1964			1964-I ⎭		1964-IV ⎭	
Percent stabilizing	66.7	71.4		100.0		100.0

[a]For descriptions and sources of the studies, see text.
[b]This study covers State of Massachusetts, only.

with this subject. Indeed, there is reason to believe that in some instances, particularly as regards short cycles of about three years' duration, experience rating acts in a cyclically stabilizing fashion more often than not" [146, p. 209].

Clinton Spivey [147]. This 1958 study investigated the period 1946–55, making use of annual data. For each state, Spivey compared changes in tax rates with changes in benefit payments. He found that in thirty-seven of the fifty-one states (73 percent) the coefficient of correlation was negative, and therefore countercyclical; the tax rate declined when unemployment benefits increased and increased when unemployment benefits declined. For the reserve-ratio states, this proportion was twenty-six out of thirty-three (79 percent). In the great majority of states, therefore, the direction of change was stabilizing. However, the degree of correlation in most states was weak. Only six states met Spivey's criterion of significance, a coefficient of correlation equal to at least 0.576. This led Spivey to conclude "there appears little evidence that the existing experience-rating systems are capable of producing countercyclical tax effects" [147, p. 90], but he avoided the erroneous positive statement of some of his predecessors that experience rating had procyclical, or destabilizing, tax effects.

Arnold H. Raphaelson [148]. This study was limited to the experience of Massachusetts during the period 1948–61. Using annual data, Raphaelson compared changes in total wages with changes in tax revenues. For the period taken as a whole, the relationship between changes in taxes and in total covered wages showed a positive correlation—that is, taxes were stabilizing—and the coefficient of correlation (0.587) was statistically significant.

The changes in tax revenues were destabilizing only twice, during the downswings of 1949 and 1958. The rise in taxes during the downswing of 1949 was contrary to the national experience and was directly traceable to the Massachusetts requirement that the reserve fund equal the highest amount of benefits paid in any one of the previous ten years. This period included the abnormal amount of benefits paid in 1945 and 1946.

The year 1955 illustrates the difficulty in putting the proper interpretation on the behavior of data during an upswing. Because Massachusetts taxes decreased slightly (about 10 percent) while wages increased, the effect was by definition destabilizing. But since the first quarter of 1955 was close to the trough of the depression in Massachusetts and the rest of the year marked the early stages of recovery, it is probable that the delay of a tax rise in 1955 was desirable rather than otherwise. As a matter of fact, since even these decreased taxes exceeded benefits in 1955, the effect of the program as a whole was deflationary at this time.

In 1951 Massachusetts changed its experience-rating plan from the benefit-wage-ratio type to the reserve-ratio type. According to Raphaelson, experience under the two plans was substantially similar, with neither being destabilizing.

Although recognizing the limitations of annual data, Raphaelson concludes that his measures "do serve as rough guides" and that "on the basis of these measures the net effect of the system was generally countercyclical with respect to changes in covered employment and in unemployment rates" [148, pp. 101, 102].

George E. Rejda [142]. This study covers the period 1945-64 and utilizes two types of relationships. It first relates cyclical changes in collection ratios to cyclical changes in the national income (not shown in Table 11-1). The collection ratio—not to be confused with the average employer tax rate—is the ratio of actual taxes collected to taxable wages. Using annual data, Rejda computed correlation coefficients and found them to be positive (stabilizing) for the entire period (1945-63) and for each of the four downswings covered by this period. He also computed correlation coefficients for employer tax *rates* and national income (not shown in Table 11-1). Although these coefficients were lower than for the collection ratio, they were also positive (stabilizing). He concluded: "Although the correlation coefficients are low, indicating that the relationship between tax rates and national income is not strong, the absence of negative correlation suggests that tax rates tend to move in the proper countercyclical direction for the period between 1945 and 1963" [143, p. 202].

The study also utilizes the "more meaningful comparison" between absolute changes in unemployment taxes and absolute changes in national income.[3] Using quarterly data and marking off periods of upswing and downswing, he compared the dollar change in national income with the dollar change in unemployment insurance taxes during each cyclical movement. The results are shown in Table 11-1. Rejda concluded that "unemployment taxes have moved in a desirable contracyclical fashion during all cycle downswings and upswings; that is, absolute unemployment taxes have declined with national income during cycle downswings and have increased with national income during cycle upswings" [143, p. 202].

Rejda also made a quarter-by-quarter study of the periods of downswing taken separately. In the entire period there were fourteen quarters of downswing; taxes moved in a desirable contracyclical manner during eleven of the fourteen quarters. A correlation analysis revealed that the correlation between national income and taxes was stronger on the downwsing than on the upswing. This latter is an important finding in view of the special significance of the downswing as explained above.

Neil A. Palomba [150].[4] This study sought to improve on the techniques of the previous studies, all of which "had at least one of the following weaknesses: (a) use of annual data instead of quarterly data; (b) use of only peak and trough

---

3. This measure was used earlier by M. O. Clement [149] and was duplicated later by Neil A. Palomba [150, p. 36].

4. Palomba presents some of his results in more condensed form in [151].

quarters, with the exclusion of other quarters; and (c) no use of a multiplier model to get at the multiple effects of unemployment benefits and unemployment collections" [152, p. 35]. Palomba used a measure of variance.[5] This measure compared the variance of the actual gross national product with the variance of the gross national product in the absence of unemployment insurance taxes. If the taxes reduced the variance in gross national product, they were stabilizing. If they increased the variance in the gross national product, they were destabilizing. Palomba used two multiplier models, that of Okun and that of Harberger, but found little difference between them.

This variance measure was applied to quarterly data for gross national product and unemployment insurance tax collections for the period 1948-64, which included the four business cycles shown in Table 11-1. Palomba found that unemployment insurance taxes were stabilizing for the period as a whole and for each of the four cycles taken separately. When this variance measure was applied to each of the five different experience rating plans, no significant differences appeared: under each, the tax changes were stabilizing in all of the four cycles.

Palomba also applied the measure of variance to an assumed situation without experience rating. That is, he calculated what taxes would have been under a fixed uniform tax of 2.7 percent levied on the actual taxable payrolls in each quarter of the same period. He concluded that "the stabilizing effect of the actual collections and the 2.7 percent collections is virtually the same" [150, p. 48]. (If the 2.7 percent tax had actually been in operation during this period, the states would have added an *additional* $18.5 billion to their reserves. Politically, of course, this is a completely unrealistic supposition.)

Palomba also applied his measure of variance to an assumed tax that varied between 2.7 and 0.5 percent. That is, it was assumed that in all quarters of all upswings the tax was 2.7 percent, while in all downturns the tax was 0.5 percent. Again, he found that the stabilizing effect was "virtually identical" [150, p. 49].

Finally, Palomba applied his measure of variance to each of the five experience rating plans taken separately. For each plan he compared the stabilizing effect of the actual taxes with what would have been the effect if the tax had been either a stable 2.7 percent or had varied between 2.7 and 0.5 percent. The result for each of the five plans was the same as for all of them taken together; there was no significant difference. "Thus, one's conclusion that the five experience rating formulas are the same, from a stabilizing point of view, would be justified on every count" [150, p. 58].

These five studies return a generally favorable verdict on the experience-rated effect of the unemployment insurance tax. They provide no basis for the charge that experience rating normally operates to aggravate the business cycle; on the

---

5. The variance of a series is the average of the squared deviations of each member of the series from the mean of the series.

contrary, they indicate that up to the present, at least, the experience-rated unemployment insurance tax has operated countercyclically.

This favorable result is not necessarily attributable to experience rating as such. In all probability, much the same timing pattern would have accompanied a uniform variable tax. The two chief factors that have accounted for the counter-cyclical impact of the unemployment insurance tax up to the present have been the brevity of the historical cycles and the timing lag inherent in the tax mech-anism.[6] The postwar cycles have been relatively short; short enough so that the delayed action of the tax mechanism has produced a countercyclical movement. By the time the tax has begun to rise, the recession has run its course and the economy has begun to recover.

In a deeper and more prolonged depression period, the unemployment insur-ance tax would eventually have a procyclical effect; that is, the tax would begin to rise while the economy was still depressed. But this is not a problem of experience rating as such. It is a problem of any system that does not wish to use deficit financing. A uniform, variable tax system would have essentially the same problem if it had to operate in the same political context.

The measure of variance used by Palomba detected no significant difference in the stabilizing effects of a wide variety of different tax patterns. This result presumably reflects the smallness of the unemployment insurance tax changes as compared with the changes in the gross national product and the insensitivity of the measure of variance to such small magnitudes. According to this measure, it would make no perceptible difference during a downswing if employers were to pay a tax of 2.7 percent or a tax of 0.5 percent [150, pp. 49–50]. Whether or not this is true on the macro level, it is much less likely to be true on the micro level.

Micro Effect

During a business cycle, not all firms have the same economic experience at the same time. A cyclical movement merely means that the greater part of economic activity is waxing or waning. But while the majority of firms are moving in one direction, many others will be moving in the opposite direction. Even the firms that are moving in the same direction will have started at different times and be moving at different speeds.

Furthermore, cyclical unemployment is not the only kind of unemployment. Insofar as it is possible to differentiate unemployment by its causes, cyclical movements apparently account for not more than about a third of all unemploy-ment.[7] Seasonal, secular, and "other" causes account for the remainder. Adjust-

6. A brief explanation of the timing lag is provided later in this chapter. For an illus-trated description of the timing mechanism, see [146].

7. See, for example, [153], [154].

ment of the unemployment insurance tax to cyclical movements does not ensure its adjustment to all other changes in unemployment.

Nature of Effect

Since the fortunes of individual firms differ markedly from one another, and since firms do not share a common pocketbook, what is most important in the matter of timing is that the tax rate of the individual firm fluctuate according to the economic needs of that firm. Without experience rating, changes in the tax over time would have to be on a statewide basis. This would not necessarily fit the experience and needs of individual firms. With experience rating, the timing pattern of the tax can be arranged to fit the pocketbook to which it is most relevant, namely, that of the individual firm.

The administrators of employment security, accustomed as they are to dealing with the individual firm, have always been sensitive to this aspect of the timing problem. Their 1940 statement was quoted earlier in this chapter. Typical also is this statement of the 1950 committee of the Interstate Conference of Employment Security Agencies: "Higher rates in the fat years should aid stability; and lower rates in the lean years should help employers to maintain jobs. In lean years, even a difference of only one-half percent on payrolls may loom large compared to profits in many lines; and might turn some red figures into black" [42, VI-2]. This commonsense view of the impact of the tax is economically sound. The whole consists of its parts. That which contributes to the health of the individual firm very likely contributes to the health of the general economy. If a business recession is something like an epidemic, the spread of the infection among the general population will be limited partly by the healthy vigor of the individuals composing the population.

The following examples of the timing pattern of individual firms are intended to be illustrative rather than representative. They serve as reminders that there is a micro aspect to the timing problem. They also provide an opportunity to review some of the principles of the unemployment insurance mechanism.

Both examples reflect the operation of the reserve-ratio system, which operates as explained in Appendix B, according to the formula:

$$\frac{\text{Taxes - Benefits (=Reserves)}}{\text{Taxable payrolls}}$$

As a help to understanding the tables, it may be well to review briefly the mechanics of that system. Taxable payrolls are a measure of the potential claims that a firm's employees might make on the fund. A firm's reserve is a measure of the firm's ability to meet such a drain. The ratio between them determines the firm's tax rate. The reserve, of course, is simply the cumulative difference between taxes that have been paid in and benefits that have been drawn out. When benefit payments increase, it is usually at a time when covered employment is decreasing and when taxable payrolls are therefore also decreasing. The increase in benefit payments tends to decrease the numerator (reserves) and to result in a higher tax rate for the firm. But the decline in payrolls works in the opposite direction: it shrinks the denominator, which tends to result in a lower tax rate for the firm. If benefit payments increase faster than taxable payrolls decrease, the result is likely to be an increase in the tax rate. Contrariwise, if taxable payrolls shrink faster than benefit payments increase, a firm's tax rate may actually decline at a time of heavy benefit drains.[8] An employer's shrinking payrolls may therefore decrease his taxes in two ways: They may lower his tax rate and they always lessen the base against which the tax rate is applied.

In the two most prevalent systems of experience rating—reserve ratio and benefit ratio—payroll changes have opposite effects on tax rates. In the reserve-ratio system, the correlation is positive: an increase in payrolls tends to increase a firm's tax rate, while a decrease in payrolls tends to decrease a firm's tax rate. In the benefit-ratio system, the correlation is negative: an increase in payrolls tends to decrease the tax rate, while a decrease in payrolls tends to increase the tax rate. As a result, the interval between a decline in payrolls and the consequent rise in tax rates is likely to be longer in the reserve-ratio system than in the benefit-ratio system. Although the actual situation is much more complex than appears in this simplified description, it is generally correct to say that during short business cycles, such as have marked the postwar period, the reserve-ratio system tends to produce the better countercyclical tax pattern.

The tax normally applies to a calendar year, say for 1970. The determination of this tax is made at some prior time, say June 30, 1969. Thus, under most state systems a new experience rate does not begin to apply until six months after the close of the experience period. Because of this timing lag, much of the relevant experience may have occurred a year or more before the new rate applies.

If the state uses, as most do, a three-year average of taxable payrolls, the impact of the most recent year is modified by whatever may have been the payrolls of the other two years. If, as happened in California during the period covered by Table 11-2, the state law changes the proportion of total wages that are taxable,[9] the denominator of the formula will be correspondingly changed, and the individual firm's tax rate will be moved up or down independently of the firm's individual experience.[10] Finally, the conditions of the reserve of the

---

8. A California study came to the conclusion: "The evidence indicates that high tax rates are associated with increases in payrolls, while low tax rates are associated with declining payrolls" [155, p. 1].

9. In 1960 California increased the taxable wage base from $3,000 to $3,600; in 1962 to $3,800; and in 1966 to $4,100. In 1967 the taxable wage base was reduced again to $3,800. It remained at this lower level through the recession of 1970-71.

10. An increase in taxable payrolls will have a temporary tendency to increase the firm's tax rate, while a decrease in taxable payrolls will have a temporary tendency to decrease his tax rate. In the long run, the tax will tend to return to the equilibrium level, that is, where tax income equals benefit outflow (Appendix B). At this new equilibrium level, an em-

Table 11-2. NORTH AMERICAN ROCKWELL: Unemployment Insurance Tax
and Benefit Experience, 1960-70

Fiscal year ending June 30	Benefit charges		Taxes[a]		Tax rate[a,b]	Average monthly employment	Taxable payroll: percent change in year	Reserve account balance: percent change in year
	Amount (000's)	Percent change in year	Amount (000's)	Percent change in year				
	(1)	(2)	(3)	(4)	(5)	(6)	(7)	(8)
1960	$ 1,032	− 25.4	$4,017	+ 13.8	2.1	56,474	+ 23.3	+ 20.7
1961	1,195	+ 15.8	3,146	− 21.7	1.2	67,630	+ 33.6	+ 11.2
1962	959	− 19.8	6,071	+ 92.9	2.1	80,074	+ 15.2	+ 26.4
1963	1,692	+ 76.4	8,513	+ 40.2	2.3	87,949	+ 25.1	+ 27.9
1964	2,360	+ 39.5	8,572	+ 0.7	2.3	89,282	+ 0.7	+ 19.8
1965	3,525	+ 51.5	7,445	− 13.2	2.2	85,262	− 9.8	+ 10.5
1966	1,689	− 52.1	5,466	− 26.6	1.6	75,622	+ 1.7	+ 9.1
1967	2,632	+ 55.9	4,108	− 24.8	1.3	74,168	− 9.6	+ 0.3
1968	2,061	− 21.7	3,846	− 6.4	1.3	68,314	− 4.3	+ 3.8
1969	6,308	+ 206.0	1,493	− 61.2	0.6	54,920	− 21.7	0.0
1970	10,450	+ 65.7	1,108	− 25.8	0.6	47,969	− 12.7	− 9.9

Source: Data furnished by firm.

[a]Excludes balancing tax.

[b]Average tax rate for fiscal year.

state as a whole may move all firms onto a higher or lower tax schedule and thus change a given firm's tax rate independently of its own individual experience.[11]

Examples of Effect

North American Rockwell. Table 11-2 shows the financial experience of this California aerospace company, whose experience with administration was described in Chapter 8. At the beginning of fiscal 1960, this company had a reserve (not shown in the table) of $14,398,887. The reserve grew rapidly through 1965, then more slowly through 1968, when it amounted to $48,425,390. This was an amount sufficient to pay benefits for thirteen years at the highest annual rate in its past experience. This healthy balance was to stand the firm in good stead in later years, when benefit charges became extremely heavy. As columns 6 and 7 show, the company grew through 1964, but then experienced a gradual decline which became precipitous toward the end of the period.

In the eleven-year period covered by the table, there were seven years in which the firm's benefit charges increased. The tax rate and taxes of the firm fell

ployer's reserve will be larger and his tax rate lower than before the change in taxable payrolls.

11. Thus in California during the period covered by the table, the low schedule was replaced by the high schedule in 1962, which was replaced in turn by the low schedule again in 1969. The low schedule remained in operation through the recession of 1970-71.

in five of these years, remained level in another, and rose in only one. Hence, on the whole, the tax mechanism acted in a clearly "stabilizing" manner. An examination of the details of the table strengthens this general impression.

The 1961 recession touched this firm only lightly. Although benefit charges rose by 15.8 percent, average monthly employment also increased, by 20 percent. Since both benefits and taxable payrolls were increasing at this time, a rise in the tax rate might have been expected. The sharp drop in the tax rate that actually occurred reflected the favorable condition of the firm's reserve.

In 1963 a substantial increase of about 76 percent in benefit charges was accompanied by a large increase of about 40 percent in taxes. This is the one year in which there was a substantial movement of taxes in the same direction as benefits. Although technically this constitutes a "destabilizing" movement, its significance is diminished by accompanying circumstances. The large percentage increase in benefit charges reflected the unusually low benefits in the year before, rather than any financial difficulties in 1963. Both covered employment and taxable payrolls rose significantly that year. This was probably as good a time as any for the firm to build up the reserve called for by this enlarged potential liability. Also, the increase in taxes was due partly to the independent factor of state legislation. California had legislated an increase in the taxable wage base in both 1960 and 1962. This automatically lowered the reserve ratios of all firms and tended to raise their tax rates.

In 1964 and 1965 substantial increases in benefits were accompanied by stable or declining taxes—the result of a steadily growing reserve. From 1965 on, the firm's employment began to shrink, slowly at first and then rapidly, until by 1970 it was half of its 1965 size. Throughout this same period the firm's taxes decreased, dropping from over $7.0 million to about $1.5 million. This favorable movement of taxes was primarily due to the firm's very large reserves. In these lean years it was truly living off the fat it had stored up in the good years.

The declining tax rate is to be explained also by the declining payrolls, which in turn are explained by the shrinking employment and by a 1967 reduction of the taxable wage base from $4,100 to $3,800. Helping also was a statewide shift in 1969 to the low tax schedule, the result of a growing statewide reserve. Even the tremendous benefit increases in 1969 and 1970 were accompanied by low tax rates. When interviewed, the firm's officers expressed their considerable relief at not having to carry a heavy burden of taxes at this time.

Company E. This is a large firm engaged in durable manufacturing and operating in a state with the reserve-ratio system. Its experience is shown in graphic form in Charts 1 and 2.

The charts enable us to see the size as well as the direction of movements and thus to gain a more realistic view of the actual operations of the program. For example, the only "destabilizing" movement of taxes—as defined in the studies summarized earlier—occurred in the downswing of 1958, when taxes rose along

Chart 1.

ANNUAL BENEFIT COSTS AND TAX PAYMENTS

1956 — 1965

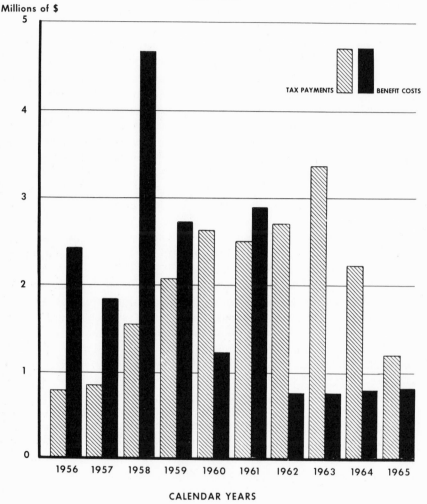

CALENDAR YEARS

with benefits. In the recession of 1961, on the contrary, the movement of taxes was "stabilizing" because, as compared to the previous year, taxes declined as benefits rose. But as is immediately evident from Chart 1, the combined effect of taxes *and* benefits was more countercyclical in 1958 than in 1961. Although in both years the system operating through Company E put more money into the hands of private spenders than it took away from them, the difference was much greater in 1958. Experience in 1959 illustrates the same danger of relying

Chart 2.

CUMULATIVE BENEFIT COSTS AND TAX PAYMENTS

1956 — 1965

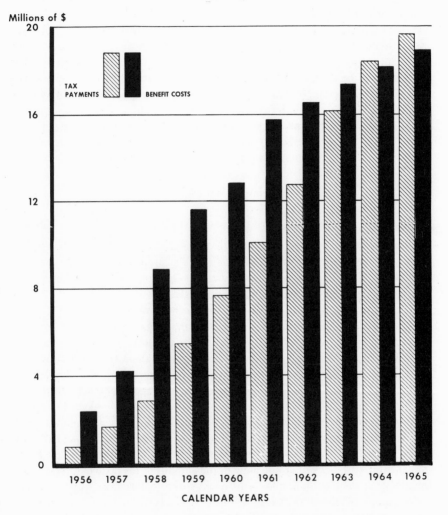

simply on the direction of change. Since benefits declined and taxes rose in 1959, the movement was by definition "stabilizing." But was it really desirable that the company's taxes rose, when its benefit outflow remained so high, even though lower than in 1958?

During the prosperous years that followed 1961, taxes stayed high and the system quickly began to recoup its losses. By the end of the period, as may be seen in Chart 2, the company had contributed a little more to the fund than it had taken out. Its reserve, which had amounted to $4.8 million at the beginning of 1956 and which had been totally depleted midway through the period, had been built up again to $5.5 million by the end of 1965.

As may be seen in Chart 1, benefits exceeded taxes during the first four years and in 1961, whereas taxes exceeded benefits in 1960 and in the last four years. As a result, as may be seen in Chart 2, over the entire period benefits and taxes about balanced. This is a good picture of how the experience-rated part of the system probably works for most firms.[12] Although the fluctuations in benefits and taxes will be less extreme for less cyclically sensitive firms, the general picture will usually be one of a rise in benefits followed by a lagged gradual increase in taxes until equilibrium is restored. Feldman came quite close to predicting the actual events when he said, back in 1939, that the increase in tax rates in bad times "will probably be gradual, will rarely be drastic, and may be postponed if the employer has a good previous record and a large reserve" [9, p. 50].

Proposals for Change

Description

Over the years, various proposals have been made to improve the timing pattern of the experience-rated tax. Some of the proposals have been put into practice for shorter or longer periods of time, while others have remained only suggestions. There have been five major proposals.

1. *Increase taxable payrolls.* To the extent that taxable payrolls are less than total payrolls, the countercyclical impact of the tax is lessened. This is because cyclical swings are reflected more in the upper part of the wage distribution than in the lower part. Because much of the cyclical variation in payrolls occurs in the part above $3,000, taxable payrolls vary less than total payrolls and constitute a smaller percentage of total payrolls in prosperous times than in depressed times.

An employee might be unemployed two months in the year and still easily earn the required amount of taxable wages, In such a case, although the employee's increased unemployment would show in the diminished amount of his annual total wages, it would not show in the amount of his taxable wages. In the same way, an increase in employment might not affect taxable wages. On both the upswing and the downswing, therefore, the tax formula will not respond fully to changes in unemployment. One solution is to increase taxable wages so that they more closely approach total wages.[13] If the payroll base were expanded,

12. Company E made two contributions to the unemployment insurance fund which were not experience-rated and which do not appear in the chart. These were the interest earned by its reserves and the taxes it paid into the state's Common Account.

13. The employment security amendments of 1970 raised the federal taxable wage base from $3,000 to $4,200, beginning in 1972. Some states have restructured their tax sched-

employers would contribute proportionately more in good times as payrolls grew and would pay less in periods of contracting payrolls.

Taxable wages that are less than total wages have another timing effect. They tend to concentrate the actual payment of taxes in two quarters of the year. The greater part of taxable wages are earned in the first and second quarters of the year, and taxes on these wages are paid in the second and third quarters, respectively. As a result, about two-thirds of the year's taxes are paid in the second and third quarters. (This has obvious implications for any study that compares changes in taxes and national income by *quarters*.)

2. *Accelerate tax on upswing.* When payrolls are rising at an unusually rapid rate, the potential liability of the fund may grow more rapidly than the fund itself. On the assumption that rising payrolls indicate growing economic strength, it has been proposed to accelerate the tax rise in such a situation. The outstanding example of this technique is furnished by the "war risk taxes"[14] which were operative in twelve states during the period 1942–45. These taxes applied only to employers with rapidly expanding wartime payrolls, which were expected to result in heavy postwar benefit claims. The fact that these additional taxes could in most instances be passed on to the federal government through cost-plus contracts provided an additional inducement. Whoever was the originator of the technique, its most effective salesman was Paul A. Raushenbush of Wisconsin.

Eight of the states levied the war risk tax only on that part of the payroll which was estimated to be caused by abnormal war activity. However, four of the states (Kansas, Maryland, Ohio, and Wisconsin) levied the tax on the entire payroll. In ten states this tax was in lieu of regular tax, but in two states (Minnesota and Ohio) it was in addition to the usual rate.

Although it was suggested (by Paul A. Raushenbush) that the technique might be usable in other situations when payrolls were expanding with unusual rapidity, it has never actually been used except in the war period. Indeed, in 1968 California moved in the opposite direction by providing a lower tax to any employer whose payroll had increased by 25 percent over the previous year.[15] This difference of approach illustrates the ambiguity mentioned earlier regarding the "proper" steps to be taken during an economic upswing.

---

ules to prevent this otherwise desirable change from causing undesirable changes in the cost-tax ratios of the individual firms.

14. Alabama, Florida, Georgia, Illinois, Iowa, Kansas, Maryland, Minnesota, Missouri, Ohio, Oklahoma, and Wisconsin. For more information see [156, pp. 71–78].

15. The late Tom Harris of the California Teamsters was largely responsible for this provision. He said he wished to provide an offset to what he considered the undesirable stabilizing effect of experience rating. He welcomed, also, the possibility that this provision would blur somewhat its other effects.

3. *Decelerate tax on downswing.* There are two methods of applying this technique, both of which may be illustrated in the experience of Wisconsin. The first is to limit the size of the rise that may occur in the tax rate in any one year. For example, since 1947 the Wisconsin law has provided that for employers whose reserves were adequate increases in taxes would be limited to 1 percent of taxable payroll in any one year.

The second method is triggered by statewide experience, rather than by the experience of individual employers, and has been tried only by Wisconsin. In 1951 Wisconsin enacted a provision whereby the state would move to a lower schedule of rates for all employers when statewide gross wages dropped 5 percent or more from one year to the next. Later (1958), Wisconsin recognized that, given inflation and population growth, total wages would rarely drop that much even in a recession and amended its law to provide for an alternative trigger: the lower tax schedule would go into effect whenever benefit payments exceeded a stated level. This provision was instrumental in lowering the average employer tax rate in 1959. However, the provision was difficult to coordinate with the requirements of solvency and was subsequently repealed in 1963.

4. *Use only one year of payroll as base.* This proposal has in view the reserve-ratio system, in which as the fraction (reserves/payrolls) increases the tax rate decreases.[16] The covered payrolls in the base of this formula may be either the most recent year or the average of two or more years. If the most recent year is used as the base, the formula becomes more cyclically sensitive. It tends to produce higher tax rates on the upswing more quickly and to produce lower tax rates on the downswing more quickly. As of January 1971, seven states used the most recent year.[17]

5. *Grant tax credits.* Under this system, two calculations are made for each employer—the dollar amount of taxes he would pay if his tax rate were the standard 2.7 percent and the dollar amount of taxes he needs to pay to maintain his reserve at some stipulated level. If the latter amount is smaller, the difference (in dollars) is granted to the employer as a credit against the taxes he would pay next year, if his payrolls were taxed at 2.7 percent.

Clearly, if in the next year his payrolls decline, this fixed amount of credit becomes a greater tax relief—expressed as a percentage of his current payrolls. On the contrary, if his payrolls rise, the credit becomes a lesser tax relief, percentagewise. Thus tax credits provide a kind of automatic countercyclical movement.

16. In the benefit-ratio system, by contrast, as the fraction (benefits/payrolls) increases the tax rate increases. Since this movement is "destabilizing" there is reason here to adopt the opposite technique and to use more than one year of payrolls in the base of the formula.

17. These seven, all reserve-ratio states, were Massachusetts, Michigan, New York, Rhode Island, South Carolina, Tennessee, and Wisconsin. Rhode Island used the most recent year of the last three years, whichever percentage was smaller.

New York enacted such a provision in 1945 but abandoned it in the major revision of its tax system that occurred in 1951. The state of Washington had such a provision during the period 1947-70.

Other plans. In 1958 a plan was outlined by Nathan Morrison, executive secretary of the New York State Advisory Council, in which a uniform surtax, independent of experience rating, was triggered by an economic indicator [14, p. 351]. More recently, in 1969, Walter B. Jessee submitted a plan to the Benefit Financing Committee of the Interstate Conference of Employment Security Agencies which would utilize as countercyclical tools the Federal Unemployment Tax and a special federal "countercyclical fund" [157, pp. 3-5].

From time to time the suggestion is made to abandon the effort to make the tax countercyclical and adopt the "level premium" method of insurance. The goal of this plan is a statewide average tax rate which remains constant, or at most fluctuates within narrow limits during both the upswings and downswings of the cycle. Arizona, for example, has aimed explictly at this objective [158] and has been reasonably successful in achieving it. During the period 1954-63, the Arizona average tax varied only between 1.26 and 1.50.

Evaluation of Proposals

The unemployment insurance tax may be assigned multiple objectives, not all of which are mutually compatible. Hence the use of a particular device that might enable the system to be more countercyclical in its impact may be limited by the tendency of the device to limit the attainment of other objectives—specifically, solvency or an effective degree of experience rating.

The use of a taxable payroll that approached more closely to total payrolls could only aid solvency. It might increase, lessen, or leave untouched the degree of experience rating in the system, depending on a number of other variable factors. Likewise it would be possible to make use of the tax credit system without threatening solvency or lessening the degree of experience rating.

A limitation on the increase that may occur in an employer's tax rate in any year and the use of only one year of payrolls in the base of the reserve-ratio formula are more debatable devices, but are probably free of any serious objection on the score of their effect on solvency or experience rating.

The devices of shifting to a higher tax schedule on the upswing and to a lower tax schedule on the downswing are difficult to use without infringing on either solvency or the degree of experience rating. However, there have been situations in which both devices have been used successfully.

The proposal to abandon any effort to achieve a countercyclical movement of the taxes stems usually from a belief that the unemployment insurance tax tends to be destabilizing and to aggravate the cycle. In this view, the best that can be done with the system is to keep it from doing harm. This proposal loses its appeal, however, when the unemployment insurance system is seen as usually operating countercyclically. Some degree of countercyclical influence is better than none.

Conclusions

On the macro level, experience rating as such does not seem to have great significance; the effect of a uniform, variable tax would probably be very similar to that of an experience-rated tax. Insofar as the two might differ, the tax variations under experience rating would have the advantage of being more automatic. However, because the effect of experience rating on the business cycle is both small and uncertain, it is not a major factor in the social debate over its desirability. Experience rating does not stand or fall by reason of its effect on the business cycle.

Studies made of the postwar period have shown that the movement of the experience-rated unemployment insurance tax during the course of a business cycle is usually in a desirable direction, especially during downswings, when a countercyclical impact is particularly important. During almost all recessions, the average tax has fallen, or at least not risen significantly.

This happy result has come about largely because the postwar recessions have been short enough to be turning the corner by the time the taxing mechanism has begun to reflect their impact, and thus higher taxes have not made their appearance until the economy was on the mend again. In a longer recession, the tax would begin to rise before the recession had ended. In this respect, as in most others, the unemployment insurance system is structured to function only as a "first line of defense" [159, p. 8].

It is not possible to set up the tax mechanism in such a way that it will *automatically* function countercyclically during both short and long business cycles. The present tax structure tends to function well in short recessions, but probably would not function equally well in a long recession. If we must choose between the two, our present choice is probably the wiser one. Short recessions seem to be the current pattern. Moreover, a prolonged recession would probably bring into operation large-scale stabilizing efforts, such as public works, compared to which the stabilizing or destabilizing effect of the unemployment insurance tax would be negligible.

In its countercyclical impact, the reserve-ratio system seems to have a clear advantage over its nearest rival, the benefit-ratio system. The advantage stems primarily from the longer delay allowed in the reserve-ratio system between a decline in payrolls, usually a sign of economic trouble, and a rise in tax rates.

On the micro level, the level of the individual firm, an experience-rated tax has a distinct advantage over a uniform variable tax. Experience rating can and usually does adapt the timing patterns of the tax to the economic changes experienced by the individual firm. Since firms vary greatly in their speed and direction of change, this is a clear timing advantage of experience rating.

Postscript

The employment security amendments of 1970, whatever effect they may have on the degree of experience rating in the system, are likely to increase its countercyclical impact in two ways. The amendments increase the federal wage base from $3,000 to $4,200, beginning in 1972. The amendments also provide a system of extended benefits which trigger in when claims loads are considerably heavier than usual. These added benefits—which will of course have a counter-cyclical effect—are to be 50 percent state financed. About half of the states have arranged to charge these extended benefits to the accounts of individual firms and thus make them a part of the state's regular experience-rating system, while the remainder have arranged to make these benefits a pooled cost (for the list of states, see Chapter 2, footnote 8). The net countercyclical impact of the method of charging is likely to be negligible.

$$12.$$

Internal
Experience
Rating

Nature and Extent

Internal experience rating is the practice by a firm of allocating its unemployment insurance tax among its operating units in some relation to the benefit experience of each unit. Thus, if Unit A has a higher benefit-cost rate than Unit B, it is charged with a higher proportion of the firm's total tax. The practice is entirely internal (the state taxes the firm, not the units) and is limited to firms having multiple cost centers. The practice is more likely to be adopted by large firms having multiple operating units, such as a manufacturing firm with a number of plants, or a retail chain with a number of stores.

If the unemployment insurance costs of these units are pooled, so that each unit has the same tax rate (the firm's rate) no matter what its individual experience, the separate units tend to see the unemployment insurance tax as a fixed overhead cost rather than as a variable operating cost. To the extent that they adopt this view, each unit is in effect faced with a uniform, not an experience-rated, tax. If each of the operating units sees the unemployment insurance tax as uniform, then in many respects the tax becomes uniform for the firm as a whole. This is especially true for those effects of experience rating which depend on employer motivation, such as the effects on administration and employment stabilization. As a consequence, the impact of experience rating on the large firm may be greatly diminished. Since large firms account for a considerable proportion of total covered employment,[1] any such dulling of the impact of experience rating on large firms would mean a notable lessening of experience rating (for good or bad) throughout the system.

One of the earliest adoptions of internal experience rating seems to have been that by the General Motors Corporation toward the end of 1946. During the reconversion period following World War II, Michigan, with its concentration of durable manufacturing, experienced more than the average degree of dislocation of its labor market and of its unemployment insurance system.[2] In addition,

1. In New York, for example, in 1969 firms with taxable payrolls in excess of $2.5 million accounted for 34.8 percent of all taxable payrolls. See also Table 5-11.
2. For a description of the problems of the reconversion period, see [102, Chapters 3 and 4].

284

General Motors experienced a prolonged strike extending from November 1945 into March 1946. Becoming aware of what it considered loose administration of unemployment insurance on its own part and on the part of the state (for example, some of the General Motors strikers incorrectly received unemployment benefits), the company appointed a high-level committee to review the corporation's relations to unemployment insurance. In the course of this review, the committee reached the logical conclusion that if experience rating was good for the country and for the state of Michigan, it ought to be good for General Motors as well. It therefore proposed that experience rating be applied internally to the corporation's operations. The proposal aroused considerable opposition from various quarters and had to be carried to the top of the corporation for settlement. It was finally approved by the corporation's Operations Policy Committee, composed of the president and vice-presidents. Introduced in 1947, internal experience rating is currently (1971) used in all the seventeen states where General Motors has a major manufacturing activity.

No one knows the extent of the practice of internal experience rating, but my contacts with firms in many states have left me with the impression that the practice is relatively rare. In an attempt to get a better fix on this general impression, I distributed a questionnaire to a sample of employers in the states of Massachusetts and New York. The samples were not representative of employers generally, but were limited to those firms which seemed more likely to use internal experience rating. The questionnaire was short and easy to answer. It was sent by name to a carefully selected individual in each firm and was accompanied by a covering letter from the president or executive secretary of the employers' association to which the firm belonged. In these circumstances, a nonresponse was very likely to indicate that the firm had nothing to say.

In Massachusetts the questionnaire was limited to 39 large firms which had multiple units in Massachusetts and which had requested the state to report benefit charges separately for each unit. Hence, each of these firms had all the data needed for applying internal experience rating. Of these 39 most likely candidates (they were large, they had multiple units in the state, and they received benefit charges from the state separately for each unit) 20 replied to the questionnaire, of whom 4 reported that they used internal experience rating. These 4 firms represented 10.5 percent of those who received the questionnaire, 20.0 percent of those who returned it.

The New York questionnaire spread its net somewhat more broadly. It was sent to 200 of the largest firms which had multiple operations in the state. The questionnaire was returned by 76 firms, of which 8 reported that they used internal experience rating. These 8 firms represented 4.0 percent of those who received the questionnaire, 10.5 percent of those who returned it. Since firms using internal experience rating would have been more likely than others to reply, it seems reasonable to conclude that if all the questioned firms had answered, the proportion reporting internal experience rating would not have been much higher than 4 percent.

In general, the results of these two questionnaires bear out my own impression, gained from numerous informal contacts, that the proportion even of large firms that use internal experience rating is quite small. Possible reasons for this limited application of the system are discussed later.

Structure

To inaugurate a system of internal experience rating, a firm must first of all obtain from the state the essential data, namely, the benefit charges according to operating unit.[3] The firm must also determine the size of the unit whose experience it wishes to measure. Most commonly, the unit will be that used for the calculation of profitability ("profit centers"), for it is at this point that a variable tax may be expected to influence policy. The most usual unit is the plant or the store, but the unit could be broader, such as an entire company in a conglomerate corporation, or it could be narrower, such as diverse functions within a plant. Administrative convenience is an important consideration influencing the choice of unit.

Finally, the firm must decide on a method for linking the experience of the units with a set of tax rates. In general, two alternatives are available. Under the first alternative, the firm simply adopts whatever system is used by the state in which the firm is operating—the reserve-ratio system in a reserve-ratio state, the benefit-ratio system in a benefit-ratio state, and so forth. A national organization might thus use several different systems of internal experience rating, depending on the states in which it was operating.

By way of example, we might consider the method of General Motors in a reserve-ratio state like Michigan. Essentially, this system requires the calculation of a primary and a secondary tax rate, whose sum constitutes the experience-rated part of each unit's tax. In addition, the unit is required to pay a (nonexperience-rated) share of Michigan's subsidiary "solvency" tax.

The primary tax rate is calculated in the same way as the state calculates the tax rates of individual firms. That is, the firm calculates for each unit a reserve, a reserve ratio, and a resulting tax rate. The schedule of tax rates is the same as that used by the state and hence does not go beyond the maximum tax rate of the state. Since for some units this maximum tax rate may not cover the unit's true cost to the firm's reserve, the total taxes raised by the primary tax rates of all the units may not equal the total tax imposed on the firm by the state. The sum raised by the primary tax may therefore leave a deficit. The firm spreads this deficit among all its units by means of a secondary tax which is also experi-

---

3. Some states, like Florida, assign separate account numbers to each location, identify each benefit charge by this account number, but show the charges classified by social security number. In such states the firm must reclassify the benefit charges according to account number. Other states, like New York, show charges classified directly by separate account numbers.

ence-rated. The deficit is allocated to the units in proportion to each unit's primary tax rate. Thus, if unit A has a 2 percent primary tax rate, while unit b has a 1 percent primary tax rate, A will pay twice as much of the deficit as B. There is no maximum on the secondary tax.

If a state has a subsidiary tax, like Michigan's solvency tax, this is not experience-rated. Since this tax is not experience-rated as between firms, General Motors does not experience-rate it as between units, but divides it among the units in proportion to each unit's payroll. Thus the total contribution of each unit consists of the unit's primary tax, its secondary tax, and its share of the common tax. This total tax charged against a unit by the firm may be higher than the maximum tax charged against any firm by the state.

New units are not included in the internal experience-rating system until they have been in operation for a specified period of time—whatever period is specified in the state law before a new firm may be experience-rated. If a unit is closed out, its reserve, positive or negative, is held as an inactive account, the effect of which is felt by the other units in the state through the secondary tax rates. Thus the other units have a direct financial incentive to hire as many as possible of the displaced employees of the closed unit.[4]

A system like that of General Motors in Michigan has the advantages of accuracy and equity, but has the disadvantage of requiring detailed cost accounting. When I pressed this disadvantage upon the General Motors people responsible for keeping the accounts, they answered that setting up the system originally had been difficult, but that once programmed it ran itself. They estimated that it required less than one-half of a man-year of time (the General Motors accounting system is highly computerized). These people were not in the unit responsible for unemployment insurance and hence had no vested interest to defend. They were in the unit from which objections to internal experience rating most frequently arise.

Deere and Company, a manufacturer of farm equipment, which adopted internal experience rating in 1955, has made a somewhat different adaptation of the reserve-ratio system for the purposes of internal experience rating. A detailed arithmetic example—entirely hypothetical—of this system is provided in Appendix F. In substance, the firm calculates for each operating unit a reserve, a reserve ratio, and a tax rate, just as the state does for individual firms. The taxes that would be produced by these tax rates are then totaled (col. 4) and the proportion of the total that is attributable to each unit is calculated (col. 5). Thus, in the example, unit B is charged with over a third of the total, while unit A is charged with none of it. If the company did not have internal experience

4. In 1968 I attended a meeting of the General Motors New Jersey Unemployment Compensation Operating Committee (ch. 8, fn. 11) at which one item of business was the prospective closing of a New Jersey plant. The other units were given advance notice and reminded that they could save themselves money by arranging to hire some of the displaced workers.

rating, the charge against unit A would be $10,000 (instead of zero) and against unit B would be $40,000 (instead of $105,400). The relative profitability of the two units would be distorted by $75,400 ($105,400 versus $30,000).

This system used by Deere and Company does not recognize a maximum limit on any unit's share of the total tax. It can happen, therefore, that a unit's share of the tax will represent a tax rate higher than the maximum set in the state law. Thus, in the arithmetic example given in Appendix F, unit B paid $164,114 in taxes. In terms of its taxable payroll of $4 million, this payment represented an effective tax rate of 4.1 percent. Actually, in 1964 one of the Deere units had an internal tax rate of 8.4 percent.

In an attempt to lessen the amount of bookkeeping involved in systems like those in General Motors and Deere, some firms have devised simpler though less accurate methods. The commonest of such methods is to divide the firm's total tax among the units in proportion to the benefits charged against each unit during the preceding year. This is essentially the system used, for example, by Swift and Company (begun in 1957), Montgomery Ward (begun in 1963), and Macy's of California (begun in 1966). In such a system, if unit A accounts for one-third of the benefits charged against the firm in the course of a year, unit A will be charged with one-third of all the taxes paid by the firm for that year. In the following numerical example supplied by Swift and Company in explanation of its system, the firm's total tax in a given state in a given year is assumed to be $100,000. This total is then allocated to the units as shown.

Unit	Benefits charged		Taxes allocated
	Amount	Percent	
A	$10,000	13.33	$ 13,333
B	20,000	26.67	26,667
C	15,000	20.00	20,000
D	25,000	33.33	33,333
E	5,000	6.67	6,667
Total	$75,000	100.00	$100,000

This kind of plan typically accumulates a tax liability for each unit as the tax year progresses by applying the firm's overall tax rate to each unit's covered payroll. At the end of the tax year, adjustments are made, allocating additional charges to some units and giving other units corresponding credits.

Some plans carry this process through only up to a specified maximum, usually the maximum tax rate in the state law. Benefits charged against a unit that are not covered by this maximum represent a deficit which is absorbed in some fashion by the firm as a whole. Other plans, however, do not recognize any maximum rate; theoretically one unit could find itself paying the firm's total tax.

The Swift system, which began in 1957, operated through most of its existence within the limits of the minimum and maximum tax rates of the states in which it was operating. No unit was charged more than the state's maximum tax rate, nor was any unit charged less than the state's minimum tax rate. Any resulting deficit was allocated to "miscellaneous costs" and carried as a general expense account on the corporation's books. Beginning in 1969, however, Swift dropped these limitations and required each unit to pay the full amount of its share of the firm's taxes.

Although less complicated than the reserve-ratio system, these simpler systems are also less exact. Governed entirely by the events of a single year, their allocation of costs may be capricious. To make this point clear, let us assume an extreme example. Assume a reserve-ratio state which has just come through a recession during which benefit charges had been heavy and reserves had been depleted, while taxes had been relatively light. As explained in Chapter 11, taxes normally lag behind experience in the reserve-ratio system. Now comes a prosperous year P in which the bills for the previous heavy benefit drain come due for payment. The firm finds itself assigned a high tax rate designed to replenish its depleted reserves. Assume further that in year P units A and B of the firm have no benefit charges while unit C has some small benefit charges. Since unit C accounts for 100 percent of the benefit charges in year P, it will be required to pay 100 percent of the firm's total taxes for that year. Since most of these taxes reflect the earlier periods in which units A and B made heavy drains on the firm's reserve, the inequity of this allocation is obvious.

If the total state tax includes a subsidiary tax needed to cover the deficits of other firms throughout the state, the inequity is compounded. The degree of inequity will be the greater if there is no maximum limit on the internal experience-rating system; but even if there is a limiting maximum, the burden on unit C will still be greatly out of proportion. Of the half-dozen firms which use this system and which I interviewed, only one reported that the system had actually produced a markedly inequitable distribution, and then only once.

In choosing the structure of internal experience rating, the employer finds himself struggling with all the major questions of experience rating itself. What objectives does he wish to attain, and what system will most effectively attain them? If all desirable objectives cannot be attained equally, which ones shall be given the preference? If a low-cost unit cries "unfair" because it has to subsidize a high-cost unit, while the high-cost unit cries "unfair" because it is asked to pay a higher tax to cover costs over which it has no control—how is the firm to choose between the conflicting claims? What should be the minimum and maximum tax rates for the internal system? If one method (reserve-ratio) is more accurate than others, but is more costly to administer, is the greater accuracy worth while? These and similar questions arise and must be answered by the firm that decides to set up an internal experience-rating system. Nothing educates an employer more throughly in the major issues of experience rating than to answer the question: "Shall I apply experience rating to the internal operations of my own firm?"

Here may be the appropriate place to mention a kind of substitute for internal experience rating which is used by some firms. This is to keep a record of the benefit-cost rates of the separate operating units and to circulate this record with comments by someone at central headquarters. Low-cost units are thus publicly commended for their contribution to keeping down the corporation tax rate, while high-cost units are exposed to view. Because managers are sensitive to their comparative performances, this technique secures some of the results of internal experience rating, even though the units are not charged with their respective costs. Managers sometimes believe, not understanding all the complexities of the unemployment insurance tax system, that they are actually being charged with these costs. For examples of firms and service companies that keep records of benefit costs by individual units see Chapter 8. Firms that have internal experience rating usually add to its impact by circulating among all the units a list of their respective tax rates.

Effects

The effects by which internal experience rating must be evaluated are almost identical with those of experience rating itself. *Solvency* in internal experience rating means the adequacy of the firm's reserve account. Solvency is even less of an issue for internal experience rating than it is for experience rating in general. The obligation to maintain an adequate reserve is imposed by the state on the legal entity which is the entire firm. It is the entire firm which is responsible for the payment of the tax, regardless of how the firm may divide this tax burden among its own units. The division of the tax is entirely an internal matter.

Internal experience rating affects the *allocation of resources* insofar as it tends to produce a more accurate cost accounting. Without internal experience rating, a firm does not have a true picture of the relative costs of its various units. (The ability or inability of the unit to control its costs is, of course, irrelevant to this consideration.) Whether the increased accounting accuracy is worth the added accounting expense depends largely on the size and regularity of the differences in the cost rates of the firm's units. The larger and more regular the differences are, the more justification there is for recognizing these differences in cost accounting procedures.

As usual, data on cost rates are rare, but tax rates may serve as approximations. Table 12-1 shows the range in tax rates for three companies which have internal experience rating. Two of the companies are in durable manufacturing, while the third is in retail trade. The table shows the average tax rate of the lowest-cost unit and of the highest-cost unit of each company.[5] In General

---

5. In the case of Deere and Company, since it does not limit the maximum tax that may be imposed on a unit, these tax rates are practically equivalent to long-run cost rates.

Table 12-1. Average Internal Tax Rates of Lowest and Highest Units
for Selected Firms

Company and location	Average internal tax rate	
	Of lowest unit	Of highest unit
General Motors Corporation (1958–68)		
State J		
Group A	1.7	4.0
Group B	0.7	3.0
Group C	0.9	2.8
Deere and Company (1955–69)		
State B	0.2	2.3
State D	0.6	2.5
Sears Roebuck and Company (1959–69)		
State B	0.1	1.5
State E	0.2	1.5

Source: Data supplied by firms.

Motors Corporation the greatest difference was 2.3 percent of taxable payrolls. In Deere and Company it was 2.1 percent; in Sears, Roebuck 1.4 percent. It should be noted that these are long run tax rates and represent the average differences between the units year after year. In any one year, the system may produce much greater differences. As would be expected, the range of rates was greater in manufacturing than in retail trade.

By way of further illustration: Swift and Company reported that in Texas in 1970 two of the company's units had a tax rate of 4.5 percent, seventeen had a tax rate of 0.1 percent, while the remaining fourteen units were scattered between these two extremes. A large midwest firm in durable manufacturing supplied the following illustrative data. In 1963, when the tax rate of the firm was relatively high, the tax rates of the units ranged from 1.3 percent to 7.5 percent. In 1967, when the tax rate of the firm was low, the tax rates of the units varied from 0.7 percent to 3.0 percent. I was permitted to examine the data in detail and could see that during a period of ten years roughly the same units were in the high and low categories in all years. If I had calculated averages, the results would have been very similar to those shown in Table 12-1.

Firms that have internal experience rating report that such tax differentials are sufficient to interest the units. High-cost units complain about the system, just as low-cost units used to to complain before the system was introduced. Units often keep records of their own and protest when a mistake is made by the central office.[6] When General Motors first introduced internal experience rating

6. By contrast, the unemployment insurance administrator of a large national chain of retail stores that does not use internal experience rating reported that in five years he had received only one question from one store about its tax rate.

I happened to be in Detroit. As I recall events at that time, the first allocation resulted in a high tax rate for Fisher Body and a low tax rate for Chevrolet. At this, Fisher Body became greatly concerned, protesting that its high benefit costs were the fault of Chevrolet, which had been "blowing hot and cold" in its demand for auto bodies. But no one had expressed any such concern until the differential costs were imposed.

Some firms without internal experience rating made some estimations, at my request, of the difference that might result from the introduction of such a system. One national food manufacturer reported that it had two plants in Georgia which regularly showed a very different experience. In the three-year period 1965–67, a simple form of experience rating, (allocating taxes in proportion to benefits charged) would have caused unit A to pay $160,000 more in taxes and would have caused unit B to pay $160,000 less in taxes. Thus internal experience rating would have made a difference of $320,000 in their relative profitability. On the other hand, in Massachusetts the same system would have made a difference of only $75,000 in the profitability of the two units operating in that state. One of the largest manufacturing firms in Massachusetts reported that for the five-year period, 1964–68, a simple form of internal experience rating would have decreased the taxes of one unit by $1.1 million and raised the taxes of another unit by $0.9 million, for a combined difference in profitability of $2 million.

Table 12-2 provides a detailed picture of a national retail chain of stores (J. C. Penney) in three large states. It shows the difference in taxes that would have been paid by each store if a simple form of experience rating (taxes apportioned according to benefits charged) had been in operation. The data show five-year totals for the period 1964–68. In state F, the largest difference in profitability (between store 5 and store 6) would have been about $26,000. In state G, the largest difference (between store 8 and store 12) would have been about $9,900. In state H, the largest difference in profitability (between store 17 and store 18) would have been about $11,800. The tax rates of this company, as for most companies in retail trade, were low. Most large companies would probably show greater differences.

The last columns in Table 12-2 illustrate how internal experience rating brings the cost-tax ratios of the various units closer to uniformity. Thus in state F the cost-tax ratio of store no. 6 would have been lowered from 70 to 44, while the ratios of all the other stores would have been raised from about 25 to 44. Similar changes may be observed in the stores in the other two states.

An important issue may be illustrated by store no. 6, which would have paid, under internal experience rating, almost $20,000 more in taxes than it actually did. By one norm this would seem to be a gain in equity, since it brought the cost-tax ratio of this unit into balance with the other units. But by another norm, the effect might be questioned. Store no. 6 accounted for benefit charges of $22,802, but it paid taxes of $32,310. Since it was already more than paying its

Table 12-2. J. C. PENNEY COMPANY: Comparison of Taxes Payable with and without Internal Experience Rating (IER) for Operating Units in Three Large States, Five-Year Totals, 1964–68

Company unit	Benefits charged		Taxes payable[a]					Cost/tax ratio	
			Without IER		With IER				
	Amount	Percent of total	Amount	Percent of total	Amount	Percent of total	Decrease (−) or Increase (+) in tax	Without IER	With IER
	(1)	(2)	(3)	(4)	(5)	(6)	(7)	(8)	(9)
State F									
1	$ 922	2.7	$ 3,533	4.6	$ 2,091	2.7	− 1,442	26.1	44.1
2	1,316	3.9	4,776	6.2	3,021	3.9	− 1,755	27.6	43.6
3	1,405	4.1	5,621	7.3	3,176	4.1	− 2,445	25.0	44.2
4	3,107	9.1	13,836	17.8	7,049	9.1	− 6,787	22.5	44.1
5	4,536	13.3	17,380	22.4	10,302	13.3	− 7,078	26.1	44.0
6	22,802	66.9	32,310	41.7	51,817	66.9	+ 19,507	70.6	44.0
All units	34,088	100.0	77,456	100.0	77,456	100.0	0	44.0	44.0
State G									
7	$ 420	1.4	$ 2,284	3.3	$ 980	1.4	− 1,304	18.4	42.9
8	1,327	4.6	10,174	14.5	3,220	4.6	− 6,954	13.0	41.2
9	1,580	5.5	4,039	5.8	3,850	5.5	− 189	39.1	41.0
10	2,504	8.6	3,329	4.8	6,020	8.6	+ 2,691	75.2	41.6
11	5,420	18.7	10,282	14.7	13,090	18.7	+ 2,808	52.7	41.4
12	17,720	61.2	39,890	56.9	42,838	61.2	+ 2,948	44.4	41.4
All units	28,971	100.0	69,998	100.0	69,998	100.0	0	41.4	41.4

(continued on next page)

Table 12-2. (Continued)

Company unit	Benefits charged		Taxes payable[a]					Cost/tax ratio	
			Without IER		With IER				
	Amount	Percent of total	Amount	Percent of total	Amount	Percent of total	Decrease (–) or Increase (+) in tax	Without IER	With IER
	(1)	(2)	(3)	(4)	(5)	(6)	(7)	(8)	(9)
				State H					
13	$ 50	0.5	$ 3,759	7.4	$ 253	0.5	– 3,506	1.3	19.8
14	732	7.1	3,196	6.3	3,595	7.1	+ 399	22.9	20.4
15	1,590	15.5	6,928	13.7	7,848	15.5	+ 920	22.9	20.3
16	1,627	15.8	9,224	18.2	8,000	15.8	– 1,224	17.6	20.3
17	2,213	21.5	3,275	6.5	10,886	21.5	+ 7,611	67.6	20.3
18	4,072	39.6	24,250	47.9	20,050	39.6	– 4,200	16.8	20.3
All units	10,284	100.0	50,632	100.0	50,632	100.0	0	20.3	20.3

Source: Data supplied by firm.

[a]Taxes exclude subsidiary taxes.

way, why should it be asked to pay additional taxes? The answer is, of course, that during this period the firm as a whole was paying much more in taxes than it was drawing out in benefits. Most of the additional taxes went to build up the unemployment insurance fund; the rest went to subsidize firms that were not paying their way. Without internal experience rating, the other stores in state F were bearing a disproportionate share of this burden of reserve-building and subsidy. Internal experience rating would have caused all units to share more proportionately in the total tax burden.

That internal experience rating tends to increase participation in the *administration* of the unemployment insurance law is obvious. Without internal experience rating the manager of any given plant is for all practical purposes faced with a uniform tax. Although his bonus usually depends on the profitability of the operation under his charge, the manager sees only a remote, indirect relationship between his unemployment insurance activities and the plant's profitability. But when the cost of unemployment insurance charged against his operations is determined primarily by his own experience, he is more likely to take an interest in controlling such a cost. Although the person charged with administering unemployment insurance in the plan may not be as sensitive to profits as the manager, his performance will probably be scrutinized by the manager. This is particularly likely if the firm circulates to all its units a list of the tax rates paid by the respective units. This gives each manager a norm against which to compare the performance of his own unit.

Theoretically, at least, employer participation in *legislation* may also be influenced by internal experience rating. State legislators come from particular districts in their state. In that district the manager of a large plant may be a relatively important person. If his interest in unemployment insurance has been sharpened by internal experience rating, he may on occasion contact his representative in the legislature when bills affecting unemployment insurance are before the legislature. He may also contact an employer representative on the state's advisory council.

If experience rating is to have an effect on the *stabilization* of employment, it must operate at the plant level. Internal experience rating greatly increases the likelihood of interest and action at the plant level. In one of the better manuals intended for the guidance of employers the statement is made: "By compelling department heads to figure the potential liability of unemployment insurance benefit charges into their budgets, some control administrators have driven home in dramatic fashion the advantages of a flexible, versatile labor pool. It has also made department heads more cooperative in supplying administrators with advance information on expected production schedule changes" [99, p. 27].

The impact of internal experience rating on the *timing* of the tax for the individual units must remain largely speculative. Data are probably available, at least in a few firms, but have never been assembled. It seems reasonable, however, to suppose that where the tax is allocated internally on the same principles as govern the external application of the tax, the timing effect would be much the same. That is, the tax of the operating unit is likely to be highest when it is best able to bear the burden and lightest when it is least able. Just as experience rating brings the state tax into some conformity with the needs of the individual firm, so internal experience rating brings the corporation's tax into some conformity with the needs of its individual operating units.

Causes

The small proportion of firms that have a system of internal experience rating leads naturally to the questions: "Why do any firms use internal experience rating?" "Why don't more firms use it?"

The first and fundamental precondition for the adoption of internal experience rating is the existence of sizable differences in the benefit-cost rates of the units. Differences in benefit-cost rates determine the possible differences in tax rates, which must be sufficiently large to justify the administrative expense involved in internal experience rating. Examples of such differentials were given earlier, in the discussion of the allocative effect of internal experience rating.

The average tax rate and the variations around the average tend to be greater for some industries, such as durable manufacturing, than for others, such as retail trade. But even in industries with samller-than-average differentials between units, there were some firms which judged that the differences justified the adoption of internal experience rating. In several instances, this judgment was based on more than a decade of experience. When firms which did not have internal experience rating were asked—in interviews and in the questionnaire described above—why they did not have it, the commonest answer was that the range of cost rates among the firm's units was not sufficient to justify the administrative expense involved in internal experience rating.

The administrative structure of firms affects the way they regard internal experience rating. Firms that are decentralized are more likely to see advantages in internal experience rating than firms that are highly centralized. This especially applies to the organization of the firm's profit centers. The extent to which a firm's cost accounting is computerized also is a factor.

Firms in the construction industry reported that they would find the administration of internal experience rating especially difficult because by the time the amount of benefits connected with a given project are known the books on the project have normally been closed out. Some firms reported that they did a substantial part of their business with the government, and they thought the government would balk at including in the contract any other unemployment insurance rate than the general corporation rate imposed by the state. However, there are companies with government contracts that use internal experience rating.

In one company's experience, it was the government that insisted on internal experience rating. The Union Carbide Corporation has long had a contract with the Atomic Energy Commission (AEC) in Tennessee. Over the years, unemployment insurance taxes paid by Union Carbide to the state and charged against the AEC have built up large reserves. Since the company's AEC operations comprise the larger part of the company's total operations in the state, the AEC early insisted that its contributions to the company's reserve be segregated for accounting purposes and that a separate internal tax rate be calculated for the AEC part of the company's total operation.

Other obstacles to the adoption of internal experience rating have been more substantive than technical, more a matter of principle than a matter of feasibility. The finance officers who discussed internal experience rating with me usually approached the subject from the viewpoint of the overall profitability of the firm. Their primary concern was whether the system could be expected to lower the firm's tax rate. They were interested in how much added incentive the system would provide for managers of units to avoid unemployment (stabilization issue) and to police claims (the administration issue). They rarely mentioned the issue of allocation of costs and resources. When I raised that issue the interviewees generally reacted in one of two ways. Most often they recognized the validity of the issue. They admitted that they were rigorous in allocating much smaller costs to the individual operating units and ought, logically, to thus allocate the cost of unemployment benefits. It was at this point that they often added: "However, the gain in more accurate cost accounting would not be worth the cost of the additional record keeping required."

A less frequent but not rare reaction to the proposal to allocate costs in this way was to say that it would be "unfair." Inquiry revealed that it was considered unfair to charge some units more than others when the high-cost units were not "responsible" for their higher costs. Some unemployment was not controllable by the individual units.[7] When this reason was offered in an interview, I would point out that other costs over which a unit had no control were allocated to each unit by a strict system of cost accounting. I would also observe that the principle involved in this objection could be and often was used against experience rating in general. If the employer was one who favored experience rating, he usually abandoned this reason, at least in principle, and fell back on other reasons, such as the administrative expense involved.

However, the employer sometimes maintained his position. Where one firm might have a policy of sharpening the sense of competition between its units, another might have the opposite policy of fostering a sense of unity. Such firms varied accordingly in their estimate of the value of internal experience rating to

7. Several firms mentioned the example of layoffs followed by "bumping." These firms had negotiated liberal seniority arrangements, whereby employees laid off by one operating unit could displace employees in another unit. It seemed undesirable to charge one unit with benefits occasioned by layoffs in another unit when the cause of the shift was a company-negotiated seniority policy. These firms, if they had a system of internal experience rating, would probably want to "noncharge" such benefits.

the corporation. Within the corporation itself, internal experience rating was more likely to be regarded favorably by the finance department than by the personnel department. The location of the unemployment insurance unit was thus sometimes a decisive factor. If it was located in the personnel department (the more usual arrangement) any proposal for internal experience rating that the unemployment insurance administrator might make was less likely to receive a hearing than if the unemployment insurance unit was located in the tax department.

The experience of one large manufacturing company is particularly interesting because after having used internal experience rating for over a decade, the company abandoned the practice. Its reasons for adopting internal experience rating originally had been three: "To encourage employment stability, to control improper payments, and to promote an interest in effective U.C. legislation by local management" [160].

The company's reasons for abandoning internal experience rating were also three, though not the same three. "First, the various plants were able to recover the added internal costs through intra-Company prices, so were not truly held accountable as a profit center for unfavorable experience" [160]. This is essentially the same argument as was discussed in Chapter 3. The original taxpayer (in this case, the unit) is assumed to shift the tax to someone else (in this case, another unit). Since the unit which shifts the tax is presumed not to feel the tax, it could not be motivated to do any of the things which the tax was supposed to promote. Although some unit finally bears the burden of the tax, the increased cost of this unit does not stem directly from unemployment benefits; hence, neither is this unit motivated to stabilize employment or police claims more closely. This line of argument, though logical in itself, has two limitations. It depends on uncertain assumptions regarding the shifting and final incidence of the tax, and it ignores the allocative effect of internal experience rating.

The second reason given by the company for abandoning internal experience rating was connected with the program of supplemental unemployment benefits (SUB), which it had negotiated earlier. Originally, the company's contribution to the SUB fund was experience-rated, but beginning in 1964 the union insisted that the company pay the full contribution in one form or another, no matter how favorable the company's experience might have been. From this time on the company ceased, of course, to use internal experience rating for SUB contributions. Since it had to abandon internal experience rating for the SUB part of unemployment benefit costs, the company thought it logical to abandon internal experience rating for the unemployment insurance part also.

The third reason given was: "The administrative workload to handle experience rating became burdensome" [160]. The company was emphatic that this was not the principal reason for abandoning internal experience rating. A fourth reason seems to have been complaints made by one large unit about the amount of record-keeping involved and the unfairness of the resulting tax rates.

Among the factors that explain the presence or absence of internal experience rating there are the unpredictable but frequently decisive forces of circumstances and personalities. The adoption of internal experience rating by General Motors, for example, cannot be explained apart from these two factors. Without the general uproar over unemployment insurance during the reconversion period, and without the long (1945-46) General Motors strike, the attention of top management in the corporation could not have been attracted to the unemployment insurance program. These circumstances prepared the way for internal experience rating, but they were only a preparation. This historical context itself would not have produced internal experience rating without the vigorous leadership of several individuals, especially Arthur S. Thornbury, within the firm.

Although I cannot document the proposition, I am inclined to believe that in most companies the introduction of internal experience rating is traceable to the strong leadership of some individual. I know that was so, for example, in Montgomery Ward and in Macy's of California. For another example: A large firm that made and sold matches comprised a lumbering operation with a high benefit-cost rate and a retailing operation with a low benefit-cost rate. Internal experience rating was introduced into the firm when it got a comptroller who had come from the retailing side of the business.

The factor of personality has the greater scope because internal experience rating, like experience rating itself, involves a choice of values, which vary with individuals. The tensions within the firm (between the low-cost and the high-cost units, or between the personnel and the finance divisions) closely resemble the external conflicts between firms. In both cases, a choice must be made whether to emphasize the things that unite or the things that divide the parts of the larger whole and to seek long run efficiency by requiring each policy decision to bear its own cost or by requiring one operation to subsidize another.

Is it possible for an employer to favor experience rating as between firms, while not favoring its use internally in his own firm? The answer is yes. While internal experience rating is a microcosm of the larger issue of experience rating itself, the two are not identical. They differ in at least four substantial respects.

First of all, within the large area of the state, the units to be taxed (the individual firms) differ sufficiently in their cost rates to establish a realistic potential for experience rating. This was the clear conclusion of Chapter 4. But for any given firm this precondition of internal experience rating may not be fulfilled. A utilities firm, for example, with a very low corporate tax rate and with homogeneous units provides much less potential for differentiated tax rates than does the state employment insurance system as a whole.

Second, the individual unit is not lost in the experience of the firm to the same extent that the individual firm is lost in the experience of the state. The unit is more likely to perceive and to feel at least some relationship between its own actions and the tax rate of the firm, and hence its own tax rate. Also, the unit is subject to the firm's control in matters affecting production, personnel, and unemployment insurance administration, while the firm is not similarly subject to the state.

Third, even though the units of a firm differ significantly in their benefit-cost rates, the firm may prefer not to require each unit to meet its own costs. The final norm is the profitability of the entire firm, not of any one unit. If the long-run profit picture of the firm is improved by pooling costs—whether in order to carry a weak unit through a difficult period, or to safeguard morale, or merely to lessen accounting expenses—then it becomes logical not to adopt internal experience rating. While the state may also reach this conclusion and require some firms to subsidize others for the good of the state as a whole, such a decision is reached much more readily when it affects the relationships of units within a firm, which share a common profit goal, than when it applies to relationships between firms, which are in competition over profits.

Finally, the administrative cost of experience rating is relatively less when the operation it covers is larger and more computerized. Since in this respect the average state has a substantial advantage over the average firm, the negative value of administrative cost may weigh more in the scales of internal experience rating than in those of experience rating in general.

My overall impression is that the absence of internal experience rating among large firms is attributable not so much to the firms' having carefully considered the system and rejected it but rather to the firms' never having seriously adverted to the possible advantages of the system. Most large firms do not know what the respective unemployment insurance cost rates of their various units are. For the firm to know benefit-cost rates by unit, the state must furnish benefit charges by unit. Since states do this only on request, and some states very reluctantly, the decision to adopt—or at least consider seriously—internal experience rating often must proceed on an assumption of significant cost differences between the units.

Where firms have given serious consideration to the possibility of using internal experience rating, the final decision has been influenced chiefly by the size of the benefit cost differentials among units, by the form of the accounting procedures in use, and by the degree of understanding of the principles of experience rating itself. Furthermore, where internal experience rating has been adopted, it has usually been after a protracted campaign on the part of someone very knowledgeable in unemployment insurance and in circumstances that favored consideration of the idea.

13.

**Experience
Rating
Revisited**

The Issue

This study has been concerned with the social debate over the desirability of experience rating in the unemployment insurance system. The study has accepted this system as it has operated historically and as it is likely to continue to operate in the foreseeable future: a federal/state system in which each state is free to determine the substance of its own program and which is supported almost entirely by a payroll tax levied on employers. With regard to this system the study has sought to answer the question: Is experience rating a desirable method of allocating the tax burden among employers?

Historically, the discussion of experience rating has been obscured by the introduction of several spurious issues. The question of whether to have separate state programs or a single federal program is one such issue. Although intertwined in the early years with the debate over experience rating, it is not currently relevant. Whether there is a single federal program or separate state programs, a decision must still be made in either program to have a uniform or an experience-rated tax. Interstate competition is another such spurious issue. Interstate competition results directly from the existence of separate state programs and would exist even if each state had a uniform tax.[1]

But the most serious of these spurious issues relates to the level of the average state tax. There is no basis for the assumption that in the absence of experience rating the average state tax would always and everywhere be at least 2.7 percent. Although historically experience rating has been the only way to vary the tax below 2.7 percent, in its absence some other method would have been found to achieve the same result. The McCormack amendment of 1938 (p. 13) exemplifies the general line of action that would have been followed. The 2.7 percent tax was chosen originally on the basis of extremely meager information about patterns of unemployment. It would have been an extraordinary piece of luck if this first rate had turned out to be the desired long-term average rate. Indeed, any fixed rate that might be chosen could be maintained only by predicting with

---

1. In fact, as explained in Chapter 3, if experience rating has any relationship to interstate competition it is to mitigate it.

301

absolute accuracy the future pattern of unemployment or by varying benefits to absorb all but no more than the revenue produced by the fixed rate. Neither alternative is practical. Any realistic appraisal would expect the rate to vary over time.

Given a system of separate state programs, the rate must be expected to vary also as between states. The variations in cost rates, and therefore in tax rates, between states stem partly from differences in benefit provisions but chiefly from differences in unemployment patterns. Even if all states were required to meet federal benefit standards, some might have to levy twice as high a tax as others because they regularly experience more unemployment. (Table A-3 shows how different the long-run cost rates of the states have been.)

The only practicable alternative to an experience-rated tax is not a uniform, fixed tax of 2.7 percent, but a tax that is uniform as between employers but variable over time and between states. Proper understanding of this proposition should tend to reduce both the opposition to experience rating and support for it. It should reduce opposition to experience rating insofar as that opposition is based on an assumption that an experience-rated tax necessarily produces less money than the "standard" tax. It is instructive to note how during the decade 1957-67 the average tax rates in California, New York, and Pennsylvania were practically the same as would have been produced by a uniform tax at the standard rate (Table A-5). Similarly, support for experience rating among employers should be reduced insofar as that support is based on an assumption that in the absence of experience rating all employers would be paying a tax rate of 2.7 percent. In the absence of experience rating, all employers in a given state would be paying a uniform tax, but in most states this tax would be much less than 2.7 percent. (However, a state's average tax would probably be somewhat lower if experience-rated than if uniform because of the effects of experience rating on administration, legislation, and stabilization.)

To discuss the genuine issues involved in experience rating it is necessary to examine its major effects, as was done in Chapters 2 through 11. With respect to each of these it is necessary to ask two questions: How much of an effect did experience rating have? Was the effect desirable? The present chapter summarizes the answers to these questions.

Allocation of Costs and Resources

As compared with a uniform tax, experience rating changes the relative profitability of high-cost and low-cost firms. In effect, it takes money away from high-cost firms and gives it to low-cost firms and by so doing changes the allocation of resources among firms. This effect is distinct from all its other effects. If experience rating had no other effects whatsoever, there would still be the question to answer: What is its impact on the allocation of resources, and is this effect desirable?

Size of Effect

The impact of experience rating on the allocation of costs and resources is as great potentially as the differentials in benefit-cost rates among individual firms and as great actually as the differentials in their tax rates. Data on cost rates, tax rates, and their relationships provide the necessary basis for a judgment on the size of this effect of experience rating. Such data also help to establish the limits within which all its other effects may occur.

Benefit-cost rates. As was explained in Chapter 4, if the investigator of experience rating could have only one piece of information, he would probably choose information about benefit-cost rates, which are the building blocks of an experience-rated system. Knowledge about benefit-cost rates is essential to an intelligent decision on whether to have an experience-rated system at all, and, if so, what degree of experience rating to have.

The situation which most favors the choice of an experience-rated system is one in which the cost rates of firms differ significantly and regularly. In order to adjust the premium to the risk, which is the essence of experience rating, the insurer must be able to calculate the risk; and to do that he must be able to find significant and regular differences in experience. The larger and the more regular the differences, the more reason there is to see the unemployment insurance tax as an insurance premium which, like other normal costs of doing business, should be integrated with the market.

The long-run cost rates of the various industry divisions differ considerably among themselves (Table A-5). For example, in Massachusetts the long-run rate of construction was 6.2 percent, while that of finance was only 0.8 percent, making a differential of 5.4 percent. Since these are averages for large industry divisions, individual firms would have had long-term cost rates both above and below these averages. (Some idea of the range of cost rates for individual firms in a single year is provided by Table 4-1.)

Tax rates. Although cost rates determine the potential degree of experience rating, the actual degree is determined by tax rates. All the effects which are attributed to experience rating are dependent upon the pattern of tax rates. The limits within which the desirable and undesirable effects attributed to it can possibly occur are set by the degree of experience rating in the system, which in turn is determined by the pattern of tax rates. The larger and the more regular the tax differentials, the more likely it is that experience rating has significant effects.

A detailed view of tax differentials is provided by Table 4-7 and Table 4-8.[2] As may be seen in Table 4-7, about one-fifth of all taxable wages were at the

2. Three appendix Tables, A-15, A-16, and A-17 provide further data on the distribution of tax rates of individual firms. These tables show tax rates distributed *within* industry divisions and groups.

upper end of the tax spectrum, while about two-fifths were at the lower end. The tax difference between these two groups averaged about 2-3 percent of taxable wages. Since taxable wages were $3,000 in most states, this difference amounted to something less than $100 per employee per year. This is a measure of the competitive advantage or disadvantage produced by (limited) experience rating for the employer groups between whom the difference was greatest. Of course, these are averages, and the firms at the two extremes of the distribution show differences twice this size, but these firms are very few. For example, in 1967 only 2.6 percent of taxable wages were at the minimum tax rate and 2.5 percent were at the uppermost tax rate—a total of 5.1 percent of taxable wages affected by the widest differential of about 4.0 percent. This differential would amount to $120 per employee per year.

How important is such a differential? The answer must vary with the kind of firm (it is more important to a labor-intensive firm that to a capital-intensive firm) and with the profitability of the firm (it is more important to a firm with a low profit rate). The answer must vary especially with the different effects of experience rating. A differential that might be too small to affect the location of a firm might be large enough to affect a firm's employment policy; and a differential that might be too small to affect a firm's employment policy might be large enough to affect its participation in unemployment insurance administration. Moreover, for the effects on administration and stabilization, another type of calculation is appropriate. For these effects the significant comparison is between the total benefits payable to a claimant, which may amount to two or three thousand dollars, and the cost of doing whatever is needed to prevent that benefit cost—controlling claims or stabilizing employment—for that particular employee. This key comparison is as important as it is frequently overlooked.

It is obvious from Table 4-7 that the states vary considerably in the extent to which they use experience rating. Wisconsin and Florida, for example, show wide ranges of tax rates, while Utah and Washington show narrow ranges. The alleged effects of experience rating, good or bad, cannot possibly be as significant in the one group of states as in the other.

The significance of the tax differentials produced by experience rating depends not only on their size but also on their regularity. The most desirable sort of data for the purpose of measuring regularity would be the tax rates of individual firms averaged over a long period of time. This sort of data is, however, practically nonexistent. A small sample of such data (Table 4-9), compiled for this study, indicates that in Massachusetts, over a nine-year period, about half (43.9 percent) of all the firms in the sample maintained their same general relationship to the state average, remaining either below or above that average throughout the entire period.

Other data that throw some light on the regularity of tax differentials are the data showing average tax rates by industry division or group. Such data are shown in some detail in appendix Tables A-5 through A-9. The general picture is one of substantial regularity. One can predict with a high degree of probability, for example, that in state after state, and year after year, most firms in the construction industry will have higher tax rates than will most firms in the industry of finance-insurance-real estate. That within construction, the special trades group will have lower tax rates than will other groups. That within the special trades, electrical work and plumbing will have lower tax rates than will painting and plastering. One can predict that the service industries will have higher tax rates than finance-insurance-real estate but lower tax rates than manufacturing. One can predict that within manufacturing, heavy durables, like steel and autos, and seasonal activities, like canning and apparel, will have higher tax rates than printing or chemicals or instruments. One can safely predict that within apparel manufacturing men's suits and women's undergarments will have lower tax rates than hats, or fur goods, or women's outerwear. The differences among the industry averages clearly are rooted in the natures of the respective economic activities. It seems logical, therefore, to assume that similar differences exist to a significant extent at the level of the individual firm.

It will be recalled from Chapter 3 how Rubinow expected that "some ten percent or twenty percent would be between the legal minimum and maximum limits and the rest either below the minimum or over the maximum" [20, p. 83]. On the basis of such an estimate, he very reasonably asked: "What is the scientific or social value of such a limited degree of rate adjustment?" Tables 4-6 and 4-7 indicate that the degree of rate adjustment is much greater than Rubinow had anticipated. The proportions of payrolls falling between the minimum and maximum limits are always well above 50 percent. Furthermore, the assumption that is implicit in Rubinow's statement is not entirely correct. It is not correct that experience rating has no meaning for firms whose cost rates are above the maximum tax rate or below the minimum tax rate. Although firms in these "zones of indifference" might have no incentive to participate in administration or to make efforts toward stabilization, they would be affected by experience rating as regards their profits and the allocation of resources.

Everything that I have seen has led me to believe that the size of the tax is of some importance to employers. One recalls the battles in the legislature over the structure of the tax, including struggles between representatives of the various industries over the distribution of the total tax burden; or the concern shown by the financial officers of corporations over small increases in the tax; or the willingness of many firms to incur the expense of setting up a centralized unemployment insurance unit in order to control claims, or of hiring a service company to perform this function. Many other similar indications might be mentioned, among them the decision of some firms to make use of internal experience rating. (See also pp. 95-96.)

Perhaps the simplest way of summing up in general terms the market significance of the tax differentials produced by experience rating is to say that if private companies sold unemployment insurance policies, as the Metropolitan Life Insurance Company once proposed to do, they would certainly charge differentiated premiums. Furthermore, a firm seeking to purchase such a policy would certainly concern itself with the premium charged and would choose among competing insurance companies partly on the size of the premium. The premium differential would not be considered a negligible quantity by either the seller or the buyer.

Cost/tax ratios. To what extent is the potential for experience rating, as revealed in benefit-cost rates, realized in the existing structure of tax rates? The question is important for several reasons. First, to evaluate experience rating as such it is essential to know to what extent the effects being investigated reflect experience rating and the extent to which they reflect its absence. Also, to make an intelligent decision to maintain or change the degree of experience rating it is very helpful to know the existing degree. If the undesirable effects of experience rating are judged to outweigh its desirable effects, presumably a decision would be reached to limit further its degree in the system. Contrariwise, if the desirable effects are judged to outweigh the undesirable effects, this could reasonably lead to a decision to use the existing potential of experience rating to a greater degree than has been done. Finally, to the extent that benefits and taxes do not balance, it is helpful to know who is subsidizing whom and by how much.

In the few states that employ the device of the "Common Account" there is available a fairly complete measure of the extent to which the potential of experience rating has *not* been actualized. As explained in Chapter 2, the Common Account reflects all those activities in the program which are not experience-rated. By this measure, in 1969 the proportion of the program not experience-rated was almost half in California (Table 5-1), and over half in Massachusetts (p. 102). In view of the original leadership roles played by Wisconsin and Ohio, it is ironical to note that in Wisconsin over one-fifth of the program was not experience-rated, while in Ohio the program was almost completely experience-rated. Since very few states have a Common Account, it is necessary to examine other data to gain some idea of the general situation.

One of the two main roots of limitations on experience rating are noncharged benefits. In 1966 in thirteen states having 12 percent of all covered workers, noncharged benefits represented over 20 percent of all benefits paid (p. 104). At the other end of the range, in twenty states, having 55 percent of all covered workers, noncharged benefits represented less than 10 percent of all benefits paid. In South Carolina, noncharged benefits have at times represented over 40 percent of all benefits paid, whereas in Michigan and New York noncharged benefits have been practically nonexistent.

The second, and in most states the more important, limitation on experience rating is the extent of ineffectively charged benefits. Tables 5-5 through 5-9 offer a succession of views of negative-balance firms, which in reserve-ratio systems are a direct reflection of the extent of ineffectively charged benefits.

The ideal measure, of course, of the extent of experience rating would be cost-tax ratios for individual firms averaged for each firm over a long period of time. But cost-tax ratios for individual firms are available only for single years, and such data are too ambiguous to be very useful. Cost-tax ratios averaged over long periods of time are available only for industry groups, not for individual firms. Such industry data are shown in Tables A–5 through A–9 and show that long-term cost-tax ratios vary greatly between industry divisions and between groups within industry divisions.

From the data on the operations of the Common Account, on noncharged benefits, on ineffectively charged benefits, and on industry cost-tax ratios, it is clear that the unemployment insurance system as a whole is very far from being completely experience-rated. The departures from experience rating are numerous and large. Hence the effects studied in this review are not the effects of "pure" experience rating, but of a very modified form of it. Hence also there is considerable room for an increase in experience rating if that should be desired.

It is clear that the degree of experience rating varies greatly as between states. States like Ohio and Michigan, for example, are marked by a much greater degree of experience rating than are states like Massachusetts and South Carolina. While it is tempting to hazard a generalization of the degree of experience rating in the system as a whole—to say, for example, that the system is one-half or two-thirds experience-rated—the great state differences, in a system where each state is independent and decides on the nature of its own program, make such generalizations of no practical value. All practical decisions to decrease, maintain, or increase the degree of experience rating must be made separately by each state in terms of its own unique experience.

Desirability of Effect

In the absence of specific evidence to the contrary, the allocative effect of experience rating is presumed to be desirable. The argumentation supporting this proposition was developed at length in Chapter 3 and is based primarily on our society's choice of the market as its principal mechanism for the allocation of resources. Experience rating is in accord with the market insofar as it brings about a more accurate allocation of the social costs of unemployment. The notion of "social cost" is currently in the forefront of public consciousness as economic activities that result in polluted air and water are being asked to bear more of the costs attendant on a polluted environment. Similarly, economic activities that result in unemployment are required by experience rating to bear more of the cost of this form of social "pollution." The presumption of desirability enjoyed by the allocative effect of experience rating has been challenged with respect to certain types of firms. Specifically, experience rating has been criticized for putting too great a burden on small firms, on new firms, and on seasonal firms.

The relationship between experience rating and *small firms* may be summed up in three propositions. (1) Since the great majority of small firms have a tax rate below the state average tax, they would be burdened with a heavier rate under a uniform tax than they are under experience rating. (2) Their tax rates are subject to greater fluctuations under experience rating than they would be under a uniform tax. Although small firms tend to congregate at the lower end of the tax spectrum, they can move very quickly to the upper end. (3) As groups, the smallest firms have the highest cost-tax ratios (Table A-10 and Table A-11). That is, the smallest firms are the subsidized and the largest firms are the chief subsidizers.

It is sometimes said that "*new employers* bear a disproportionate share of the cost of unemployment insurance under experience rating" [14, p. 343]. Four observations are relevant to this criticism. (1) New firms must accumulate experience during one to three years, depending on the state law, before they are "rated," that is, are eligible for an experience-rated tax. During this period they pay the standard tax (usually 2.7 percent), which may be higher or lower than the tax paid by their established competitors. Hence during this period new firms may be disadvantaged or advantaged with respect to the older firms, depending largely on whether they are in a low-cost or high-cost industry. Although most new firms will be disadvantaged, not all will be. (2) In reserve-ratio states, the advantage or disadvantage is temporary. If a new firm pays in more or less than its benefit costs during the preliminary period, its taxes will be correspondingly lower or higher in later periods. If a state wishes, it may shorten the preliminary period to one year.[3] (3) The employment security amendments of 1970 (H.R. 14705) provided that any state may, if it sees fit, assign to new firms reduced rates (down to 1 percent) on some other basis than experience with unemployment. (4) Because new firms have a higher failure rate than established firms, they account for more than their share of deficit firms. They do, indeed, bear a "disproportionate" share of the cost but in the opposite sense intended by the criticism.

Experience rating is charged with imposing too great a burden on *seasonal* firms. This charge is based on the argument that if seasonal firms are required to pay their own costs, their activity will be curtailed and they will provide less employment. Although seasonal firms do tend to pay a higher tax under experience rating than they would under a uniform tax, many still do not pay their way but enjoy a subsidy paid for by other firms. The cost-tax ratios of Chapter 5 provide illustrative data on the extent of this subsidy. Whether the existing subsidies are too small or too large must be decided by each state for itself in the light of its own economic situation.

The payment of unemployment benefits for "seasonal unemployment" has always posed and probably will always pose a problem for the system. "It is therefore desirable," Paul Douglas wrote in 1939, "to exclude a very large proportion of chronic seasonal unemployment from compensation" [27, p. 319], and Merrill Murray found the issue still very much alive in 1971.[4] But

---

3. As of January 1971, twenty-five states rated firms after one year of experience.
4. The W. E. Upjohn Institute for Employment Research is currently preparing for publication a monograph by Murray on this topic.

instead of excluding seasonal workers from benefits, another solution is to charge seasonal firms (more of) what they cost the fund. While this solution tends to increase the opposition of the seasonal firms, it tends to decrease the opposition of the much more numerous nonseasonal firms. Which force is greater depends on the politics of each particular situation, but from the viewpoint of a society concerned with the allocation of resources there is clearly less reason to question the payment of benefits for seasonal unemployment when the cost of such benefits is more fully reflected in the prices under which the seasonal firms operate. Similarly, experience rating may forestall objections that might otherwise be raised to the payment of benefits in situations involving a liberal interpretation of the eligibility of seasonal claimants. Other firms are less likely to find such policies objectionable if the firms that reap the benefits also bear the cost. The Wisconsin law has a provision that brings out this point of view very clearly: If an employer requests the agency to ignore certain circumstances which if considered might result in the disqualification of the claimant, the state agency may honor the request if the employer is paying his way, but may not honor the request if his firm is deficit.

In summary, it must be concluded that the allocative effect of experience rating is not only sizable but is also desirable—on the assumption that market effects are desirable effects unless there is specific evidence to the contrary.

Employer Participation in Administration

Size of Effect

This effect ranks high, probably second, among the reasons advanced by the advocates of experience rating. It is of considerable importance, also, to the critics of the system, who charge that the kind of employer participation elicited by experience rating hinders rather than helps in the proper administration of unemployment insurance.

There is no doubt that experience rating can elicit a very active participation on the part of employers, as exemplified by the firms described in Chapter 8. Several respondents to the opinion survey reported experience similar to the following:

> With the beginning of merit rating (within the past 5 years) there has been a definite increase in employer participation. Previously employers (top management) expressed interest only in cases when they had "strong feeling" for or against payment to a specific worker. Clerical workers or assistant personnel staff were available for limited information, and little interest was otherwise expressed. Since merit rating, calls for information regarding separation and merit rating charges have greatly increased from the supervisory level, and more explicit information, and rebuttal information, is promptly given upon request.

The potential for employer participation in the administrative process may be measured in various ways. The most general measure is provided by the proportion of separations from employment that represent layoffs for reasons other than lack of work. It is only with regard to these that the employee's eligibility might be in question and the employer's participation required. Although such data are lacking for the covered workforce, for the workforce as a whole separations other than layoffs can explain the greater part of labor turnover. In 1969 such separations accounted for 76 percent of all labor turnover; even in 1970, a recession year, they accounted for 62 percent [161, p. 98].

Employer participation in administration is practically limited to initial claims that give rise to a nonmonetary determination involving a separation issue. The analysis of the experience of Massachusetts (Chapter 7) revealed that less than one-fifth of initial claims gave rise to nonmonetary determinations and that only about two-thirds of these involved separation issues. Thus the potential for employer participation would seem to have been limited to about 12 percent of the initial claims (about 1 percent of all the claims) filed in Massachusetts during this period. Since these proportions vary over time and between states, the Massachusetts experience cannot do more than provide a starting point for one's thinking. It does suffice, however, as a guard against the mistaken notion that employer participation is needed whenever a worker is separated from employment. The Massachusetts data also show that the employer is not always needed to raise the original question regarding a claimant's eligibility. Of all the nonmonetary determinations made in a five-year period, only half (50.5 percent) were occasioned by the employer alone (Table 7-1).

The effect of experience rating on employer participation in administration is a function also of the firm's interest in controlling claims. Firms differ very much in the attention they accord this administrative task and the same company may vary over time, as the experience of companies A, B, and C illustrates (Chapter 8). At one period of their history these firms showed little interest in this administrative task, while at another period they showed considerable interest. I am inclined to think that the "average" firm resembles these companies in their earlier, rather than their later, attitude toward claims control.

In large firms the degree of interest depends very much on the extent to which the unemployment insurance function is centralized. As noted at various places in the preceding chapters, line supervision tends to neglect the unemployment insurance function unless the firm either has a centralized unemployment insurance unit or uses internal experience rating. The North American Rockwell Corporation exemplifies the efficient use of a central unit (Chapter 8), while the General Motors Corporation exemplifies the use of internal experience rating (Chapter 12).[5]

I asked a number of firms with centralized units whether they would maintain such units in the absence of experience rating. Most replied that they would

5. As a kind of substitute for a central administration unit, General Motors also makes use of unemployment insurance policy committees (Ch. 8, fn. 11).

not. The few that said they would admitted that if the firm went through a cost-cutting period the centralized unit would probably be an early fatality. I also asked these same firms how their participation in the administrative process might change in the absence of experience rating. They were in agreement that the following would probably occur: (1) The firm would appeal claims very seldom. (2) The firm would give less attention to the preparation of the forms describing the separation from employment. Sometimes the form might not be returned at all. When it was returned, borderline cases of quits and discharges might be labeled "layoffs" whenever it was inconvenient to ascertain the exact circumstances of the separation. (3) There would be an increase in the tendency to use unemployment benefits as a supplement to wages or as a way of doing a favor for an employee.

Service companies are probably the clearest indication that experience rating has an impact on employer participation in administration. Service companies exist to aid the employer in this administrative chore, and service companies would not exist except for experience rating. Firms that contract for the services of such companies have calculated that potential tax savings are worth the fee they must pay the service company. Their calculations may not be correct, but the possibility of error accompanies most business calculations.

Desirability of Effect

To provide a basis for judging whether employer participation in administration was desirable or not, experienced deputies and referees were asked whether such participation helped or hindered them in their task of administering the law. If any persons in the entire program have an opinion worth considering, it should be the deputies and referees, who are in constant contact with claimant and employer, serving as the bridge between them and arbitrating their disputes about claims—day after day, year after year.

This group was asked the question: "Does employer participation in the administrative process help or hinder you in your job of carrying out the unemployment insurance law of your state?" All but one of the thirteen items in the questionnaire asked this central question in one form or another. The answers received were distributed as follows:

	Percent
Favorable to employer participation	74.0
Unfavorable to employer participation	15.0
Neutral	11.0

While these answers do not link employer participation to experience rating as such, they reflect a situation in which experience rating was actually operative. In the judgment of the program's deputies and referees, the gains from employer participation clearly outweighed the losses.

Over half (57.5 percent) of all respondents wanted more employer participation, while 15.1 percent expressed their general satisfaction with the existing
situation. Only 4.8 percent expressed a wish for less employer participation.[6]
The most frequently expressed desires for changes in employer participation
were that employers would provide more detailed information in their original
protests, that they would appear at the hearings initiated by claimants, and that
they would bring to all hearings, whether initiated by themselves or by claimants, "percipient witnesses," that is, those persons who could give first-hand
testimony regarding the issues involved in the appeal.

In the response to a question about historical changes in employer particpa-
tion, only 1.7 percent of all respondents (nearly all of them in state B) felt that a
change for the worse had occurred. About one-quarter (26.4 percent) reported
no significant change in employer participation. The rest (about 72 percent) felt
that employer participation had increased and improved. A Michigan referee
summed up the historical change thus:

> Younger personnel or labor-relations representatives are more alert, better
> educated, less contentious, prone to present pertinent original records for
> inspection by a referee, with copies available for substitution as exhibits,
> and less apt to state "the law is not fair" or "the employer doesn't have a
> chance." They are cooperative in arranging for presence of witnesses who
> have personal knowledge of incidents that resulted in discharge etc., and
> less apt to take the position that the employer's statements should not be
> doubted or questioned.

Many respondents commented on what seemed to them to be the inherent
dilemma of the situation. They were convinced that to elicit adequate employer
participation it was necessary to employ the tax incentive, but they also perceived that some of the participation elicited by this method was of an undesirable nature. They recognized that to increase employer participation by means of
experience rating was to increase both the desirable and the undesirable forms of
participation. However, in balancing the gains and losses of increased employer
participation through experience rating, the great majority of them chose increased employer participation. It is clear that in general the deputies and referees of the country do not see "too much" employer participation as a major
problem. They desire to maintain at least as much employer participation as there
has been in the past; moreover, the increase in employer participation that has
marked the recent past is viewed by them as a good development which they
would like to see prolonged into the future.

One question (#3) asked the opinion of the respondents on the specific
charge that employers harassed claimants by filing "frivolous" protests and
appeals. Of the respondents, one-fifth reported that this happened often,

---

6. Even this low proportion chiefly reflected the answers in one state (State B) where the
proportion was 44.9 percent.

meaning in 10 to 20 percent of disputed claims, while one-half reported that it happened seldom, meaning in less than 5 percent of disputed claims.

A special study made of the Massachusetts experience (Chapter 7) provided a clearer answer to this somewhat ambiguous question for at least this one state. During the five-year period, 1963-67, the outside possible limit of employer harassment in Massachusetts would seem to have been something much less than 1 percent of initial claims and an even tinier fraction of all claims.

In Chapter 8 the experience of a number of individual firms was described in some detail. These were firms which a preliminary investigation had determined to be more than ordinarily active in claims control. Such firms could be expected to reflect the maximum impact of experience rating. It was expected that here, if anywhere, the advantages and disadvantages of experience rating would be discernible. The record of these firms was, on the whole, good. It corresponded with the answers returned by the deputies and referees in the opinion survey. These firms tended to protest a high proportion of claims when the labor market was tight and a low proportion when the labor market was loose. Moreover, whether the proportion of protests was high or low, the firms' win-ratio remained consistently high. A high proportion of claims protested in combination with a high proportion of protests won would seem to indicate that there was a substantial function for the firm to perform and that the firm performed the function responsibly.

Chapter 8 also reported on the experience of some of the service companies. Since service companies are the direct product of experience rating and would not exist without it, they, like the most active firms, can be expected to reflect its effects most clearly. While service companies vary greatly in quality, the older and larger companies, which have most of the business, seem to be efficient, responsible firms. Their win-ratio both at the level of initial protest and at the appeal level is usually high. Also, they seem to enjoy a fairly good reputation with the majority of deputies and referees. In the questionnaire, while three-quarters of the respondents expressed a preference for dealing with employers directly rather than through service companies, three-quarters also gave a guarded vote of approval to service companies.

Employer activity at the appeal level is probably the most sensitive aspect of employer participation in administration. The decade of experience summarized in Table 8-7 shows that employer appeals were relatively infrequent, averaging only 0.26 percent of new spells of unemployment, and that employers won 41.9 percent of the appeals they filed. (For purposes of comparison, claimant appeals averaged 1.62 percent of new spells of unemployment and claimants won 27.3 percent of the appeals they filed.)

In conclusion, it seems reasonably clear that experience rating has a perceptible effect on employer participation in administration and that on balance this participation is desirable insofar as it helps the deputies and referees in their task of administering the law.

Employer Participation in Legislation

Size of Effect

The issue here is accurately expressed in the question: Has experience rating caused employers to work more effectively (from their point of view) in the area of legislation? The question is difficult to answer because experience rating is only one of the many factors influencing unemployment insurance legislation. Any tax levied solely on employers, whether uniform or experience-rated, would probably occasion considerable legislative activity on the part of the employers. However, the weight of seasoned opinion seems to be affirmative. Because of experience rating there is probably more effective employer participation in the legislative process, especially in the area of disqualification provisions.

The widespread practice of noncharging is striking proof of the conviction of many persons close to the program that experience rating does affect the attitude of employers toward disqualification provisions. It may be significant, also, that Utah and Washington, which have a minimum degree of experience rating, do not have the strictest forms of disqualifications. However, it is not possible to decide to what extent the absence of stricter disqualifications is a result of the absence of experience rating and to what extent both are the results of a common cause, namely, the political climate of the state. Given the different political complexions of the various states, they would probably differ considerably in their disqualification provisions even if none of them used experience rating.

Except for disqualification provisions, it is not at all clear how experience rating affects employer participation in legislation. As a matter of fact, most employers have a lesser financial incentive to oppose liberalization when the tax system is experience-rated than when it is uniform (pp. 222-24).

Desirability of Effect

In the final judgment on experience rating, the desirability of this effect must be given considerable weight. Certainly fear of undesirable effects on legislation is the chief source of opposition to experience rating. If there were no fault to find with experience rating on the score of its effect on legislation, opposition might be relatively light. It is probable that the effects of experience rating on the allocation of resources and on administration, for example, are feared by some primarily because these initial effects are expected to have undesirable secondary effects on legislation.

In attempting to evaluate the desirability of employer participation in administration, an objective norm was available in the form of the unemployment insurance law. "Desirability" could be given a meaningful definition in terms of whether employer participation helped or hindered the attainment of the objectives of the law. But here the issue is the desirability of the law itself. What norms are available for evaluating whatever effect experience rating may have on the law? At this level, the appropriate norms are the systems of social values, only once removed from the absolute values of philosophy and theology, upon which each society builds its social structures.

In the area of disqualification provisions, where experience rating probably has its chief effect, a number of prior attitudes are likely to provide the mediate norms of evaluation. On the positive side there are the widely accepted principles that the individual should be free of legal constraint in choosing his way of making a living and that welfare programs (programs established to aid persons in difficulty) should be interpreted liberally. The acceptance of these principles places the burden of proof on whoever argues for the desirability of stricter disqualification provisions.

On the negative side, two other social judgments are relevant to the task of evaluation. One is society's judgment on the amount of "abuse" in the program. Polls taken in the United States have uniformly found that the general populace was under the impression that claimant abuse in unemployment insurance was widespread. A 1970 survey of public opinion by the Canadian government found that the most frequently mentioned desirable change in the unemployment insurance program was "reduce the possibilities of people to cheat" [115, p. 8]. Although it probably is exaggerated, this public attitude must be considered in assessing the desirability of employer participation in legislation. One long-experienced state administrator gave as his main reason for favoring experience rating that indirectly it results in more liberal benefits. He meant that the willingness of legislators to provide more liberal benefits will always be in some proportion to the effectiveness of administration in controlling what the public considers "abuse."

A second and more fundamental value judgment that enters into the evaluation of this effect of experience rating is one's judgment of the "proper" balance of power to be maintained between labor and management. Rubinow early remarked on "the very close connection of the question of unemployment with the entire matter of the struggle between the employer and labor, and the grave problems raised by state intervention in the struggle" [119, p. 24]. As explained in Chapter 9, unemployment insurance differs from the other social security programs in being more closely intertwined with labor-management tensions because it is more closely linked to the competitive market. To have a competitive market and a free economy it is necessary to allow for the possibility of unemployed resources. To allow for the possible unemployment of the labor resource it is necessary to set some limits on unemployment benefits. One of the essential limits is provided by disqualification provisions. Hence one's evaluation of the effect of experience rating on disqualifications will be critically influenced by one's judgment of the broader issue of employee/employer relationships and the role played in that relationship by the possibility of unemployment. This broader issue is obviously outside the scope of the present investigation, but anyone who ventures on an evaluation of experience rating must have made a prior judgment on the proper balance to be maintained between labor and management.

It would help greatly toward an evaluation of the effect of experience rating on legislation if there were available more information on the results produced by the existing disqualification provisions. But this area has not yet been adequately researched.

Stabilization of Employment

Size of Effect

As explained in Chapter 10, experience rating is related to the goal of unemployment prevention through three of its effects—on the allocation of resources, on the business cycle, and on the policies of management. Although all three are genuine forms of employment stabilization, the term, unless otherwise specified, usually refers to the management effect, that is, to the incentive provided by experience rating for the manager of a firm to avoid layoffs.

Three formal studies have attempted to measure this effect. The results, summarized in Chapter 10, are generally similar. It would seem that about one-quarter of the firms surveyed, having about one-third of the covered employees, were influenced to some appreciable degree by the incentive of experience rating. The remaining three-quarters of the firms, with two-thirds of the covered employees, were affected by the incentive very little or not at all—either because they were already stable or because the cost of stabilization would have outweighed any gain of lower unemployment insurance taxes. All three studies emphasized the uncertainty of their findings and the difficulty of arriving at firmer estimates.

The chief limitation on the extent to which experience rating may be expected to provide an incentive for stabilization is simply that most unemployment insurance costs are not entirely within the control of the firm. Most layoffs are occasioned by economic forces that to some extent are outside the individual employer's control. The predictable differences in cost rates and tax rates between the various industries are primarily explainable not by differences in managerial skill but simply by differences in the economic activities involved.

The individual employer's control over his unemployment insurance costs is further restricted by limits on experience rating. As shown in Chapter 5, the unemployment insurance tax system is far from completely experience-rated. The tie between an employer's stabilization efforts and his tax rate is thus weakened, with a consequent weakening of the incentive to stabilize employment. This factor, or course, admits of considerable modification. If desired, the degree of experience rating could be increased. If the degree of experience rating were increased enough, some patterns of employment that are thought to be fixed would be found to be changeable.

Besides its direct financial impact, experience rating has the psychological effect of focusing attention on the prevention of unemployment. Other costs of unemployment may more easily be overlooked, especially if responsibility for them is diffused, but the unemployment insurance tax is a distinct cost for which the employer must write a check and which is directly traceable to one cause, unemployment. Most observers and all three of the stabilization studies emphasize this aspect of the experience-rated tax.[7]

In the case of large firms, this psychological impact of experience rating is frequently diminished by a diffusion of responsibility. Large firms operate through separate departments, such as finance, accounting, sales, production and personnel. The stabilization of employment is a function of all these departments but is the specific obligation of none of them. Each department is open to the moral hazard of ignoring the impact of its actions on the corporation's tax rate and of using unemployment benefits as a costless way of achieving its own objectives more easily.[8] The only effective guards against this development are internal experience rating, or the establishment of a centralized unemployment insurance unit, or, what is roughly the same, the hiring of a service company.

The numerous examples given in Chapter 10 help to make more concrete this generalized and theoretical description of the potential of experience rating for influencing employment stabilization. While such examples do not represent employer practice generally, they serve as a reminder (1) that experience rating is a force constantly at work, like gravity, adding to a firm's incentive to avoid unemployment and (2) that at least in some circumstances this force has a perceptible effect. The unemployment insurance tax, experience-rated, is thus a constant pressure working throughout the economy punishing (mildly) businessmen who become careless or who are simply inefficient in their use of manpower.

Desirability of Effect

The New Emphasis was and continues to be a good emphasis. Since the time of Justice Louis D. Brandeis much progress has been made and much more remains to be done in the prevention of unemployment. Like an infectious disease, unemployment is containable only by a policy of continuous attention and effort. In this unending struggle to lessen unemployment, unemployment benefits can be a hindrance as well as a help. The availability of unemployment benefits constitutes a "moral hazard" for the employer, inviting him to accept

7. This is the reason for the strong statement by Marion Folsom regarding the attention businessmen accord the unemployment insurance tax (p. 254).

8. One of the reasons that Russia has shown a new interest in a wider use of the profit motive has been the tendency of plant managers to hoard labor. When surplus labor is costless, from the viewpoint of the plant, managers hold on to workers as insurance against possible increased workloads. The result is a large number of partially employed workers and a resultant decrease in labor productivity.

more unemployment than he otherwise would. Experience rating turns this hindrance into a help, giving the employer an incentive to avoid unemployment.

The objection used to be raised that the attainment of stability through experience rating tends to divide the labor force into two groups—the steadily employed and the steadily unemployed. Popular in the depression years, this argument is rarely heard today except as directed specifically to the use of overtime. Experience rating may encourage the use of overtime, but whether this is desirable or undesirable depends on the circumstances of each concrete situation. It would seem that the excessive use of overtime (however such excess is defined) is better controlled by increasing the price of overtime than by eliminating a possible source of needed stability.

All three of the stabilization studies reviewed in Chapter 10 examined the charge that because of experience rating employers artificially manipulated their employment patterns and achieved, not genuine employment stabilization, but simply a form of tax avoidance. All three studies encountered instances of such manipulation, but found them to be rare.

It may be concluded that the effect of experience rating on the prevention of unemployment, while minor as compared to other economic forces, is nevertheless significant and very desirable. If this were the system's only effect, it would constitute a solid reason for having experience rating.

Timing of the Tax

Size of Effect

As was explained in Chapter 11, the effect of experience rating on the business cycle is both small and uncertain. Hence it is not a major factor in the social debate over the desirability of experience rating. Experience rating does not stand or fall by reason of its effect on the business cycle. It would be hard to find a historical situation in which its impact on the business cycle was an important factor in any decision affecting experience rating.

Desirability of Effect

In the early years of the program it was frequently assumed that the effect of experience rating was to aggravate the business cycle and was therefore undesirable. However, a number of studies made of the postwar period found that the movement of the experience-rated unemployment insurance tax was nearly always countercyclical, especially during downswings, when a countercyclical impact is particularly important. During almost all recessions, the average tax has fallen or at least not risen significantly. The timing pattern produced by experience rating has been clearly countercyclical and therefore desirable.

On the macro level—the level of the total economy—the difference between an experience-rated tax and a uniform variable tax is probably not significant. That is, a uniform tax would probably perform as well as the experience-rated tax has performed. But on the micro level—the level of the individual firm—an experience-rated tax has a distinct advantage over a variable uniform tax. Experience rating can and usually does adapt the timing patterns of the tax to the economic changes experienced by the individual firm. Since firms vary greatly in their individual patterns of development, this is a clear timing advantage of experience rating. Of all the systems of experience rating, the reserve-ratio system will usually have the most desirable timing pattern whether on the macro level or on the micro level.

Solvency of the Fund

Size of the Effect

As explained in Chapter 2, the effect of experience rating on solvency is largely a spurious issue. Any amount needed for benefits, and hence for solvency, may be raised as well by an experience-rated tax as by a uniform tax. The issue in experience rating is not the size of the average state tax but only its distribution among the taxpayers. However, to the extent that a tax system is only partially experience-rated—that is, to the extent that it provides for non-charged and ineffectively charged benefits—solvency requires that there be a source of funds other than that triggered by the experience of the individual firm. Of the various ways of providing such funds, the Common Account is perhaps the least incompatible with experience rating insofar as this device increases the visibility of the deficit created by the operations of some firms and requires such firms to make an additional contribution.

Desirability of Effect

If the device of the Common Account or one of its many equivalents is used, any undesirable effect of experience rating on solvency is practically eliminated. There remains only the desirable effect of a degree of automatic adjustment in the tax inflow to balance the benefit outflow. A somewhat greater degree of automaticity can be achieved with experience rating than without it. The judgment on the net effect of experience rating on solvency must therefore be that it is desirable—but not important.

A Last Look

Looking Back

The diagram below is a distant, hill-top view of the terrain traversed in the preceding chapters. While such a view does not substitute for the detailed, painstaking mapping provided by the separate chapters, and may be used safely only by one who recalls the many distinctions and qualifications applying to all the diagram's monosyllabic answers, it serves a useful function. It enables one to see at a glance the principal answers to be returned to the twin questions that guided the exploration: Are the effects produced by experience rating of sufficient importance to be worth consideration? In their net impact, are these effects desirable?

Effect on	Sizable?	Desirable?
1. Allocation	Yes	Yes
2. Administration	Yes	Yes
3. Legislation	Disqualifications: Yes	?
	Other: ?	?
4. Stabilization	Perhaps	Yes
5. Timing	Macro: ?	Yes
	Micro: Yes	Yes
6. Solvency	No	Yes

In general, the effects of experience rating are sizable. The tax differentials produced by experience rating belong among that category of costs which are too small to be decisive but not so small as to be disregarded. In general, also, its effects are desirable. The effects are appropriate to our kind of unemployment insurance system, in which benefits are proportioned to wages and funds are obtained almost exclusively from employers. The effects are appropriate, also, to our kind of economy, in which the market is the main mechanism for the allocation of resources.

The above diagram groups the effects in a rough order of magnitude and desirability. The effects on the *allocation* of resources and on employer participation in *administration* are among the larger and the more clearly desirable effects. The effects on *legislation* and on *stabilization* are somewhat less sizable; also, while the effect on stabilization is clearly desirable, some of the effects on legislation are open to dispute. The effects on the *timing* of the tax and on the *solvency* of the fund are the least important; but they are clearly desirable insofar as they occur.

In the course of this investigation, I wrote a personal, confidential letter to each of the state directors of unemployment insurance asking them the simple question: If your state were free to choose between a uniform tax and an experience-rated tax, which would you hope your state would choose? Thirty-nine of the directors had a definite opinion which they were willing to express. Of these, thirty-four (87 percent) replied that they would want their states to choose experience rating. These thirty-four states accounted for 73 percent of total covered employment. The directors of the other five states, which accounted for 16 percent of covered employment, expressed a preference for a uniform tax.[9] Thus the great majority of the program's directors, who combine

9. One of the five gave as his chief reason that experience rating is too hard on small firms; another, that most unemployment is not within the control of the individual em-

in a unique way technical and political awareness, were in accord with the general conclusion reached in this investigation, that, on balance, experience rating seems desirable.

Looking Forward

A number of future developments in the unemployment insurance program and in the labor market are likely to affect the desirability of experience rating, mostly by increasing it. Six of these developments are worth noting, three in the unemployment insurance program and three in the labor market.

Currently (1971), the unemployment insurance program is in the process of being further liberalized. Coverage is being expanded to include the smallest firms and also nonprofit institutions. The potential duration of benefits provided by the system continues to grow on both ends—as the waiting period is shortened or eliminated and as the number of available weeks is increased. As of January 1972, all states provided a maximum duration of at least twenty-six weeks, and nine states provided a longer duration.

The continued growth in the potential duration of benefits raises a problem of principle for experience rating. For how long after the employment relationship has been severed should the resulting unemployment benefits be considered the responsibility of the individual employer, rather than of the economy as a whole? The problem is presented in its most acute form in connection with the "extended" benefits that have accompanied all recessions since 1958. During the most recent recession, benefits were made available in some states for as long as fifty-two weeks. The extended benefits provided by the employment security amendment of 1970 are to be financed half by the federal government and half by the states. The "emergency benefits" of 1971–72 are to be financed entirely by a federal payroll tax. The federal taxes are not experience-rated but as of March 1972, twenty-eight states with 52 percent of the covered employment had arranged to charge their share of extended benefits to the accounts of individual firms and thus make them a part of the state's regular experience rating system.

Even if extended benefits continue to be financed by a payroll tax levied on employers (itself a debatable issue), the propriety of using experience rating becomes increasingly questionable. Most students of the program feel an unease with the automatic extension of the traditional tax structure to cover these new developments. A growing body of opinion holds that for benefits extending beyond a specified limit—perhaps twenty-six or thirty-nine weeks—a different source of revenue and a different type of tax would be more appropriate. The average benefit check, which has fluctuated between 30 and 40 percent of statewide average weekly wages during the past thirty years, seems likely to

---

ployer; a third that the difference in cost(taxes) between individual firms is too small to be worth the administrative bother; the remaining two did not give reasons.

increase in the future. Pressure in this direction will come from four sources: the example set by those states which have recently raised their maximum substantially, a steadily growing sentiment for a federal standard regulating the maximum benfit, the operation of the more liberal private programs of supplemental unemployment benefits, and the inauguration of some kind of universal guaranteed family income plan. For unemployment insurance to maintain its favored position vis-à-vis welfare programs, it will have to maintain a substantial benefit differential.

Enacted in 1970, H.R. 14705 provides a new federal standard that limits the states in their use of the severe penalty consisting of cancellation of benefits. The 1971 decision of the United States Supreme Court in the *Java* case (Chapter 6) would seem to eliminate most of the delays in the payment of benefits occasioned by employer appeals. This development removes one of the chief sources of criticism of employer participation in administration.

Since these changes in the unemployment insurance program will make for increased costs, they tend to increase the importance of the allocative and stabilizing effects of experience rating. They will also tend to increase the propriety of employer participation in administration and legislation.

In 1972 the tax base will increase from $3,000 to $4,200. It is not possible to predict how this change will affect experience rating. In principle it is possible to readjust the tax schedule so as to get about the same total income while increasing, decreasing, or maintaining the existing degree of experience rating.[10] It seems probable that the net effect of the increase in the tax base will be to increase the degree of experience rating nationally, but such an effect may not apply in all states.

The labor force also shows several trends that have significance for experience rating. Women workers, service workers, and part-time workers are becoming a larger proportion of the total labor force. All of these are traditionally sources of some administrative problems for unemployment insurance. The growth in "fringe benefits" (especially vacation, early retirement, severance, and SUB plans) will also have a tendency to increase the administrative problems of unemployment insurance. Both developments will increase the importance and probably the desirability of employer participation in administration.

The growth in manpower programs in aid of the disadvantaged worker has an implication for experience rating that is just being recognized. As the public employment service has become more involved in these programs, it has found itself in many states—for example, in Ohio [162]—giving less attention to "regular" workers and therefore filling a smaller proportion of the open jobs in the competitive market. Never very effective in applying the job test, the public employment service may become even less so and may need even more the

10. New York, for example, will readjust its tax schedule so as to (1) obtain roughly the same income in 1972 as would have been produced by the smaller tax base and (2) increase the degree of experience rating in the system.

assistance represented by employer participation in administration. Such employer participation may also hasten the return of a full-functioning employment service for all claimants.

One final development may be noted—the growing use of the computer for the program's administrative chores. This development has significance for the additional administrative cost occasioned by experience rating. It is difficult to obtain a reasonably reliable estimate of this additional cost. The direct, measurable cost seems to be in the neighborhood of 4 percent of total unemployment insurance administrative expenses, but there are additional indirect costs connected with experience rating which cannot easily be isolated for measurement. However, several long-experienced state administrators have said that the task of administering experience rating has become progressively easier with the growing use of more mechanized equipment. With the advent of the computer, this trend is being greatly accelerated. (It will be recalled from Chapter 12 that General Motors gave the same answer to a question about the costs of the corporation's system of internal experience rating.)

Degree of experience rating. To quote from the conclusion of Chapter 1: "Probably the simplest and most satisfactory way of conceiving the focus of this study is to assume the position of the state legislator who must decide whether to increase or decrease the degree of experience rating in his state's law." If such a legislator agrees with the conclusion of this study that the net effect of experience rating seems to be generally desirable, and if he further concludes that this general proposition applies to his own state, he is likely to judge that the degree of experience rating in his state should be retained or increased.

Among the steps open to a state wishing to increase the degree of experience rating are the following: (1) Adopt the reserve-ratio system if another system is currently in operation. (2) Raise the maximum tax rate.[11] (3) Lower the minimum rate to zero. This would avoid any "zone of indifference" at the lower end of the tax schedule.[12] (4) Lessen or eliminate noncharged benefits. (5) Increase the sensitivity of the tax schedule by providing that a smaller change in the employer's reserve will result in a change in his tax rate. (6) Improve the forms

11. A higher maximum tax becomes politically more feasible in proportion as the approach to it is made more gradual. A state law might provide, for example, that after a firm's tax rate reached 3.5 percent, it would not be increased by more than 0.5 percent of taxable wages in any one year. If the maximum were then placed at 6.0 or 7.0 percent, a firm would have five or seven years in which to adjust its operations to reflect this growing cost.

12. The establishment of a Common Account should facilitate the adoption of a zero minimum rate, since the Common Account tax assures that all firms, even those with a zero tax rate, contribute to making up the deficit resulting from noncharged benefits and ineffectively charged benefits. (This contribution is in addition to the interest earned by the reserves of the firms with low tax rates.) The Common Account also increases the visibility of such a deficit and provides a fairly accurate measure of the extent to which the system is *not* experience-rated.

that are provided for the use of employers in describing the conditions under which the claimant was separated from employment. Many deputies and referees who responded to the questionnaire (Chapter 6) touched on this point. (7) Hold training sessions to acquaint employers with the unemployment insurance law and to instruct them in the proper use of the forms. (8) For firms that request it, provide benefit charges on the basis of the firm's operating units. Such information facilitates control of claims and is essential to any firm wishing to install internal experience rating. (9) Provide weekly or monthly notice of benefit charges. (10) Grant to service companies the full power to represent their clients.

Looking Within

Experience rating stems from and strengthens the market mentality. It conforms to and confirms a system which makes each state responsible for its own costs, which draws its revenues almost entirely from a tax on covered employers, which restricts benefits to those employees whose employers are required to make contributions, and which proportions those benefits to the claimant's wages. The effect of experience rating on the market mentality may be one of the more significant effects of the system. It is quite possible that experience rating is something like a cement that holds this entire structure together.[13]

The chief significance of experience rating may lie as much in its roots as in its fruits. Where experience rating may begin to have something like major significance is in its relationship to the deep tension that exists in every society between the individualistic and the socialistic approaches to the solution of problems. Experience rating epitomizes the individualistic, competitive approach. By definition, it is the distilled essence of individualism. There is no mistaking its import: its whole being says, "individual responsibility."[14] The deepest meaning of a shift away from experience rating would be that our society's values had shifted along the scale from individual responsibility in the direction of social responsibility.

In recent years, the general individualistic/socialistic issue has developed in a way that has particular relevance for experience rating. A debate has arisen over the relative merits of (1) a single, universal program of aid available to everyone simply because he is a citizen and (2) a set of differentiated programs, some of which would provide earned benefits while others would provide free gifts, or "welfare." Although up to the present our society has chosen to distinguish between categories of need, as reflected in the difference between programs of

13. Some such judgment on the key role of experience rating seems to underlie the following statement of Eveline Burns, made in 1945: "The most significant of the obstacles to the adoption of a consistent unemployment insurance system which would have some prospect of stability, because reflecting social and economic realities, is the existence of experience rating" [40, p. 12].
14. The reference here is to the experience-rating principle (experience rating as such) and not to its historical forms, all of which are mixtures of experience rating and other principles.

social insurance and programs of social assistance, it is a choice that has often been challenged.

Some years ago, when Canada was making a thorough review of its social security system, the government actuary, A. D. Watson, spoke specifically on this question and advised the Canadian government to retain the distinction between social insurance and social assistance:

> And there may be some who, with the best intentions, are anxious to blur the distinctions between social insurance and the other social instrumentalities, including social assistance, in the mistaken notion that by so doing social objectives may be attained the more quickly and effectively. As against such views it is sobering to recall that in the administration of justice it is necessary to have distinct courts and procedures for different purposes, and that commericial banks, admirable as they may be to serve the current purposes of business, trade and commerce, are unsuited to answer the long term needs for credit. Special banks have to be organized for specialized functions. Hence, one may safely conjecture that, throughout the whole economic, industrial and social system, separate and distinct instrumentalities for separate and distinct purposes, co-ordinated and functioning side by side, will probably be found essential to sound progress for a long time to come [163, p. 15].

Without attempting to judge the soundness of Watson's analysis, it is sufficient to point out that the future of experience rating will depend very much on how this choice is made. The further we move in the direction of the undifferentiated demogrant, available to everyone who belongs to the "demos," the less sense experience rating will make. On the other hand, if we choose to maintain a set of income maintenance programs that are closely geared to the market and operate like deferred wages, with benefits proportioned to wages and with taxes levied solely on payrolls and employers, unemployment insurance as presently constituted will be a necessary part of such a system and experience rating is likely to be considered a desirable part of unemployment insurance.

Tables

Table A–1. Type of Experience-Rating Plan Provided for in State Unemployment Insurance Laws, for Selected Years[a]

State	1938	1939	1940	1941	1945	1948	1949	1951	1954	1955	1958	1960	1962	1964	Plan in 1969	Percent of U.S. coverage 1969
Total–states with plans	40	39	39	38	45	51	51	51	51	50	50	51	51	51	51	99.6[b]
Number of states by plan:																
Reserve ratio (RR)	32	26	26	23	28	29	30	31	32	32	32	32	32	32	32	66.0
Benefit ratio (BR)		2	2	3	7	6	6	6	5	5	5	6	6	7	9	18.5
Benefit-wage ratio (BWR)		5	5	8	8	8	7	5	6	6	6	6	6	6	5	10.6
Payroll decline (PD)						5	5	5	5	4	4	4	4	4	3	2.3
Compensable separations (CS)		1	1	1	1	1	1	1	1	1	1	1	1	1	1	2.0
Other[c]					1	2	2	2	2	2	2	2	2	1	1	0.2
Plan undetermined (PU)	8	5	5	3												
No provision (NP)	11	12	12	13	6					1	1					
Alabama	PU			BWR											BWR	1.1
Alaska	PU			NP		PD						PD			PD	0.2
Arizona	RR														RR	0.7
Arkansas	RR									NP					RR	0.6
California	RR														RR	10.9
Colorado	RR														RR	0.9
Connecticut	RR	CS													CS	2.0
Delaware	RR	BWR													BWR	0.3
District of Columbia	PU		BR		RR										RR	0.7
Florida	RR														BR	2.4

State								
Georgia	NP					RR	RR	1.8
Hawaii	NP	RR					RR	0.4
Idaho	RR	NP					RR	0.2
Illinois	RR	BWR					BWR	6.8
Indiana	RR						RR	2.8
Iowa	RR						RR	1.0
Kansas	RR						RR	0.7
Kentucky	RR						RR	1.1
Louisiana	PU		NP			RR RR	RR	1.3
Maine	NP						RR	0.4
Maryland	NP		BR				BR	1.6
Massachusetts	NP	BWR			RR	RR	RR	3.2
Michigan	RR	BR			RR		RR	5.5
Minnesota	RR	BWR	BR				BR	1.8
Mississippi	NP		BR	PD			BR	0.6
Missouri	RR						RR	2.2
Montana	PU	NP		c			c	0.2
Nebraska	RR						RR	0.5
Nevada	PU		BR	RR			RR	0.3
New Hampshire	RR						RR	0.3
New Jersey	RR						RR	4.1
New Mexico	RR		c			RR	RR	0.3
New York	NP	RR					RR	12.0
North Carolina	NP						RR	2.0
North Dakota	RR						RR	0.1
Ohio	RR		BWR				RR	6.1
Oklahoma	RR					BR	BWR	0.8
Oregon	RR			PD			BR	1.0
Pennsylvania[d]	NP		BWR	PD		BR	BR[d]	6.3
Rhode Island	NP					RR	RR	0.5

Table A-1. (Continued)

State	1938	1939	1940	1941	1945	1948	1949	1951	1954	1955	1958	1960	1962	1964	Plan in 1969	Percent of U.S. coverage 1969
South Carolina	RR														RR	0.9
South Dakota	RR														RR	0.1
Tennessee	RR			NP	RR										RR	1.5
Texas	RR	BWR													BR	4.5
Utah	RR	BR	NP			PD									PD	0.4
Vermont	PU		RR												BR	0.2
Virginia	NP		BWR												BWR	1.6
Washington[e]	PU		NP			PD									PD[e]	1.7
West Virginia	RR														RR	0.7
Wisconsin	RR														RR	2.2
Wyoming	RR	PU			BR										BR	0.1

Sources: Plans: 1938 and 1939—"Current Experience Rating Research," Bureau of Employment Security, April 1, 1940, p. 65; 1940 through 1969—"Comparison of State Unemployment Compensation Laws," Bureau of Employment Security. Coverage: "Unemployment Insurance Statistics," Bureau of Employment Security, February 1968, p. 9.

[a]The years selected are those for which source material was available from the Bureau of Employment Security, as indicated above. Where a change of plan is indicated, the new plan is listed under the year of the "Comparison" in which it was first reported.

[b]Puerto Rico (0.4 percent), which did not have an experience rating plan as of 1969, is not included.

[c]Montana: Payroll decline, duration of liability, and ratio of benefits to contributions, 1948–69. New York: Payroll decline and age factor, 1945–47; payroll decline and benefit-wage ratio, 1948–50; payroll decline and reserve ratio, 1951–62.

[d]Pennsylvania in 1969 combined reserve ratio with a benefit ratio system.

[e]In 1970 Washington adopted a new experience rating plan, which combines payroll decline with a benefit ratio system.

Table A-2. Years for Which States Suspended Experience Rating, 1950-66

Year	Alaska	Massachusetts	Nevada	New York	Oregon	Pennsylvania	Rhode Island	Washington	West Virginia	Wyoming	Totals by year
1950	[a]			X			X	X			3
1951	[a]	X		X			X				3
1952	X[a]	X					X				3
1953	X	X					X				3
1954	X						X				2
1955	[b]						X				1
1956	[b]						X				1
1957	[b]						X				1
1958	[b]				X[c]		X	X[d]			3
1959	[b]				X[c]	X	X	X			4
1960	[b]				X		X	X	X		4
1961		X[e]			X		X	X	X		5
1962					X		X	X	X		4
1963			X		X		X	X	X	X	6
1964			X				X	X		X	4
1965							X	X			2
1966											0
Totals by state	3	4	2	2	6	1	16	9	4	2	49

Sources: Handbook of Unemployment Insurance Financial Data, BES No. U-73, 1946-67, Bureau of Employment Security; The Labor Market and Employment Security, June 1951, July 1952, December 1953, September 1954, April 1955, May 1956, November 1959, March 1962, Bureau of Employment Security; Unemployment Insurance Review, December 1964, November-December 1965, February 1968, Bureau of Employment Security; Variable Tax Rate Structures and Unemployment Insurance Financing in Alaska, Alaska Employment Security Commission, January 1959.

[a] Alaska's suspension of experience rating, originally scheduled to become effective as of July 1, 1950, was overruled by the courts and did not become effective until July 1, 1952.

[b] Alaska repealed experience rating January 1, 1955, and restored it October 1, 1960.

[c] Oregon suspended experience rating for the last three quarters of 1958 and 1959.

[d] Washington suspended experience rating as of July 1, 1958.

[e] Massachusetts suspended experience rating for the latter half of 1961.

Table A-3. Average Benefit-Cost Rates, 1940–68, and
Average Insured Unemployment Rates, 1947–67, by State,
Ranked by Cost Rate

State	Percent of covered employment in U.S. June 1967	Benefit[a] cost rate	Rank	Insured unemployment[b] rate	Rank
United States	100.0	1.0		3.9	
Alaska	0.1	2.1	1	8.6	1
Rhode Island	0.6	1.7	2	6.2	2
California	9.6	1.4	3	4.9	9
New Jersey	3.8	1.4	4	4.7	13
Washington	1.6	1.3	5	5.5	4
Nevada	0.3	1.3	6	4.1	22
Massachusetts	3.4	1.3	7	4.4	16
North Dakota	0.2	1.3	8	3.8	23
New York	11.2	1.3	9	4.7	14
Oregon	1.0	1.2	10	5.2	8
Idaho	0.3	1.2	11	4.2	21
Montana	0.3	1.2	12	4.3	18
Maine	0.5	1.2	13	5.8	3
Pennsylvania	6.6	1.2	14	4.7	15
Kentucky	1.2	1.2	15	5.4	6
Vermont	0.2	1.1	16	4.2	19
Michigan	4.7	1.1	17	4.2	20
Tennessee	1.8	1.0	18	5.2	7
West Virginia	0.7	1.0	19	5.5	5
Mississippi	0.7	1.0	20	4.7	12
Wyoming	0.1	1.0	21	2.6	41
New Hampshire	0.4	1.0	22	4.8	11
Maryland	1.8	1.0	23	3.2	32
Louisiana	1.4	1.0	24	3.6	26
Arkansas	0.8	1.0	25	4.8	10
Connecticut	1.9	0.9	26	3.5	27
Utah	0.4	0.9	27	3.1	36
Alabama	1.3	0.9	28	4.3	17
Hawaii	0.4	0.9	29	3.2	33
North Carolina	2.4	0.8	30	3.8	24
New Mexico	0.4	0.8	31	2.8	39
Minnesota	1.8	0.8	32	3.3	29

Table A-3. (Continued)

State	Percent of covered employment in U.S. June 1967	Benefit[a] cost rate	Rank	Insured unemployment[b] rate	Rank
Ohio	5.6	0.8	33	2.9	38
Oklahoma	0.9	0.8	34	3.8	25
Kansas	0.8	0.8	35	2.5	43
Wisconsin	2.2	0.8	36	2.6	42
Illinois	6.3	0.8	37	3.2	34
South Carolina	1.1	0.8	38	3.2	31
Georgia	2.0	0.7	39	3.1	35
Missouri	2.3	0.7	40	3.4	28
Arizona	0.6	0.7	41	3.3	30
Delaware	0.3	0.7	42	2.4	44
Indiana	2.7	0.6	43	2.8	40
South Dakota	0.2	0.6	44	2.2	45
Nebraska	0.6	0.6	45	1.9	47
Colorado	0.9	0.6	46	1.8	51
Florida	2.5	0.6	47	3.1	37
Iowa	1.1	0.5	48	1.9	49
District of Columbia	0.7	0.5	49	1.8	50
Virginia	1.9	0.4	50	2.1	46
Texas	4.7	0.4	51	1.9	48
Puerto Rico	0.7	c	c	c	c

Sources: Percent of covered employment: *Unemployment Insurance Statistics*, February 1968, U.S. Department of Labor, Manpower Administration. Benefit-cost rate calculated from figures taken from Ohio Bureau of Employment Services, Division of Research and Statistics, Table, *Benefits Paid Plus Reserves for Future Benefits per $100 of Total Payroll Covered under State Unemployment Compensation Laws Ranked by State, 1940-1968* (Columbus, Ohio, 8-29-69). Insured unemployment rate calculated from *Handbook of Unemployment Insurance Financial Data*, U.S. Department of Labor, Bureau of Employment Security.

[a]Benefit payments as percent of *total* covered payroll.

[b]Average weekly insured unemployment as percent of average monthly covered employment.

[c]Puerto Rico data excluded.

Table A-4. Taxable Wage Base, All States, Year 1969[a]

State	$3,000 base	Above $3,000	Dates of increases or decreases
Alabama	X		
Alaska		7,200	1955-3,600; 1957-4,200; 1960-7,200
Arizona		3,600	1965-3,600
Arkansas	X		
California[b]		3,800	1960-3,600; 1962-3,800; 1966-4,100; 1967-3,800
Colorado	X		
Connecticut[b]		3,600	1968-3,600
Delaware		3,600	1955-3,600
District of Columbia	X		
Florida	X		
Georgia	X		
Hawaii[b]		5,500	1962-3,600; 1965-4,200; 1966-4,300 1967-4,600; 1968-4,800; 1969-5,500
Idaho		3,600	1963-3,600
Illinois	X		
Indiana	X		
Iowa	X		
Kansas	X		
Kentucky	X		
Louisiana	X		
Maine	X		
Maryland	X		
Massachusetts		3,600	1962-3,600
Michigan		3,600	1963-3,600
Minnesota		4,800	1966-4,800
Mississippi	X		
Missouri	X		
Montana	X		
Nebraska	X		
Nevada		3,800	1954-3,600; 1965-3,800
New Hampshire	X		
New Jersey		3,600	1968-3,600
New Mexico	X		

Table A-4. (Continued)

State	$3,000 base	Above $3,000	Dates of increases or decreases
New York	X		
North Carolina	X		
North Dakota[b]		3,800	1968-3,300; 1969-3,800
Ohio	X		
Oklahoma	X		
Oregon		3,600	1956-3,600; 1960-3,800;1965-3,600
Pennsylvania		3,600	1964-3,600
Rhode Island		3,600	1956-3,600
South Carolina	X		
South Dakota	X		
Tennessee		3,300	1963-3,300
Texas	X		
Utah		4,200	1964-4,200
Vermont		3,600	1964-3,600
Virginia	X		
Washington	X		
West Virginia		3,600	1962-3,600
Wisconsin		3,600	1966-3,600
Wyoming		3,600	1968-3,600
Totals	29	22	

Sources: *Handbook of Unemployment Insurance Financial Data*, and *Comparison of State Unemployment Insurance Laws*, BES No. U-141, U.S. Department of Labor, Bureau of Employment Security.

[a]Beginning in 1972, the minimum for all states becomes $4,200.

[b]Taxable wage base is $3,800 when total revenue equals total disbursements during any twelve-month period ending on computation date, $4,100 when total disbursements exceed total revenue (California); increases to $3,900 if ratio of fund balance to three-year payroll is 3.5 percent or more (Connecticut); taxable wage base computed annually at 90 percent (Hawaii) and 70 percent (North Dakota), of state's average annual wage for the one-year period ending June 30.

Table A - 5. Eleven-year Average Benefit-Cost Rates,[a] Tax Rates,[b] and Cost/Tax Ratios, Selected States, Years 1957-67, by Industry Divisions

State	All industry divisions[c]			Agriculture, forestry and fisheries			Mining, including quarrying			Construction		
	Cost rate	Tax rate	Cost/tax ratio	Cost rate	Tax rate	Cost/tax ratio	Cost rate	Tax rate	Cost/tax ratio	Cost rate	Tax rate	Co ta rat
California[c]	2.7	2.6	105.1	7.1	3.0	235.4	2.3	2.6	86.7	5.5	3.1	17
Maine[c]	2.0	–	–	4.3	–	–	5.4	–	–	4.5	–	–
Massachusetts[d]	2.4	2.2	106.2	–	–	–	–	–	–	6.2	3.0	21
New Jersey[e]	–	–	99.3	–	–	236.6	–	–	104.0	–	–	14
New York[f]	2.5	2.5	98.8	–	–	–	–	–	–	5.7	3.2	17
Ohio[d]	1.8	1.7	106.9	5.6	2.4	232.8	2.9	2.0	148.3	5.5	2.9	18
Oregon[g]	1.7	2.0	87.2	–	–	–	–	2.2	105.1	3.2	2.4	13
Pennsylvania	2.4	2.7	88.4	–	–	–	6.7	3.1	212.8	5.3	3.4	15
Utah[h]	1.0	1.0	108.3	–	–	–	1.0	0.8	120.2	2.8	1.4	20
Virginia	0.7	0.9	77.5	1.8	1.4	124.3	1.6	1.4	108.4	1.2	1.5	7
Washington[i]	2.1	2.4	86.6	8.6	2.5	347.9	3.1	2.4	129.5	3.7	2.5	14

Note: Cost rate = benefit payments as percent of taxable payrolls; tax rate = taxes as percent of taxable payrolls; cost/tax ratio = benefit payments as percent of taxes.

Sources: The data for benefit payments, taxable payrolls, and contributions, on which the rates shown this table were based, were derived mainly from periodic and special reports issued by the employment security agencies of the respective states. In some cases, where the data were not available in publish form, they were supplied by the agency as requested.

[a]Benefits include state-extended benefits paid in California; they exclude some $60 million of su benefits paid in Ohio in 1958-59 and the relatively minor amount paid in New York in 1959. They not include payments under the TUC and the TEUC programs.

[b]Tax rates include supplementary taxes not credited to employer reserves. No attempt was made adjust tax rates for the increases in FUTA taxes resulting from TUC and TEUC programs.

[c]The Standard Industrial Coding Manual on which distributions by industry were based was revised 1957, affecting the industrial distributions of benefits and taxes cited in this report. In the case industrial divisions, it is believed that the revisions have not significantly affected the eleven-year average California departs from the SIC in two minor ways not significant for the purpose of the table. Maine da were adapted to include in the manufacturing division benefits chargeable to multi-industry establis ments.

Manufacturing			Transportation, communication, and utilities			Wholesale and retail trade			Finance, insurance, and real estate			Services		
Cost rate	Tax rate	Cost/ tax ratio	Cost rate	Tax rate	Cost/ tax ratio	Cost rate	Tax rate	Cost/ tax ratio	Cost rate	Tax rate	Cost/ tax ratio	Cost rate	Tax rate	Cost/ tax ratio
.8	2.5	111.6	1.6	2.2	75.3	2.3	2.6	89.1	1.2	2.3	51.7	2.5	2.8	89.3
.2	–	–	1.0	–	–	1.0	–	–	0.5	–	–	1.6	–	–
.5	2.3	109.2	1.5	1.9	79.8	1.6	2.0	79.5	0.8	1.7	48.5	1.7	2.2	74.2
–	–	103.4	–	–	70.0	–	–	82.8	–	–	63.8	–	–	96.9
.2	2.6	122.6	1.4	2.1	66.7	1.7	2.4	68.3	0.9	2.0	43.1	1.9	2.6	73.9
.9	1.8	105.3	1.0	1.1	86.9	1.1	1.5	76.3	0.6	1.1	52.2	1.2	1.7	72.7
.1	2.1	102.6	0.8	1.7	49.0	1.1	1.9	58.7	0.6	1.8	34.0	1.3	2.0	64.4
.6	2.9	88.5	1.2	2.3	53.2	1.6	2.5	64.7	0.8	2.1	35.7	1.8	2.5	69.6
.9	0.8	110.8	0.4	0.8	56.4	0.8	1.0	84.0	0.5	0.9	54.3	1.1	1.2	95.7
.8	0.9	83.7	0.3	0.6	44.9	0.3	0.7	49.6	0.2	0.6	30.8	0.3	0.8	43.7
.2	2.4	91.6	1.5	2.4	61.5	1.7	2.4	71.0	1.2	2.4	48.5	1.7	2.4	70.3

[d]Massachusetts and Ohio pay dependents' allowances; they are included in benefit costs and in the computation of the cost/tax ratio.

[e]The ratio shown for New Jersey is for the period from January 1, 1939 (when payments began in that state), through 1966; taxes paid prior to that date have been included in the calculation of the ratio. Excluded were benefit costs of and contributions paid by establishments which, in June 1967, were no longer "active."

[f]For New York, the rates shown for the service division are inclusive of benefit costs and taxes relating to agriculture, forestry and fishing, mining (including quarrying), and miscellaneous other establishments not elsewhere classified."

[g]Data for Oregon covered the thirty-two-year period 1936 through 1967. Benefit payments began January 1, 1938; contributions prior to that date were included in the calculation of average tax rates and average cost/tax ratios.

[h]Data for Utah represent eight-year averages based on *total* wages for the years 1960 through 1967.

[i]Data for Washington based on benefits paid and cash contributions received during the years 1939 through 1967.

Table A-6. Benefit-Cost Rates,[a] Tax Rates,[b] and Cost/Tax Ratios,[c] Selected States, 1961[d] and 1967, by Industry Divisions

	All industries						Mining (including quarrying)					
	1961			1967			1961			1967		
State	Cost rate	Tax rate	Cost/ tax ratio	Cost rate	Tax rate	Cost/ tax ratio	Cost rate	Tax rate	Cost/ tax ratio	Cost rate	Tax rate	Cost/ tax ratio
All states	2.9	2.4	121.6	1.3	1.6	80.7	–	2.0	–	–	1.5	–
Alaska	2.9	2.8	91.4	2.1	2.8	59.9	4.0	2.9	102.5	1.5	3.1	40
Maine[e]	2.9	2.0	146.1	1.2	1.2	88.2	3.5	2.6	133.3	6.4	2.3	280
Massachusetts	3.2	2.6	108.3	1.7	2.1	80.0	–	–	–	–	–	–
Michigan[f]	2.4	3.0	81.6	1.3	1.6	83.7	5.6	3.1	182.3	2.3	1.8	127
Minnesota	2.4	1.6	146.5	0.7	1.3	57.2	8.9	2.7	344.0	2.9	2.5	117
Mississippi	2.5	2.0	125.7	0.8	0.9	83.6	2.5	2.0	122.5	0.6	1.0	62
Pennsylvania	4.2	3.3	125.6	1.0	2.5	39.8	11.6	3.7	324.2	1.8	3.2	55
Utah	1.8	1.4	125.9	1.5	1.5	99.3	2.2	1.3	163.6	1.2	1.3	93
Wisconsin	3.3	1.4	218.1	–	1.5	–	9.2	2.2	436.2	–	3.4	–

	Transportation, communication, and utilities						Wholesale and retail trade					
All states	–	1.9	–	–	1.3	–	–	2.1	–	–	1.5	–
Alaska	1.1	2.3	38.2	1.3	2.5	40.7	1.5	2.5	49.2	1.2	2.5	38
Maine[e]	1.4	1.6	86.7	0.6	0.9	71.5	1.5	1.8	84.3	0.5	1.1	44
Massachusetts	2.1	2.2	81.4	1.2	1.8	64.3	2.3	2.4	82.8	1.1	1.9	58
Michigan[f]	1.5	1.8	84.6	0.8	1.1	74.9	1.6	1.9	80.1	0.6	1.5	38
Minnesota	1.4	1.3	107.6	0.3	1.0	34.8	1.5	1.3	117.4	0.4	1.0	35
Mississippi	1.3	1.8	74.6	0.4	0.7	66.9	1.5	2.0	76.1	0.4	0.7	60
Pennsylvania	1.8	2.8	64.8	0.4	2.0	19.8	2.5	3.0	83.8	0.6	2.2	26
Utah	1.1	1.3	85.5	0.5	1.3	38.5	1.5	1.4	102.8	1.1	1.4	76
Wisconsin	1.7	0.9	192.1	–	1.2	–	1.2	1.0	115.4	–	1.2	–

Sources: The data in this table were derived mainly from periodic and special reports issued by the employment security agencies of the respective states. In some cases where the data were not available in published form they were supplied by the agency as requested. Rates for "all states" were obtained from U.S. Department of Labor, Bureau of Employment Security, *Unemployment Insurance Tax Rates by Industry*, 1962, 1967.

[a]Cost rate = benefit payments as percent of taxable payrolls. Benefits do not include payments under the TEUC program.

[b]Tax rate = taxes as percent of taxable payrolls. Tax rates include supplementary taxes not credited to employer reserves. No attempt was made to adjust tax rates for the increases in FUTA taxes resulting from the TUC and TEUC programs.

	Construction						Manufacturing					
	1961			1967			1961			1967		
	Cost rate	Tax rate	Cost/ tax ratio	Cost rate	Tax rate	Cost/ tax ratio	Cost rate	Tax rate	Cost/ tax ratio	Cost rate	Tax rate	Cost/ tax ratio
	–	2.9	–	–	2.5	–	–	2.5	–	–	1.6	–
	4.8	3.5	168.9	3.9	3.5	91.5	3.5	3.1	96.4	2.6	3.1	66.9
	7.0	2.6	265.2	3.3	2.4	143.5	3.2	2.0	160.6	1.3	1.3	95.2
	8.5	3.4	217.9	5.2	2.9	177.5	3.5	2.7	110.1	1.6	2.1	76.9
	8.9	3.9	230.2	3.6	3.0	120.9	2.3	3.6	65.2	1.4	1.4	101.5
	6.5	2.6	245.5	3.0	2.8	107.3	2.1	1.6	123.1	0.5	1.1	44.9
	5.2	2.5	207.6	1.5	1.9	76.9	3.0	2.0	149.8	0.9	0.9	98.6
	9.7	3.8	248.7	2.5	3.4	73.6	4.7	3.5	132.0	1.1	2.5	42.5
	3.8	1.8	204.9	5.1	2.1	243.3	1.7	1.3	129.5	1.3	1.4	89.6
	7.0	2.6	281.9	–	2.9	–	3.3	1.6	187.2	–	1.5	–

	Finance, insurance, and real estate						Services					
	–	1.9	–	–	1.2	–	–	2.4	–	–	1.8	–
	1.0	2.1	36.6	0.8	2.0	31.1	1.6	2.6	45.0	1.3	2.6	40.8
	0.8	1.7	48.4	0.2	0.8	28.6	2.4	2.2	112.7	0.9	1.6	55.5
	1.1	2.1	43.9	0.7	1.6	44.3	2.2	2.5	75.5	1.0	2.1	49.1
	0.5	1.4	35.7	0.3	1.1	27.6	2.0	2.3	89.6	0.8	1.8	45.6
	0.5	0.9	55.6	0.1	0.8	14.7	1.5	1.2	122.5	0.3	1.1	31.8
	0.5	1.6	31.4	0.1	0.4	31.3	1.2	2.0	63.5	0.5	0.8	59.7
	1.0	2.5	38.3	0.3	1.9	13.6	2.7	3.0	86.9	0.7	2.3	30.5
	0.8	1.4	59.6	0.7	1.3	49.2	1.7	1.6	105.7	1.4	1.6	87.7
	0.3	0.7	48.7	–	0.8	–	1.2	1.1	107.2	–	1.4	–

[c] Cost/tax ratio = benefit payments as percent of taxes.

[d] For 1961 the tax rates and cost/tax ratios shown have been based on 1962 tax data.

[e] Maine data were adapted to include in the manufacturing division benefits chargeable to multi-industry establishments.

f Cost rates for Michigan are based on benefits charged to active employer accounts in the twelve months preceding the June or December computation date in 1961 and 1967. Rates were computed by the state agency.

Table A-7. Eleven-Year Average Benefit-Cost Rates,[a] Tax Rates,[b] and Cost/Tax Ratios, Selected States, Years 1957–67, for Selected Industry Groups

Industry (SIC)[c]	New York[a,d]			Ohio[a,d]			Pennsylvania[a]		
	Cost rate	Tax rate	Cost/tax ratio	Cost rate	Tax rate	Cost/tax ratio	Cost rate	Tax rate	Cost/tax ratio
Total–all industries	2.5	2.5	98.8	1.9	1.8	107.5	2.4	2.7	88.4
Contract construction	5.7	3.2	178.0	5.5	2.9	186.7	5.3	3.4	159.1
15 General building contractors[e]	6.1	3.3	183.6	5.5	3.1	180.8	5.0	3.7	133.6
16 Other general contractors[e]	8.9	3.4	263.4	8.6	3.3	258.8	7.0	3.9	179.7
17 Special trade contractors[e]	4.7	3.1	148.6	4.4	2.8	158.8	4.3	3.5	121.2
Manufacturing	3.2	2.6	122.6	2.0	1.8	107.2	2.6	2.9	88.5
19 Ordnance and accessories	1.3	2.3	57.6	1.0	2.7	38.7	f	f	f
21 Tobacco products	1.2	1.9	62.0	2.5	2.0	122.9	4.9	3.4	143.2
22 Textile mill products	5.4	3.0	180.8	2.8	2.1	131.1	3.9	3.0	130.4
23 Apparel, other finished fabric products	7.1	3.2	223.8	2.5	1.9	132.6	3.6	3.1	116.0
25 Furniture and fixtures	2.9	2.7	103.8	2.5	2.0	127.5	2.6	2.9	90.1
27 Printing and publishing	1.4	2.1	64.0	0.6	1.0	62.9	0.9	2.2	41.9
28 Chemicals and allied products	1.3	2.1	64.5	0.9	1.2	71.6	1.4	2.5	55.0
31 Leather and leather products	5.0	3.0	170.2	1.7	1.4	123.5	3.1	2.9	107.5
33 Primary metals	3.0	2.6	115.2	3.1	2.2	138.6	3.1	3.1	97.9
36 Electrical machinery[e]	2.0	2.7	77.0	2.0	2.2	91.9	1.6	3.2	50.1
37 Transportation equipment[e]	3.0	2.8	108.3	2.3	2.2	105.7	2.4	3.3	72.9
38 Instruments, optical goods, clocks	1.4	2.1	67.3	1.6	1.9	83.0	1.3	2.5	52.2
Transportation, communication, and utilities	1.4	2.1	66.7	1.0	1.1	87.4	1.2	2.3	53.2
41 Passenger transportation[e]	0.8	1.9	43.1	0.8	0.8	95.8	1.1	2.3	47.5
42 Motor freight transportation, warehousing	2.2	2.6	85.3	1.5	1.6	94.6	1.9	2.6	74.2
48 Communication[e]	0.6	1.6	35.2	0.3	0.7	45.0	0.6	2.2	25.9
49 Electric, gas, sanitary services[e]	0.5	1.5	33.7	0.3	0.6	47.1	0.5	2.3	22.4

	Cost rate	Tax rate	Benefit payments	Cost rate	Tax rate	Benefit payments	Cost rate	Tax rate	Benefit payments
Wholesale and retail trade									
55 Automotive dealers, gasoline stations[e]	1.7	2.4	68.3	1.1	1.5	75.6	1.6	2.5	64.7
	1.3	2.4	51.8	1.0	1.5	65.7	1.3	2.6	50.9
56 Retail apparel and accessories	2.2	2.6	86.9	1.2	1.5	76.3	2.4	2.6	90.6
Finance, insurance, real estate									
65 Real estate	0.9	2.0	43.1	0.6	1.1	52.2	0.8	2.1	35.7
	1.7	2.5	70.0	2.2	2.1	104.1	2.1	2.7	78.4
Services[f]									
70 Hotels, motels, and camps	1.9	2.6	73.9	1.3	1.7	71.8	1.8	2.5	69.6
	3.1	2.8	111.5	1.7	2.1	84.0	2.6	2.8	91.8
75 Automobile repair services, garages	1.4	2.6	52.6	1.5	1.9	76.5	1.6	2.4	67.7
80 Medical and other health services[e]	1.0	2.6	36.9	0.6	1.8	32.9	0.7	2.3	30.6

Note: Cost rate = benefit payments as percent of taxable payrolls; tax rate = tax rates as percent of taxable payrolls; cost/tax ratio = benefit payments as percent of taxes.

Sources: The data for benefit payments, taxable payrolls, and contributions, on which the rates shown in this table are based, were derived mainly from periodic or special reports issued by the employment security agencies of the respective states. In some cases where the data were not available in published form they were supplied by the agency as requested.

[a]Benefits exclude state-extended benefits paid in Ohio (some $60 million in 1958–59), and New York (a relatively small amount paid in 1959). They also exclude payments made under the TUC and TEUC programs. Dependents' allowances are included in the Ohio figures.

[b]Tax rates include supplementary taxes not credited to employer reserves. No attempt was made to adjust tax rates for increases in FUTA taxes resulting from TUC and TEUC programs.

[c]The Standard Industrial Coding Manual, on which distributions by industry were based, was revised in 1957, affecting the industrial distributions shown in this table. In the case of industry *divisions*, it is believed that the revisions have not significantly affected the long-term averages. For Ohio, averages for the major industry *groups* are based on a ten-year period which omits 1959, when coding shifts were in process. For Pennsylvania, the eight-year averages are based entirely on the revised coding manual.

[d]Supplementary taxes were included in the data for Ohio and New York.

[e]The Pennsylvania averages shown for these industry groups are based on data for the eight-year period, 1960–67.

[f]Data were not reported as a separate item in the agency reports. The New York figures for service include mining; also agriculture, forestry and fishing.

341

Table A-8. Average Benefit-Cost Rates,[a] Tax Rates,[b] and Cost/Tax Ratios, Selected States, 1961 and 1967, for Selected Industry Groups

	California					
	1961			1967		
Industry division and group (SIC)[c]	Cost rate	Tax rate	Cost/ tax ratio	Cost rate	Tax rate	Cost/ tax ratio
All industries	3.3	3.1	97.8	2.4	2.8	86.2
Contract construction	6.1	3.3	168.0	8.3	3.5	237.2
15 General building contractors	7.9	3.3	214.5	10.0	3.5	281.3
16 Other general contractors	5.6	3.4	153.4	8.9	3.6	247.9
17 Special trade contractors	5.3	3.3	146.3	6.9	3.4	202.9
Manufacturing	3.5	3.1	103.1	2.1	2.8	75.2
19 Ordnance and accessories	0.5	3.0	10.2	0.5	2.6	19.3
20 Food and kindred products	5.8	3.2	175.2	5.2	3.0	173.1
21 Tobacco manufactures	3.3	3.3	60.0	INA	3.5	–
22 Textile mill products	3.3	3.2	90.8	2.6	3.1	83.6
23 Apparel, other finished fabric products	6.4	3.3	180.7	4.9	3.4	142.1
24 Lumber and wood products except furniture	8.3	3.3	242.1	6.9	3.3	206.9
26 Paper and allied products	2.3	3.1	68.2	1.1	2.7	40.7
27 Printing, publishing, allied industries	1.5	2.9	47.0	1.2	2.5	49.8
28 Chemicals and allied products	1.8	3.0	59.4	1.4	2.5	54.4
30 Rubber and miscellaneous plastic products	4.1	3.1	116.1	1.5	2.9	51.8
31 Leather and leather products	5.2	3.3	145.5	3.1	3.3	93.8
33 Primary metal industries	3.5	3.2	101.6	2.2	2.8	78.6
35 Machinery, except electrical	2.6	3.1	75.9	1.1	2.7	38.9
37 Transportation equipment	4.3	3.1	138.8	1.4	2.7	52.6
38 Instruments, optical goods, clocks	2.0	3.1	62.6	1.3	2.7	46.1
Transportation and utilities	2.3	2.9	73.5	1.4	2.4	57.2
41 Passenger transportation	2.9	2.9	93.7	1.3	2.5	54.6
42 Motor freight, warehousing	4.0	3.1	117.3	3.0	2.8	107.5
45 Transportation by air	1.4	2.9	42.9	0.6	2.2	26.1
48 Communication	0.8	2.8	28.5	0.7	2.0	33.3
49 Electric and gas services	1.1	2.8	38.0	0.7	2.1	32.5
Wholesale and retail trade	2.9	3.0	88.0	1.9	2.8	69.6
50 Wholesale trade	2.6	3.0	78.8	2.0	2.7	73.7
52 Retail trade–building materials	3.0	3.0	96.8	2.8	2.8	99.3
54 Retail trade–food	2.7	3.0	84.0	1.5	2.6	58.9
55 Automotive dealers, gasoline stations	3.0	3.0	89.6	1.6	2.8	57.0
56 Retail apparel and accessories	2.7	3.1	82.8	2.0	2.9	67.1
57 Retail trade–furniture	3.5	3.0	107.2	2.7	2.9	92.4
58 Retail trade–eating and drinking	4.4	3.2	128.4	2.8	3.2	85.6
Finance, insurance, real estate	1.2	2.9	36.4	1.1	2.4	47.1
60 Banking	0.7	2.9	23.0	0.6	2.2	29.3
63 Insurance carriers	1.1	2.9	34.7	0.9	2.2	41.8
65 Real estate	2.7	3.0	78.6	2.6	3.0	87.2
Services	2.8	3.1	82.0	2.1	3.0	69.8
70 Hotels, motels and camps	4.3	3.2	127.1	3.2	3.3	97.3
75 Automobile repair, automotive services	3.5	3.1	101.3	2.0	3.0	66.7
78 Motion pictures	4.5	3.2	144.2	4.8	3.3	144.9
79 Amusement services except motion pictures	4.5	3.3	126.7	3.1	3.3	94.2
80 Medical and other health services	1.4	3.0	40.4	0.9	2.7	34.3
81 Legal services	0.9	2.9	27.3	0.9	2.5	36.1

Note: Cost rate = benefit payments as percent of taxable payrolls; tax rate = taxes as percent of taxable payrolls; cost/tax ratio = benefit payments as percent of taxes. Cost/tax ratios and tax rates shown above for "1961" are based on benefits paid in that year of heavy unemployment and the increased taxes which ensued in 1962.

Sources: The data for benefit payments, taxable payrolls, and contributions, on which the rates shown in this table were based, were derived mainly from periodic and special reports issued by the employment security agencies of the respective states. In some cases, where the data were not available in published form, they were supplied by the agency as requested.

| Massachusetts | | | | | | Minnesota | | | | | |
| 1961 | | | 1967 | | | 1961 | | | 1967 | | |
Cost rate	Tax rate	Cost tax ratio	Cost rate	Tax rate	Cost tax ratio	Cost rate	Tax rate	Cost tax ratio	Cost rate	Tax rate	Cost tax ratio
3.2	2.6	108.3	1.7	2.1	80.0	2.4	1.6	146.5	0.7	1.3	57.2
8.5	3.4	217.9	5.2	2.9	177.5	6.5	2.6	245.5	3.0	2.8	107.3
–	–	–	–	–	–	5.8	2.7	205.9	2.4	2.9	81.4
–	–	–	–	–	–	11.2	2.9	415.0	6.7	4.0	169.3
–	–	–	–	–	–	4.2	2.3	168.9	1.4	2.1	66.4
3.5	2.7	110.1	1.6	2.1	76.9	2.1	1.6	123.1	0.5	1.1	44.9
–	–	–	–	–	–	1.3	1.2	112.4	0.2	0.7	26.9
3.0	2.4	110.9	1.6	1.8	90.0	2.0	1.7	113.8	0.7	1.4	49.9
–	–	–	–	–	–	–	–	–	–	–	–
4.9	3.2	137.6	2.3	2.5	92.4	3.3	1.5	204.5	0.7	1.3	53.6
8.0	3.5	207.7	4.9	2.9	167.4	5.0	2.2	210.9	1.4	1.8	80.7
–	–	–	–	–	–	6.7	2.5	278.8	1.4	1.7	86.7
1.7	2.1	70.1	0.8	1.6	50.9	0.6	0.8	73.9	0.2	0.8	26.6
1.5	2.1	60.5	0.9	1.7	51.9	1.1	1.2	88.7	0.3	0.9	33.3
1.7	2.3	65.5	1.1	1.6	67.9	1.7	1.5	104.1	0.5	1.1	42.0
2.9	2.8	83.6	1.9	2.1	90.4	2.8	2.1	112.9	0.3	1.0	33.3
6.0	3.3	169.2	3.1	2.6	118.8	2.3	1.3	168.5	1.1	0.9	125.0
3.2	2.7	96.5	0.9	2.0	47.9	3.8	2.1	164.5	0.6	1.5	40.8
2.3	2.6	76.1	1.1	1.9	56.3	1.5	1.7	74.0	0.2	0.7	28.6
3.4	3.0	115.4	0.8	2.4	35.4	5.1	2.5	197.5	0.9	1.3	63.3
2.2	2.7	64.9	0.6	1.8	33.3	0.7	1.1	65.2	0.1	0.7	16.1
2.1	2.2	81.4	1.2	1.8	64.3	1.4	1.3	107.6	0.3	1.0	34.8
–	–	–	–	–	–	1.3	1.0	124.8	0.4	0.8	45.0
–	–	–	–	–	–	2.0	1.5	131.3	0.4	1.0	42.7
–	–	–	–	–	–	2.2	2.4	93.0	0.1	0.7	8.8
–	–	–	–	–	–	0.6	0.9	65.2	0.1	0.8	12.3
–	–	–	–	–	–	1.1	1.1	101.4	0.3	0.8	34.4
2.3	2.4	82.8	1.1	1.9	58.8	1.5	1.3	117.4	0.4	1.0	35.8
2.3	2.4	85.5	1.2	1.9	61.5	1.4	1.3	101.1	0.3	1.0	32.0
–	–	–	–	–	–	2.3	1.4	157.2	0.7	1.4	49.2
1.7	2.3	67.5	0.9	1.7	53.6	1.2	1.0	116.9	0.3	0.9	30.8
1.9	2.3	72.4	0.8	1.8	42.6	1.4	1.3	105.1	0.3	0.9	33.9
2.6	2.6	89.9	1.5	2.1	69.6	1.3	1.3	98.2	0.4	1.0	37.0
–	–	–	–	–	–	2.0	1.3	158.5	0.2	1.0	23.5
3.4	2.7	112.6	1.8	2.3	76.0	2.3	1.4	155.9	0.5	1.3	41.0
1.1	2.1	43.9	0.7	1.6	44.3	0.5	0.9	55.6	0.1	0.8	14.7
–	–	–	–	–	–	0.3	0.8	29.5	0.1	0.8	7.2
–	–	–	–	–	–	0.4	0.8	48.4	0.0	0.8	11.3
–	–	–	–	–	–	1.9	1.4	132.5	0.5	1.3	38.0
2.2	2.5	75.5	1.0	2.1	49.1	1.5	1.2	122.5	0.3	1.1	31.8
3.8	2.8	128.8	2.5	2.5	100.2	2.3	1.3	172.1	0.6	1.1	52.9
–	–	–	–	–	–	2.0	1.2	152.3	0.2	1.1	20.9
–	–	–	–	–	–	2.2	1.5	142.2	0.3	1.0	28.0
–	–	–	–	–	–	3.0	2.1	138.1	0.8	2.0	40.2
–	2.4	–	0.6	2.0	28.0	0.6	0.8	63.5	0.2	0.9	18.8
–	–	–	–	–	–	0.3	0.8	37.5	*	0.8	3.6

*Less than 0.05 percent.

aBenedit-costs include state-extended benefits paid in California in 1967, but not those paid in 1961; they do not include benefits paid in the three states under the TEUC program in 1961.

bTax rates include supplementary taxes not credited to employer reserves (California). No attempt was made to adjust tax rates for the increases in FUTA taxes resulting from TUC and TEUC programs.

cIndustrial classifications are based on the Standard Industrial Coding Manual (1957 revision). California departs from the SIC in two minor ways not significant for purposes of this table.

Table A–9. Average Benefit-Cost Rates, Tax Rates, and Cost/Tax Ratios—1967, California, Massachusetts, and New York, for Selected 3-Digit Industry Groups

Industry Group (SIC)	California[a]			Massachusetts[b]			New York[a]		
	Cost rate	Tax rate	Cost/Tax ratio	Cost rate	Tax rate	Cost/Tax ratio	Cost rate	Tax rate	Cost/Tax ratio
17 Construction—special trade contractors	6.9	3.4	202.9	3.6	2.8	131.9	4.1	2.8	137.0
171 Plumbing				1.3	2.4	56.4	2.1	2.8	71.8
172 Painting and papering				9.0	3.3	274.1	7.4	3.1	221.2
173 Electrical work				0.7	2.4	31.8	1.1	2.0	54.6
174 Masonry and Plastering				7.1	3.3	218.7	7.6	3.1	223.4
175 Carpentry				3.9	2.8	141.8	4.1	2.9	135.5
176 Roofing and sheet metal work				3.3	2.9	115.0	3.5	2.8	114.7
177 Concrete work				4.9	3.2	156.2	7.5	3.2	217.0
178 Water well drilling				1.7	1.9	84.2	2.5	2.3	100.0
20 Food and kindred products	5.2	3.0	173.1	1.2	1.9	67.9	1.7	1.7	105.5
203 Canning and preserving fruits, vegetables, sea food	10.0	3.5	282.8	5.2	3.0	174.8			
206 Sugar	7.1	3.1	230.2	1.3	2.2	61.9	5.5	2.6	212.6
23 Apparel and other finished products made from fabrics and similar materials	4.9	3.4	142.1	4.4	2.9	151.0	5.8	2.8	201.6
231 Men's and boys' suits and coats				3.1	3.0	107.8	3.4	2.3	145.3
232 Men's and boys' furnishings				2.9	2.6	112.3	4.6	2.5	190.0
233 Women's and misses' outerwear	6.0	3.5	169.4	6.0	3.0	199.2	6.4	3.0	212.0

Code	Industry	Benefit payments	Cost rate	Tax rate	Benefit payments	Cost rate	Tax rate	Benefit payments	Cost rate	Tax rate
234	Women's and children's undergarments				84.0	2.2	2.7	100.1	2.7	2.7
235	Hats, caps, and millinery				347.0	11.9	3.4	459.7	15.1	3.2
236	Children's, infants' outerwear				136.5	4.4	3.3	188.5	5.3	2.9
237	Fur goods				233.3	9.3	3.3	379.2	12.3	3.2
24	Lumber and wood products, except furniture	206.9	6.9	3.3	48.3	0.9	1.9	82.4	1.9	2.2
241	Logging camps and logging contractors	488.8	17.9	3.7	66.7	1.4	2.1			
242	Sawmills and planning	188.5	6.4	3.4	40.0	0.7	1.9			
37	Transportation equipment	52.6	1.4	2.7	34.4	0.9	2.6	84.6	1.8	2.5
371	Motor vehicles and motor vehicle equipment	90.1	2.8	3.1	58.0	1.1	1.9			
372	Aircraft and parts	35.9	0.9	2.6	21.3	0.4	2.0			
373	Ship and boat building and repairing	124.3	4.4	3.5	28.2	0.6	2.2			
50	Wholesale trade	73.7	2.0	2.7	41.0	0.7	1.9	53.1	1.1	1.8
504	Groceries and related products	152.1	4.4	2.9	58.1	1.2	2.1			

Note: cost rate = benefit payments as percent of taxable payrolls; tax rate = contributions as percent of taxable payrolls; cost/tax ratios = benefit payments as percent of taxes.

Sources: California Department of Employment, Research and Statistics, Report 352, no. 26 (Sacramento, August 1968); tabulations furnished by the Massachusetts Division of Employment Security (Boston 1969); Unemployment Insurance Tax Rates, 1968, New York State Department of Labor, Division of Employment, Research and Statistics Office (Albany, January 1969).

[a]Rates shown for California and New York are limited to industries for which data were published by the state agency. The "balancing" and "subsidiary" taxes levied by California and New York are included in the tax figures. For these two states, cost rates are based on all benefits paid, not merely on those charged to employer reserves.

[b]Cost rates for Massachusetts are based on benefits charged during the twelve months ended September 30, 1967–not on total benefits paid. In this state 18 percent of all benefits paid during that period were noncharged.

Table A-10. NEW YORK: Average Benefit-Cost Rates, Tax Rates, and Cost/Tax Ratios, 1962–67, by Size of Firm

Size of taxable payroll	Average benefit-cost rates						Average tax rates[a]						Average cost/tax ratios					
	1962	1963	1964	1965	1966	1967	1962	1963	1964	1965	1966	1967	1962	1963	1964	1965	1966	1967
Averages—all size groups	2.6	3.0	2.5	2.2	1.8	1.7	3.4	3.3	2.7	3.0	2.6	1.9	75.6	76.7	93.3	72.6	70.6	88.1
Under $5,000	3.3	4.5	4.3	3.8	}2.5	}2.3	3.8	3.6	2.8	3.1	}2.6	}2.1	88.0	125.0	152.5	123.4	}95.1	}112.2
$5,000– 9,999	2.9	2.9	3.0	2.7			3.6	3.4	2.8	3.1			80.3	84.5	107.5	86.0		
10,000– 19,999	2.7	2.7	2.7	2.4	}2.1	}2.0	3.5	3.4	2.8	3.2	}2.8	}2.1	77.1	79.9	96.4	75.7	}76.7	}92.5
20,000– 49,999	2.9	2.9	2.9	2.5			3.5	3.4	2.9	3.2			82.4	85.3	101.8	77.4		
50,000– 99,999	3.6	3.5	3.4	3.0	2.7	2.5	3.6	3.5	3.0	3.3	2.9	2.3	99.7	100.0	114.5	89.8	93.1	110.6
100,000– 199,999	3.7	3.6	3.6	3.3	}2.4	}2.3	3.7	3.6	3.0	3.4	}2.8	}2.2	101.4	101.4	119.2	96.8	}82.7	}102.3
200,000– 999,999	2.9	2.8	2.9	2.5			3.6	3.4	2.9	3.2			81.7	82.4	101.8	77.4		
1,000,000–9,999,999	2.1	2.1	2.0	1.7	1.3	1.3	3.4	3.2	2.6	2.9	2.3	1.7	62.3	66.7	78.4	59.2	56.5	75.7
10,000,000 and over	1.3	1.3	1.1	0.8	0.6	0.7	3.1	2.8	2.2	2.5	2.0	1.4	41.9	46.4	50.2	32.0	31.0	51.8

Note: Cost rate = benefit payments as percent of taxable payrolls; tax rate = contributions as percent of taxable payrolls; cost/tax ratios = average benefit cost rates as percent of average tax rates.

Sources: Unemployment Insurance Tax Rates, New York State Department of Labor, Division of Employment, Years 1963–1968.

[a]Include subsidiary taxes.

Table A–11. MASSACHUSETTS: Average Benefit-Cost Rates, Tax Rates, and Cost/Tax Ratios, Rated Employers by Size of Taxable Payroll, Year Ending September 30, 1967, Positive- and Negative-Balance Accounts

Size of taxable payroll	All rated employers					Positive-balance accounts					Negative-balance accounts				
	Number	Percent of total	Cost rate	Tax rate	Cost/tax ratio	Number	Percent of size group	Cost rate	Tax rate	Cost/tax ratio	Number	Percent of size group	Cost rate	Tax rate	Cost/tax ratio
Total–all size groups	103,404	100.0	1.3	2.1	61.5	86,919	84.1	0.6	1.9	32.4	16,485	15.9	6.6	3.4	197.1
Under $10,000	54,296	52.5	2.5	2.1	120.6	44,933	82.8	0.2	1.8	14.8	9,363	17.2	14.2	3.4	418.6
10,000- 24,999	23,551	22.8	1.6	2.1	75.6	20,163	85.6	0.4	1.9	22.9	3,388	14.4	8.4	3.4	251.3
25,000- 49,999	11,407	11.0	1.6	2.1	72.4	9,803	85.9	0.5	1.9	28.2	1,604	14.1	7.6	3.4	228.2
50,000- 99,999	6,658	6.4	1.6	2.2	72.4	5,696	85.6	0.6	2.0	32.4	962	14.4	7.0	3.4	208.8
100,000- 249,999	4,523	4.4	1.6	2.3	70.9	3,787	83.7	0.6	2.0	32.4	736	16.3	6.2	3.4	186.6
250,000- 499,999	1,531	1.5	1.6	2.2	72.7	1,276	83.3	0.7	2.0	36.8	255	16.7	6.1	3.4	181.6
500,000- 999,999	805	0.8	1.3	2.1	58.9	689	85.6	0.6	1.9	33.0	116	14.4	4.9	3.3	149.4
1,000,000- 2,499,999	410	0.4	1.2	2.1	59.7	362	88.3	0.7	1.9	38.6	48	11.7	5.3	3.3	162.2
2,500,000- 4,999,999	126	0.1	0.8	2.0	42.4	118	93.7	0.6	1.9	34.6	8	6.3	3.9	3.3	120.6
5,000,000- 9,999,999	58	0.1	0.9	2.0	46.6	54	93.1	0.7	1.9	40.3	4	6.9	3.0	3.2	95.9
10,000,000-24,999,999	29	*	0.8	1.8	43.5	28	96.6	0.6	1.8	38.9	1	3.4	4.7	3.3	143.9
25,000,000 and over	10	*	0.5	1.9	24.0	10	100.0	0.6	1.9	24.0	0	0.0	–	–	–

Note: Cost rate = benefit charges as percent of payrolls; tax rate = contributions as percent of taxable payrolls; cost/tax ratio = benefit charges as percent of taxes. (During the year ending September 30, 1967, 18 percent of all benefits paid were noncharged.)

Sources: Tabulations furnished by the Massachusetts Division of Employment Security (Boston 1969).

*Less than 0.05 percent.

Table A-12. States Having Maximum Possible[a] Tax Rate above 2.7 Percent, Selected Years, 1938–69

State	1938	1939	1940	1941	1945	1948	1949	1951	1954	1955	1958	1960	1962	1964	1969
Alabama	4.0												3.6	3.6	3.6
Alaska													4.0	4.0	4.0*
Arizona	3.6	3.6	3.6	3.6											2.9*
Arkansas	4.0	4.0	4.0	4.0										3.3	4.0
California					3.6							3.0	3.5	3.5	3.7*
Colorado	3.6	3.6	3.6	3.6	3.6	3.6									3.6
Connecticut															*
Delaware	4.0	4.0	4.0	4.0									4.5	4.5	4.5*
District of Columbia	4.0	4.0	4.0	4.0	3.0	3.0	3.0	3.0	3.0	3.0	3.0	3.0			
Florida[a]											2.9	2.9	2.9	3.5	4.5
Georgia														4.2	4.5
Hawaii		4.0	4.0												3.0*
Idaho										3.25	3.25			5.1	5.1*
Illinois	3.6	3.6	3.6	3.6	3.6	3.6						4.0	4.0	4.0	4.0
Indiana	3.7	3.7	3.7												3.2
Iowa	3.6	3.6	3.6	3.6	3.6	3.6	3.6								4.0
Kansas	3.6	3.6	3.6												
Kentucky	3.7	3.7	3.7	3.7					3.7	3.7	3.7				
Louisiana	3.6	3.6	3.6									4.2	4.2	4.2	4.2
Maine															3.7
Maryland												3.7	3.9	4.2	3.6
Massachusetts	4.0	4.0	4.0	4.0	4.0	4.0	4.0	4.0	4.0	4.0			4.1	4.1	4.1*
Michigan											4.5	4.5	4.5	4.6	6.6*
Minnesota	3.2	3.2	3.2	3.25	3.25	3.25		3.0	3.0	3.0	3.0	3.0	3.0	3.0	4.5*
Mississippi														3.2	
Missouri	3.6	3.6	3.6		4.1	4.1	4.1	4.1	4.1	4.1	3.2	3.6	4.4	5.0	4.1
Montana	3.6														3.1

348

State															
Nevada				4.5											3.0*
New Hampshire	3.6	3.6	3.6	3.6	3.6	3.6	3.6	3.6	3.6	3.6	3.6	3.6	3.6	4.0	4.3
New Jersey	3.6	3.6	3.6	3.6	3.6	3.6	3.6	3.6	3.6	3.6	3.6	3.6	4.2	4.2	4.2*
New Mexico	3.6	3.6	3.6	3.6	3.6	3.6	3.6	3.6	3.6	3.6	3.6	4.2	4.2	3.6	3.6
New York	3.7	3.7	3.7	3.7	3.7	3.7	3.7	3.7	3.7	3.7	3.7	3.7	3.7	3.7	4.2
North Carolina			3.7	3.7	3.7	3.7	3.7	3.7	3.7	3.7	3.7	3.7	4.2	3.7	4.7
North Dakota			4.0	4.0			3.7	3.7	3.7	3.7	3.7	3.7	4.2	4.2	4.2*
Ohio	4.0	4.0	4.0	3.5	4.0		3.2	3.2	3.2	3.2	3.2	3.2	3.2	4.7	4.7
Oklahoma	3.6	3.6	3.6	4.0											
Oregon	4.0	4.0	4.0	4.0					3.0						*
Pennsylvania[a]												4.0	4.0	4.0	4.0*
Rhode Island													3.3	3.3	4.0*
South Carolina	3.6	3.6	3.6	3.6	3.6								4.1	4.1	4.1
South Dakota	3.6	3.6	4.0	3.3					3.0	3.0			4.1	4.1	4.1
Tennessee	3.6	4.0	4.0	3.3				3.0	3.0	3.0	3.0	3.0	3.5	4.0	4.0*
Texas	3.6				3.3								7.2	7.2	7.2
Utah	3.6	3.2													*
Vermont														3.2	4.4*
Virginia															
Washington	3.6	3.6													
West Virginia	3.6	4.0	4.0	4.0		4.0		4.0	4.0	4.0	4.0	4.0	4.0	4.0	3.3*
Wisconsin	4.0	4.0													4.4*
Wyoming[a]	3.6	3.6	3.6	3.6	3.5									3.2	*
Totals	27	27	27	21	16	13	10	8	9	11	12	16	23	32	39

Sources: 1938–39—*Current Experience Rating Research*, U.S. Department of Labor, Bureau of Employment Security; 1940–69—*Comparison of State Unemployment Insurance Laws*. (*See also* Table A–4.)

*Taxable wage base above $3,000 in 1969.

[a]The "maximum possible" rate is the highest rate payable under the least favorable rate schedule plus the highest possible supplementary rate. For Florida, Pennsylvania, and Wyoming supplementary taxes are not included.

Table A-13. States Having Possible[a] "0" Tax Rate, Selected Years, 1938-69

State	1938	1939	1940	1941	1945	1948	1949	1951	1954	1955	1958	1960	1962	1964	1969
Alabama															
Alaska															
Arizona															
Arkansas															
California						X						X			X
Colorado	X						X	X	X	X	X	X	X	X	
Connecticut	X														
Delaware															
District of Columbia															
Florida								X	X	X	X	X	X		X
Georgia															
Hawaii		X	X	X	X	X	X	X	X	X	X	X	X	X	
Idaho	X														
Illinois	X														
Indiana	X														
Iowa						X	X	X	X	X	X	X	X	X	X
Kansas										X	X	X	X	X	X
Kentucky	X	X	X	X	X	X	X	X	X						
Louisiana										X	X	X	X	X	X
Maine															
Maryland													X		
Massachusetts														X	
Michigan											X	X	X	X	X
Minnesota															
Mississippi															X
Missouri	X	X	X	X	X	X	X	X	X	X	X	X	X	X	X
Montana	X	X	X	X	X	X	X	X	X	X	X	X	X	X	X

Nebraska															
Nevada		X													
New Hampshire															
New Jersey															
New Mexico															
New York						X	X	X	X		X	X	X	X	X
North Carolina															
North Dakota											X			X	X
Ohio											X			X	X
Oklahoma								X	X		X	X	X	X	X
Oregon															
Pennsylvania											X		X	X	
Rhode Island									X		X	X	X	X	X
South Carolina															
South Dakota	X	X	X	X	X	X	X	X	X	X	X	X	X	X	X
Tennessee					X										
Texas	X														
Utah	X														
Vermont															
Virginia															
Washington								X	X		X	X	X	X	X
West Virginia						X	X	X	X		X	X	X	X	X
Wisconsin						X	X	X	X		X	X	X	X	X
Wyoming										X	X	X	X	X	X
Totals	10	5	6	4	5	8	9	11	12	14	15	15	15	15	15

Sources: 1938–39—*Current Experience Rating Research*, U.S. Department of Labor, Bureau of Employment Security; 1940–69—*Comparison of State Unemployment Insurance Laws.*

[a]The states shown as having a "possible '0' rate" are those for which no tax is payable under at least one of their more favorable schedules.

Table A-14. Average Tax Rates,[a] by States, Calendar Years 1957 through 1967

	1957	1958	1959	1960	1961	1962	1963	1964	1965	1966	1967
Average rate—all states[b]	0.85	0.84	1.06	1.15	1.24	1.39	1.34	1.26	1.18	1.05	0.86
States with average rates above all-state average for all (11) years											
Alaska	2.03	1.92	1.90	2.48	2.45	2.31	2.38	2.39	2.34	2.21	2.18
Massachusetts	1.04	0.99	1.14	1.16	1.29	1.72	1.61	1.68	1.59	1.49	1.18
Nevada	1.49	1.59	1.56	1.53	1.65	1.55	1.77	1.71	1.27	1.24	1.26
New York	1.09	0.94	1.16	1.29	1.61	1.87	1.73	1.39	1.53	1.25	0.91
Oregon	1.09	1.70	1.90	1.98	1.94	1.88	1.86	1.54	1.23	1.20	1.16
Pennsylvania	0.99	1.25	1.67	1.79	1.92	1.88	1.79	1.89	1.78	1.61	1.40
Rhode Island	2.10	2.00	2.02	1.99	1.96	1.91	1.87	1.82	1.77	1.45	1.38
Washington	1.40	1.65	1.66	1.61	1.56	1.53	1.48	1.44	1.42	1.24	1.18
States with average rates at or above all-state average for six to ten years (as indicated)											
California (9)	0.85	0.80	1.21	1.28	1.39	1.97	1.90	1.83	1.77	1.75	1.58
Idaho (9)	0.95	0.93	1.02	1.12	1.55	1.60	1.51	1.48	1.49	1.31	1.21
Maryland (7)	0.68	0.69	1.39	1.67	1.89	1.92	1.85	1.63	1.28	0.95	0.63
Michigan (10)	1.20	1.20	1.43	1.55	1.55	1.52	1.66	1.44	1.22	1.12	0.80

State											
Mississippi (9)	1.30	1.27	1.51	1.45	1.45	1.46	1.66	1.59	1.42	0.84	0.59
New Jersey (7)	1.08	1.16	1.18	1.26	1.36	1.37	1.29	1.21	1.18	1.12	1.05
North Dakota (10)	1.08	0.89	1.00	1.34	1.45	1.58	1.55	1.51	1.41	1.29	1.18

States with average rates at or below all-state average for six to ten years (as indicated)

State											
Arizona (8)	0.91	0.90	0.82	0.83	0.82	0.84	0.88	0.83	0.86	0.90	0.93
Arkansas (8)	0.89	0.90	0.97	0.96	1.01	1.03	1.04	1.04	1.07	1.06	0.81
Connecticut (9)	0.76	0.71	1.10	1.22	1.19	1.16	1.12	1.09	1.08	1.03	0.86
Delaware (7)	0.43	0.40	1.14	1.48	1.20	1.44	1.35	1.22	0.96	0.56	0.48
Georgia (9)	0.91	0.91	0.97	0.94	0.90	0.93	0.89	0.82	0.77	0.71	0.66
Hawaii (7)	0.75	0.72	0.76	0.81	0.81	0.89	1.21	1.51	1.32	1.20	1.13
Kentucky (6)	1.43	1.34	1.58	1.44	1.36	1.36	1.25	1.14	1.11	0.81	0.83
Louisiana (10)	0.98	0.75	0.75	0.99	0.98	1.13	1.17	1.13	1.03	0.97	0.71
Maine (6)	1.19	1.13	1.13	1.15	1.23	1.34	1.41	1.29	1.09	0.91	0.73
Montana (6)	0.87	0.85	0.88	1.48	1.56	1.03	0.97	0.95	0.95	0.89	0.89
New Hampshire (8)	1.18	1.09	1.14	1.15	1.09	1.07	1.05	1.04	1.02	0.73	0.61
North Carolina (7)	1.13	1.12	1.20	1.16	1.07	1.04	1.12	1.02	0.96	0.82	0.81
Ohio (9)	0.44	0.45	0.80	0.84	0.77	1.14	1.10	1.45	1.22	1.02	0.63
South Carolina (9)	0.93	0.88	0.81	0.84	0.82	0.78	1.00	0.94	0.90	0.85	0.83
Tennessee (6)	1.24	1.22	1.18	1.15	1.15	1.15	1.18	1.17	1.15	1.08	0.91
Utah (8)	0.88	0.90	0.82	0.90	0.86	0.85	1.13	0.96	1.01	0.99	0.99
Vermont (6)	0.98	0.83	0.87	0.89	1.03	1.06	1.13	1.33	1.54	1.89	1.55
West Virginia (6)	0.73	0.75	1.24	1.63	1.60	1.77	1.74	0.72	0.77	0.81	0.83
Wyoming (6)	0.79	0.74	0.84	0.86	0.86	1.05	1.78	1.92	1.33	1.22	0.99

Table A–14. Average Tax Rates,[a] by States, Calendar Years 1957 through 1967 (continued)

	1957	1958	1959	1960	1961	1962	1963	1964	1965	1966	1967
States with average rates at or below all-state average for all (11) years											
Alabama	0.74	0.63	0.71	0.79	1.01	1.22	1.26	0.98	0.78	0.68	0.61
Colorado	0.45	0.46	0.28	0.33	0.67	0.79	0.76	0.89	0.70	0.64	0.25
District of Columbia	0.46	0.39	0.50	0.51	0.50	0.62	0.49	0.48	0.52	0.50	0.42
Florida	0.47	0.55	1.03	0.77	1.03	1.19	0.88	0.81	0.70	0.52	0.40
Illinois	0.61	0.46	0.61	1.15	1.14	1.18	1.07	0.98	0.68	0.39	0.19
Indiana	0.65	0.67	0.80	0.73	0.65	0.75	0.69	0.65	0.59	0.63	0.57
Iowa	0.48	0.50	0.53	0.38	0.40	0.47	0.46	0.44	0.39	0.31	0.32
Kansas	0.73	0.70	0.68	0.67	0.66	0.75	0.74	0.82	0.82	0.79	0.67
Minnesota	0.55	0.49	0.74	0.67	0.63	0.86	0.78	0.72	0.73	0.88	0.81
Missouri	0.65	0.64	0.67	0.63	0.88	0.87	0.82	0.77	0.75	0.68	0.34
Nebraska	0.66	0.56	0.75	0.68	0.73	0.77	0.78	0.74	0.59	0.54	0.54
New Mexico	0.81	0.83	0.84	0.81	0.78	0.81	0.81	0.78	0.77	0.75	0.69
Oklahoma	0.65	0.54	0.63	0.76	0.83	1.14	1.11	0.87	0.80	0.63	0.40
South Dakota	0.69	0.69	0.71	0.54	0.65	0.85	0.71	0.62	0.58	0.51	0.46
Texas	0.42	0.36	0.48	0.56	0.57	0.56	0.53	0.54	0.51	0.47	0.35
Virginia	0.38	0.30	0.90	0.59	0.73	0.85	0.79	0.56	0.47	0.41	0.34
Wisconsin	0.70	0.64	0.64	0.83	0.85	0.78	0.84	0.82	0.86	0.86	0.84

Source: *Handbook of Unemployment Insurance Financial Data, 1946–1967*, U.S. Department of Labor, Bureau of Employment Security.

[a]Based on *total* wages.
[b]Excludes Puerto Rico, for which comparable data were not available for the entire period.

Table A-15. NEW YORK: Percent Distribution of Rated Employers by 1967 Tax Rates[a] within Industry Divisions

Tax rate	Totals all divisions		Contract construction		Manufacturing		Transportation and utilities		Wholesale and retail trade		Finance, insurance, and real estate		Services	
	Number		Number		Number		Number		Number		Number		Number	
Totals—all rates	393,232		32,409		41,851		12,245		138,881		42,281		117,563	
Insufficient period of coverage	43,451		2,355		1,575		663		7,864		1,423		25,679	
Rated employers	349,781		30,054		40,276		11,582		131,017		40,858		91,884	
Percent distribution by rates		Percent		Percent		Percent		Percent		Percent		Percent		Percent
All rates[b]		100.0		100.0		100.0		100.0		100.0		100.0		100.0
0.8	97,806	28.0		10.9		15.9		22.8		29.8		43.7		30.7
0.9	8,747	2.5		0.8		1.9		2.4		2.6		3.5		2.8
1.0	8,988	2.6		0.9		2.1		2.5		2.7		3.2		2.9
1.2	8,896	2.5		0.8		2.4		2.7		2.7		2.9		2.8
1.4	8,596	2.5		0.9		2.3		2.5		2.7		2.7		2.7
1.6	8,389	2.4		0.9		2.3		2.8		2.6		2.4		2.6
1.8	8,211	2.3		1.2		2.2		2.8		2.5		2.3		2.5
2.0	8,203	2.3		1.3		2.3		2.5		2.5		2.2		2.5
2.2	7,932	2.3		1.3		2.0		2.7		2.4		2.2		2.5
2.3	10,364	3.0		1.8		2.5		3.0		3.1		2.8		3.4
2.4	9,772	2.8		1.8		2.4		3.0		2.9		2.6		3.2
2.5	7,794	2.2		1.5		2.2		2.5		2.4		2.0		2.4
2.6	7,453	2.1		1.6		2.0		2.4		2.2		1.7		2.3
2.7	6,175	1.8		1.3		1.9		2.1		1.9		1.3		2.0
2.8	13,442	3.8		4.1		3.2		3.9		4.2		3.8		3.7
2.9	4,801	1.4		1.3		1.7		1.7		1.4		0.9		1.4
3.0	56,801	16.2		21.5		20.0		19.4		16.2		10.8		15.0
3.1[c]	24,824	7.1		12.6		5.1		7.2		7.0		5.2		6.8
3.3[d]	42,587	12.2		33.5		25.6		11.1		8.2		3.8		7.8

Source: Unemployment Insurance Tax Rates 1968, New York State Department of Labor, Division of Employment (Albany, April 1968).
[a]The average tax rate for 1967 was 1.93.
[b]Inclusive of subsidiary tax of 0.1 percent.
[c]Accounts with negative balance for one year.
[d]Accounts with negative balance for two years and accounts delinquent in reporting.

Table A-16. OREGON: Percent Distribution of Employers by 1967 Tax Rates[a] within Industry Divisions

Tax rate	Total all industry divisions		Agriculture, forestry and fisheries		Mining		Contract construction		Manufacturing		Transportation and public utilities		Wholesale and retail trade		Finance, insurance, real estate		Services	
	Number	Percent	Number	Percent	Number	Percent	Number	Percent	Number	Percent	Number	Percent	Number	Percent	Number	Percent	Number	Percent
Total—all employers	40,437		444		179		4,832		4,282		1,912		15,400		2,891		10,384	
All rates		100.0		100.0		100.0		100.0		100.0		100.0		100.0		100.0		100.0
1.2	16,549	40.9		40.5		12.3		17.8		19.8		28.7		42.6		59.9		55.7
1.5	3,411	8.4		6.8		8.4		7.1		9.7		12.1		9.5		7.7		6.6
1.8	1,009	2.5		1.3		2.2		2.6		3.3		3.2		2.7		1.6		2.0
2.0	1,309	3.2		2.5		2.8		3.2		4.6		6.0		3.5		1.9		2.2
2.2	1,754	4.4		4.1		2.2		4.5		6.4		5.7		4.7		3.1		3.2
2.4	1,952	4.8		4.7		7.8		6.2		6.9		4.8		5.0		3.4		3.5
2.6	3,261	8.1		7.2		18.5		13.4		11.3		7.8		7.8		4.1		5.7
2.7	11,192	27.7		32.9		45.8		45.2		38.0		31.7		24.2		18.3		21.1

Note: The 1967 Legislature has since increased the number of tax schedules from 4 to 8, with the minimum rate reduced from 1.2 to 0.8.

Sources: Distribution of Employers by Rate Group and Industry, 1967 Oregon Unemployment Insurance Tax Rates, 1966.

Tax Year, Oregon Department of Employment, Research and Statistics (Salem, March 29, 1968); Handbook of Unemployment Insurance Financial Data, Significant Measures, 1967.

[a]The average contribution rate for 1967 was 1.94 percent.

Table A–17. MASSACHUSETTS: Distribution of Rated Employers by 1968 Tax Rates within Industry Divisions

1968 tax rates	Total all divisions		Agriculture, forestry and fishing		Mining and quarrying		Contract construction		Manufacturing		Transportation and public utilities		Wholesale and retail trade		Finance insurance, real estate		Services	
	Number 103,404	Percent 100.0	Number 1,463	Percent 100.0	Number 84	Percent 100.0	Number 12,775	Percent 100.0	Number 9,996	Percent 100.0	Number 4,071	Percent 100.0	Number 39,124	Percent 100.0	Number 8,220	Percent 100.0	Number 27,671	Percent 100.0
Total–all rates	103,404	100.0	1,463	100.0	84	100.0	12,775	100.0	9,996	100.0	4,071	100.0	39,124	100.0	8,220	100.0	27,671	100.0
Positive-balance employers:	86,919	84.1		49.7		56.0		54.2		83.7		83.3		89.9		93.0		89.0
0.7	18,361	17.8		6.2		7.1		8.3		13.5		13.0		20.2		24.6		19.6
0.9	4,560	4.4		1.4		3.6		1.6		4.2		3.4		5.1		6.0		4.7
1.1	5,074	4.9		1.7		1.2		1.7		5.1		4.1		5.7		6.6		5.0
1.3	5,137	5.0		1.8		6.0		1.6		5.6		4.9		5.6		6.1		5.3
1.5	4,817	4.7		1.5		3.6		1.6		5.4		4.4		5.3		5.5		4.9
1.7	4,610	4.5		2.0		—		1.8		5.3		5.0		4.9		5.1		4.6
1.9	4,207	4.1		2.5		1.2		1.9		5.2		4.0		4.5		4.2		4.1
2.1	3,668	3.5		1.9		2.4		1.7		3.8		4.6		3.8		3.4		3.9
2.3	3,376	3.3		2.0		—		1.7		3.6		3.1		3.5		3.5		3.5
2.5	2,977	2.9		1.4		2.4		1.8		2.9		3.6		3.0		2.7		3.2
2.7[a]	5,309	5.1		4.0		6.0		5.3		4.2		5.4		4.8		6.2		5.5
2.9	24,823	24.0		23.4		22.6		25.2		24.7		27.6		23.6		19.2		24.8
Negative-balance employers:	16,485	15.9		50.3		44.0		45.8		16.3		16.7		10.1		7.0		11.0
2.7[a]	1,307	1.3		2.3		—		4.3		0.9		1.3		0.7		0.8		0.8
3.1	3,472	3.4		5.7		6.0		6.7		4.1		4.0		2.7		1.9		2.8
3.3	1,219	1.2		2.7		4.8		2.9		1.7		1.1		0.9		0.5		0.8
3.5	10,487	10.1		39.6		33.3		31.8		9.8		10.3		5.8		3.8		6.6

Source: Tabulations furnished by the Massachusetts Division of Employment Security (Boston 1969).

[a] A Massachusetts employer who has had no taxable payroll during the year ending at the computation date is assigned a rate of 2.7 percent for the ensuing year, whether his reserve balance is positive or negative.

357

Table A–18. OHIO: Percent Distribution of Rated Employers in Selected Size-of-Taxable-Payroll Groups, by Tax Rates, 1967

Tax rate[a] for 1967	Total—all rated employers		Size of taxable payroll					
			Below $20,000		$20,000 to $999,999		$1,000,000 and over	
	Number	Percent of total	Number of employers	Percent of total	Number of employers	Percent of total	Number of employers	Percent of total
Total—all rates	86,394	100.0	48,167	100.0	37,297	100.0	930	100.0
4.2[b]	6,974	8.1	4,812	10.0	2,130	5.7	32	3.4
4.1[b]	1,009	1.2	633	1.3	371	1.0	5	0.5
4.0	1,121	1.3	713	1.5	396	1.1	12	1.3
3.8	1,153	1.3	698	1.5	448	1.2	7	0.8
3.5	1,314	1.5	780	1.6	522	1.4	12	1.3
3.1	1,624	1.9	907	1.9	708	1.9	9	1.0
2.8	1,920	2.2	988	2.1	909	2.4	23	2.5
2.5	2,386	2.8	1,081	2.2	1,271	3.4	34	3.6
2.1	3,553	4.1	1,455	3.0	2,065	5.5	33	3.5
1.6	6,001	6.9	2,175	4.5	3,733	10.0	93	10.0
1.1	12,331	14.3	6,082	12.6	6,082	16.3	167	18.0
0.8	9,896	11.5	4,107	8.5	5,602	15.0	187	20.1
0.6	8,329	9.6	4,206	8.7	4,009	10.7	114	12.3
0.5	5,658	6.5	2,974	6.2	2,608	7.0	76	8.2
0.4	4,457	5.2	2,559	5.3	1,849	5.0	49	5.3
0.3	3,530	4.1	2,161	4.5	1,341	3.6	28	3.0
0.2	2,698	3.1	1,764	3.7	918	2.5	16	1.7
0.1	12,440	14.4	10,072	20.9	2,335	6.3	33	3.5

Source: Calculated from tabulation issued by Division of Research and Statistics, Ohio Bureau of Unemployment Compensation, Table RS 204.3 (Columbus, 1967).

[a] Include 0.1 percent mutualized tax rate.
[b] These rates were assigned to negative-balance firms.

Table A-19. NEW YORK: Cost/Tax Ratios[a] for Selected Three-Digit
Industries, Years 1964 through 1967

S I C	Industry	1964	1965	1966	1967
17	Construction–special trade contractors	158.2	147.8	132.8	137.0
171	Plumbing and heating	107.9	117.4	92.3	71.8
172	Painting and papering	211.0	223.4	210.8	221.2
173	Electrical work	53.4	47.6	35.1	54.6
174	Masonry and Plastering	234.3	251.1	212.6	223.4
177	Concrete work	275.0	293.2	178.3	217.0
178	Water well drilling	92.2	43.1	74.2	100.0
20	Food and kindred products	106.9	89.9	94.2	105.5
203	Canning and preserving fruits, vegetables, and sea food	249.6	191.3	181.4	212.6
23	Apparel	195.9	156.3	166.2	201.6
231	Men's and boys' suits and coats	153.7	91.5	112.6	145.3
233	Women's and misses' outerwear	210.3	187.0	187.6	212.0
234	Women's, children's under garments	116.3	95.8	84.8	100.1
235	Hats, caps, and millinery	366.1	311.1	347.5	459.7
237	Fur goods	305.6	245.9	248.0	379.2
239	Miscellaneous fabricated textile products	177.8	139.3	145.5	168.8

Sources: Benefit payments: Annual reports on Unemployment Insurance Tax Rates, 1965, 1966, 1967, and 1968, published by the Division of Employment, Department of Labor, State of New York. Taxes paid: years 1964 through 1966–estimates based on tabulation furnished by the Research and Statistics office of the Division of Employment; year 1967–estimates based on annual report on Unemployment Insurance Tax Rates, published by Department of Labor, State of New York.

[a]The cost/tax ratio is the ratio of benefit payments to taxes paid, inclusive of subsidiary taxes. For the year 1967 subsidiary taxes have been estimated.

Table A-20. Benefits Charged to Negative-Balance Firms, as Percent of Benefits Charged to All Firms,[a] by Industry Divisions and Selected Groups, Selected States, 1967

S I C	Industry	Massachusetts[b]		
		Benefits charged to all firms	Benefits charged to negative-balance firms	
		Amount (in 000's)	Amount (in 000's)	Percent of benefits charged to all firms
Totals—all industries		$72,517	$41,149	56.7
Agriculture, forestry and fisheries		1,634	1,479	90.5
Mining		193	144	74.6
Contract construction		16,676	15,150	90.8
Manufacturing		31,889	15,867	49.8
Transportation and public utilities		3,159	853	27.0
Wholesale and retail trade		10,748	3,961	36.9
Finance, insurance, real estate		2,139	468	21.9
Services		6,078	3,228	53.1
17-Construction—special trade contractors		6,929	5,903	85.2
171-Plumbing		592	199	33.6
172-Painting and papering		1,749	1,728	98.8
173-Electrical work		244	66	27.0
174-Masonry and plastering		1,881	1,829	97.2
175-Carpentry		390	339	86.9
176-Roofing and sheet-metal work		407	343	84.3
177-Concrete work		203	192	94.6
178-Water well drilling		16	9	56.3
179-Miscellaneous contractors		1,447	1,198	82.8
203-Canning and preserving fruits, vegetables, and sea foods		680	641	94.3
23-Apparel		7,694	6,727	87.4
231-Men's and boys' suits and coats		677	565	83.5
232-Men's, boys' furnishings and related products		557	448	80.4
233-Women's and misses' outerwear		4,023	3,660	91.0
234-Women's, children's undergarments		283	191	67.5
235-Hats, caps, millinery		805	803	99.8
236-Children's, infants' outerwear		232	223	96.1
237-Fur goods		7	7	100.0
238-Miscellaneous apparel and accessories		488	382	78.3
239-Miscellaneous fabricated textile products		622	448	72.0

Sources: The data in this table were derived mainly from periodic and special reports issued by the employment security agencies of the respective states. In cases where the data were not available in published form, they were supplied by the agency as requested.

[a]Excluded are benefits charged to accounts which lapsed during the year.

| | Michigan[c] | | | New York | |
| Benefits charged to all firms | Benefits charged to negative-balance firms | | Benefits charged to all firms | Benefits charged to negative-balance firms | |
Amount (in 000's)	Amount (in 000's)	Percent of benefits charged to all firms	Amount (in 000's)	Amount (in 000's)	Percent of benefits charged to all firms
$60,244	$20,968	34.8	$294,202	$174,588	59.3
515	463	89.9	d	d	d
1,085	856	78.9	d	d	d
13,555	9,513	70.2	54,301	48,252	88.9
31,460	4,462	14.2	139,405	82,199	59.0
2,818	1,745	61.9	13,176	5,055	38.4
6,207	1,841	29.7	41,648	16,337	39.2
666	95	14.3	8,903	2,664	29.9
3,938	1,994	50.6	36,421[d]	19,799[d]	54.4[d]
4,442	2,769	62.3	25,144	20,968	83.4
			2,988	1,760	58.9
			4,227	4,065	96.2
			1,073	179	16.7
			6,513	6,159	94.6
			1,746	1,535	87.9
			1,093	835	76.4
			2,767	2,716	98.2
			45	27	60.0
			4,692	3,690	78.6
			3,204	2,761	86.2
456	189	41.4	52,553	45,914	87.4
			3,136	2,344	74.7
			2,844	2,456	86.4
			25,571	22,932	89.7
			2,077	1,271	61.2
			3,926	3,858	98.3
			2,760	2,298	83.3
			3,542	3,440	97.1
			3,414	2,962	86.8
			5,282	4,353	82.4

[b]Data are for rated firms. Benefit charges are for the twelve-month period ending September 30, 1967. Some 18 percent of benefit payments in Massachusetts in that fiscal year were noncharged.

[c]Data cover the twelve months preceding the computation date for the 1967 rate year. Figures for industry-group subdivisions were not available for Michigan.

[d]Data for "agriculture, forestry and fishing," and "mining and quarrying" are combined with "services."

Table A-21. Benefits Charged to Negative-Balance Firms As Percent of Benefits Charged to All Firms,[a] by Size of Taxable Payroll, Selected States, Year 1967

Size of taxable payroll	Massachusetts[b]			Michigan[c]			New York		
	Benefits charged to all firms Amount (in 000's)	Benefits charged to negative-balance firms Amount (in 000's)	Percent of benefits charged to all firms	Benefits charged to all firms Amount (in 000's)	Benefits charged to negative-balance firms Amount (in 000's)	Percent of benefits charged to all firms	Benefits charged to all firms Amount (in 000's)	Benefits charged to negative-balance firms Amount (in 000's)	Percent of benefits charged to all firms
All size groups	$72,517	$41,149	56.7	$60,244	$20,968	34.8	$294,202	$174,588	59.3
Under $10,000	5,671	5,157	90.9	1,637	1,382	84.4	18,784	16,351	87.0
$10,000- 24,999	5,909	4,534	76.7	3,647	2,652	72.7	22,918	16,281	71.0
25,000- 49,999	6,206	4,323	69.7	4,178	2,685	64.3	26,892	17,690	65.8
50,000- 99,999	7,264	4,756	65.5	4,579	2,376	51.9	38,190	26,803	70.2
100,000- 249,999	11,057	7,257	65.6	7,037	3,607	51.3	57,267	40,356	70.5
250,000- 499,999	8,521	5,269	61.8	5,971	3,014	50.5	32,812	21,110	64.3
500,000- 999,999	7,004	3,978	56.8	4,836	1,834	37.9	23,308	13,280	57.0
1,000,000- 2,499,999	7,714	3,590	46.5	7,094	2,831	39.9	22,588	10,610	47.0
2,500,000- 4,999,999	3,665	953	26.0	3,366	587	17.4	16,445	9,034	54.9
5,000,000- 9,999,999	3,563	828	23.2	1,780	0	0	} 34,998	3,073	8.8
10,000,000-24,999,999	3,435	505	14.7	2,411	0	0			
25,000,000 and over	2,510	0	0	13,708					

Sources: The data in this table were derived mainly from periodic and special reports issued by the employment security agencies of the respective states. In some cases where the data were not available in published form, they were supplied by the agency as requested.

[a]Excluded are benefits charged to accounts which lapsed during the year.

[b]Data are for rated firms. Benefit charges are for the twelve-month period ending September 30, 1967. Some 18 percent of benefit payments in Massachusetts in that fiscal year were noncharged.

[c]Data cover the twelve months preceding the computation date for the 1967 rate year.

Table A–22. CALIFORNIA: Cumulative Deficits of Selected[a] Negative-Balance Employers as of June 30, 1966,[b] and Increases in Such Deficits during the Fiscal Year Ending at That Date, As Percents of 1965 Taxable Wages

SIC	Industry and title	Number of accounts	Negative reserve cumulative to June 30, 1966		Increase in negative reserve during year ending June 30, 1966	
		(1)	Amount (2)	As percentage of 1965 taxable wages (3)	Amount (4)	As percentage of 1965 taxable wages (5)
	Total, all rated negative-reserve accounts	47,828	$564,215,637	26.3	$92,225,745	4.29
	Total, selected large accounts	740	358,339,260	47.9	39,578,172	5.28
071	Agricultural services	15	10,570,104	182.9	697,964	12.07
151	Building construction—general contractors	75	18,039,519	31.1	2,777,240	4.78
161	Highway and street construction (except elevated highways)	47	19,153,457	36.2	3,010,063	5.69
162	Heavy construction (except highway and street construction)	60	21,796,453	27.3	3,433,770	4.30
201	Meat products	8	3,460,431	63.4	316,436	5.79
203	Canning; preserving fruits, vegetables, and sea food	104	156,075,142	99.0	16,330,571	10.35
206	Sugar refining	4	7,746,913	37.9	1,050,652	5.14
233	Women's, misses', and juniors' outerwear	32	8,716,839	61.5	1,011,463	7.13
241	Logging camps and logging contractors	22	3,685,401	104.6	445,364	12.63
242	Sawmills and planning mills	19	4,055,499	43.8	238,405	2.57
422	Public warehousing	10	3,279,439	131.0	200,044	7.98
504	Assemblers of farm products (including fruits and vegetables)	152	39,636,267	130.0	3,264,556	10.71
505	Farm products—raw materials	6	6,995,994	115.0	777,648	12.78
781	Motion picture production	10	5,727,238	10.0	215,870	0.37
794	Sports promoters and miscellaneous recreation services	8	1,937,046	28.6	244,404	3.61
	All others	168	47,463,518	19.9	5,563,722	2.33

[a] Active rated accounts with negative balances of $100,000, or more in selected industries.

[b] Cumulative since 1938. All negative balances were canceled as of July 1, 1966.

Source: State of California, Department of Employment, Research and Statistics, Report 285 #29, California Rated Employers With Negative Reserve Balances, Rating Year 1967, Table 7, Financial experience of rated employer accounts active on June 30, 1966 with negative balance of $100,000 or more as of June 30, 1966, by selected industry (July 17, 1967).

Table A-23. Reserve-Ratio States Ranked According to Tax Rates and
to Selected Measures of Liberality,[a] for Year 1967

Reserve-ratio states	Average tax rate as percent of total wages	Ratio of average weekly benefit amount to average weekly total wage	Proportion of claimants:		
			Whose weekly benefit amount was *not* limited by state's maximum	Who met monetary requirements	Who met non-monetary requirements
	Rank	Rank	Rank	Rank[b]	Rank[c]
	(1)	(2)	(3)	(4)	(5)
Colorado	1	31	4.5	2	2
Iowa	2	27	6	19	6
Missouri	3	8	12	5	20
District of Columbia	4	21	20.5	7	8
South Dakota	5	19	9	8	31
Nebraska	6	20	7	24	1
Indiana	7	2	4.5	20	21
New Hampshire	8	22	30.5	22.5	14
Ohio	9	6	1.5	25	12
Georgia	10	14	24	6	3
Kansas	11	26	15	16.5	11
New Mexico	12	4	10.5	16.5	24
Louisiana	13	9	13.5	1	29
Maine	14	18	27	14	23
Michigan	15	12	1.5	27	10
Arkansas	16.5	15	28	12	18
North Carolina	16.5	3	32	18	27
Kentucky	19	16	16	11	28
South Carolina	19	17	29	4	4
West Virginia	19	1	20.5	21	7
Wisconsin	21	28	17.5	30	26
New York	22.5	10	24	29	9
Tennessee	22.5	5	24	9	32
Arizona	24	11	8	10	5
New Jersey	25	7	17.5	26	16
Hawaii	26	32	20.5	31.5	17
Massachusetts	27.5	24	30.5	31.5	30
North Dakota	27.5	30	10.5	3	22
Idaho	29	29	13.5	13	25
Nevada	30	13	3	22.5	13
Rhode Island	31	25	20.5	28	19
California	32	23	26	15	15

Table A–23. (Continued)

Reserve-ratio states	Average tax rate as percent of total wages	Ratio of average weekly benefit amount to average weekly total wage	Proportion of claimants:		
			Whose weekly benefit amount was *not* limited by state's maximum	Who met monetary require-ments	Who met non-monetary require-ments
	Rank	Rank	Rank	Rank[b]	Rank[c]
	(1)	(2)	(3)	(4)	(5)
Spearman rank correlation coefficient		0.123	0.305	0.327	0.276
Significant at 0.05 level		0.301	0.301	0.301	0.301
Significant at 0.10 level		0.295	0.295	0.295	0.295

Sources: *Handbook of Unemployment Insurance Financial Data. Unemployment Insurance; State Laws and Experience, BES No. U–198 R, Unemployment Insurance Statistics*, all published by Manpower Administration, U.S. Department of Labor.

[a]Ranks are assigned in ascending order: the greater the degree of liberality the higher the rank. Liberality is measured by the size of the ratio or proportion: the larger the ratio or proportion the more liberal the state. Fractional or identical ratings indicate ties between states.

[b]The ranking in column (4) is based only on the percents of new claimants having sufficient wage credits. (In some states a further requirement is imposed in terms of length of time worked in covered employment in the base period.)

[c]The ranking in column (5) is based on the number of claimants denied benefits as a proportion of 1,000 "claimant contacts" (the sum of initial and continued claims).

APPENDIX **B**

The Mechanics of Experience Rating

Experience Rating and "Additional" Credit

In 1935 President Franklin D. Roosevelt and the Congress feared that the United States Supreme Court would declare unconstitutional any social security legislation that imposed federal taxes for the purpose of paying unemployment benefits. To lessen this danger, the device of the tax offset was used. Although the 1935 Federal Unemployment Tax Act (FUTA) required all covered employers to pay a 3 percent payroll tax to the federal government, it provided that if a state established an approved unemployment compensation law of its own, the employers of that state could use the taxes they paid to the state as a partial offset against their gross federal tax. As provided in FUTA, this tax credit offset currently reads as follows:

SEC. 3302. CREDITS AGAINST TAX.
(a) Contributions to State Unemployment Funds.—
(1) The taxpayer may, to the extent provided in this subsection and subsection (c), credit against the tax imposed by section 3301 the amount of contributions paid by him into an unemployment fund maintained during the taxable year under the unemployment compensation law of a State which is certified for the taxable year as provided in section 3304.

The tax credit is limited to 2.7 percent. The rest of the tax must be paid to the federal government, which uses the proceeds to meet its own and the states' expenses in administering the program.[1]

Since FUTA made no provision for the payment of federal unemployment *benefits*, if a state did not establish an unemployment insurance program of its own, its employers would pay the federal tax, but its workers would receive no benefits from it. Under this stong inducement, all states have enacted unemployment insurance laws. These laws must begin by imposing a "standard" rate of 2.7 percent of taxable payrolls on all covered employers, but may reduce this rate for those employers whose experience with unemployment seems to warrant a reduction. This is "experience rating," the only method available to a state to achieve a reduced rate for any employer and an average state tax of less than 2.7 percent.

To provide for experience rating in a system that uses a tax offset, it is necessary to employ the cumbersome device of "additional credit." (Otherwise a

---

1. The original 3.0 percent federal tax was later increased to 3.1 percent and more recently to 3.2 percent; but the tax credit has remained at 2.7 percent. Hence the federal share has increased from 0.3 percent to 0.5 percent.

366

reduced state rate would be nullified by an increase in the employer's federal tax payment.) Under the provision of Section 3302(b) of the Act shown below, an employer who qualifies for a reduced rate under the experience-rating provisions of the state unemployment insurance law is allowed to deduct not only his actual contribution to the state but also the additional tax (up to 2.7 percent) which would have been payable if he had not qualified for a reduced rate.

[3302] (b) Additional Credit.—In addition to the credit allowed under subsection (a), a taxpayer may credit against the tax imposed by section 3301 for any taxable year an amount, with respect to the unemployment compensation law of each State certified for the taxable year as provided in section 3303 (or with respect to any provisions thereof so certified), equal to the amount, if any, by which the contributions required to be paid by him with respect to the taxable year were less than the contributions such taxpayer would have been required to pay if throughout the taxable year he had been subject under such State law to the highest rate applied thereunder in the taxable year to any person having individuals in his employ, or to a rate of 2.7 percent, whichever rate is lower.

However, the employer is granted this additional credit only if the experience-rating provisions of his state meet specified conditions:

SEC. 3303. CONDITIONS OF ADDITIONAL CREDIT ALLOWANCE.
    (a) State Standards.—A taxpayer shall be allowed an additional credit under section 3302(b) with respect to any reduced rate of contributions permitted by a State law, only if the Secretary of Labor finds that under such a law—
    (1) no reduced rate of contributions to a pooled fund or to a partially pooled account is permitted to a person (or group of persons) having individuals in his (or their) employ except on the basis of his (or their) experience with respect to unemployment or other factors bearing a direct relation to unemployment risk during not less than the 3 consecutive years immediately preceding the computation date.

In this provision the key phrase is "on the basis of his experience with respect to unemployment."
    A simple illustration may help to clarify the essential operation of the system. The example assumes an employer whose taxable payroll is $1,000,000 and who is required to pay a state experience-rated tax of 1 percent.

Total federal tax (3.2% × $1,000,000)	=	$32,000
Less credit for state tax actually paid		
(1.0% × $1,000,000)	= $10,000	
Less additional Credit[2] (1.7% × $1,000,000)	= 17,000	
Total credit (2.7% × $1,000,000)	=	27,000
Net federal tax due (0.5% × $1,000,000)	=	$ 5,000

Thus, instead of paying a tax of $32,000, the employer actually pays a total of only $15,000 ($10,000 to the state, $5,000 to the federal government).

Systems of Experience Rating

At present there are five distinct systems of experience rating, usually identified as reserve-ratio, benefit-ratio, benefit-wage-ratio, compensable separations,

2. For the state tax that would have been paid except for experience rating.

and payroll-decline formulas. A few states use combinations of two or more systems.

In spite of significant differences, all systems have certain common characteristics. All formulas are devised to establish the relative experience of individual employers with unemployment or with benefit costs. To this end, all have factors for measuring each employer's experience with unemployment or benefit expenditures, and all compare this experience with some measure of relative exposure—usually payrolls. However, the five systems differ greatly in the construction of the formulas, in the factors used to measure experience and the methods of measurement, in the number of years over which the experience is recorded, in the use of other factors, and in the relative weight given the various factors in the final assignment of rates.

1) *Reserve-ratio formula.* This system is, essentially, cost accounting. For each employer an account is set up to which his contributions are credited and against which benefits paid to his former employees are charged. The ratio of the resulting balance to the employer's annual payroll is then determined. This is the reserve-ratio. The balance carried forward each year under the reserve-ratio plan is ordinarily the difference between the employer's total contributions and the total benefits received by his workers since the law became effective, or other date as may be specified by a particular state law.

The payroll used to measure the reserves is ordinarily the last three years, but some states use the last year's payroll only, while a few use more than three years.

The employer must accumulate and maintain a specified reserve ratio before his rate is reduced. Then rates are assigned according to a schedule of rates for specified ranges of reserve ratios: the higher the ratio the lower the tax rate. The formula is designed to ensure that no employer will be granted a rate reduction unless over the years he contributes more to the fund than his workers draw in benefits. Also, fluctuations in the state fund balance affect the rate that an employer will pay for a given reserve; an increase in the state fund may signal the application of an alternate tax rate schedule in which a lower rate is assigned for a given reserve and, conversely, a decrease in the fund balance may signal the application of an alternate tax schedule in which a higher rate is assigned for a given reserve.

As of January 1, 1971, thirty-two states, with 66 percent of all covered employment, used the reserve-ratio system.

2) *Benefit-ratio formula.* The benefit-ratio formula also uses benefits as the measure of experience, but eliminates contributions from the formula and relates benefits directly to payrolls. The ratio of benefits to payrolls is the index for rate variation. Rates are further varied by the inclusion in the formulas of three or more schedules, effective at specified levels of the state fund in terms of dollar amounts or a proportion of payrolls or fund adequacy percentage.

Unlike the reserve ratio, the benefit-ratio system is geared to short-term experience. Only the benefits paid in the most recent three years are used in the determination of the benefit ratios.

As of January 1, 1971, nine states, with 18.5 percent of covered employment, used the benefit-ratio formula.

3) *Benefit-wage-ratio formula.* The benefit-wage formula makes no attempt to measure all benefits paid to the workers of individual employers. The relative

experience of employers is measured by the separations of workers which result in benefit payments, but the duration of their benefits is not a factor. "Frequency" is accurately measured, but "severity" is only approximated. The number of such separations from an employer, times the total wages that have been paid to the separated workers during their "base-periods," are recorded for each employer as his "benefit wages." The ratio of these "benefit wages," totaled over the last three years, to his total payroll during this period is determined once a year for each employer. This is the employer's "experience factor." Next, a "state experience factor" is determined by calculating the ratio of total benefit payments to total benefit wages in the state in the preceding three years. Each employer's tax rate is then determined by multiplying his experience factor by the state experience factor, and relating the product to a table of tax rates.[3]

As of January 1, 1971, five states, with 10.6 percent of all covered employment, used the benefit-wage system.

4) *Compensable-separations formula*. Like the benefit-wage formula, this formula requires less record keeping because it uses compensable separations as the measure of an employer's experience with unemployment. A worker's separation is weighted by his weekly benefit amount, and that amount is entered on the employer's experience-rating record. The employer's aggregate payroll for three years is then divided by the sum of the entries over the three years to establish his index. Rates are assigned on the basis of an array of payrolls in the order of the indexes, the lowest rates to those with the highest indexes. One of a number of different tax rate schedules is applied, according to the size of the fund. This formula is used only by Connecticut.

5) *Payroll-decline formula*. Under this system, tax rates are determined on the basis of variations in payrolls, without any reference to whether benefits were paid to the employer's former workers. An employer's experience with unemployment is measured by the decline in his payrolls from quarter to quarter or from year to year. The declines are expressed as a percentage of payrolls in the preceding period: the firms with the smallest declines are eligible for the largest proportional reduction in their tax rates.

As of January 1, 1971, three states, with 2.3 percent of covered employment, made some use of this formula, but only Utah used it exclusively.

Natural Tax Rate

In the reserve-ratio system there is a fundamental relationship known as the "natural tax rate." This is an equilibrium rate toward which the system constantly tends. For all employers whose benefit chargeback rate is less than the maximum tax and more than the minimum tax, the tax rate tends to stabilize at the point where it equals the benefit chargeback rate.

If this equilibrium is disturbed, it tends to reestablish itself. If, for example, the rate of benefit charges grows, the tax rate will increase to match it. Likewise, if taxable payrolls increase—because a higher tax base is legislated or because

---

3. Because this formula requires less record keeping, it is simpler to administer. Ease of administration was the main purpose of its most active salesman, Frank B. Cliffe, then of the General Electric Company, and was its chief merit in the eyes of the states which adopted it in the early days of the program, when the difficulties of all phases of administration loomed large.

firms grow in size—or if a higher tax schedule goes into operation, the tax rate of an affected employer will increase, but only temporarily. Eventually the tax rate of such an employer will return to its "natural" or equilibrium level, where it equals the rate of benefit charges. (When the disturbance in the equilibrium is caused by an increase in taxable payrolls, the firm's reserve will be larger and its tax rate lower at the new equilibrium point.)

A homely example, making use of the "bathtub theorem," may help to make this relationship clearer. The tub is like the fund; the water level in the tub is like the reserve ratio; the spigot letting water into the tub is like the inflow of taxes; the drain letting water out of the tub is like the outflow of benefits, of which part is metered, part is not. The metered part consists of benefits that are charged to some employer's account; the nonmetered part consists of non-charged and ineffectively charged benefits. What the principle of the natural tax rate says is that the inflow from the tax spigot tends to equal the metered outflow through the benefit drain. Or in other terms, the natural tax rate tends to equal the benefit chargeback rate.

From this fundamental relationship there follow many interesting conclusions, some of which are developed in a series of technical papers published by the California unemployment insurance agency [164]. Here, however, it suffices to point out that the natural or equilibrium tax rate is the basis for the general principle that every dollar of benefits charged against a given firm will have to be replaced by that firm, all other factors remaining unchanged, if the firm's long-run tax rate is between the minimum and the maximum. (The operation of this principle is reflected in Chart 2, Chapter 11, which shows the cumulative benefit costs and tax payments of company E for the decade 1956–65.)

Tax Avoidance

Tax avoidance is not to be confused with tax evasion, which by definition is illegal. Attempts at tax avoidance follow tax legislation as inevitably as mechanical breakdowns follow machinery. In unemployment insurance, some forms of tax avoidance are common to uniform and experience-rated taxes alike, but some are peculiar to experience rating. Among the latter, some affect the payment of benefits while others—like the devices of payrolling and the joint account—affect only the distribution of the tax burden. These last two are the subject matter of Appendix C.

Payrolling

If one part of a firm's operations tends to generate much higher unemployment insurance benefit costs than another, the firm may arrange to place the employees of this operation on a separate payroll, as though they worked for a separate firm. By this device, instead of paying at a single tax rate on the combined payroll the firm pays at different tax rates on separate payrolls. In some situations, the firm thus achieves a permanent saving in taxes, while in other situations the tax payment is at least delayed so that the firm has the use of its cash for a longer time. The gain to the firm is likely to be greatest when one part of the payroll has a benefit-cost rate higher than the maximum tax rate. In this situation there will likely be some benefits charged ineffectively against the high-cost payroll which would have been charged effectively against the combined payroll. The tax saving represented by these ineffectively charged benefits will be permanent in three situations: if the high-cost payroll is taxed at the maximum rate indefinitely; if the state has a policy of writing off negative balances; or if the high-cost operation goes out of (legal) existence while its reserve balance is still negative.

The allocation of high-cost employees to a separate payroll may be achieved in three ways. (1) A firm may hire such employees, not directly, but through a manpower agency that performs most of the ordinary functions of an employer with respect to such employees—recruiting them, setting their rates of pay, determining their working hours, etc. Although this arrangement may permit the client firm to avoid part of the unemployment insurance tax,[1] the practice is unobjectionable since the manpower agency is by all ordinary tests the real employer of these workers and as such is properly responsible for the payment of all payroll taxes.[2]

1. Usually the avoidance of the unemployment insurance tax is a minor reason among many reasons for the use of the manpower agency.
2. These manpower agencies are not necessarily deficit firms; in fact, the majority of them are not. The majority pay a tax rate below the maximum and are concerned with controlling claims. Some even hire service companies for this purpose.

2) In recent years some manpower agencies have expanded their traditional functions and have offered to carry on their payrolls high-cost employees hired and completely controlled by the client firm. The manpower agency performs the bookkeeping functions connected with the payroll, including the payment of payroll taxes, but that is all. The client firm performs all the other functions of an employer.

3) A corporation may be reorganized into separate legal entities so as to concentrate all high-cost employees on one payroll. The reorganization may represent a genuine change in the operations of the firm or merely the creation of another corporation established solely for the purpose of reducing tax costs.

Administrators in some states have begun to challenge the second and third types of payrolling on the ground that the actual employer, for the purposes of the unemployment insurance law, is not the manpower agency or the dummy corporation, but is the firm that hires, fires, sets wages and working conditions, and in other ways completely controls the working relationship. In a number of instances, the challenged firm has agreed to make restitution of the taxes in exchange for the administrator's promise of immunity from possible penalties and prosecution. These administrative rulings have not yet been tested thoroughly in the courts.

There is little information on the extent of payrolling. In 1968, the Unemployment Compensation Committee on the Interstate Conference of Employment Security Agencies studied the problem briefly and invited all the states to report on the prevalence of the practice. A half-dozen states supplied a number of interesting examples but were unable to say how representative they might be. The Committee reached the tentative conclusion that the practice of payrolling was not widespread.

An article on payrolling which appeared in the *Wall Street Journal* [165] mentioned the example of the firm of Mattel, Inc., a Los Angeles toy-maker, which had reorganized its subsidiaries in such a way that most high-cost employees were concentrated on one payroll. Apprised of the situation by the journal article, the California unemployment insurance agency forbade the company to continue the practice. Later the company transferred its seasonal high-cost operations to a new plant just across the border in Mexico. As a result, the firm continued to avoid the tax and California lost a sizable number of seasonal jobs. It is hardly likely that the firm made the move primarily to lower its unemployment insurance tax rate, but the prohibition against payrolling may have been a contributing factor. The location of the high-cost operation in a separate plant across the border may indicate that the original reorganization was more than a payrolling device and that the agency might properly have allowed the divided operation.

Joint Account

This device has essentially the same objective as payrolling but uses the opposite technique. Instead of separating units, it joins them for the sake of avoiding taxes. This practice seems to have been concentrated largely in New York. As of 1967, according to a survey made by New York [166], only fourteen states made any provision for joint accounts,[3] of which only three permitted firms to

3. Arizona, California, Colorado, Connecticut, Delaware, Hawaii, Missouri, New Jersey, New York, Ohio, Oregon, Washington, West Virgina, Wyoming.

join and dissolve at will, and only two had any substantial experience with the device.

For many years the New York law has provided that two or more firms could combine their experience for the sake of obtaining a common tax rate. The provision seems to have arisen from the original interest in employment stabilization. Two seasonal firms might have complementary employment patterns, one hiring while the other was laying off, and if they had a common tax rate they would have an inducement to organize their hiring patterns in such a way as to employ one another's laid-off workers. The provision was used very little for this or any other purpose until recently, when its tax-avoidance potentialities began to be recognized.

The device utilizes excess reserves, which one firm in effect rents out to another. A firm with a very low tax rate and "excess" reserves will agree to accept a joint tax rate with a firm that has a higher tax rate. In this context, excess reserves are those above the amount needed to maintain a minimum tax rate.[4] The potential of the joint account is thus in direct proportion to the existence of excess reserves, which in turn depend on a state's tax structure. There is much less inducement to set up a joint account in Ohio, for example, than in New York, where the truncated structure of the lower tax intervals results in large amounts of "excess" reserves. From the viewpoint of the firm, these are idle funds which the firm would prefer to put to work for its own benefit. The firm's reserve may be so excessive that even when combined with the lower reserve of a high-cost firm, the resulting joint tax rate is greater than the tax rate it would have if it stood alone. There is thus the possibility of the two firms coming to some mutually advantageous agreement.

The joint account could be, and usually was, dissolved at the end of one year. It could then be reestablished or not at the pleasure of the two parties and in view of the expected developments of the coming year. If the joint account was dissolved, each firm resumed its own total experience and was assigned a tax rate based on this lifetime experience—just as though neither firm had ever entered into a joint-account arrangement. Thus the low-cost firm assumed practically no risk.

The gain accruing to the high-cost firm would be temporary or permanent under much the same conditions as were listed above in connection with payrolling. In its analysis of experience under joint accounts, the New York Division of Employment contended that the gains were only temporary. It presented several examples of firms which had saved two-tenths of a percentage point on their 1966 tax rate, but which had paid a 1967 tax rate two-tenths percent higher than they would have paid if they had not gone into the joint account the year before. Although, these examples proved that the advantage was temporary, they did not disprove the existence of some advantage. The firms had the use of more funds during 1966 than they otherwise would have had. The gain to the high-cost firm was worth at least what the use of the tax for that year was worth. In other examples developed by the agency, three years of successive tax increases were required before the gain achieved during the year of joint accounting was wiped out. In many cases, a permanent gain seems to have been

4. The calculation may be made even more finely. For example, in New York the tax rate increases as the reserve ratio of the firm decreases in multiples of 0.5 percent. Thus a change in a reserve ratio of less than 0.5 percent will not result in a tax rate change, and to this extent there is an "excess" reserve available for use in a joint account.

made because of the closer claims control that resulted from the arrangement (see below).

Until about 1964 little if any use was made of the joint account for the purposes of tax avoidance. For one reason, the average firm lacked the technical knowledge required. In 1964 The Association Services Corporation (ASC), a service company[5] in New York, recognized the potentialities of the device and interested a number of its clients in making use of it. The ASC acted as a kind of marriage broker, bringing together suitable low-cost and high-cost firms. Typically, the uniting firms belonged to the same trade association and were small or medium-sized. In 1967, of all of the firms entering into a joint account under the guidance of this service company, 90 percent had less than 100 employees. While the ASC was the chief promoter of this device, many joint accounts were entered into independently of this service company.

The growth of joint accounts in New York state was rapid. The number of new accounts established in the course of a year grew from 110 in 1964 to 1,088 in 1967 [167, p. 6]. Nearly all of those established during a given year were dissolved a year later. Contending that the practice frustrated the intent of experience rating and threatened the solvency of the fund, the New York agency acted to restrict the use of the device by requiring (through an amendment to Rule 12, effective March 15, 1967) that a joint account have a minimum life of three years. Since a three-year commitment would increase the risk for the low-cost partner, the agency expected that fewer such arrangements would be made. This expectation was fulfilled, at least in part. The 1,175 joint accounts active in 1967 shrank to 336 in 1968 and thereafter (through 1971) remained at about 400. However, the ASC reports that although it has formed fewer joint accounts since 1967, the number of firms in its joint accounts has continued to increase. To offset the increased risk represented by the three-year rule, the ASC has sought safety in numbers and has greatly increased the size of the groups.

Evaluation

The devices of payrolling and the joint account may be evaluated by two norms. The first norm is simply the law, and by this norm the joint account is clearly legal, while the more extreme forms of payrolling probably are not. But the legal norm is not final. If the practices are deemed undesirable in themselves, the law can be changed to make them illegal. If, on the contrary, the practices are deemed desirable, the law can be changed to favor them. Arizona amended its law in 1969, for example, to legalize a wider use of payrolling.

Are the devices desirable in themselves? Without attempting to provide a final answer to this question, it is sufficient here to point out the relationship of these devices to experience rating. Payrolling in the second and third forms described above probably diminishes the degree of experience rating in the system. Like the uniform tax, payrolling results in some firms escaping full responsibility for their own unemployment and passing part of the burden on to other firms.

The effect of the joint account on experience rating differs as seen from the viewpoint of the low-cost or the high-cost firm. For the low-cost firm, the effect of the joint account is to increase, slightly, the degree of experience rating. In

5. In this study, the term "service company" means a firm that supplies managerial services to other firms, especially with respect to the operations of unemployment insurance.

exchange for loaning its excess reserves to its high-cost partner, the low-cost firm must gain some advantage which decreases its own costs in some manner. It is a desire for more experience rating for itself that moves the low-cost firm to enter into the joint-account arrangement.

For the high-cost firm, the effect of the joint account on experience rating is uncertain, but is probably neutral more often than not. If the high-cost partner is a deficit firm, its tax gain may or may not be permanent; if its tax gain is permanent, experience rating has been diminished. But the ASC, at least, never admits a deficit firm to a joint account. The high-cost firm must have a tax rate below the maximum and therefore subject to the law of the "natural tax rate" (Appendix B). In cases where the firm's tax gain is only temporary, the state fund suffers no permanent loss of revenue. In cases where the tax gain is permanent, this must be because improved economic conditions or tighter claims control have resulted in a lessened benefit outflow.

It is probable that the device of the joint account as administered by the ASC has the effect not only of delaying the payment of taxes into the fund but also of diminishing permanently the payment of benefits out of the fund. This is because, as a result of the joint account, the claims control exercised by both partners probably is tighter. The low-cost firm is practically always in the "zone of indifference" which prevails at the lower end of any tax scale with a minimum tax above zero. It has very little, if any, financial incentive to control claims. The ASC takes over the entire task of administering the claims filed against the account of this company. In most cases this probably results in closer claims control than existed previously. The ASC supplies this service free of charge to the low-cost firm, which thus is freed of all administrative costs connected with unemployment insurance. According to the ASC, this is the only inducement offered the low-cost firm to enter into the joint account.[6] The high-cost firm is also serviced by the ASC and is required to take an active interest in claims control and employment stabilization under penalty of being excluded from the arrangement the following year. The ASC uses as one of its norms of a satisfacory arrangement whether the combined *reserves* of the partners increase in the course of a year. The members of the joint account must therefore contribute more to the state fund than their employees take out.

One final observation is pertinent to the crucial question often raised, whether the tax differentials produced by experience rating are large enough to be significant to a firm. The interest that firms show in avoiding or even postponing some of the tax would seem to indicate that the differences in costs caused by experience rating are not negligible. Since the differences in tax rates resulting from either of these devices is usually less than one-half of one percent, the much larger differences regularly produced by experience rating (see the section on tax rates in Chapter 4) would, *a fortiori*, be perceived and felt as a distinct business cost.

---

6. According to the ASC, the members of a joint account do not know what other companies are grouped with them and have no way of communicating with one another.

Policy Statement, Wisconsin Unemployment Compensation Law

"108.01 PUBLIC POLICY DECLARATION. Without intending that this section shall supersede, alter or modify the specific provisions hereinafter contained in this chapter, the public policy of this state is declared as follows:

"(1) Unemployment in Wisconsin is recognized as an urgent public problem, gravely affecting the health, morals and welfare of the people of this state. The burdens resulting from irregular employment and reduced annual earnings fall directly on the unemployed worker and his family. The decreased and irregular purchasing power of wage earners in turn vitally affects the livelihood of farmers, merchants and manufacturers, results in a decreased demand for their products, and thus tends partially to paralyze the economic life of the entire state. In good times and in bad times unemployment is a heavy social cost, directly affecting many thousands of wage earners. Each employing unit in Wisconsin should pay at least a part of this social cost, connected with its own irregular operations, by financing compensation for its own unemployed workers. Each employer's contribution rate should vary in accordance with his own unemployment costs, as shown by experience under this chapter. Whether or not a given employing unit can provide steadier work and wages for its own employes, it can reasonably be required to build up a limited reserve for unemployment, out of which benefits shall be paid to its eligible unemployed workers, as a matter of right, based on their respective wages and lengths of service.

"(2) The economic burdens resulting from unemployment should not only be shared more fairly, but should also be decreased and prevented as far as possible. A sound system of unemployment reserves, contributions and benefits should induce and reward steady operations by each employer, since he is in a better position than any other agency to share in and to reduce the social costs of his own irregular employment. Employers and employes throughout the state should co-operate, in advisory committees under government supervision, to promote and encourage the steadiest possible employment. A more adequate system of free public employment offices should be provided, at the expense of employers, to place workers more efficiently and to shorten the periods between jobs. Education and retraining of workers during their unemployment should be encouraged. Governmental construction providing emergency relief through work and wages should be stimulated.

"(3) A gradual and constructive solution of the unemployment problem along these lines has become an imperative public need."

—

Railroad
Unemployment Insurance

Originally a part of the general social security system, the railroad industry, largely at the insistence of its unions, persuaded Congress to establish a separate system for railroad employees. It was argued that the interstate nature of the industry made a single federal system with uniform provisions more appropriate than a system of separate and different state programs. The Railroad Unemployment Insurance program (RUI) went into operation on July 1, 1939.[1]

Like the state programs, RUI is financed by a tax on covered employers, but the tax is uniform on all railroads. Thus for over thirty years there has been operating side by side with the experience-rated state system a substantial program that has never been experience-rated.[2] A brief review of the similarities and differences between the two systems may throw some additional light on the alleged effects of experience rating.

At the outset it is helpful to note two characteristics of the railroad industy in relation to RUI. The first is the long-term decline in railroad employment. Total annual employment declined from 3 million in 1945 to about 2 million in 1950 and to about 1 million in 1960. Thereafter employment continued to decline but more slowly. This characteristic is a part of the explanation of nearly all aspects of RUI.

The second general characteristic is the relatively greater influence of the railroad unions in Congress as compared with the influence of other unions either in the state legislatures or in Congress. Beginning with the establishment of the separate RUI system itself, many aspects of the system such as the availability of benefits to strikers, are attributable to union influence rather than to the absence of experience rating. Indeed, the absence of experience rating is itself attributable to this source. It is very unlikely that any increased employer interest that might have been generated by experience rating would have changed significantly the balance of power between railroad labor and railroad management.

Solvency

The history of RUI is here very instructive. During the war years, RUI reserves expanded greatly as the result of an unchanged uniform tax rate of 3

---

1. Taxes already paid by the companies to the various states were recovered by the federal government and used to begin the railroad trust fund.
2. Although the tax rate does not vary between employers, there is a kind of experience rating for the industry as a whole in the obligation of the industry to raise its own taxes and pay its own way. This can have some of the effects of experience rating, especially in the area of legislation.

percent.[3] To limit this growth of the fund, taxes might have been lowered or RUI benefits might have been increased further. Instead, in 1946, Congress established a system of cash sickness benefits, to be paid out of the same fund as unemployment benefits. But the reserves continued to grow, and in 1948 Congress abolished the principle of a fixed tax rate and substituted a sliding scale of rates from 0.5 to 3.0 percent of taxable payroll, depending on the size of the fund. This is a picture of what would inevitably have happened to the state programs in the absence of experience rating.

Then, much as in the case of Pennsylvania, reserves were allowed to decline to a point where, in 1959, RUI had to borrow from the Railroad Retirement Fund in order to meet its obligations. In 1963 the maximum tax was increased to 4.0 percent, and the financial position of the fund gradually improved. As of 1971, the RUI debt was still about $61 million, down from its peak of $300 million.

Allocation

In all probability there has been considerable subsidization of one railroad by another, but since no regular records have been kept of benefit-cost ratios, there is no way to measure the extent of the subsidy. A special study made of the experience of two years showed that the ratio of benefits to taxes varied for the individual railroads from 10 percent to 160 percent in fiscal 1967 and from 10 percent to 270 percent in fiscal 1968. In both years the great majority of companies fell in the bracket 10–40 percent. In all probability, experience rating would make a considerable difference in the amount of the taxes paid by most of the railroads, increasing the taxes of some and lowering the taxes of others.

These cost/tax differentials seem to have attracted little attention in the industry. Certainly they have not been an important issue. The lack of interest may be explainable by a number of factors. In the first place, there has been no readily available information on the extent of the differentials. Further, in a regulated industry like the railroads, where rates are set by the national government and wages are bargained with a national union, competition between the individual firms is not as keen as in the economy generally. Moreover, because the railroads tend to see their labor force as one large family protected by a variety of insurance programs to which all the roads contribute, there is less inclination to distinguish sharply between one program and another. If an employee is not cared for by one program, he is likely to end up on another; in either case, the railroads pay the cost. Thus cash benefits during sickness are paid out of the same fund as are unemployment benefits. Finally, since contributions to all the other employee insurance funds are uniform, the roads tend to accept a uniform tax in RUI as "natural."

Administration

Here the difference between the railroad and the state systems is considerable. Claims for benefits are taken by a "claims agent," a railroad employee, usually a clerk who performs this task as a minor addition to his regular work.[4]

---

3. The taxable wage base, originally $3,000, was raised in successive steps to $3,600, $4,200, and, finally, in 1959, to $4,800. (In this appendix, the description of RUI provisions may not always be technically accurate, but it is given in a form to facilitate comparison with the state unemployment insurance programs.)

4. The Railroad Retirement Board pays the railroad fifty cents for each claim processed. This was the amount originally set, and it has never been changed.

The agent forwards the claim with the necessary information to a regional office of the Railroad Retirement Board, where the determination is made to allow or to deny it. The claimant has the right to appeal a denied claim, but the employer does not have the right to appeal an allowed claim. The entire administrative process is in the hands of the claims agent, normally a union member, and the Railroad Retirement Board, whose members are appointed by the President. The agent receives his training from the Board. Given this administrative structure, it is doubtful that experience rating would make an appreciable difference in the extent of employer participation in administration.

Legislation

The provisions of RUI are determined by the Congress, usually in consultation with the unions' Railway Labor Executives Association and management's Association of American Railroads. Congress has acted frequently to amend RUI, at least as frequently as the states have amended their laws.[5]

Like the states, Congress has continually extended the duration of benefits, but has gone further than any of the states. Since 1968, railroad employees with fifteen years of service have been eligible for a year of unemployment benefits. This extension of benefits was in response to the protracted decline in railroad employment and was in a long railroad tradition going back at least to the Washington Job Protection Agreement of 1936, which made some employees eligible for five years of unemployment benefits.

As to the benefit amount, it is approximately correct to say that in comparison with the state programs the RUI was less liberal during the first few years of its separate existence, was more liberal during most ot the period following thereafter, and in recent years has been about the same as the state programs. The RUI benefit has been limited chiefly by the failure of the maximum benefit to keep pace with the higher-than-average wages in the railroad industry.[6] For the last decade, over 90 percent of RUI beneficiaries have been limited by the maximum. As a result, the benefit-wage ratio has usually been below 40 percent, sometimes much below. In 1952, for example, benefits averaged only 24 percent of earnings. This history of limitations on the benefit amount in a nonexperience-rated situation illustrates how factors other than experience rating may be at work determining the content of legislation. In the case of RUI, the chief limiting factor was simply the heavy cost of the system. The same long-term employment decline that explains the extension of the duration of benefits also explains the limited liberalization of the benefit amount.

The disqualification provisions of RUI have always been less severe than those of the average state program. According to a Department of Labor analysis, "usually 5 to 10 percent of RUI beneficiaries are unemployed for reasons that would disqualify them for benefits under most state programs" [168, p. 15]. It is questionable whether this situation has resulted from the absence of experience rating. More likely, both the milder disqualifications and the absence of experience rating are the result of a common cause, the political influence of railroad labor. The clearest example is probably the RUI provision that makes

5. A detailed historical comparison of the benefits provided by RUI and by the states may be found in [168].

6. As of January 1, 1971, thirteen states, with 37 percent of all covered employment, provided a maximum weekly benefit higher than RUI's $63. An additional five states, with 19 percent of all covered employment, provided a maximum higher than RUI's for claimants with dependents.

benefits available to strikers.[7] There is no reason to think that this provision is attributable to the absence of experience rating. Experience rating has not been needed to supply employers with an incentive to oppose this provision. The nonexperience-rated railroads have tried repeatedly, though unsuccessfully, to repeal the provision—just as New York's experience-rated employers have tried repeatedly but unsuccessfully to repeal that state's somewhat similar provision.

The increase in the RUI tax that occurred in 1956 and 1957 made the railroad industry as a whole much more conscious of the cost of unemployment benefits and led to a demand, which Congress heeded, for stricter disqualifications in cases of voluntary quitting and discharge for misconduct. Thus, even apart from experience rating, employers may take an active interest in disqualification provisions.

Although in general the railroad worker is better off today under RUI than he would be if he were still covered by the state programs, this is not necessarily, or even probably, because of the absence of experience rating. The same proposition holds, for example, with regard to retirement benefits: The railroad worker is better off today under his separate program than he would be if he were still covered under the general social security retirement system.

Stabilization

A 1957 study of the railroad industry found that "great opportunities for stabilization on a practical and economical basis exist" [137, p. 223] and observed: "The RRUI system does not appear to provide the individual carrier with a significant stabilization incentive. Whether or not a system of individual "experience rating" would provide such an incentive, the present uniform industry-wide rate means that the stabilization record of any one carrier has no significant effect on its level of contributions" [137, p. 228]. Partly with a view to increasing the carriers' stabilization incentive, the study recommended the inauguration of a supplemental unemployment benefit program: "An exceedingly strong case exists for the development of a system of private Supplementary Unemployment Benefits . . . [which] . . . will compel serious attention to layoffs and create a clear relationship between layoff avoidance and lower Supplementary Unemployment Benefits costs" [137, p. 231].

Although experience rating was never introduced into the RUI system, nor was a supplemental unemployment benefits program added, the industry has in recent years moderated the seasonal swings in employment of its maintenance-of-way operations. The change has come about partly under the influence of a high RUI tax rate (4 percent on a $4,800 base) and partly through increased mechanization.

Conclusions

The railroad industry, a world to itself, differs from the rest of industry in so many major ways that the effect of a minor difference like the absence of experience rating cannot be isolated. However, it is possible to draw an instructive negative conclusion. The difference in experience rating did not prevent certain similar developments in the history of RUI and the state system. Among

7. One justification offered for the provision is the legal limitation on the freedom of the railroad unions to strike. Benefits are paid only if the strike has met all the legal requirements. Because railroad strikes tend to be infrequent and short-lived, the direct cost of this provision has been small. Over the life of the program, less than 1 percent of total benefits have been paid to claimants on strike.

the similarities were the demand for a way to reduce the tax as reserves grew; the fall into insolvency as the result of reducing taxes while increasing benefits; the steady liberalization of the duration provisions; the lag of the maximum benefit behind the increase in wages; and the demand for stricter disqualifications as experience was gained and as costs rose. Such similarities afford another opportunity to apply the "principle of limits:" The effects properly attributable to experience rating cannot be greater than are compatible with this similarity in history between experience-rated and nonexperience-rated systems.

A Hypothetical Example of Internal Experience Rating

Premises:

1. A company has five units in state D. Its three-year average annual payroll is $33,000,000.

2. Its reserve balance (total contributions less total benefits charged) on the computation date is $1,388,000 for a reserve ratio to average annual payroll of 4.2 percent.

3. A ratio of 4.2 percent on the computation date in state D establishes an unemployment tax rate of 1 percent of the calendar year's taxable wages.

4. Its total taxable wages for the calendar year is $31,000,000, and, accordingly, its contribution for that year is $310,000 (1 percent of 31 million).

Application:

The company spreads the $310,000 among its five units by using experience rating in the following manner:

Unit	Taxable wages for calendar year	Tax rate[1]	Col. 2 × col. 3	Col. 4 as a percent of total of col. 4
(1)	(2)	(3)	(4)	(5)
A	$ 1,000,000	0	0	0
B	4,000,000	2.7	$108,000	34.0
C	6,000,000	.7	42,000	13.2
D	9,000,000	1.0	90,000	28.4
E	11,000,000	.7	77,000	24.4
Total	$31,000,000		$317,000	100.0

Column 5 indicates each unit's percentage share of the company's contribution of $310,000 for all units. Using those percentages, each unit will be charged amounts computed as follows:

1. Each unit's tax rate is determined by its reserve ratio in the same manner that the tax rate would be determined by the state if the units were separate entities, with one exception: the company does not recognize a maximum rate when making calculations to arrive at the rates indicated in column 3. Each unit's share of the company's contribution is added to its reserve, from which benefits paid to its employees are deducted.

Unit	Percentage share of total contribution	Total contribution	Each unit's share
A	0	$310,000	0
B	34.0	310,000	$105,400
C	13.2	310,000	40,920
D	28.4	310,000	88,040
E	24.4	310,000	75,640
	100.0		$310,000

Memorandum of Company X:
Centralization vs. Decentralization of the Unemployment Insurance Operation

The following are the principal reasons why the processing of unemployment insurance claims and the handling of appeals to Referees and the Appeals Board should be done in the Group Executive Office, that is, should be centralized:

1. The employment insurance tax rate is levied against the corporation as a whole rather than by divisions. This tax rate can be affected by the manner in which unemployment insurance claims and appeals are handled. Improper handling by one division can result in a higher tax rate for all divisions.

2. If the unemployment insurance function should be decentralized, it would become a part-time responsibility of several people in the divisions. It is not likely that the same degree of expertise in claims and appeals handling, which the unemployment insurance staff now has, could be developed on the part of division personnel who would continue to have other major responsibilities. Further, changes in personnel in the divisions could make a continuous training process necessary.

(Decisions as to eligibility for unemployment insurance benefits are based on precedent decisions handed down by the Appeals Board and the courts during the past twenty-eight years. We must be thoroughly familiar with these decisions to do the most effective job. Further, we must keep up with new precedents.)

3. Examining and cross-examining of witnesses in a hearing requires a great deal of skill. (In some states, only lawyers are permitted to do this.) This skill is best acquired and maintained through a full-time participation in hearings.

4. The preparation of briefs and the presentation of oral arguments before the Appeals Board requires considerable skill. Some employers retain lawyers for this purpose. Decentralization would make it necessary to train five individuals to do this; it is the responsibility of only *one* individual now.

5. It is assumed that if the operation were decentralized, there would be monitoring of activity in the divisions. A report of activity would not reveal the quality of the job being done. This could be determined only by a review of claim files, transcripts of appeal hearings, briefs, etc. Executive office staff would be required for this.

6. Experience is a very important factor in the effectiveness of appeals handling. Each referee has his own personal peculiarities as well as his own ideas as to the conduct of hearings. Representatives attending quantities of hearings become familiar with these and act accordingly.

7. A centralized system permits the unemployment insurance staff to determine over a period of time changes in the philosophy of the state agency in regard to benefit payments and to spot inconsistency in the decisions of deputies and referees. Steps can be taken by the Unemployment Insurance Manager to remedy situations which are adverse to the Company's interest.

8. A centralized function ties in with the activity of the Executive Office in preparing and presenting material concerning unemployment insurance matters for the consideration of various employer and legislative groups.

References

1. Witte, Edwin E. "Development of Unemployment Compensation." *Yale Law Journal*, vol. 55, no. 1 (December 1945).
2. U.S. Congress, House, Committee on Ways and Means, *Unemployment Compensation, Hearings on H.R. 8282*, 89th Cong., 1st Sess., 1965 (Parts 1, 2, 3, 4, and 5).
3. Walgrave, J. H., P.P. *Newman the Theologian*. New York: Sheed and Ward 1960, pp. 122-23.
4. Witte, Edwin E. *The Development of the Social Security Act*. Madison: The University of Wisconsin Press, 1962.
5. Altmeyer, Arthur J. *The Formative Years of Social Security*. Madison: The University of Wisconsin Press, 1968.
6. Raushenbush, Paul A. "Starting Unemployment Compensation in Wisconsin." *Unemployment Insurance Review* (April-May 1967). Washington: U.S. Department of Labor, Bureau of Employment Security.
7. Nelson, Daniel. *Unemployment Insurance: The American Experience, 1915-1935.* Madison: The University of Wisconsin Press, 1969.
8. Lubove, Roy. *The Struggle for Social Security, 1900-1935*. Cambridge: Harvard University Press, 1968.
9. Feldman, Herman, and Smith, Donald M. *The Case for Experience Rating in Unemployment Compensation and a Proposed Method*. New York: Industrial Relations Counselors, Inc., 1939.
10. Lester, Richard A., and Kidd, Charles V. *The Case Against Experience Rating in Unemployment Compensation*. New York: Industrial Relations Counselors, Inc., 1939.
11. Malisoff, Harry. "The Emergence of Unemployment Compensation." *Political Science Quarterly* 54 (June, September, and December 1939), and 55 (June 1940).
12. Burns, Eveline M. *The American Social Security System*. Boston: Houghton Mifflin Company, 1949.
13. _____. *Social Security and Public Policy*. New York: McGraw-Hill Book Company, Inc., 1956.
14. Haber, William, and Murray, Merrill G. *Unemployment Insurance in the American Economy*. Homewood, Illinois: Richard D. Irwin, Inc., 1966.
15. Raushenbush, Paul A. Presentation to the International Association of Government Labor Officials. Chicago: September 15, 1933.
16. _____. "The Wisconsin Idea: Unemployment Reserves." *Annals* (November 1933).
17. Raushenbush, Paul A. and Elizabeth B. *Oral History, Social Security Project*. New York: Columbia University, October 1966.

18. Rubinow, I. M. "The Ohio Idea: Unemployment Insurance." *Annals* (November 1933).

19. _____. *The Quest for Security*. New York: Henry Holt and Company, 1934.

20. _____. "State Pool Plans and Merit Rating." *Law and Contemporary Problems*, vol. 3, no. 1 (Duke Station, Durham, N.C.: January 1936).

21. Beveridge, William H. *Unemployment: A Problem of Industry*. London: Longmans, Green and Co., 1930.

22. Becker, Joseph M., S.J. *Shared Government in Employment Security: A Study of Advisory Councils*. New York: Columbia University Press, 1959.

23. Barbash, Jack. "John R. Commons and the Americanization of the Labor Problem." *Journal of Economic Issues*, vol. 1, no. 3 (September 1967): 161 (Reprint Series No. 92, The University of Wisconsin, Industrial Relations Research Institute).

24. Raushenbush, Paul A. "The Wisconsin Unemployment Reserve Law," reprinted from *Quarterly Bulletin of the New York State Conference on Social Work* (April 1933).

25. Bureau of Employment Security, Employment Security Memorandum No. 9, *Standards for the Interpretation of Section 1602(a) (1) of the Internal Revenue Code*. U.S. Dept. of Labor, July 1940.

26. Raushenbush, Paul A. "Federalization Threatens Experience Rating and State Laws," talk to American Photo-Engravers Association. Madison: Industiral Commission of Wisconsin, 1941.

27. Douglas, Paul H. *Social Security in the United States*. New York: McGraw–Hill Book Company, Inc., 1939.

28. Green, William "Merit Rating Will Bankrupt Funds and Menace Benefits." *American Federationist*, (January 1939).

29. Interstate Conference of Employment Security Agencies, *Proceedings of the Fourth Annual Meeting*. Washington, D.C.: October 1–4, 1940.

30. O'Brien, James. "The Shocking Erosion of the Jobless Pay System." *American Federalist* (January 1969).

31. Interstate Conference of Employment Security Agencies, Report of the Committee on Employer Experience Rating, *Volume I–Unanimous Report, Experience Rating under Unemployment Compensation Laws*. Washington, D.C.: September 1940.

32. Interstate Conference of Employment Security Agencies, *Statements Presented by Representatives of Several Interest Groups at a Meeting of the Committee on Employer Experience Rating*. February 13, 1940. (mimeo.).

33. Interstate Conference of Employment Security Agencies, Report of the Committee on Employer Experience Rating. *Volume II–Majority Report, An Evaluation of Experience Rating in Relation to Federal Standards and the Broad Social and Economic Effects of Variable Rates*. Washington, D.C.: September 1940.

34. Interstate Conference of Employment Security Agencies, Report of the Committee on Employer Experience Rating. *Volume III–Joint Minority Report, State Unemployment Compensation Laws and Experience Rating*. Washington, D.C.: October 2, 1940.

35. McQueeny, Robert P. "Experience Rating–A New Opportunity to Improve Our Industrial Climate," paper presented at 41st Annual Convention of Puerto Rico Manufacturers Association, October 23–26, 1969. San Juan: 1969.

36. Miller, Taulman A. *The Kansas Unemployment Insurance System*. Report submitted to the 1961 Legislature by the Special Committee on Unemployment Compensation, Kansas Legislative Council, February 1961.

37. U.S. Bureau of Unemployment Compensation, Division of Legislative Standards. *Experience Rating Under State Unemployment Compensation Laws*. Washington: December 8, 1938 (mimeo.).

38. U. S. Bureau of Employment Security. *Draft Legislative Provisions for Employer Experience Rating Under Pooled Fund Laws* (1943) (mimeo.).

39. U.S. Department of Labor, Bureau of Employment Security. *Comparison of State Unemployment Insurance Laws*, BES No. U-141.

40. McKean, Eugene C. *The Taxable Wage Base in Unemployment Insurance Financing*. The W. E. Upjohn Institute for Employment Research, December 1965.

41. Burns, Eveline M. "Unemployment Compensation and Socio-Economic Objectives." *Yale Law Journal*, vol. 55, no. 1 (December 1945).

42. Interstate Conference of Employment Security Agencies. *The Long-Range Financing of Unemployment Benefits Under State Unemployment Compensation Laws*. Washington, D.C.: October 1950, Supplement, October 1951.

43. Wermel, Michael T. *Factors Affecting the Cost of the Maryland Unemployment Insurance System and Solvency of the Unemployment Fund*. Paper presented at a staff meeting of the Maryland Department of Employment Security, Baltimore, Md., May 15, 1952 (mimeo.).

44. Woytinsky, W. S. *Principles of Cost Estimates in Unemployment Insurance*. Washington: Bureau of Employment Security, 1948.

45. Malisoff, Harry. *The Insurance Character of Unemployment Insurance*. The W. E. Upjohn Institute for Employment Research, 1961.

46._____. *Cost Estimation Methods in Unemployment Insurance, 1909-1957*, New York State Department of Labor, Division of Employment. New York: June 1958.

47. Williamson, W. R. "State Actuarial Problems in Unemployment Compensation." *Law and Contemporary Problems*, vol. 3, no. 1 (January 1936).

48. Eberling, E. J. "Financial Policy in a Period of Low Unemployment Insurance Disbursements." *Employment Security Review* (December 1951).

49. Horwitz, James W. *The Risk of Unemployment and Its Effect on Unemployment Compensation*. Cambridge, Mass.: George F. Baker Foundation, Harvard University, Publication of the Graduate School of Business Administration, vol. 25, no. 5, July 1938.

50. Teple, Edwin R., and Nowacek, Charles G. "Experience Rating: Its Objectives, Problems and Economic Implications," *Vanderbilt Law Review*, vol. 8, no. 2 (February 1955).

51. Social Security Board. *Social Security Bulletin*. Washington: January 1944.

52. U.S. Department of Labor, Bureau of Employment Security, *Manual of State Employment Security Legislation*, revised September 1950. Washington, D.C.: 1950.

53. Brandeis, Elizabeth. "The Employer Reserve Type of Unemployment Compensation Law." *Law and Contemporary Problems*, vol. 3, no. 1 (January 1936).

54. Delehanty, John A. *Financing Unemployment Insurance Benefits in Indiana: Final Report*. Indianapolis, Indiana: Indiana Employment Security Division, December 1960.

55. Newton, Shirley King. *The Role of Experience Rating in Unemployment Compensation*. M.A. thesis, Aug. 7, 1964 released by Research & Statistics Section, Dept. of Employment Security, State of Tennessee, October 1964.

56. *Financing Methods—Benefit Structure—Costs of Michigan Unemployment Insurance*, A Report of the Michigan Employment Security Commission. Detroit: February 3, 1953.

57. State of New York. *Report of the Joint Legislative Committee on Unemployment Insurance* (Legislative Document No. 79, 1951).

58. California Department of Employment. *California Unemployment Compensation Fund*, Report of the Actuaries for Calendar Year 1966. Woodward and Fondiller, Inc., September 1967.

59. Leontief, Wassily. "Theoretical Assumptions and Nonobserved Facts." *American Economic Review*, vol. 61, no. 1 (March 1971).

60. Arnold, Almon R. "Experience Rating." *Yale Law Journal*, vol. 55, no. 1 (December 1945).

61. Myers, Charles A. "Employment Stabilization and the Wisconsin Act." *American Economic Review*, vol. 29, no. 4 (December 1939).

62.———. "Experience Rating in Unemployment Compensation." *American Economic Review* 35 (June 1945): 337–54.

63. Lester, Richard A. *The Economics of Unemployment Compensation*. Princeton: Industrial Relations Section, Princeton University, 1962.

64. Brittain, John A. "The Incidence of Social Security Payroll Taxes." *American Economic Review* (March 1971).

65. Shoup, Carl S. *The Prospects for a Study of the Economic Effects of Payroll Taxes*. (Washington, D.C.: Committee on Social Security of the Social Science Research Council, November 1941).

66.———. *Public Finance*. Chicago: Aldine Publishing Company, 1969.

67. Pigou, A. C. *The Economics of Welfare*. London: MacMillan and Co., Ltd., 1950.

68. Bowman, Mary Jean, and Bach, George Leland. *Economic Analysis and Public Policy*. New York: Prentice–Hall, Inc., January 1950.

69. Cartwright, Philip W. "Unemployment Compensation and the Allocation of Resources," *The Allocation of Economic Resources*. Stanford, California: Stanford University Press, 1959.

70. *The American System of Social Insurance* eds.: William G. Bowen, Frederick H. Harbison, Richard A. Lester, Herman M. Somers. New York: McGraw–Hill Book Company, June 1967.

71. Beveridge, William H. *The Past and Present of Unemployment Insurance*. London: Oxford University Press, 1930.

72. Pigou, A. C. *Industrial Fluctuations*. New York: Kelley, 1929.

73. Weiss, Harry. "Unemployment Prevention Through Unemployment Compensation." *Political Science Quarterly* vol. 53, no. 1 (March 1938).

74. Brandeis, Louis D. "The Right to Work as Formulated Long Since." *Survey Graphic*, April 1929, Special Issue.

75. Groves, Harold M., and Brandeis, Elizabeth. "Economic Bases of the Wisconsin Unemployment Reserves Act." *American Economic Review* (March 1934).

76. Letter of Paul A. Raushenbush to George E. Bigge, Social Security Board, November 14, 1938 (Raushenbush Collection: Madison, Wisconsin).

77. Nelson, Daniel. "The Origins of Unemployment Insurance in Wisconsin." *Wisconsin Magazine* (Winter, 1967–68).

78. Schmidt, Emerson P. "Experience Rating and Unemployment Compensation," *Yale Law Journal*, vol. 55, no. 1 (December 1945).
79. Nelson, Daniel. *The Development of Unemployment Insurance in the United States, 1915–1935* (MS, University of Wisconsin, January 1968).
80. U.S., Congress, Subcommittee of the Committee on Interstate and Foreign Commerce, *Hearings on H.R. 10127, Unemployment Insurance for Railroad Employees*, 75th Cong., 3rd Sess., 1938.
81. Weinberg, Nat. "The Thinking Behind the UAW-CIO Guaranteed Employment Plan." *Michigan Business Review* 7 (March 1955).
82. *California Unemployment Insurance Act*, as amended, 1945. Sacramento: Department of Employment.
83. *Social Security Perspectives: Essays by Edwin E. Witte*, Robert J. Lampman (ed.). Madison: The University of Wisconsin Press, 1962.
84. Matscheck, Walter, and Atkinson, Raymond C. *Problems and Procedures of Unemployment Compensation in the States*. Chicago, Illinois: Committee on Social Security, Social Science Research Council, Public Administration Service No. 65, 1939.
85. State of Ohio, *Report of the Ohio Commission on Unemployment Insurance*, Part I, Conclusions and Recommended Bill. Columbus: November 1932.
86. Douglas, Paul H. *Standards of Unemployment Insurance*. Chicago: The University of Chicago Press, 1933.
87. Clague, Ewan. "Economics of Unemployment Compensation." *Yale Law Journal*, vol. 55, no. 1 (December 1945).
88. *Information Please Almanac*, 1970.
89. *A Report on Unemployment Compensation Benefit Costs in Massachusetts*. Boston: Massachusetts Division of Employment Security, August 1950.
90. Andrews, William H., Jr., and Miller, Taulman A. *Employment Security Financing In Indiana*. Bloomington, Indiana: Bureau of Business Research, School of Business, Indiana University, 1956.
91. Kehoe, John Kimball, S.J., *One Company's Incentives to Stabilize Employment and to Police Claims Under Experience Rating*, presented to the faculty of the Graduate School of St. Louis University in partial fulfillment of the requirements for the degree of Master of Arts, 1964.
92. *American Economic Security*, February–March 1948. Washington, D.C.: U.S. Chamber of Commerce.
93. *A Group Contribution Rate for Small Employers in Unemployment Insurance*. New York: Department of Labor, Division of Employment, October 1956 (mimeo.).
94. Statement of Harold Keller at *Public Hearing on Proposed Change of Joint Account Rule 12*, held by New York Division of Employment, Albany, New York, March 6, 1967.
95. Dodd, Walter F. "Administering Unemployment Compensation Benefit Claims," *Law and Contemporary Problems*. Duke Station, Durham, N.C.: January 1936.
96. State of Connecticut, *Merit Rating*, Report of the State Advisory Council on Employment Security. Hartford: January 1969.
97. State of New York, *Report of the Joint Legislative Committee to Investigate the Administration of the Unemployment Insurance Law to The Legislature of the State of New York* (Legislative Document No. 14, March 31, 1967).

98. General Motors Corporation, *Unemployment Compensation in Ohio* (a reference booklet of information of interest to General Motors' Supervisors in the State of Ohio) 1953.

99. *Controlling Your Non-Working Payroll Costs: Unemployment Insurance.* New York: Associated Industries of New York State, Inc., 1961.

100. Devine, Bobbie. *What Management Should Know about Unemployment Insurance.* El Segundo, California: North American Rockwell Corporation, Aerospace and Systems Group, 1968.

101. Jacoby, George. "The Significance of Employer Interest in Good Administration," address at the National Institute of Unemployment Compensation, U.S. Chamber of Commerce, Washington, D.C., March 31, 1949.

102. Becker, Joseph M., S.J., *The Problem of Abuse in Unemployment Benefits.* New York: Columbia University Press, 1953.

103. Pauly, Mark V. "The Economics of Moral Hazard: Comment." *American Economic Review* (June 1968).

104. California Department of Human Resources Development v. Java, 402 U.S. 121 (1971).

105. Letter of H. L. Hutcherson, General Counsel, Mississippi Employment Security Commission, December 28, 1966.

106. Hayes, A. J. International President, International Association of Machinists, "Labor's Views on the Employment Security Program and its Administration," *Proceedings of the 23rd Annual Meeting of Interstate Conference of Employment Security Agencies*, October 12-15, 1959. Washington, D.C.: 1959.

107. Zecca, Paschal C. "Interstate Impact of UI Taxes on Plant Location Decisions." *Unemployment Insurance Review* (U.S. Department of Labor: May 1968).

108. McKean, Eugene C. *Unemployment Insurance Costs of the ABC Corporation in Michigan and Nearby States.* Kalamazoo, Mich.: The W. E. Upjohn Institute for Employment Research, August 1962.

109. Interstate Conference of Employment Security Agencies, *Report of Sub-Committee on Disqualifications.* Washington, D.C., October, 1944.

110. "Twenty Years of Unemployment Insurance in the U.S.A., 1935-1955." *Employment Security Review* (August 1955). Washington, D.C.: U.S. Department of Labor, Bureau of Employment Security.

111. Warden, Charles, Jr., "Unemployment Compensation: The Massachusetts Experience," *Studies in the Economics of Income Maintenance*, ed. Otto Eckstein. Washington, D.C.: The Brookings Institution, 1967.

112. UAW-CIO Education Department, *Steady Work, Steady Pay, Questions and Answers about the UAW-CIO Guaranteed Employment Plan.* Detroit: UAW-CIO, Publication No. 330.

113. Simrell, Earle V. "Employer Fault vs. General Welfare as the Basis of Unemployment Compensation." *Yale Law Journal*, vol. 55, no. 1 (December 1945).

114. Canada, Unemployment Insurance Commission, *Extract from Study to Update Unemployment Insurance Act*, Chapter XVII: Implications from the Attitude Survey for the Proposed Schema. Ottawa: November 1970.

115. Lamphier, C. Michael, Portis, Bernard M., and Golden, Malcolm. *An Analysis of Attitudes Toward Unemployment Insurance.* Ottawa, Canada: Unemployment Insurance Commission, July 1970.

116. "Welfare: Trying to End the Nightmare," *Time*, February 8, 1971.

117. *Wall Street Journal*, January 26, 1971, p. 1.
118. Mesa-Lago, Carmelo. "Unemployment in a Socialist Economy: Yugoslavia." *Industrial Relations*, vol. 10, no. 1 (February 1971). Berkeley, California: Institute of Industrial Relations, University of California, p. 49.
119. Rubinow, I. M. *Social Insurance*. New York: Henry Holt and Company, 1916.
120. Beveridge, William H. *Social Insurance and Allied Services*, American Edition. New York: The MacMillan Company, 1942.
121. Burns, Eveline M. "Social Insurance In Evolution." *American Economic Review*, vol. 34, Supplement (March 1944): 199-211.
122. Rector, Stanley. "The Frailty of the 'Fallacy' of Experience Rating." *Labor Law Journal* (May, 1951).
123. National Association of Manufacturers. *Unemployment Compensation in a Free Economy*, Economic Policy Division Series, No. 52. Washington, D.C.: July 1952.
124. *Unemployment and Income Security: Goals for the 1970's*. A Report of the Committee on Unemployment Insurance Objectives Sponsored by the Institute. Kalamazoo, Michigan: The W. E. Upjohn Institute for Employment Research, July 1969.
125. Peterson, Florence. *Survey of Labor Economics*. New York: Harper & Brothers, 1951.
126. Reynolds, Lloyd G. *Labor Economics and Labor Relations*. New York: Prentice-Hall, 1959.
127. Reder, Melvin W. *Labor in a Growing Economy*. John Wiley and Sons, Inc., 1957.
128. Turnbull, John G., Williams, C. Arthur, Jr., Cheit, Earl F. *Economic and Social Security*. New York: The Ronald Press Co., 1957.
129. Daugherty, Carroll R., and Parrish, John B. *The Labor Problems of American Society*. Boston: Houghton Mifflin, 1952.
130. Special article by Paul Wohl, written for *The Christian Science Monitor*, October 28, 1969.
131. Industrial Relations Research Association, *Proceedings of the Twelfth Annual Meeting*. Washington, D.C., 1959.
132. Myers, Charles A. *Employment Stabilization and the Wisconsin Act*, Bureau of Employment Security Memorandum No. 10. Washington, D.C.: September 1940.
133. Letter to author from Clyde W. Summers, Chairman of Connecticut Advisory Council on Employment Security, April 23,1969.
134. Myers, Robert J., and Swerdloff, Sol. "Seasonality and Construction," *Monthly Labor Review* (September 1967).
135. *Seasonal Operation in the Construction Industries*, Report on Recommendations of a Committee of the President's Conference on Unemployment. New York: McGraw-Hill, 1924.
136. Confidential report by Personnel Director of a New York manufacturing firm, 1960.
137. Haber, William, Carroll, John J., Kahn, Mark L., and Peck, Merton J. *Maintenance of Way Employment on U.S. Railroads*. Detroit: Brotherhood of Maintenance of Way Employees, 1957
138. Wisconsin Industrial Commission, *The First Wisconsin Conference on Steadier Jobs*, Milwaukee, Wisconsin, June 21, 1940. Madison: 1940.
139. *To Make Jobs More Steady and to Make More Steady Jobs*, Minnesota American Legion Foundation, 360 pages. St. Paul: 1943.

140. New York State, *Report of the New York Unemployment Insurance State Advisory Council on the Subject of Experience Rating*, March 1940, Part 1.

141. Ficek, Karel F. *Contribution Rate Variation in Unemployment Insurance*. Address delivered at the Eastern Spring Conference of Controllers, Controllers' Institute of America. New York: May 20, 1940.

142. Rainwater, P. L. "The Fallacy of Experience Rating," *Labor Law Journal* (February 1951).

143. Rejda, George E. "Unemployment Insurance as an Automatic Stabilizer." *Journal of Risk and Insurance* (June 1966).

144. Hart, Albert G. *Money, Debt, and Economic Activity*. New York: Prentice-Hall, Inc., 1948.

145. Larson, Arthur. "The Economic Function of Unemployment Insurance," *Industrial Relations Research Association, Proceedings of Seventh Annual Meeting*. Detroit, Michigan: 1954.

146. Andrews, William H., and Miller, Taulman A. "Unemployment Benefits, Experience Rating, and Employment Stability," *National Tax Journal* (September 1954).

147. Spivey, Clinton. *Experience Rating in Unemployment Compensation*. Urbana, Illinois: University of Illinois, 1958.

148. Raphaelson, Arnold H. "Massachusetts Unemployment Compensation, 1948-1961, A Study in Countercyclical Finance," *Research Report—Federal Reserve Bank of Boston*, no. 32 (1966).

149. Clement, M. O. "The Quantitative Impact of Automatic Stabilizers," *Review of Economics and Statistics* (February 1960).

150. Palomba, Neil Anthony. "A Measure of the Stabilizing Effect of the Unemployment Compensation Program—With Emphasis on the Experience Rating Controversy." Ph.D. dissertation, University of Minnesota, 1966.

151._____. "Unemployment Compensation Program: Stabilizing or Destabilizing," *Journal of Political Economy* (January–February 1968).

152._____. "Experience Rating: A 30-Year Controversy," *Labor Law Journal* (January 1968).

153. Warden, Charles. *Unemployment Insurance*, M.A. thesis, Harvard University, Cambridge, Mass., September 1963.

154. New York State, *An Analysis of Registered Unemployment in New York State, 1959-1965*, Research Bulletin 1966-8, Department of Labor, Division of Employment, Albany, April 1966.

155. State of California, *Employer Account Reserve Ratio and Payroll Trend in Experience Rating Base Period, Rate Years 1954-1959*, Technical Papers, Series R #21, December 15, 1959. Sacramento: 1960.

156. *Comparison of State Unemployment Compensation Laws*, U.S. Department of Labor, Bureau of Employment Security (December 1945).

157. *Countercyclical Financing of Unemployment Insurance*, a report by Walter B. Jessee for the second meeting of the Benefit Financing Committee, Interstate Conference of Employment Security Administrators (July 15–17, 1969).

158. *Arizona's Third Planning Period for Financing Unemployment Insurance*, Arizona Employment Security Commission. Phoenix: November 1964.

159. *Report to the President of the Committee on Economic Security*. Washington: U.S. Government Printing Office, 1935.

160. Letter of Company's Insurance Department to J. M. Becker, S. J., dated June 1, 1971.

161. U.S. Department of Labor, Bureau of Labor Statistics, *Monthly Labor Review*, April 1971.
162. State of Ohio, *Nonagricultural Employment and Placements, 1965–1967*, Research Memo No. 69. Columbus: Bureau of Employment Services, Research and Statistics Department, April 1, 1968.
163. Watson, A. D. *The Principles Which Should Govern the Structure and Provisions of a Scheme of Unemployment Insurance*. Ottawa: The Unemployment Insurance Commission, February 1948.
164. California State Department of Employment, Technical Papers, Series R #8 (1955), R #19 (1959), R #24.1 (1961), R #24.2 (1962).
165. Steiger, Paul E. "Payroll Ploy." *Wall Street Journal*, Monday, October 23, 1967.
166. Statement of William L. O'Toole at *Public Hearing on Proposed Change of Joint Account Rule 12*, held by N.Y. Division of Employment, Albany, New York, March 6, 1967.
167. Dorkin, Murray. "Joint Accounts," *Employment Review*, New York State Department of Labor, Division of Employment, September 1967.
168. Riche, Martha F. "Railroad Unemployment Insurance." *Monthly Labor Review*, November 1967, p. 9.

Index

THE JOHNS HOPKINS UNIVERSITY PRESS

This book was composed in Press Roman Medium type by the Jones
Composition Company. It was printed by Universal Lithographers, Inc.
on S. D. Warren's 60-lb. Sebago paper in text shade, regular finish. The book
was bound by L. H. Jenkins, Inc. in Holliston Roxite cloth.